# FREA

"*Freak Kingdom*...sheds new light on Thompson's [political] awakening and reporting—and the toll it took on him and his later work and life. Few books this season will give you a stronger and more chilling sense of déjà vu....The book chronicles, in absorbing day-by-day detail, how Thompson intersected with history more than some may recall." —*Rolling Stone*

"Denevi...crafts his biography like a nonfiction novel, letting his research unfold in a captivating narrative that places readers at some of the most important episodes of Thompson's career. Denevi's work reminds us that the persistent concern about totalitarianism overwhelming free speech isn't something new. And fifty years ago, one journalist decided to do something about it." —*Associated Press*

"Through meticulous research and recreated in novelistic detail, Denevi chronicles Thompson's scramble to create a viable career out of the instability of freelance writing....If you've ever felt Thompson a bit much to read on his own, *Freak Kingdom* makes a handy and stabilizing companion text: the behind-the-scenes details of how his big stories came together make it impossible to dismiss Thompson as the pop culture caricature he was later made out to be." —*Salon*

"Terrifically redemptive...The first book about Thompson to be written during the Trump presidency....Denevi gives a charmingly sensational account of Thompson's life in order to prove his point that Thompson actually conducted himself as quite a serious person." —*PopMatters*

"Denevi's writing does more than just bring the period alive, it makes one want to be there as if it were brand new....There has never been a Hunter S. Thompson biographer who has captured Thompson's work as well....Simply put, *Freak Kingdom* does justice to Hunter S. Thompson." —Counterpunch

"*Freak Kingdom*...is one of the most important books of this election season. Despite the word 'Trump' not appearing in it once, it is somehow present on every page." —Mashable

"By dramatizing the key decade in Thompson's life, *Freak Kingdom* brings his weird journey into clear and vivid focus." —TruthDig

"Given the state of America today, the true story of Thompson's life could not be more timely—and just might inspire the next generation of fearless and ferocious voices." —WestWord

"Sober and serious...Lively and well-researched...Denevi writes in clean and unadorned prose." —*Aspen Times*

"Scrupulously researched in a way that Thompson would admire." —LEO Weekly

"*Freak Kingdom* moves this iconic figure from the Gonzo parody and arms him with a wife, a moral code, and in some sense, an origin story. It's a wonderful though painful read for the Thompson admirer and historical enthusiast alike." —*Leavenworth Times*

"A thorough, timely, tautly written, and credible volume certain to be assigned by scores of journalism professors and a great new book for fans ready to move past Thompson's alter ego, Raoul Duke, to the next level." —*Kirkus Reviews*

"A spirited account...including 100 essential pages of notes containing samples of the journalist's work....Fans of Thompson, those unfamiliar with him, as well as journalists and scholars will enjoy this breezy but ultimately cautionary tale." —*Library Journal*

"Timothy Denevi's *Freak Kingdom* is a high-octane and elegantly written study of Hunter S. Thompson's fatwah against fascism. The damn thing is alive with anarchistic and climactically redemptive Gonzo mischief. A fierce resistance fable for our troubled times!"

—Douglas Brinkley, Katherine Tsanoff Brown Chair in Humanities and professor of history at Rice University, author of *Cronkite*

"Hunter Thompson is back and very much alive in this sympathetic and sharply written 'best years of his life' bio. I loved it."
—Terry Gilliam, director of *Fear and Loathing in Las Vegas*

"Based not on the Upper West Side or in West Hollywood but in Woody Creek, Colorado, Hunter S. Thompson got onto the page more of the 1960s and 1970s than any of his contemporaries. In this painstaking, exquisitely detailed, and impressively balanced book, Timothy Denevi conveys at what extraordinary cost to Thompson such Herculean work was accomplished. If a writer doesn't aim to cause trouble, why even bother?"

—David Shields

"Surreal, astonishing, and at times deeply disturbing, *Freak Kingdom* is a welcome and timely revision to the popular hagiography of the larger-than-life Hunter S. Thompson depicted by popular culture. A necessary read for anyone who wishes to understand our current political moment."

—Jennifer Percy, winner of the National Magazine Award and author of *Demon Camp*

"Timothy Denevi shines a long-overdue light the powerful idealism that underlies all of Hunter S. Thompson's best writing, and he proves to us that Hunter's writing is just as relevant and important today as it was in the early 1970s. This book is a must-read for anyone concerned about our current political situation and shows why Hunter's books continue to inspire new generations of readers."

—Juan F. Thompson, author of *Stories I Tell Myself: Growing Up with Hunter S. Thompson*

# FREAK KINGDOM

# FREAK KINGDOM

Hunter S. Thompson's Manic
Ten-Year Crusade
Against American Fascism

## TIMOTHY DENEVI

PUBLICAFFAIRS
New York

PublicAffairs
Hachette Book Group
1290 Avenue of the Americas, New York, NY 10104
www.publicaffairsbooks.com
@Public_Affairs

Printed in the United States of America

Originally published in hardcover and ebook by PublicAffairs in October 2018
First Trade Paperback Edition: September 2019

Published by PublicAffairs, an imprint of Perseus Books, LLC, a subsidiary of
Hachette Book Group, Inc. The PublicAffairs name and logo is a trademark of the
Hachette Book Group.

The publisher is not responsible for websites (or their content) that are not owned
by the publisher.

Essays, literary analysis, and political writing that served as an intellectual starting
point for this book originally appeared online in the magazines *American Short
Fiction*, *Literary Hub*, *Scoundrel Time*, and *The Paris Review*.

Print book interior design by Jeff Williams

The Library of Congress has cataloged the hardcover edition as follows:

Names: Denevi, Timothy, author.
Title: Freak kingdom : Hunter S. Thompson's manic ten-year crusade against
American fascism / Timothy Denevi.
Description: New York : PublicAffairs, [2018] | Includes bibliographical
references and index.
Identifiers: LCCN 2018015549 (print) | LCCN 2018021767 (ebook) | ISBN
9781541767959 (ebook) | ISBN 9781541767942 (hardcover)
Subjects: LCSH: Thompson, Hunter S. | Presidents—United
States—Election—History—20th century. | Political campaigns—United
States—History—20th century. | United States—Politics and
government—1945–1989. | Nixon, Richard M. (Richard Milhous), 1913–1994. |
Politicians—United States.
Classification: LCC JK524 (ebook) | LCC JK524 .D465 2018 (print) | DDC
070.92 [B] —dc23
LC record available at https://lccn.loc.gov/2018015549

ISBNs: 978-1-5417-6794-2 (hardcover), 978-1-5417-6795-9 (ebook);
978-1-5417-6801-7 (trade paperback)

LSC-C

10 9 8 7 6 5 4 3 2 1

For Brett

# CONTENTS

I'm not at all embarrassed at the use of
the word freak. I think the way things
are going in this country today, it's a very
honorable designation, and I'm proud of it.
To be abnormal, to deviate from the style of
government that I deplore in America today,
is not only wise but necessary.

—HUNTER S. THOMPSON,
Pitkin County Sheriff's Debate, October 24, 1970

# AUTHOR'S NOTE

The career of Hunter S. Thompson, in its bright arc across the second half of the previous century, continues to exist today in many forms. From his own prodigious output of personal narrative, to a wealth of auxiliary material such as interviews, films, and biographies, he has managed to pass an astonishing amount of his experience onto the printed page.

As such, we've arrived at a point in the present where *multiple* versions of Hunter Thompson appear to coexist simultaneously: versions that in his own writing he both encouraged and also fought back against; that have been amplified in the subsequent biographical works on his life and times; and that remain part of our popular culture, complicating our perspective on who, at different moments in his life, he might've actually been.

The book you're about to read is, among other things, an attempt to reevaluate Thompson's role as a *political* writer—as a literary journalist in the essayistic tradition whose activism remains underappreciated.

To be sure, it constitutes one version among many: my own, a take that's been composed amid the very specific political climate we currently find ourselves inhabiting. To write this book—in addition to the years of research and interviews that went into its construction—I attended the 2016 political conventions in Cleveland and Philadelphia, and afterward reported on election night, the 2017 inauguration, and various protests in Washington, DC. I'm only bringing up this series of events now to acknowledge the specific lens through which I've arranged everything you're about to read.

Which is to say: in writing about the past I'm of course expressing, in some manner, my own concern for the current state of our institutions and ideals—for the Constitution, participatory democracy, and the independent press—that Hunter Thompson fought so tirelessly to defend.

His perspective on the American republic remains as valuable as ever. In these pages I've tried to dramatize his political evolution in the manner a novel might—while also citing every detail and quote along the way—with the hope of expressing, for you, the *effort* he put out as a writer and thinker to combat institutional injustice.

In the end his effort came at a dire personal cost. But, during the period of time spanning John F. Kennedy's murder to Richard Nixon's resignation, it also set the real Hunter Thompson apart from the more outlandish versions we've come to identify with him.

From the start he understood better than most the possibilities and dangers inherent to the system of government that he liked to refer to as "that fantastic possibility . . . the last best hope of man."

And whether you're already familiar with his fascinating career or happen to be coming to his story for the first time, I hope that you'll see in his perspective a timeless and necessary rigor—something worth considering every day, especially today.

# FREAK KINGDOM

## CHAPTER ONE

# THE VALLEY
# OF THE MOON

## 1963–1964

## From the Emptiness of the Sky Itself

On an autumn afternoon in 1963, Hunter S. Thompson, a twenty-six-year-old journalist living in a small rented cabin with his wife, Sandy, was startled by a knock at the door.

This was on Woody Creek Road, just outside of Aspen, Colorado. He and Sandy had been staying there since the end of the summer, a temporary arrangement; Thompson had recently been offered the position of West Coast correspondent for the *National Observer*, a weekly general-interest newspaper owned by the Dow Jones Company, and the current plan was to save up enough money for a more permanent move to California. At the time Sandy was six months pregnant.

Thompson went to the door and opened it. Their neighbor, a rancher by the name of Wayne Vagneur, was standing on the porch. Something was up. You could see it in this man's eyes: a pressing, expectant look.

Vagneur got right to the point. There'd been violence, he said. Down in Dallas. John F. Kennedy had been shot. What's more, he was dead. *Murdered.*

Thompson let out a sob. In the next moment he started swearing. He swung his eyes at Vagneur, briefly hoping that what he'd just heard might in fact be the setup to some outrageous punch line, but no: this pioneer-family rancher wasn't the joking type.

November 22, 1963. That afternoon the information traveled the continent, occupying everything, a lament of incontestable volume. Thompson found out the way most people did—*personally*. Only later did you switch on the radio or television for confirmation.

This much was clear: the head of the American government had been cut down by rifle fire in the broad Texas daylight. And the perpetrator, it was beginning to appear, came from the left of the political spectrum: a deranged *communist* with ties to Cuba and the Soviet Union who'd coiled himself on the sixth floor of a nearby building to strike as if from everywhere at once—from above, from a sniper's distance, from the emptiness of the sky itself, his bullets shattering the famous young leader's body and head.

Really, what had taken place was something more than an assassination; it amounted to both an act of terror *and* a violent regime change. The country would be under the command of Lyndon Baines Johnson, that ancient, lifelong politico whom Kennedy had sped past on his way to the nomination in 1960, and who would now be asked to stand in memoriam during the upcoming election cycle, with no guarantee of either continuity or victory.

Hunter Thompson had become a Kennedy enthusiast three years earlier after watching the first televised presidential debate during a 1960 hitchhiking trip through California and the Pacific Northwest. With a friend he'd caught a ride at the Oregon turnpike to a small-town bar—a place he must've known he'd never pass through again—where, on the television, he watched what he instantly understood to be the visual turning point in the battle between the country's conservative and liberal factions. JFK, while at times affected and calculating, had come to represent, for Thompson and for many others, the least-terrible option American politics had seen in a generation: a leader who wouldn't be corrupted by the enormous degree of power he sought, and who, as a result, suggested a future in which the collective hopes of the country might for once outweigh the ruthless, cheap, small-minded, glaringly hypocritical ambition that so many other candidates had relied upon for victory.

From Thompson's perspective there'd been plenty to doubt in the three years since, but at least with Kennedy, progress on civil rights and in international affairs seemed possible; for once, it felt as if the better sentiments of the American character had gotten a foot in the door.

On that Friday afternoon in November, after Vagneur delivered the terrible news and departed, Thompson grabbed his reporter's notebook and headed into town, where, as if from behind the lens of a camera, he began collecting firsthand testimony. He talked to everyone he could find. He copied out their reactions verbatim. People were shocked and scared and pessimistic for the future. They told him so. With pen and paper he bore witness to the country's roaring pain.

That night, back at the cabin, as the radio reports gave way to a series of previously recorded Billy Graham sermons, he couldn't sleep. For a while he worked on compiling the quotes he'd gathered, polishing them into a thousand-word article he could then send to his editor at the *National Observer*, but eventually he switched to a more intimate form of expression: personal letters.

"It is a triumph of lunacy, of rottenness, the dirtiest hour in our time," he wrote to Paul Semonin, an old friend from Louisville. "The shits were surely killing us, and now they have killed the only hope on the American horizon."

He was afraid to fall asleep, he added, sure that he'd wake up to news of a full-scale attack on Cuba or some other communist satellite. It was as if the future itself could be redrawn in the blue silences of each new hour that passed. He finished the first letter and started another, and as the night gave way to morning—sunrise at eight thousand feet, a rarefied, alpine light—he kept thinking about the long-term *political* ramifications of the assassination.

For Thompson, Kennedy's murder was nothing short of a challenge to the soul of the Republic itself. America's duly elected leader had been removed from his post with violence. Such a thing had happened before, yes, but this current situation was altogether new; in an era of mutually assured nuclear destruction, it didn't necessarily matter if the assassin was a lone maniac or the agent of a wider plot. The result was the same: power was being transferred across discreet, unmonitored channels. And the official narrative, emanating now like a deadly fog from the various outlets of the postwar media apparatus, suggested a familiar target—*communists*. In short: America had suffered an attack from the very threat its most conservative politicians had been shouting about, as a means to advance their own careers, for decades.

"The political clock has been turned back to Eisenhower & McCarthy," he wrote. "It will almost surely mean a Goldwater victory in '64, a wild reaction against 'The Reds.'"

Such a thing had seemed impossible only a few days earlier. But all of sudden, Barry Goldwater—the conservative senator from Arizona who, in his campaign for the Republican nomination, advocated a policy of more direct confrontation with the Soviet Union that could very quickly lead to nuclear war—appeared poised to embody the country's desire for retaliation. For vengeance. It would play out both at home and abroad: against domestic groups like the Fair Play for Cuba Committee, and in shows of force against weaker communist governments the military would be looking to make an example out of.

And as he considered these ramifications, Thompson found himself hung up on a single word: *Shitrain*.

This was what he imagined. A deluge of human barbarity that would swirl and descend and dirty itself in endless succession. At last, the worst aspects of mankind were coming together to submerge the very best in us all. There was nowhere to hide, let alone run.

The unique horror of Kennedy's death was that, at the time, it appeared to offer the ideal catalyst for national suicide. In the aftermath of such an extreme event, how long would it be until constitutional rights were suspended, journalists were silenced, individual expression was criminalized, and, in the name of safety and security, the last remnants of open political dissent were eradicated from the national stage?

Thompson had already seen it happen elsewhere. The previous year, traveling up and down South America as a stringer for the

*Observer,* he'd written extensively on the subject in articles with titles like "Democracy Dies in Peru, but Few Seem to Mourn Its Passing," and "It's a Dictatorship, but Few Seem to Care to Stay and Fight." Of late he'd begun to believe that America was much more vulnerable to fascistic, populist, militaristic forces than most of its citizens cared to think.

In this sense, Barry Goldwater wasn't the only homegrown threat on the horizon. During the long funereal week that followed the assassination, as the major news outlets provided unverified updates that felt indistinguishable from speculation, Thompson's thoughts turned to the prospects of another right-wing politician, a man who'd also relied on the previous decade's climate of communist fearmongering to propel a national career.

"And now," Thompson wrote later that week, "with a hairy animal called Nixon looming once again on the horizon, I am ready to believe that we are indeed in 'the time of the end.'"

It was inconceivable. Only a year before, on November 7, 1962, Nixon had stood in front of reporters at the Biltmore Hotel in Los Angeles and, while ostensibly delivering a concession speech to mark the end of his failed bid for the California governorship, proceeded to openly reveal himself as the petulant, narcissistic hypocrite he'd always worked so gratuitously to hide. This speech lasted fifteen minutes: throughout it he lamented how his opponent had treated him; how biased the press coverage had been, going so far as to single out certain reporters in particular; and how, in summary, everyone had conspired to give him what he referred to as "the shaft." It was a spectacular meltdown. Here was a politician who'd previously painted himself, in often garish strokes, as the humblest of civil servants acting solely out of love for God and country and who, in a fit of victimhood and rage, was throwing a match to all of it. "You won't have Nixon to kick around anymore," he finally bleated, "because, gentlemen, this is my last press conference."

But now, after the president's murder in Dallas at the hands of a maniac communist, *all* bets, including those on Nixon's future, were suddenly off. For Thompson, the very mention of the name *Richard Nixon* was itself a testament to the horrific ramifications of Kennedy's death. "There is no explanation for the durability of that man," he added. "He is like a hyena that you shoot and gut, then see a few hours later, loping along in his stinking way, oblivious to the fact that he is not only dead, but gutted as well."

The 1964 Republican Convention was only nine months away; it would be held in San Francisco. And while Thompson had been working on a move from Colorado to California for a while, the assassination clarified the matter: the political climate was in flux, and as a West Coast journalist based in the Bay Area, he figured he'd be able to best participate in the fight that was to come. It would be an ugly, unprecedented battle, but he needed to do *something*. It was up to him to get closer to the action. "I don't mind saying that my primary motive," he explained, "is to keep that man Nixon out of the presidency."

The tragedy provided Thompson a fresh burst of determination. For the past half decade he'd been trying to break through as a journalist and also as a fiction writer, and by twenty-six he'd already written two unpublished novels while steadily climbing the ranks as a freelancer. But neither had paid off; he knew it was finally time to make a decision.

So on that tragic long-ago Friday in November, as news reports on the radio confirmed the president's assassination and not much else, he wrote in a letter to the novelist William Kennedy, his close friend: "Fiction is dead." Instead, from here on out, he vowed to devote himself to journalism—his own way of influencing, however subtly, the political and cultural direction in which the country might go. "The stakes are now too high," he added, "and the time too short."

In the same letter he offered a personal articulation of the tragedy: "There is no human being within 500 miles to whom I can communicate anything," he wrote, "much less the fear and loathing that is on me after today's murder."

*Fear:* for America's core democratic values, for the safety of his family in a society that appeared to be going mad.

And *Loathing:* for the power-hungry figures who were willing to sacrifice the basic tenets on which the Republic was founded.

Looking back, this appears to mark his first recorded usage of that short phrase he'd make famous. It's a striking description of the tragedy's true shape: the absence that the murder had created in millions of individual American hearts and in the collective heart of the nation as well, a grave blow to everything the country hadn't yet become but still someday might. What happens when an idealistic young leader is replaced by a sense of bottomless distress forged from equal parts terror and hatred?

Into the emptiness of this new space anything might flow: doom, fate, the future, or maybe Richard Milhous Nixon. Something, at any rate, was coming. And Hunter Thompson planned to be there when it finally emerged; the least he could do was document its progress.

## Sunrise in Sonoma

The Thompsons moved to California three months after John F. Kennedy's assassination. They'd hoped to leave before that, but there'd been lingering financial questions, and by the time they secured the money for a down payment and headed west, hauling a trailer across twelve hundred miles of dirty snow, it was the middle of winter, February 1964.

They made the trip in a 1959 Rambler Custom, a cream-colored sedan with brown piping and bench seats, a wedding present from Sandy's mother. Agar, their purebred Doberman, rode along with them. Sandy was eight months pregnant. Their destination was a small town fifty miles north of San Francisco: Glen Ellen, located in the Sonoma Valley.

They'd been married for less than a year. In retrospect, their relationship at the time seemed, for all intents and purposes, healthy.

They were young and intimate and, together, they'd found a path to create a life they could both share.

Sandy had just turned twenty-six. She had dark eyebrows and striking hazel eyes. Her hair was long and blond, parted down the middle. She'd been born in New York and attended Goucher College, an all-girls university in Baltimore known then for its conservative curriculum. They'd first met in 1958, on Christopher Street in Greenwich Village during the Thanksgiving holiday—at the time she was engaged to someone else—and in the years since they'd lived together in places like San Juan and Big Sur and Rio de Janeiro and Louisville.

Now, in the winter of 1964—arriving in Glen Ellen with a baby on the way—they'd arranged to rent a roomy cottage just down the road from Jack London State Park. But when they finally crossed California and pulled into this secluded valley north of the state's famous bay, they were told, much to their disbelief, that there'd been a misunderstanding: the cottage they were to live in had, in fact, been promised to someone else.

Suddenly they had nowhere to go. The only other option was a small tin-walled structure at the top of the main property—what was, for all intents and purposes, a hillside shack—but they had no choice but to accept.

It could've been worse. This shack consisted of two rooms, one large and one small, along with a kitchen, and it had running water and electricity. The mattress was set up on box springs. At night Agar slept in the bed between them.

To prepare for the baby, they purchased what furniture they could afford from the local thrift shop. In the winter the valley was a vast windless depression of intermittent sunlight, the mountains holding the fog from the coast. *The Valley of the Moon,* Jack London had called it. Only a few of the roads were paved. The fields smelled like manure. Many of their neighbors were former Oklahomans, transplants from the Dust Bowl: a conservative population

that tended to view a professional occupation like Thompson's—
*writer*—with suspicion.

Sandy's water broke early on a morning in March. By the time
they made it to the hospital in Santa Rosa the baby was ready.
"You could've given birth in a field," the doctor said afterward. It
was a boy. They named him Juan Fitzgerald—for the fallen president, whose murder continued to shadow the present, and also for
F. Scott, the author of *The Great Gatsby,* which was one of Thompson's favorite books.

Suddenly they were a family, three humans and a bed-sleeping
dog, all of them residing in the tin-walled shack. Shortly after the
delivery Juan had suffered a health scare—there'd been a complication regarding blood types—but now he was gaining weight. At
night he fell asleep to the sound of Hunter Thompson's typewriter.

Years later, Sandy would reflect on these first months in Sonoma
as some of the very best in her life. She was surrounded by everything in the world she loved most. It was a period of stillness and
safety, the future stretching outward with the same startling clarity
that marked the present.

But for Hunter Thompson, it was the opposite: the move to
California was quickly evolving into one of the great crises of his
young life.

In the wake of Kennedy's death, all he could focus on were the
things he hadn't yet accomplished. Everywhere he looked he saw
impediments, signs that revealed his coming failure. He didn't have
enough time or money or support to become the writer he'd spent
his adult life fashioning himself into. The editors at the *National
Observer* may have given him a lofty title but they still paid him
no salary, only a fee for each article. What's more, they kept reject-
ing his pitches. He wasn't allowed to write about the free-speech
movement in Berkeley, which he perceived (correctly, in retrospect) as a vibrant indicator of the upheaval to come. Three times
a week he drove to the Dow Jones office in San Francisco and was
shocked by the incurious nature of his colleagues. It didn't seem to

matter that he was married to a beautiful woman who loved him; that they'd had a child, a son; that by moving to Sonoma he was acting on a moral imperative, living a life he felt called to answer; or that, at last, he was supporting himself and his family as a writer.

"I am deep in the grip of a professional collapse that worries me to the extent that I cannot do any work to cure it," he wrote in an April 7 letter. "A failure of concentration, as it were, and a consequent plunge into debt and depression."

A week later, he was considering moving his young family to Los Angeles, or New York, even Mexico City—anywhere to escape the "deep ugly funk" he found himself in—when, on a weekday afternoon, Sandy was walking with Juan through Sonoma's large central square when she happened to cross paths with a woman and her infant daughter.

The woman's name was Terri Geiger; she lived nearby in a condo complex that, due to a remodeling project, was currently unoccupied. Together they started talking, and as the sun descended behind the western mountains and evening came on—as they began to realize just how much they appeared to have in common—Terri went so far as to make a spontaneous offer: what did Sandy think about bringing her family by, that night, for dinner?

A few hours later, the Thompsons arrived at the condo complex in their Rambler. They were greeted by Terri's husband, Dr. Robert C. Geiger, a thirty-three-year-old orthopedist who'd recently opened his first family practice in Sonoma—no small feat—and who also, just that week, had published his debut novel *Ask for Me Tomorrow*, about a Californian surgeon preparing to ship out to South Vietnam.

Bob Geiger had been told that their guests that night included a young journalist, but he had no idea what to expect. And as Hunter Thompson emerged from the driver's side—tall and long-limbed, his jaw sharp, his elbows bent, a jetty of hair receding above the broad high slope of his forehead—Geiger was struck by an additional detail:

Thompson exited the car slowly. A tiptoed step: he swung himself forward on his left foot, his hip revolving, a barely perceptible movement that a man of Geiger's training could tell, after only a few strides, was the result of uneven legs—the left one nearly half an inch shorter than the right.

The two families gathered inside. After a few preliminary drinks the conversation began, and as if on cue, Bob Geiger and Hunter Thompson began discussing politics, and sports, and writing.

Both young men had qualities the other envied. Thompson was younger and had traveled all through South America, where he'd reported on government abuses and student demonstrations for a national periodical. He was making a living as a writer, if barely; he was politically savvy. Geiger, besides his medical and novelistic feats, also happened to be an amazing athlete, a college quarterback at Berkeley and for the semiprofessional Cal Ramblers.

But their first interaction wasn't colored by envy. Instead, Geiger and Thompson stayed up together until the sun rose, long after Sandy and Juan had fallen asleep in the guest bedroom. The next morning they were still talking and drinking, even as the sky above the Valley of the Moon brightened and lifted, a valley that on certain mornings could feel as isolated as its namesake and no less beautiful, especially when the dawn struck the shadows from the mountains and the day shaped itself forward, California emerging again as if from the ocean beyond.

∗

After their first dinner together, as spring gave way to the dry season, the Thompsons and the Geigers found themselves spending much of their time in each other's company.

For Sandy, this new friendship was like a ballast; now, when her husband traveled on assignment for the *National Observer,* she had people looking out for her and Juan—and a friend in Terri.

And for Hunter Thompson, Bob Geiger provided a fresh, careful perspective on the world around them. Throughout April and

May, they'd often head over to the nearby high school in the afternoon, where they'd throw the football around. Or they might drive to the coast with Agar. At night there were family dinners, a chance to extend their ongoing conversation. They talked about political activism—about what they could do, personally, to make a difference—and for a while they genuinely considered making a trip down to Mississippi to register voters with the Freedom Riders. They also discussed the upcoming presidential contest and the differences between fiction and reporting, how Thompson might use the skills he'd developed as a novelist to liven up his articles, which would remain "true" in the sense that they accurately represented his interpretation of what had happened. *Impressionistic Journalism:* this was the term Thompson had begun using to describe the hybridized, dramatized nature of his writing.

They both liked to drink, especially together. For nearly a decade, ever since he was in high school, Thompson had been a functioning alcoholic. At the age of twenty-six he was still young enough to recover the next day—both physically and mentally—but the long nights of bourbon and beer inevitably took a toll. It didn't help that his writing schedule lacked structure; he liked to work late at night, often until daybreak, all the while drinking steadily—a balance that, at certain points in the past, he'd managed to pull off surprisingly well. But in Sonoma, in the wake of such a stressful move, not to mention the arrival of his first child—as well as the budding editorial disagreement with the *National Observer*—he found himself writing sparingly, sleeping poorly, and drinking even more than usual. The terrifying inspiration of Kennedy's murder was beginning to abate; instead he found himself waiting, in a state of uncertainty and dread, for the advent of the societal upheaval he'd been sure the assassination would precipitate.

Dr. Bob Geiger, for his part, seemed to possess a preternatural capacity for time management. Each morning he started things off with a five-mile run, no matter the circumstances. Afterward he'd head to his orthopedic practice or to the Santa Rosa hospital for surgery. When he wasn't on call, he'd match Thompson drink for drink, going entire nights without sleep only to repeat his usual schedule the next day. He also wrote fiction, spent evenings with his family, played rugby for the Olympic Club in San Francisco, and found an hour or two each afternoon to throw the football around with his younger friend.

It was a contrast so stark, they both couldn't help but notice. And that May, Dr. Bob Geiger broached the topic with Thompson. He had an idea, something he thought might help: had Hunter Thompson ever considered Dexedrine?

In 1964 this drug, a trade version of the psychostimulant amphetamine, wasn't yet regulated as a controlled substance. Thompson had tried stimulants before—experimenting with them a year earlier, during his reporting trip to South America—but he'd never taken them regularly. What's more, a drug with Dexedrine's properties, mixed with salt and consumed in tablets, tended to have a much smoother action than uppers like cocaine or Benzedrine.

Geiger had been taking Dexedrine since medical school; many of his colleagues used it regularly as a secret weapon to make it through the insane schedule their profession demanded. To him, it was a safer alternative to the most popular stimulant of all— tobacco—which each year was responsible for the deaths of many thousand Americans. He understood that the drug was really a per-formance *sustainer,* a way for talented but presently overwhelmed individuals to bridge the gap between ambition and productivity. It had a tendency of mimicking sobriety: with Dexedrine, reality became less blurry and closer in proximity; all of a sudden you could differentiate among your demands and complete the most immediate task without freaking out. In this sense, the distance between you and what you wanted to accomplish was thinned of interference, which went a long way toward offsetting whatever larger issues of motivation you might be facing. You could stay engaged with the object of your focus for longer stretches.

After their discussion, Geiger wrote out a Dexedrine prescription for his new friend. And, over the course of the next ten years, Thompson would consume this drug daily, just as he did alcohol.

But we're getting ahead of ourselves. At the time, there were immediate concerns. In fact, the start of his Dexedrine usage coincided with a longstanding obligation: his first major reporting trip since moving West, a three-week all-expenses-paid tour of Idaho, Montana, Wyoming, and the badlands of North Dakota, during which he'd be expected to produce multiple pieces for the *National Observer*.

His editors envisioned these articles as more sanitized versions of the dispatches he'd filed from South America the year before; they wanted him to avoid expressing his personal opinions or providing political context. And for the most part he obliged them, at least on the surface. He completed four articles during the trip, three of which would be best categorized as travelogues. But the other—"What Lured Hemingway to Ketchum?"—would push much deeper, personally and culturally, to defy the sort of easy classification his editors expected.

Ernest Hemingway had killed himself in Ketchum, Idaho, three years earlier, and Thompson arrived there with the ostensible goal of answering the question posed in the headline. But his eventual article touched on a broader theme, one that had been haunting him ever since Kennedy's assassination.

"Like many another writer," Thompson wrote, "Hemingway did his best work when he felt he was standing on something solid—like an Idaho mountainside, or a sense of conviction." But what happens when the premise on which these convictions are based changes too rapidly and unpredictably? How do writers whose perspectives have been forged by their experiences within a certain time and place adjust to a *new* reality—to "the mean nature of a world that will not stand still long enough for them to see it clear as a whole?" In other words: how do you stay relevant when the moment in history you're tasked with rendering is defined by a lack of clarity? "It is not just a writer's crisis," Thompson concluded, "but they are the most obvious victims because the function of art is supposedly to bring order out of chaos, a tall order even when the chaos is static, and a superhuman task in a time when chaos is multiplying."

He finished the article with a haunting reference to Hemingway's suicide, by shotgun, at the age of sixty-one—a decision, Thompson implied, that represented a final act of agency in the face of irrelevance and deterioration. After decades of hard living, Hemingway's body and mind had broken down. In the end, his perspective on the world—that lens through which he'd so famously articulated the major events of the century—had grown too outdated and simplistic for the complex moral realities of the early 1960s. Hemingway's suicide amounted to the saddest of epigraphs: what does it mean when the only thing you have left to express is a desire to take away your ability to say anything at all?

At one point during his trip to Ketchum, Thompson was offered the chance to tour Ernest Hemingway's house. Afterward—after making his way through all the things Hemingway left behind, the detritus of this famous writer's late-life and suicide—he noticed, hanging over the entrance, the bleached, perforated skull of a ten-point elk, its antlers standing against the wall like an ancient crown. In the next moment he removed this trophy, carried it to the Rambler, and, without anyone seeing, stashed it safely away.

## Richard Nixon, Barry Goldwater, and the Deep Revolutions of the Soul

That July, Hunter Thompson drove down from Sonoma to San Francisco to attend his first major political event: the twenty-eighth Republican National Convention.

It was summer, dusk: above the bay the hills rose like surf, lantern-lit, as dense and cool as bottomless water. Downtown, the newest buildings crowded Union Square. On O'Farrell Street stood the twenty-story Hilton, opened only six weeks earlier. Across the harbor the ships were arriving. The sky was the same drained-out color of the bay, the ocean broken by wind. A city of Victorian mansions and midcentury skyscrapers. Freeways and cable cars and fleet, famous bridges.

Tuesday, July 14, 1964: Already the convention was in its second day, the evening schedule of speeches about to kick off. In anticipation, Hunter Thompson situated himself in the single-level bowl of the stands, the gallery section, high above the floor and the delegates there. Through the *National Observer*, he'd been allotted one of the 5,423 press credentials. Around him the Goldwater supporters numbered in the many thousands; they'd come to celebrate their candidate's nomination. Most of the attendees were staying on Nob Hill, but the events were being held six miles to the south at the Cow Palace, a ten-thousand-seat hangar-shaped arena located along San Francisco's border with Daly City.

The Cow Palace had been constructed twenty-five years earlier, during the Works Progress—era building boom, to hold national livestock conventions. It had hosted everything from circuses to welterweight title fights.

For the convention, the speaker's stand had been erected at the southern end atop a wood-paneled façade, behind which an enormous banner read BY THE PEOPLE. OF THE PEOPLE. FOR THE PEOPLE, a penny-shaped profile of Abraham Lincoln emblazoned alongside.

The first major speech of the evening was from Dwight Eisenhower. "I'm here with great pride because I am a Republican," the old general said. For Thompson, Ike was a lot like Hemingway: he'd been built to win the battles we were no longer interested in fighting, a relic in the truest sense. The narrative on which he defined himself had been relegated, through no fault of his own, to another era. "My deep dedication to Republicanism!" he said. Two months earlier, he had tried, along with other moderate conservatives, to steer the party away from the impending nomination of Barry Goldwater, and the majority of the crowd, made up of attendees far more radical than the old general would ever be, hadn't forgotten.

It was an amazing sight. There at the podium, the great symbol of the American 1950s—of its conformity; its communist-baiting hysteria; its prosperity—had suddenly been transformed into irrelevance.

What's more, this transformation had been initiated by none other than Goldwater, the silver-haired senator from Arizona—a man in his fifties who, in his black horn-rimmed glasses, looked more like the wealthy owner of a petroleum company than an agent for political change.

Goldwater had arrived in San Francisco ready to reiterate his answer to the question that, in the wake of Kennedy's murder, would dominate the 1964 presidential election: *How much risk is the United States willing to stomach, domestically and abroad?* He'd won the nomination by running hard to the right. He voted no on the Civil Rights Act (despite his previous opposition to segregation). Railed against big government. Refused to denounce the John Birch Society. His foreign policy positions had become increasingly extreme, effectively channeling the desire for vengeance in the wake of Kennedy's death. He'd threatened to invade Cuba. Called for an open confrontation with communism. And advocated, on multiple occasions—as a means to achieve their unconditional surrender—the right to launch a first-strike nuclear attack against the Soviet Union and its allies.

In the eyes of his fervent supporters he seemed to genuinely believe that to save the country you had to be willing to risk its destruction—and not by the means John Kennedy had employed during that famous October fortnight only two years earlier, with his bluffs and blockades. For Goldwater the battle was a matter of will; it could only be won by convincing your enemy of your ability to accept the unacceptable, a willingness to inflict death on a nuclear scale and also absorb its unending consequences across all strata of society. Unlike most populist leaders, Goldwater did not promise a return to an idealized past. What he offered, instead, was the transformation into something altogether new: an American resurrection. Like a minor desert prophet he burned coldly, and to his supporters in San Francisco, the extremes of their present-day—assassinations and missile crises and racial unrest—only confirmed what they'd heard him saying all along: *liberty with fire.*

\*

That night, Eisenhower's speech was followed by one last challenge to Goldwater's nomination: a procedural move to revise the convention platform with amendments that 1) supported civil rights, 2) disavowed the John Birch Society, and 3) clarified the chain of command on the use of nuclear weapons.

It was a gesture more than anything else—the math had been clear since the weekend—and despite a late challenge (in the form of a poorly worded letter) by Pennsylvania governor William W. Scranton, no amount of debate, however spirited, would sway the current totals. But the intended audience for this final volley wasn't so much the Republicans at the Cow Palace as the many more watching on television.

Not that the crowd saw it this way. From the start they appeared incensed. And as multiple moderates from the East Coast Establishment took the floor to denounce the extremism of their inevitable nominee, the chorus of displeasure rose . . . until, during a late-night speech by Nelson D. Rockefeller—Goldwater's main primary opponent, the governor of New York, and for the last few years the most easily identified representative of the party's mainstream—a full-blown commotion broke out.

Hunter Thompson was still in the stands up among the Goldwater supporters when it happened. Rockefeller was announced—allotted five minutes to speak on the amendments—but before he could say a word the Cow Palace erupted. "We want Barry! We want Barry!" they shouted. They booed and howled. Like geese they were hissing wildly. It was an arena-wide outburst buttressed with innumerable noisemakers: horns, Klaxons, bells, and trumpets, all of them ringing together. From somewhere distant came the martial bang of a drum. Rockefeller tried to speak. Got drowned out. Started again. Behind his heavy glasses he seemed to be smirking. His jaw was clenched. His eyes were set in an ancient, aristocratic weariness, as if, with just a look, he could offer a gesture of such unparalleled disappointment the whole world would be bound to feel it. "We repudiate the efforts of irresponsible, extremist groups," he intoned, "such as the communists, the Ku Klux Klan, the John Birch Society and others."

The thousands howling refused to let up. In them Rockefeller saw a dangerous and cavalier disregard, and by the way he raised his chin you could tell he hated them for it. Of course they hated him right back. They were having fun—together they'd become overjoyed by the fact that he'd been forced, up there on that speaker's platform, to listen.

"Our sole concern is for the future well-being of America," he said. And: "There is no place in the Republican party for such hawkers of hate, such purveyors of prejudice." And: "The Republican party must repudiate these people."

In all he was interrupted twenty-two times. When an organizer reminded him that his time was almost up, he shot back, "You control the audience, and I'll make my five minutes." But beneath the weight of their raucous human music he'd been silenced. "This is still a free country," he finally muttered.

At last Thompson was witnessing, firsthand, the tumult he'd been sure of ever since Kennedy's death. The Goldwater supporters kept screeching, their horns and cowbells ringing louder than ever even as the delegates on the floor were ordered to be quiet. Like cheap plastic the arena vibrated.

Still, the convention was only halfway done. Now that such a sound had come into being it couldn't be unmade. The Cow Palace displaced any possibility of its absence; instead, the great hangar-shaped dome of banners and blue smoke had become a portal, something into which this new expression, blaring at the same pitch of the previous year's national lament, passed fully into being.

*

Throughout the convention, Thompson's assignment for the *National Observer* was simple: they wanted him to work as a stringer, gathering reactions and quotes that his editors, who would be writing the stories, could then include in their standard who/what/when/where/why recaps. In a role like this access is key. And after finding himself confined for the most part to the gallery section during the first two days, he decided to take the matter into his own hands. It happened that a friend of his at the time, T. Floyd Smith, was working for the Pinkerton Agency, a private firm the Republicans hired to provide security. Smith had a badge that granted complete access, and when Thompson explained his desire to get closer to the action, he shrugged and said, "Take my credentials. I can go anywhere I want."

Suddenly, for Hunter Thompson, the entire arena—a labyrinthine facility of obscure tunnels and observation decks and innumerable small rooms smelling like cigars and vodka and dour, sweaty men—was open.

Throughout Wednesday and early Thursday he roamed the grounds as if to map them out. Around each new corner there existed the promise of another enthralling glimpse into the nation's political mechanics, that process through which we provide a single American with the power to instantly end all our lives. He found himself in numerous caucus rooms that would've otherwise been off-limits to the press—control centers for the Goldwater campaign and for politicians like Maine senator Margaret

Chase Smith, the first woman to be put up for nomination for president at a Republican or Democratic convention. At VIP outposts for corporations and lobbyists he ate and drank all he wanted for free. Of course he'd dressed for the part, in the sort of sport coat you'd find on a young congressional aide. He was clean-shaven. Wearing wingtips. Still he was uncomfortable, trying to fit in.

At one point he made his way to the very top of the Cow Palace, where skyboxes had been constructed to accommodate members of the television networks. It was from these precipitous sets that the notable anchors—Chet Huntley and David Brinkley at NBC, Walter Cronkite at CBS—hosted their nightly shows. For Thompson the contrast was astonishing. Huntley and Brinkley relied on an enormous staff of editors and experts to select the stories they hoped their audience would find the most interesting, while Walter Cronkite, suspended like an old philosopher king in his perch high above the arena, did all that work himself: for hours he turned his attention to a chorus of closed-circuit television monitors, contemplating the convention from a dizzying degree of physical and perceptual distance.

Thompson stayed up all night Wednesday in San Francisco, returning to the Cow Palace early Thursday afternoon for what would be the convention's main event. By this point he'd been taking Dexedrine regularly for two months. Already it appeared to be helping professionally. Amphetamine, in its effects, allowed him to stay awake longer than everyone else, with energy and focus, a supplement to the convention's frenetic environment. Suddenly he could work harder than he had before, even as normal regulators like exhaustion and hunger blared terribly. He could drink with important people and remain more functionally sober than all of them. He could explore every inch of the 1964 Republican National Convention with such cartographical thoroughness that it was as if his goal all along had been to record its exact shape for a generation of people he knew he'd never meet.

That Thursday evening, Barry Goldwater was scheduled to close out the festivities with his highly anticipated acceptance speech. What's more, he'd be introduced by none other than the former vice president of the United States, Richard Milhous Nixon, who'd returned from a short stint in the wilderness to put on his best face at this already contentious convention.

Thompson was down on the floor among the 1,308 delegates when Nixon emerged. It was the first time the two of them had been in the same room together—only a few dozen feet apart. In 1964 Richard Nixon looked like a branch-level bank president who very much enjoyed telling people that they'd failed to qualify for a loan. He was fifty-one years old. From his speaker's perch on the Cow Palace floor he gripped the podium tightly. His hair was oily and black, receding behind an evenly balanced widow's peak. He was wearing a slim navy tie to match his suit. His shirt was powder blue. His eyes flashed intelligently between the delegates below and the many thousands in the bleachers beyond. He was, and this can't be overstated, perfectly at ease, playing his favorite role of all: that of a humble, self-sacrificing idealist.

"Now I'm just a simple soldier in the ranks," he said, smiling. Thompson knew the act; it was the same hokey shtick that Nixon had been using for years, most notably during his 1952 "Checkers" speech: *I'm just the hardworking son of a poor butcher,* he liked to imply. A diligent, self-effacing Californian Quaker. The exact opposite of those East Coast Rockefeller elites.

The audience ate it up. For Thompson it had to be uncanny. To watch Richard Nixon live for the first time was to witness his one true talent: the ability to convince people who *knew* he was lying that they should trust him anyway. It's what made him such a resilient candidate; he could position himself for a future run by claiming to desire the exact opposite. He concluded his speech by gesturing theatrically. "Down this corridor will walk a man into the pages of history," he said. "He is the man who earned and proudly carries the title of Mr. Conservative, and he is the man who after the greatest campaign in history will be Mr. President. Barry Goldwater!"

And at that moment, as the silver-haired senator from Arizona strode forth to accept his party's nomination—as the band struck up "Glory, Glory Hallelujah" and the balloons came cascading down, thousands of them, many exploding loudly upon contact with the burning tips of equally numerous cigarettes—these two very different political animals basked at the podium together, hand in hand.

"I'd like to thank my good friend Dick Nixon," Goldwater said. He slid on his bulky reading glasses. And for the next forty minutes, in a calm, deliberate tone, he proceeded to enumerate the specifics of an ideology that to Thompson bordered on the apocalyptic.

The speech was heavy on terms like "liberty" and "law and order" and "security" that alluded to his most controversial positions without stating them directly. Halfway through, he seemed to throw a jab in Nixon's direction. "Small men," he said, "seeking great wealth and power, have too often and too long turned even the highest levels of public service into mere personal opportunity."

But the real surprise came just as his speech appeared to be winding down. Goldwater, after a brief silence, glanced at the podium, his jaw jutting sharply. Then, gazing out at the delegates below, he said, pausing every couple of words, "I would remind you . . . that extremism . . . in defense of liberty . . . is no vice."

In the next instant the Cow Palace erupted. Shouts, whistles, applause, cheers, also the horns and drums—at first it seemed to be the same sound as before. But after a few seconds Thompson noticed a new component. All around him, the delegates were jostling. Writhing. They banged their bodies against their chairs, their chairs against the floor, and now the floor was rumbling against their countless stomping feet.

Goldwater paused to let them have at it. "Thank you, thank you," he mouthed at the microphone. He waved. Still the sound kept rising. Thompson felt terrified. There was no mistaking it: the delegates around him were screaming and pounding *violently*. And amid them he was the only person not doing the same. How long until they turned their fervor in his direction—and what happened *then?*

Finally Goldwater resumed. He offered a companion line— "moderation in pursuit of justice is no virtue"—and as the crowd echoed and reverberated and subsided, he finished his acceptance speech for the Republican nomination, and with it this bewildering national convention.

Afterward, exhausted and frightened, Thompson left the Cow Palace along with the thousands of other attendees and, skirting the civil rights protestors who'd been camped out in the parking lot for days, he crossed the six miles back to downtown San Francisco. His Dexedrine usage had caught up with him; he'd pushed too hard for too long. Soon enough the crash would come; already he'd descended into a state of such exhaustion he'd be given a reprimand, the next day, from his editors at the *Observer*.

Still, the atavism of that moment on the floor—Goldwater's claim and the thunder that erupted, its sinister appeal—would haunt him. Four months later he'd write in a letter to a friend: "I recall standing on the floor of the convention when GW made his acceptance speech, and actually feeling afraid because I was the only person not clapping and shouting. And I was thinking, God damn you Nazi bastards I really hope you win it, because letting your kind of human garbage flood the system is about the only way to really clean it out."

In retrospect, he couldn't have asked for a more poignant contrast of political identities, especially in the wake of Kennedy's assassination. With Barry Goldwater, you knew what you were going up against: a true believer. When he suggested that to save the country you had to be willing to risk its destruction you immediately understood that he was speaking with a sort of compassion, however demented. With every bone in his body he seemed to say: *If it's liberty through fire you're looking for, then rest assured: I will be the first to burn.* A sentiment you can't fake. And the delegates that night, hearing it distilled in the line about extremism, had responded with their collective version of the same profound sincerity. Someone like Goldwater might have been espousing a dangerous ideology, but beneath it all was a consistency that hinted at something more: at promises kept, at a mutual and ancient devotion we might call, for lack of a better word, *love.*

Richard Milhous Nixon would never be loved like that. He'd always be incapable of eliciting the sincerity that Goldwater's supporters had expressed, due in no small part to the simple fact that he lacked this exact trait from the start. Then again, a politician of Nixon's emptiness—able to change his character to match whatever the electorate appeared to want—had a much better chance of appealing to a majority of Americans than a sincere extremist like Goldwater.

Thompson knew all this already, but to see it play out in person, from only a few feet away, was to be offered a glimpse into what it was that made a man like Richard Nixon so particularly evil: an innate and sinister talent for deception that the American electorate, when presented over and over again with its unabashed used-car-salesman tenor, somehow kept mistaking for an entirely different trait—ambition.

### In Trust

A few weeks after the convention, Hunter Thompson was spending the evening at his small residence in Glen Ellen with Sandy and Juan and the Geiger family, who'd come by for dinner and drinks. Much later that night, with their wives and children asleep, Thompson and Geiger found themselves walking together along the dry dark hillside. It was just past 4:00 a.m. First light was only an hour or so off, something they no doubt enjoyed waiting for—talking, as usual, about all that'd recently happened. Geiger had meant to join

Thompson at the Cow Palace for the Nixon/Goldwater speeches, but before the event he'd been at an Italian restaurant in the city when the waiter said he had a phone call. It was his answering service; there'd been a terrible car crash in Sonoma, and he was needed in surgery immediately.

Thompson had come away from the convention in a particular bind. Finally he'd seen, up close, the first act in the drama he'd been sure was coming. But as a writer for the *Observer*, he'd never be able to express his perspective on it through a literary lens—as *impressionistic* journalism. Other writers, like Joan Didion and Norman Mailer, were experimenting formally, but Thompson lacked the fame and experience to land the high-paying, feature-length assignments that would allow the artistic leeway he was searching for.

Mailer's stylistic approach served as a blueprint. Like Thompson, the famous fiction writer had also been there at the Cow Palace. On Thursday he'd bribed a guard to get down on the floor for Goldwater's speech—and his subsequent essay for *Esquire*, "In the Red Light," would encapsulate the sort of participatory experience Thompson wanted to convey. Mailer had exited the convention with the thousands of other attendees feeling the same despair that haunted Thompson: "And so their sense of crisis opens and they know like me that America has come to a point from which she will never return. The wars are coming and the deep revolutions of the soul."

That summer, Thompson began looking for a different employment venue, querying magazines like *The New Republic* and *The Nation*. He was also considering a move to San Francisco: he and Sandy and Juan would have less space and tranquility there, but he'd be able to react quickly to the Bay Area's fast-moving political and cultural developments. The day before the convention, forty thousand people had marched from the Embarcadero to the civic center, the largest civil rights protest in the city's history. At Berkeley the free-speech movement was taking off. The region itself was transitioning from its Beat-centered counterculture to something new and more overt—something that seemed be as much about personal expression as political act—and Thompson felt the need to be closer to it all.

Bob Geiger had gone to medical school in the Haight-Ashbury district, one of the neighborhoods Thompson was considering, and it's fair to speculate that at some point during their predawn walk along that Glen Ellen hillside a few weeks after the convention, the topic of moving to San Francisco would've naturally come up. Though what happened next would, in retrospect, hasten the whole process.

Just before sunrise Thompson and Geiger noticed some go-phers out beyond the shack. At first light the small, surreptitious animals were perching at their holes.

These gophers had been burrowing through the lawn at the front of the property, wrecking it, and Thompson and Geiger saw their appearance, now, as fortuitous. They went and got Thompson's shotgun. Together they crept toward the lawn. Without hesitation they fired volley after volley at their targets, which fled deep into the hill at the first deafening crack. Still they kept shooting, taking turns. At that moment it felt like a perfectly reasonable thing to do.

Suddenly they heard the shouts. The woman who owned the property was running at them. She was livid. Her home abutted the lawn the gophers had taken up residence in. To her it didn't matter *why* they'd been doing what they were doing. They'd fired on her house! She wanted Thompson and his family gone—immediately.

So that day, after being awake all night, Geiger helped Thomp-son move his small cache of possessions out of the tin-walled shack and into the empty condo complex where he was still housesitting. In his three-bedroom place there was more than enough room for the Thompson family. It was a natural decision: in retrospect he felt responsible for what had happened—at least in part—and besides, it would only be for the short term, until the coming move to San Francisco.

Still, it was the sort of gesture on which your entire future can depend—one that Bob Geiger made without hesitating, and one that Hunter Thompson accepted immediately. After all, he and Sandy and Juan and Agar had nowhere else to go.

*

For the next month the Geigers and Thompsons lived together as if on some long-planned vacation. It was August, hot. Sandy and Juan spent the days by the pool. A month of dinners and drinks, swimming and sunlight: by all accounts it was an easy-going accommodation, another miraculous moment in the Thompsons' brief Sonoma tenure.

Hunter Thompson had just turned twenty-seven. At the condo complex he continued to write at night. Sometimes Bob Geiger would stay up late, too, but he still needed to practice medicine in the morning.

By the end of the summer the Thompsons had found an apartment in San Francisco—on Parnassus Avenue, at the very top of the Haight-Ashbury district—and on a blue morning in September, Geiger rented a trailer to help his younger friend make the move.

It'd been nearly ten months since Kennedy's assassination, a period in which not much had actually changed despite the fact that nothing would be the same again. It now appeared that Barry Goldwater would lose to Lyndon Johnson by a significant margin. At the convention in July the Republican moderates had offered a test run of the strategy the Democrats would light upon in the general election, one that focused on Goldwater's hawkish approach to foreign policy and could be summed up by the attack slogan: "In your heart, you know he *might*." The majority of the country, it turned out, wasn't willing to stomach the prolonged threat of another nuclear crisis. It had already happened once, only two years earlier, when their young leader had stared down the Russians and the Cubans and his own military all at once, and improbably things had worked out—America had won. And the majority of voters in the upcoming election appreciated their winnings; they weren't about to risk their lives and double-down now, no matter how direly the Republican challenger might render the coming conflict between democracy and communism. Instead, in November, Americans would choose Johnson, a leader as perfunctory and shrewd as an ancient Roman censor, over some radical from the West. To Thompson *neither* was very appealing, but for the time at least, LBJ appeared to be the less-apocalyptic option.

That afternoon in September, the Rambler wasn't starting, so they attached the moving trailer to Geiger's car. They took off on the hour-long trip from Sonoma to the city. Soon they were crossing the Golden Gate. The new apartment on Parnassus Street actually had a view of the famous bridge; from the rear window you could see its heights, a pair of arches crowning the hills like the masts of an impossible ship.

The move Thompson was making would, in retrospect, represent one of the great transitions in his life. The first had occurred more than a decade earlier, in his hometown of Louisville, when, just before his fifteenth birthday, he watched his father die of a short, debilitating illness, leaving his mother to somehow support her three sons. The next took place in June 1955: accused of a robbery he never committed, he spent thirty days in the Jefferson County Jail—"The police lie," he wrote in one of his many letters to his mother, "injustice is rampant"—and immediately afterward he left town for good to join the Air Force, where he'd flourish as a sportswriter for the Armed Forces journalistic network. And then there'd been his reporting trip through South America, the final portion of which Sandy had flown down to join him on; they were married the month they came back to the United States, in May 1963, and that summer they'd set out for a life together in the West—for Colorado and California and whatever might come next.

Now this. The Golden Gate. The city beyond. In the blue deck of sunlight down beneath the bridge's span the water slid past. They were approaching San Francisco in September. Ahead of them, the streets climbed the hills, blocking the sky.

Thompson turned to Bob Geiger and said, "You know I wouldn't have made it without you. I feel like I've been put in trust."

## CHAPTER TWO

# THAT AWFUL EVIL HEAVY PACIFIC FOG

## 1965–1966

## Down and Out in San Francisco

It was just before midnight on Thursday, March 25, 1965, when Hunter S. Thompson stepped through the entrance to the DePau Hotel bar, located on Evans Avenue near the border to Hunters Point, a slim, worn-out lattice of auto shops and shipping cranes set along the southernmost stretch of San Francisco's rocky bayshore.

The sky was wet, fog-blurred. The water from the nearby pier smelled like machine oil. The streets were muted, lit as if from within by the city's lamps. Suddenly Thompson hesitated. In the next moment he took off his blazer, a Palm Beach madras that, with its tropical stripes, resembled nothing so much as a garishly patterned Scottish kilt. Briefly he considered shedding his tie, too, but he realized it wouldn't do much good—he was also wearing slacks and wingtips—and aside from driving the six or so miles back to his apartment and changing into jeans, there wasn't much he could do.

Inside, members of the Hell's Angels motorcycle gang's local chapter were gathering for their weekly meeting. At his arrival they all continued to do what they'd been doing—shooting pool, waiting on drinks—but with an air of menace that amplified the attention of the room in Thompson's direction.

He bought a glass of beer and sat back. His contact on this evening was Frenchy, a slight, delicately boned Angel in his twenties who was currently playing pool and had yet to acknowledge Thompson's arrival.

Hunter Thompson was here to write a feature on the motorcyclists for *The Nation,* for which he'd be paid $100—not nearly enough, in his opinion, but then again, these were desperate times.

A few months earlier, his long-simmering conflict with the editors at the *National Observer* had finally boiled over, and long story short, he'd given up his position there—a more drastic development than he'd anticipated. As of yet a steady reporting job hadn't materialized. Already he'd borrowed money from Bob Geiger and other friends to cover his rent. As a result, the political passions that motivated him for much of the past year had been thrown in stark relief by the more immediate crisis of providing for his wife and son. In this sense, the feature he'd arrived at this bar to compose represented a new crisis point in his journalistic career; if it didn't work out he'd need to consider giving up reporting altogether and find another way to support his family.

*The Nation* feature wasn't actually Thompson's idea. He'd been hoping to write a more overtly political piece about Mario Savio and the student protests across the Bay at Berkeley, but a week earlier Carey McWilliams, the magazine's prestigious editor, had sent him a query on the Hell's Angels, along with a long-awaited report on the gang compiled by California's attorney general Thomas C. Lynch. And now, thanks to a well-connected friend at the *San Francisco Chronicle*—the crime writer Birney Jarvis, who'd once been the vice president of this very Angels' chapter—Thompson was put in touch with the birdlike Frenchy and granted permission to attend the current gathering at the DePau.

For the time being, at least. Thompson hung back at the bar and watched as more Angels showed up. Finally Frenchy finished his pool game; he sunk his shot, walked over to Thompson, and said, "What do you want to know?"

For much of the next hour, Thompson asked Frenchy every question he could. About the gang's insignia, a winged death's-head set against dark denim. About their stinking, soiled outfits. About their personal backgrounds. About their resentments and expectations. About their day-to-day realities. And most of all, about the recent exposure they'd received in the national media—in articles from *Newsweek* and *Time* published just that week—most of which, because the reporting had lacked any real firsthand knowledge, relied exclusively on the testimony of law enforcement to paint the Angels in a cartoonish light: that of marauders looking to steal and rape and murder and then move on to the next town they could find.

*But is this true?* Thompson wanted to know. More specifically: *How has the press gotten things wrong?* Finally he asked Frenchy, "Has this rash of publicity affected your day-to-day activities?"

"Oh I don't know," the delicate young Angel replied. "Of course I don't like to read all this bullshit because it brings the heat down on us." He flashed a melancholic smile and added, "But since we got famous we've had more rich fags and sex-hungry women come looking for us than we ever had before. Hell, these days we got more action than we can handle."

Finally it was time for the chapter meeting. Once again Thompson slunk against the bar. Soon the conversation turned to the unexpected presence of the journalist in their midst.

"Who is this big cat?" one of the Angels demanded.

Another: "A fucking reporter?"

Another: "Beat his ass!"

Thompson stepped forward. Everyone at the meeting was about his age: young men who'd spent the day working at Frenchy's transmission shop and at the General Motors assembly line across the Bay—people who Hunter Thompson, a Louisville native without a college degree and with his own teenage history of jail time, no doubt understood more keenly than he would a roomful of, say, Princeton graduates. *Crazies recognize each other,* he reminded himself.

"Look," he said to everyone. "You guys don't know me and I don't know you." He told the Angels that he'd heard some wild things and that his goal, without any hidden agenda, was to separate fact from fiction. "I'm here to get the real picture," he explained. "I will do you the ultimate favor. I'll tell the American people the truth about you. Everything out there now is terrible." And as if on cue, he produced the recent articles from *Newsweek* and *Time*. "This is what happens when a lazy reporter does an article on rough and ready types like you guys."

As the Angels looked over this evidence he added a few additional comments about the function of the "outlaw press"—with which he aligned himself and *The Nation*—and about how, all things considered, they should keep in mind that he planned to write the article anyway . . . so they might as well cooperate.

This last point seemed to hit home—especially in the context of the current press clippings he'd passed around. "I'd go nuts if I read that stuff all the time," one of the Angels said. "It's all bullshit."

Thompson concluded his pitch on a spontaneous note: anyone who doubted his intentions was welcome to come back to his apartment, on Parnassus, for an all-night drinking bout. In the end five of the Angels accepted his offer. And when the bar closed at 2:00 a.m. they followed him on their motorcycles up across the city's hilly spine—all the way to the top of the Haight, 319 Parnassus. He arrived ahead of them and, darting inside, quickly explained the situation to Sandy. She knew he'd spent the evening reporting on the meeting, but it's fair to say that nothing could've prepared her for the arrival of half the San Francisco chapter of the notorious gang at her doorstep.

Thompson tried to calm her. Inside Juan was asleep. About the gang she'd heard horrible things. But perhaps she also understood, at least on some level, that among the many journalistic skills her husband had spent the last half decade developing, one of the most unheralded was his ability to identify threats during a crisis, especially when it came to the safety of his family and friends; in social environments he had the uncanny ability to notice *everything*—including the potential for violence. Really, he was asking her to trust him.

In the next moment Thompson moved past Sandy and grabbed the shotgun he kept in their apartment closet. From the front steps he waved the gun at the Angels, who were standing on the curb below, and shouted, "I'm not much for fist-fighting. I prefer to settle my beefs with a double-barreled 12-gauge shotgun."

This didn't do much to calm Sandy. But for his guests it seemed to make a certain kind of sense: already Thompson knew that the most dangerous thing about the Hell's Angels was their preference for *total* retaliation, meeting any perceived attack with over-the-top violence. By taking out the gun he'd raised the stakes as high as they could go. It was mutually assured destruction.

In the next moment the five Hell's Angels entered his apartment. There was Frenchy, his main contact; Filthy Phil, a former president of the San Francisco chapter who weighed over three hundred pounds; Okie Ray, a well-known burglar sporting a single gold earring and blond, Edwardian mustache; also a young man nicknamed Puff and another called Crazy Rock, who worked as a janitor at the newly opened Hilton. After a few tense moments they all settled into Thompson's chairs and couch.

Sandy retreated to the bedroom where Juan was sleeping and tried her best to go back to bed. Their apartment was long and slim. The fireplace, which no longer worked, was filled with crushed-up cans. Above it on the wall Hunter Thompson had hung a quote by Samuel Johnson, one of his favorites: "HE WHO MAKES A BEAST OF HIMSELF GETS RID OF THE PAIN OF BEING A MAN." Thompson put a record on the stereo: *The Freewheelin' Bob Dylan*. The Angels helped themselves to his alcohol: a case of beer and a gallon of cheap wine. And after a while they all found themselves talking easily together: Thompson's journalistic probing was matched, he began to realize, by a natural curiosity on the part of his guests. *Where did you get this amazing music?* they all wanted to know.

Frenchy happened to be a crack guitar player and banjoist—his young wife was a serious fan of American folk music—and listening to Dylan's album for the first time, he was struck by the elegiac ballads, by the tone of resentment and bewilderment and loss.

Together they listened to the lyrics of "Blowin' in the Wind." "Masters of War." "A Hard Rain's A-Gonna Fall." "Don't Think

Twice, It's All Right." "Talkin' World War III Blues." And "I Shall Be Free." It appeared that Thompson's impromptu late-night gesture—the invitation into his home, where his wife and one-year-old were sleeping in the room beyond—had disarmed them.

These members of the Hell's Angels would remain in Thompson's apartment drinking and talking and listening to Bob Dylan until dawn. In the bedroom Juan was still asleep. Sandy dozed, terrified; at 8:00 a.m. she needed to head downtown for her four-hour shift at a realtor's office—the family's main source of income these past few months—and the five bikers departed just as she was getting ready to leave.

Thompson spoke with her on her way out the door. Nothing terrible had happened, as he'd promised, and all in all he'd come away with the opportunity to tell a story no one else could write. It was the sort of breakthrough an actor might hope for, or a politician: the chance to stand apart from the pack. This also meant it could be a *monetary* breakthrough: if he nailed the feature there'd be the chance of jumping a whole journalistic income level, to that of, say, the *Saturday Evening Post*—an exponential raise.

Did Sandy understand? In the context of their recent financial crisis, perhaps the better question would be whether or not she'd consider a night like this—one populated by the most notoriously violent gang members in all of California—*worth it*. Would she still be able to convince herself, after the fact, that the terror she and her family had just endured was a necessary step on the path to making their life better?

Once she left for work Hunter Thompson sat down at his typewriter. Alone with his sleeping son, he felt exhilarated. Dawn in San Francisco: a fine curtain of coastal rain was drawing east. Already the day was as low and white-capped as the ocean beyond. The Dexedrine Thompson took was still working on him, and he spent the next few hours writing letters to friends on the East Coast: in a harried salesman's prose he articulated why the night he'd just experienced was so distinctly lucrative.

Though in truth there was much more at stake than money. The people he'd just met—young men who listened thoughtfully to Bob Dylan and at the same time portrayed themselves, physically and culturally, as adherents to a perverse system of violent retaliation—were so deeply contradictory that he could never have made them up.

＊

The March 1965 California attorney general's report on the Hell's Angels—fifteen pages of anecdotes, statistics, and recommendations—had been compiled over the previous six months by Thomas Lynch at the behest of a state senator from Carmel, a certain Frederick F. Farr, who'd pushed for a broader investigation into the Angels in the wake of a recent rape allegation filed against five of the gang's members in Monterey.

The final draft was overtly sensational. In lurid detail it specified nearly twenty crimes committed by the motorcycle group while implying that the real number was many times that. It's not that these accusations were unfounded—violence and assault were synonymous with the Angels for a reason—but after the Lynch report was released, national media outlets lit upon the salacious narrative to construct their own lurid full-length features. How could they not? Nothing moves the presses like a tale of indiscriminate Old West–style lawlessness.

The goal of Thompson's feature for *The Nation* was to separate the one-sided sensationalism of the attorney general's report—and the wave of cultural panic it set in motion—from the reality of the gang itself: who are these young men and, more importantly, *why* are they like this?

That March, during the week that followed the improbable all-night drinking bout at his Parnassus apartment, he did his best to immerse himself in the complex world of the Hell's Angels. Frenchy took him across the bay to the El Adobe, a bar that the Oakland chapter used as its headquarters, and set up an introduction with

Ralph "Sonny" Barger Jr., the gang's intelligent, charismatic, ruthless president. Barger, a year younger than Thompson, had recently gotten out of the Santa Rita Rehabilitation Center after serving time for marijuana possession. Unlike most of the Angels, he had a keen understanding of image control and politics, and while his own beliefs on government were surprisingly conventional—he harbored the sort of anticommunist patriotism with unapologetic nationalist leanings you'd just as soon find at a local Elks Lodge or VFW bar—his canniness was unnerving. In the wake of their meeting Thompson would write about Barger: "By turns he is a fanatic, a philosopher, a brawler, a shrewd compromiser and a final arbiter." On the whole Thompson seemed to find the week of participatory research—in its confirmations and contradictions and further demystifications—as intriguing as that first night in the Angels' company.

The final draft of his article for *The Nation* would clock in at just over four thousand words. In it he picked apart the faulty methodology and wildly overestimated membership statistics the attorney general's report had relied on. His conclusion: "The difference between the Hell's Angels in the paper and the Hell's Angels for real is enough to make a man wonder what newsprint is for."

Which isn't to say he dismissed the gang as harmless or nonexistent or culturally irrelevant. He emphasized the concept of "total retaliation for any offense or insult"—in his opinion the gang's central attribute. "The Hell's Angels try not to do anything halfway," he wrote. "Their claim that they 'don't start trouble' is probably true more often than not, but their idea of 'provocation' is dangerously broad, and their biggest problem is that nobody else seems to understand it. Even dealing with them personally, on the friendliest terms, you can sense their hair-trigger readiness to retaliate."

In the end Thompson sought to portray the Angels within a wider postwar context: how their sudden popularity was really just another manifestation of what happens when a nation like America limits economic and cultural mobility for entire groups of people; and also how, when said groups happen to be made up of formerly privileged individuals—white men without college degrees who only two decades earlier, during the wartime manufacturing boom, could've made a decent living on the unskilled labor market—the response is especially troubling.

He went so far as to characterize the Hell's Angels as representative of a disturbing trend: their outrageous behavior gave voice to a growing contingent of American society that now felt obsolete.

> Their real motivation is an instinctive certainty as to what the score really is. They are out of the ball game and they know it—and that is their meaning; for unlike most losers in today's society, the Hell's Angels not only know but spitefully proclaim exactly where they stand . . . [They] mean only to defy the world's machinery. But instead of losing quietly, one by one, they have banded together with a mindless kind of loyalty and moved outside the framework, for good or ill. There is nothing particularly romantic or admirable about it; that's just the way it is, strength in unity. They don't mind telling you that running fast and loud on their customized Harley 74s gives them a power and a purpose that nothing else seems to offer.

∗

Thompson sent a final draft of his *Nation* feature to Carey McWilliams on April 9. It was scheduled for a mid-May publication. With the $100 fee he paid off a month's worth of rent. Still, money was desperate. Their phone went dead after he repeatedly failed to pay the bill. He had to pawn his most valuable commodities—shotgun and camera. Each day he wrote on a typewriter that was unpredictable and slow, its margins off, but of course he couldn't afford another. And faced with the very real threat of eviction from his landlord—after months of overdue notices and noise complaints——he was forced to give away Agar, the family's beloved Doberman, to a game warden in Sonoma County.

Things got so bad by the end of April that, each morning before dawn—after having been awake all night trying to write—he headed out to the docks with the longshoremen in search of work. But among so many regulars he was a stranger; the old dock bosses never selected him. Next he tried delivering periodicals; at four in the morning he joined the crowd of alcoholics at Fifth Street and Folsom for the chance to hand out circulars at a dollar an hour. Only a few were ever chosen, and each time the truck pulled up he was passed over, despite being the youngest and healthiest person out there on the curb.

To date his income from the year totaled just under $500. Without Sandy's part-time job they would've lost the apartment. That spring, their first in San Francisco, the city was cold and sodden, blanketed by a senseless fog that never seemed to reach the more temperate coastal valleys. They still saw the Geigers, but the daily support from the year before was gone. Thompson continued his vampiric schedule—drinking until dawn and taking Dexedrine before finally giving up on his writing to wander the city in search of work—which only seemed to exacerbate his feelings of bleakness. He was desperately trying to finish his next *Nation* article and collect another $100 fee—this time on the free-speech movement at Berkeley.

It was the very article he'd been prevented from writing at the *National Observer,* an overtly political work that demanded both reportorial expertise and personal insight: into the movement itself, its drawbacks and strengths, and into the broader flaws of the society such a movement sought to critique. Really, his budding relationship with *The Nation* represented another long-sought step in the right direction.

But at the time, as he waited for the Hell's Angels article to come out, he felt the opposite. "I seem to be doing everything humanly possible to finish myself with booze and general physical abuse, pills, no sleep, etc.," he wrote to a friend in an April 18 letter. "The truth is, I'm in a perpetually rotten mood and rubbed raw each day by new lashings of bullshit . . . I think there is a terrible angst on the land, a sense that something ugly is about to happen, an hour-to-hour feeling of nervous anticipation. Whether it's the Bomb or a simple beating, you never know."

San Francisco, slow as always to emerge from its annual stretch of winter-in-springtime weather, only served to amplify his despair. He had felt something similar, half a decade earlier, during his first visit to the Bay Area. "City of hills and fog and water," he wrote in "Down and Out in San Francisco," an unpublished essay from October 1960. "City of no jobs . . . City of newspapers for Nixon . . . of neon bars and apartments full of people who can't pay rent or phone bills . . . where you can drink all night and jump off the bridge to beat a hangover." In a letter to Sandy composed that same month he added, "I understand the Golden Gate suicides . . . The city is merely an extension of Alcatraz, once you get here there's nowhere to go except backward, and the kind of people who flee to San Francisco don't have the guts or the time to start over."

And now, five years later, despite his modest but hard-won successes—not to mention a son and wife who depended on him—this desire for escape was building again. "I think that's the way to go out," he wrote in a letter to another friend on May 3, 1965—two weeks to the day before *The Nation* feature was slated to be published—"running the Big Sur highway on a big cycle with no lights and keep turning it over until the engine goes off in a wild scream and on one of the curves you keep going straight over, then turn on the headlight for the surf, and hold tight." In the next paragraph he seemed to echo his darkly perceptive assessment of Hemingway's suicide: "I don't claim to be invulnerable, but the one thing I insist on is that I can't be croaked except when I give the word."

Through the windows of his apartment on Parnassus there'd be one detail that the fog and rain could never completely obscure: the city's famous bridge. At all hours the red lights of the twin summits flashed, insinuating the presence of its span against the deep swift channel below, across which the boats progressed endlessly, as if on rails, their horns sounding at the transition from ocean to bay. Each night Thompson took in this view; he sat at his writing desk and looked out in the direction of the Pacific, a black-velvet amphitheater of ocean and unseen hills fluted by the slimmest passageway. In this sense the bridge *was* the city, its shape: both doorway and exit. And wherever Hunter Thompson drove that spring—in search of predawn work at the docks, or south of Market Street to pass out circulars, or across the Bay itself, to Sausalito and Berkeley and Oakland beyond—the Golden Gate would've been there, too, disappearing one moment behind avenues and buildings before rematerializing the next.

On a weekend in May, at an hour that was probably closer to dawn than midnight, Thompson was driving near the base of one of San Francisco's many bridges when he suddenly lost control of his car. Later he'd claim he passed out at the wheel. Either way, he veered into an abutment at 70 mph and was thrown into a spin. In the next instant he somehow recovered, righting himself before he could crash into anything else. The side of the Rambler was scraped and dented. Miraculously, the car still worked. And he was lucky to be alive. Afterward he found himself overcome by a sensation of what might be best described as grace: an enormous rush of gratitude to not be dead. It was an outcome so providential as to be without question unearned. A gift.

During the weeks that followed Thompson was terrified to drive. He couldn't look at the violence done to the Rambler without contemplating the reality that, for the briefest of instants, he'd come breathtakingly close to being crushed and killed and removed once and for all from the only world he'd ever known.

✳

"The Motorcycle Gangs: Losers and Outsiders" appeared in the May 17 issue of *The Nation*. At the time Thompson's phone was still disconnected—he hadn't yet paid the bill—and the only way to keep in touch with the outside world was through the postal service. So each afternoon he dragged himself down the steps of 318 Parnassus to the cramped ground-level entryway, where the mail, stuffed through a slim golden slot in the door, was piled haphazardly on the tile. He'd been banking on an immediate response, hoping, ideally, for inquiries from editors at high-paying magazines. And in the days that followed the article's release, he descended the narrow stairway to discover—amazingly—queries from *Playboy, Cavalier, Esquire,* and the *Saturday Evening Post*. They all wanted him to write something on motorcycle gangs. Each offered many times more money than *The Nation*.

The avalanche of interest didn't stop there. More people than he could've imagined had read his article on the Hell's Angels, and during those last two weeks of May, the floor of his Parnassus entryway was also flooded with long, complimentary notes from New York publishers: what did he think about turning his recent feature into a *book*?

By June he'd whittled down the field to a pair of options. The first came from Angus Cameron, a renowned fifty-six-year-old editor who, during the hysteria of the previous decade, had been accused of communist affiliations by the Pulitzer-winning author Arthur Schlesinger Jr. and blacklisted from the book publishing world—a sentence that had lasted until 1959, when he was brought back into the fold with a senior position at Alfred A. Knopf. In a June 7 letter to Thompson he wrote, "I was struck by the fact that there [are] all kinds of people 'out of the ball game' these days, and wondered if you ever thought of extending your analysis of the motorcycle version to a broader book dealing with various alienated losers and outsiders." Eventually he asked to see an outline, adding: "I think you look at things in a way that would interest people and you write well—and ironically."

The second appealing query came from Bernard Shir-Cliff, an executive editor at Ballantine Books, who had come across Thompson's feature and was blown away by the honesty, liveliness, and intimacy of the writing—so much so that he bypassed the issue of requesting a formal book proposal in favor of making an actual *offer:* a $6,000 advance against royalties on the paperback rights, with $1,500 available up front and the details of a possible hardcover still to be negotiated.

It was a tremendous sum, nearly fifty thousand dollars by today's standards. Thompson accepted.

As soon as he received the check he paid off his rent for the next two months. From the pawnshop he retrieved his shotgun and camera equipment. He contacted the Overseas Press Club to purchase a new health insurance policy for his family. Finally he could get his phone working again. There was one more thing he planned to buy: a motorcycle—a BSA 650 Lightning, as opposed to the standard Harley the Angels rode—that would allow him to differentiate himself from the subjects of his new book as he followed along on their excursions.

Afterward he wrote Angus Cameron at Knopf to explain why he'd gone with the Ballantine offer; he liked the idea of a project on "outsiders and losers" and wanted to leave the door open for a future collaboration. The decision was strictly an economic one: "I am simply damn tired of being poor." He knew that a work of participatory journalism on the Hell's Angels was an extremely risky proposition, both artistically and personally. "The depth of research will be a nightmare," he admitted. "I suspect I'll be having some medical bills by the time this thing is done." But a book steeped in such a vibrant degree of immersion offered the chance to compose a *literary* narrative—"something like George Orwell's *Down and Out in Paris and London,*" he explained, "or "Tom Wolfe's 'Junior Johnson.'"

In Thompson's view, such stylized, personal work represented a fresh iteration of the "impressionistic" nonfiction he'd been crafting the previous year. "Fiction is a bridge to the truth that the mechanics of journalism can't reach," he wrote to Cameron, before scratching out "the mechanics of" with a blue ballpoint pen. The book he hoped to write would exist at a point along just such a bridge; everything in it would be researched and witnessed and verifiable, but his ultimate goal was to dramatize it all with a novelist's skill, to render the true events through a personal, subjective perspective: his own. "In order to write that kind of punch-out stuff you have to add up the facts in your own fuzzy way," he concluded. "And to hell with the hired swine who use adding machines."

## In the Red Light of La Honda

Two months later, on a clear blue afternoon, Hunter Thompson gathered Sandy and Juan into the Rambler and together they rode south along the olive-drab ridges of San Francisco's coastal range. Their destination was La Honda, a small mountain town about forty-five minutes down the peninsula.

At the turnoff to the ranch house, they looked up to find an enormous banner painted with red, white, and blue letters: THE MERRY PRANKSTERS WELCOME THE HELL'S ANGELS. Beneath it, waiting as if to greet them, four police cars were parked in a row, their lights rotating in the low mountainside shadows of the afternoon. Thompson piloted past the banner and cops, and after spanning a long wooden bridge, he pulled to a stop in the driveway down below the house. Perhaps fifty people had gathered already.

Off to one side, more than a dozen Hell's Angels stood near their motorcycles. They'd arrived a few minutes earlier when, in a booming ceremony, biker after biker had gunned his 74-cubic-inch Harley-Davidson engine across the bridge before screeching to a stop. Now they appeared to be waiting impatiently, bearded and greasy in their sleeveless denim jackets. The whole San Francisco chapter was there—Frenchy and Filthy Phil and all the rest.

From the other part of the crowd—a group that included artists and activists and intellectuals and families with small children—a blond, broad-necked man emerged. He wore a buckskin shirt. In his hand he carried a cup of what appeared to be beer. It was Ken Kesey, the twenty-nine-year-old author who, after publishing *One Flew Over the Cuckoo's Nest* and *Sometimes a Great Notion* to broad acclaim, had purchased this ranch house and the surrounding three-acre property, living here now along with his wife and children and a close-knit group of friends known as the Merry Pranksters.

Saturday, August 7, 1965. An arid summer afternoon in the coastal mountains. The party was only just beginning.

Earlier that week, Thompson and Kesey had participated in a roundtable talk on writing for the local public-access television station, KQED, and afterward they'd decided to duck into a nearby bar for a few drinks. Thompson had been shadowing the Angels on a daily basis since June—they'd enjoyed his article in *The Nation* enough to let him continue to hang around—and he mentioned to Kesey that he planned to head over to Frenchy's transmission shop later in the day, to which Kesey responded, "Whoa, I'd like to meet those guys." So together they drove down to Hunters Point, where they spent the rest of the evening drinking with the members of the gang's San Francisco chapter. At the end of the night Kesey suggested that they all get together again for a weekend party, a chance for the parallel rails of the burgeoning Bay Area counterculture to join up.

Thompson and his family had arrived just as these two groups were feeling each other out. On the one side you had the Merry Pranksters: educated advocates of consciousness expansion who'd traveled together, the year before, on the cross-country bus trip that would become the centerpiece of Tom Wolfe's *Electric Kool-Aid Acid Test*. On the other, the working-class members of a motorcycle gang who'd recently found themselves flush with media and police attention. Both were seen as anarchic and nonconformist.

Also, both were in serious legal trouble—the Angels because of the Lynch Report and recent rape accusations in Monterey, and Kesey and his group for cultivating and consuming marijuana. Finally, both groups were made up almost exclusively of white, young, male Californians; they each constituted a version of their own idealized fraternity.

For Thompson, the party offered the potential to create a dramatic set piece for his book, and he'd arrived at Kesey's as an observer, particularly since he'd brought his wife and son. But now, as Thompson watched Kesey approach the Angels with a cup in his hand—and saw cups in the hands of many in the motorcycle gang—he began to panic. Kesey wasn't just sharing his supply of beer. He was offering his new guests lysergic acid diethylamide—LSD-25, dissolved into liquid—and the Angels, told what it was, didn't hesitate to drink it down, despite the fact that none of them had ever tried it before.

In 1965 LSD was still legal. Hunter Thompson had never done the drug himself; years earlier, while living in Big Sur, friends had warned him that acid could bring out the worst in people—especially in those with energetic, high-strung personalities—and he'd been cautioned against taking it. With the Angels the danger seemed even more pronounced. Over the last few months, Thompson had learned that once the members of the motorcycle gang started mixing alcohol with drugs—especially with the barbiturate Seconal—they tended more often than not to turn violent and unreasonable, and he'd made it a habit to leave at the first sign of trouble.

Now, standing with his son and wife in the afternoon shadow of the mountains, he tried to imagine the sort of behavior LSD might provoke in the Angels. Not that he planned to wait around and find out; at that moment, only a few minutes after he'd arrived, he hustled Sandy and Juan back into the Rambler and together they all drove off, back up the hill, through La Honda, and then down to the ocean-side town of San Gregorio to enjoy a picnic on the beach.

He'd fled out of the fear of the unpredictability, but he knew that whatever was taking place back at the ranch house would be integral to his book. So he made a decision: after their meal by the sea they'd stop in at Kesey's again so as to view, from a safe distance, the evolution of a scene they'd so hastily left.

*

A few hours later the Thompsons made their second approach on the party. Once again they passed the police, who'd been staking out Kesey's place on suspicion of marijuana cultivation for months now, though on this occasion—thanks in no small part to the enormous banner—they'd increased their contingent to four cars, the red lights of which continued to turn in the late-afternoon hillside.

Now, when he pulled to a stop on the other side of the bridge, there wasn't anyone around to greet them. Instead, the Angels, along with the other guests, were sitting peacefully—contentedly—near the house, where a giant screen had set up. The Merry Pranksters were projecting a movie: footage from their cross-country bus trip the year before. With Juan, the Thompsons exited their car and began to make their way through the grounds.

Across the three-acre property, Kesey and his Pranksters had arranged a number of enormous, high-powered sonic amplifiers. They were hidden among the branches of the sequoias, the trunks of which were painted in DayGlo neon. From the heights of these trees came a constant crash of sound. Some of the amps played music: the Rolling Stones, the Beatles, Jumpin' Joe Jackson, and more often than not, Bob Dylan. Others were rigged to live microphones, which had been set to a one-second delay and hidden in squirrels' nests, bathrooms, bedrooms, even along the bank of the rushing creek.

The total number of guests that afternoon amounted to perhaps a hundred; in addition to the Angels and the Pranksters

there were professors, writers, doctors, and psychologists. Former Harvard professor and LSD guru Richard Alpert was there,
along with the novelists Robert Stone and Larry McMurtry. Also:
members of the Grateful Dead, as well as famous figures from
the Beat generation, including Neal Cassady and Allen Ginsberg.
Nearly everyone was on acid. After the film, they all spread out
together across the property. Took turns blowing soap bubbles.
Throwing Frisbees. Playing flutes. Banging drums. Around them
the trees sounded and gleamed. Dogs wandered. DayGlo paint,
the same kind that had marked the redwoods, now masked faces;
guests were applying it to one another generously. From one
direction Bob Dylan could be heard singing "Mr. Tambourine
Man." From another, Radio KLSD, an imaginary station broadcast along the same sound system, blared a hastily composed blues
poem, the lyrics of which described the real-time actions of the
people listening below.

Kesey and most of the Pranksters had met a few years earlier
at Stanford University, where, as students and professors, they'd
resided in a section of campus known as Perry Lane. Together
they'd grown dissatisfied with what they saw as America's postwar
conformity—the political, legal, and moral power structures that
conditioned people to think and live in the manner society expected. For the most part their dissatisfaction had been expressed
through recognizable channels: art, poetry, intellectual theory, as
well as the curriculums of the college-level classes they taught.

At first Kesey had done the same. But in 1960, to augment the
creative-writing fellowship that supported him and his wife Faye,
he'd signed up for a series of trials at the Palo Alto Veterans Hospital,
where he and other volunteers were given dosages of psychedelic
compounds—substances that few people had ever experienced.
These included IT-290 amphetamine, mescaline pellets, Ditran,
and LSD, the latter of which produced in Kesey an experience
of such unfettered, cosmic immediacy—the perception of both
subjective and objective reality; of the personal and impersonal;

of what might perhaps be best described as the *infinite,* at least in conceptual terms—that he smuggled some samples to his friends, who began procuring and consuming it in more felicitous settings than those of a stark Stanford University hospital.

For them LSD made previous forms of articulation irrelevant. Something like poetry might highlight and indict the brutal logic of the American status quo, but it was still up to the reader/audience to put the pieces together and comprehend, intellectually and emotionally, the flaws they'd been shown. Now the whole process could be sidestepped. Kesey had gotten hold of a substance that created, as if magically, an entirely new perspective: it allowed whoever consumed it to see past the games and conditions of American society and, in doing so, experience the full unfettered breadth of reality—a point of view that in his opinion would make the status quo irrelevant for *everyone.*

In other words, Kesey and his friends were sure that what they'd discovered was some Prometheus-level stuff, an evolutionary leap so extreme as to change the course of mankind forever. The eventual goal of consciousness expansion was something called intersubjectivity; with LSD, each individual human point of view could be expanded outward until they all merged into a single, unifying, omniscient collective. Which was part of the reason why Kesey had recently decided to give up writing and position himself, instead, as the most trustworthy and experienced guide to their revolution of the mind: a revolution that, as opposed to the political or militaristic means usually associated with this sort of massive society-wide change, required hardly any effort at all—beyond the consumption of the drug itself.

The party that was being held on this long-ago Saturday afternoon in August—its real-time cacophony—represented the first steps in the revolution. For Kesey and the Pranksters it was a living rendering of the immediacy that they felt literature could no longer capture. For Hunter Thompson and Sandy it was unnerving and intriguing.

Toward dusk Allen Ginsberg had the Pranksters and Angels arrange in a circle. He grabbed the microphone. He was wearing finger cymbals. And he proceeded to sing *Hare Krishna,* his long beard
swaying with his hips. Later Neal Cassady, the inspiration for Jack
Kerouac's Dean Moriarty character in *On the Road,* stripped naked
and ran toward the cop cars across the highway beyond. From the
wooden bridge over the creek he cursed them. "Come on over
here and see what you get!" he screamed. "Goddamn your shit
filled souls anyway! Don't fuck with me, you sons of shitlovers!"

By 8:00 p.m. the sun had disappeared. The house was lit from
inside: a yellow chandelier, blazing. The floor vibrated, everyone
danced, the trees kept up the music, there'd been no threats (apart
from Cassady's), no violence, and as the evening turned to night,
the members of the Hell's Angels wandered about, tripping on LSD
and discovering, at various points among the redwoods, Kesey's vast
collection of sculptures. A hanged man near the creek. A thundering bird, its voice amplified with light. Even this: two metal figures
locked explicitly together, water shooting from their waists in a
single, continuous stream.

Hunter Thompson watched these developments from his relatively sober vantage point; to his surprise, the night seemed a success on every measurable front. As a result, he and Sandy decided to
stay until the next day; she and Juan could sleep in the bunks where
Kesey's children were camped out while Thompson continued to
document the party for his book.

A few hours later—now it was almost midnight—he noticed
that a number of people appeared to be beating a path up to a small
studio about a hundred feet from the main house. He walked over
to see what was going on. In the small room were about twenty
Hell's Angels, many of them naked. Together they were watching a
slim blond woman; she was having sex with four men at once. On
the wooden floor the Angels surrounded her, descending in shifts,
her loose red dress bunched up to her chest. Like the rest of the

partygoers, she'd taken LSD, and it was clear to Thompson that she was drunk to the point of incoherence.

Someone told him that she was Neal Cassady's ex-wife, but in fact she was one of Cassady's three current love interests, a visual artist named Anne Murphy who'd been living with him in Palo Alto. Earlier in the evening she'd approached two of the Angels with an invitation to join her in the shack. Her motivation for doing so was never made clear to Thompson—years later Murphy would write that her main goal was to make Cassady jealous—but by now, word of what was happening had gotten out, drawing many more participants than she'd counted on. Thompson would later describe what he saw as "somewhere between a friendly sex orgy and an all-out gang rape." And while he stops short of calling it one or the other, it's fair to say that events had reached the point where consent could no longer be given. Instead, in the shack, the Angels held all the cards. As always their power resided in their numbers: a physical manifestation of the worst sort of mob.

Eventually some of the Angels in the room, for reasons that weren't clear, went back out into the party and found Neal Cassady, who was high and naked and stumbling drunk, and dragged him into the shack where, at their behest, he eventually took his own turn on the floor with his girlfriend.

Thompson was horrified. The party had turned into an unmitigated disaster; even after he'd fled the shack and spoken with Sandy, who'd had no idea what was going on, he couldn't cast aside what he'd seen. "All these shadowy figures," he reported in his audio notes, "silhouettes is what they were, in that way, kind of surrealistically horrifying, the image was ever present . . . people kneeling, and jumping around, and bending, and getting up off of her, and getting down on her, and people holding her legs, and really . . . too much." He felt sick about it; it was due to him, after all, that the Angels were here in La Honda in the first place.

But he knew that the odds of stopping the assault were over-whelmingly against him—that the Angels would inflict total retali-ation on anyone who tried to interfere. What could he do? Instead, he tried to find a way to counter the panic he was feeling. Up till that moment, he'd avoided the acid and the alcohol, in his capac-ity as a working reporter, knowing that the success of his book would determine the future path of his career. During a previous daylong party at Kesey's—this was in May, when the stakes were social as opposed to professional—he'd consumed twenty beers, struggling to keep his car from going off the road on the drive home. And now, as everything around him fell apart and the gang rape in the shack wore on—and Sandy and Juan were safely tucked away alongside Kesey's sleeping children—he seemed to release his professional decorum.

Why hold back when the worst that can happen already has? Thompson approached Ken Kesey and asked for LSD. He drank it down just after midnight—the first dose of his life.

The party continued. The cops remained on the road; from the tops of their cars the lights continued to rotate, reddening the leaves beyond the creek. At some point Cassady and Anne Murphy returned to the main house, where they danced slowly together, despite the music's frenetic beat, surrounded by many of the men who'd raped her in the shack.

For Thompson, the effects of the LSD came on and he was sur-prised; he didn't feel violent or wild. Over the next few hours, as he wandered quietly throughout the property, he experienced an enor-mous sense of relief; the LSD, in its effects, managed to blast away the immediacy of the awful scene he'd witnessed. At the same time it failed to unleash the demons he'd always suspected he harbored. He'd finally gone to the bottom of the well, the place he feared most, and to his enduring astonishment he'd found these depths empty.

Not that the drug would ever come to represent, for him at least, a potential catalyst for political and social revolution or anything like it. In contrast to Kesey and the Pranksters, Thompson saw this drug as an end, as opposed to a means—an escape. It wasn't as if career politicians like Lyndon Johnson and Richard Nixon would suddenly sue for peace if they took acid. In fact it was the opposite: the idealism of Kesey's revolution made the Pranksters even more likely to be manipulated by those holding real power: by police, local government, and, ultimately, by politicians who believed that authority is determined, first and foremost, by an ability to manipulate the facts of the reality around them. Which was why the Hell's Angels were an even more frightening group, politically, than most people might assume. At least the Pranksters were harmless. However, if the powers that be ever stopped demonizing the Hell's Angles and decided, instead, to co-opt their gang-oriented violence—a terrifying form of which had been on display that night in the shack, stark and recurring as a nightmare, in the images of the scene Thompson had witnessed—the results would be terrifying.

Toward dawn, just as the summer sun was hitting the mountains, he and Sandy and Juan finally departed Ken Kesey's house for the final time. They drove past the cops and headed back to San Francisco, where they arrived, without incident, just after 5:00 a.m. The party they'd left behind would continue for another two full days, and over the next month the Angels and Pranksters would join together to throw several more.

That Sunday morning, as he crossed the thirty miles back to the apartment on Parnassus, the effects of the LSD were still working on him, if subtly. After getting his family home safely, he sat down at the desk overlooking the Golden Gate Bridge and recorded his notes for the book: "Tonight was Saturday, August 7th. Now it's Sunday morning, August 8th, I suppose. Ah shit. It's a long and dirty story and I'm tired and it's 5:30 in the morning and I've just driven back, from Kesey's, in that awful evil heavy Pacific fog."

## Johnson Uber Alles

By the autumn of 1965, with the investigative reporting portion drawing to a close—finally it was time to start writing in earnest—Hunter Thompson suddenly found his attention torn; he was drawn toward a rapidly evolving issue: the US military's intervention in Vietnam.

In the spring of that year Lyndon Johnson had sent the Marines into Da Nang. Operation Rolling Thunder, an extraordinarily furious bombing campaign, was in full swing. And the protest movement at Berkeley, which had previously focused on civil rights and free speech, was now centered, under the direction of activists like Jerry Rubin, on the question of America's plans for Southeast Asia.

Thompson articulated his own thoughts on the war, in a letter that he sent directly to none other than LBJ. "I refer specifically to your hysterical Vietnam policy," he wrote, "which has put the United States in a position very much resembling Nazi Germany's in the Spanish Civil War." It was an extraordinary statement—about as close as you could come to calling the leader of the free world a fascist without saying it outright. But Thompson was just getting started. "I am neither a pacifist nor an advocate of nonviolence," he wrote, "but my sensibilities are offended by the spectacle of old men whose mania for blood and bombing will inevitably cause thousands of young men to be killed for no good reason."

His tone was equal parts bewilderment and horror. "Are you getting your foreign policy advice from Goldwater and Nixon?" he asked. And: "We cannot possibly prevail in Asia, any more than Hitler could prevail in Europe." And: "If Kennedy had lived I believe he would have us on the way out of Vietnam by now, while you have us sunk to the eyeballs." He ended with a warning: "You can't win it without killing us all, and—unless you start acting like a thinking human instead of a senile political beast—you are going to end up the goat, with a belly-full of blame for your own mistakes as well as other people's." He typed all of this on letterhead featuring his Parnassus address and signed it: "Sincerely, Hunter S. Thompson."

Later, he'd worry that letters like this would draw the attention of the Secret Service and FBI, but perhaps that was part of the point he was trying to make. As he was indicating, an unjust war will always disfigure the country tasked with carrying it out. It's a thesis that Orwell hammered home again and again—especially in his essay "Shooting an Elephant"—and from the beginning Thompson understood that a folly like Vietnam wouldn't just deracinate a large portion of the American population with the twin horrors of trauma and loss; it would also, to prop up its dishonest execution, faulty rationales, and false claims of impending victory, demand the silencing of public dissent in favor of a blindly patriotic nationalism. Not that he was alone in thinking this, but he knew as well as anyone that the best way for authoritarians to undermine a representative government is to sacrifice the means of this representation under the banner of claiming to save it—from communists, from radical student groups, from civil rights activists, even from the very institutions meant to hold accountable the nation's civilian leader. The year before, Barry Goldwater had pretty much made the same argument: *You have to be willing to risk the destruction of America in order to save it.* And now LBJ, in the wake of the Gulf of Tonkin Resolution and the buildup that followed, appeared to be trapped by a similarly reductive logic.

That October, as the death toll for Americans in Asia continued to grow—it would reach 2,344 by the end of the year—Thompson headed to Berkeley to report on one of the largest antiwar protests to date: the Get Out of Vietnam demonstration and march. Ken Kesey had been invited to speak, and the plan was for a convoy of Hell's Angels and Merry Pranksters to arrive on campus together, dressed in military garb with fake guns hanging from the bus and with bike engines roaring, a faux-invasion that was meant to be both statement and prank—a fresh way to blow the minds of everyone in attendance.

The protest itself had been organized by Jerry Rubin and Paul
Krassner, founding members of the Vietnam Day Committee
(VDC) who would eventually go on to form, with Abbie Hoffman, the Youth International Party (Yippies). The protest was
scheduled to culminate in a fifteen-thousand-person march from
the university to the Oakland Army Terminal, the war effort's
major shipping point.

But on the day of the event—October 16, a Saturday—Kesey
and the Pranksters were stopped by the cops staking out his La
Honda property, and the delay caused them to miss their rendez-
vous in Palo Alto with the Angels, who'd instead cross the bay to
Berkeley on their own.

Kesey was the rally's second-to-last speaker. He took the stage
late in the afternoon, and, wearing an epauletted DayGlo vest the
same color as the sun, he told the audience of mostly white, educated students gathered there: "You know, you're not gonna stop
this war with this rally. That's what *they* do. They hold rallies and
march. That's the same game you're playing . . . their game." He
pulled a harmonica from his pocket and struck up the opening
chords to "Home, Home on the Range." He compared the gestures of the speaker preceding him to those of Benito Mussolini.
And, true as always to his belief in consciousness expansion—for
him, a protest such as this was as outmoded and primitive a form
of expression as something like writing—he offered the thousands
of attendees a final piece of advice: "There's only one thing's gonna
do any good at all . . . and that's everybody just look at it, look at
the war, and turn your backs and say: *Fuck it*. Just look at it and
turn away and say: *Fuck it!*"

The organizers were furious. All at once the energy of the rally
seemed to universally deflate. By now the sun was going down.
And it was in such a state—of agitation and dejection and nervousness—that the fifteen thousand protesters began their march
toward the Oakland Army Terminal. They carried signs that read:
JOHNSON UBER ALLES. IF GOD WERE ON OUR SIDE HE'D PUKE. VIET

CONG ASK FOR FREE ELECTIONS, U.S. ANSWER? And LBJ YOU'VE GONE TOO FAR. A windy, bay-cooled afternoon, the gusts stripping the leaves from the eucalyptus branches. Together they made it as far as Telegraph Avenue and Woolsey Street—the border to Oakland— where they were summarily greeted by nearly four hundred police officers who'd been waiting there for hours, arranged in an arrowed wedge, to prevent the marchers from continuing on to the terminal.

Hunter Thompson was waiting, too; with his press credentials and tape recorder and camera he'd come up from behind the police, on the Oakland side of the confrontation, weaving through the phalanx of dark-sleeved officers to reach the tense no-man's-land beyond, where the protest's leaders had gathered to consider their next move: Was it worth it to rush the lines and submit themselves to what everyone knew would be a vicious beating? Or should they relent, and turn the whole march around? After some debate, the decision was made to back down—no small task, considering the number of people involved—and together the members of the VDC committee were walking over to inform the Oakland police chief, Edward M. Toothman, of their plan to reverse course . . . when, from behind the wall of officers, a dozen individuals in denim vests suddenly burst forward.

At last the Hell's Angels had appeared. Together they rushed the protest's leaders. They were ordered to do so by Sonny Barger, who was acting in accordance with his conservative political beliefs. The charge was led by the Oakland chapter's sergeant at arms, a six foot five, 250-pound repo-agent nicknamed "Tiny."

"Communists!" the Angels screamed. "Traitors! Beatniks!" Tiny was as solid as a boulder; against the VDC leaders he flung himself, knocking a path as other members of the gang streamed forward to punch and kick and stomp anyone in their vicinity.

Barger followed from behind. "Why don't you people go home!" he screamed, his voice breaking. He shoved through the line of demonstrators at the front of the march—they'd all linked hands to form a barrier on the Berkeley side—and then he spun around, bouncing on the balls of his feet like a boxer. Someone on a loudspeaker implored, "Everybody sit down, sit down in this area!"

Thompson watched all of this from only a few feet away. He knew these specific Angels well. "Tiny hurts people," he would later write. "When he loses his temper he goes completely out of control and his huge body becomes a lethal weapon. It is difficult to see what role he might play in the Great Society."

For the leaders of the VDC and the thousands of protestors gathered beyond, such anger and violence made about as much sense as Kesey's speech. Over the previous month, in the wake of the party at La Honda, the Bay Area's countercultural left had come to see the Hell's Angels as fellow outsiders: an equally alienated segment of the population ready to stand up to the oppressive mainstream that had so blithely discarded them.

The police were also caught off-guard; now they found themselves tasked with protecting the people they'd spent the day preparing to fight. They quickly intervened, batons bared, and clubbed at the Angels who were attacking the students and activists. "Back off," Police Chief Toothman shouted at Barger. Just then three officers grabbed Tiny while another struck him in the head, knocking him unconscious; suddenly his huge body was stripped of its tension, and like a fleshy stone, he swung down to the ground—in the process pinning one of the cops' legs, which snapped against the sheer heft of his descent.

Hunter Thompson was one of the few people who didn't seem surprised by what was transpiring. "When push came to shove," he wrote afterward, "the Hell's Angels lined up solidly with the cops, the Pentagon, and the John Birch Society." They revealed to the antiwar movement what they were: nationalistic, authoritarian, and more than willing to violently suppress anyone whose point of view they didn't share.

*

In the wake of the violence, Allen Ginsberg and other members of the VDC met with Sonny Barger, hoping to convince him to come around to their perspective. In November Barger stayed up all night with them, taking acid and listening patiently to their arguments. But neither side appeared to be any closer to understanding the other's motivation.

On November 19—the day before the next scheduled VDC protest against the war—Barger called a press conference in Oakland at Dorothy's Bail Bonds, which advertised itself as "the Hell's Angels official bail bondsman." Barger was wearing his usual dark vest, the collar popped up, his hair greased and shining. As he read from a sheet of prepared comments he held his cigarette awkwardly, struggling to keep his eyes on the cameras. He called the antiwar protest "a despicable, un-American activity." But in the next breath he revealed that he'd decided, "in the interest of public safety and the protection of the good name of the city of Oakland," to keep his distance from future demonstrations so as to avoid violence: "We intend to absent ourselves from the scene, and we encourage all citizens to do the same."

The reporters who'd gathered to hear him out—including Hunter Thompson—weren't really sure what to make of it all. "Sonny," one of them asked, "isn't this a complete turnaround as far as the Hell's Angels are concerned? You people aren't used to doing what you're told to do."

"The thing of it is," Barger replied, "we haven't been told to do nothin'. This is our own decision. We think it's best for the country."

He went on to call the antiwar demonstrators a "mob of traitors" and refused to answer whether or not he believed in their right to march. Eventually he pulled out a telegram and, claiming that it was a copy of the one he'd just sent off to none other than Lyndon B. Johnson, he started reading from it. "Dear Mr. President," he said. His voice sounded flat and expressionless, like a child's, as if he were delivering an apology that someone in a position of authority had obviously forced him to make. The gist of the telegram went like this: Barger wanted LBJ to know that the Hell's Angels were ready to fight for their country in "behind the lines" duty in Vietnam. The motorcyclists would "demoralize" the enemy with their clandestine tactics. "We are available for training and duty immediately," he concluded.

In Hunter Thompson's view, Barger was just being himself—adhering to the coarse, conservative instincts on which he always relied. At the very least the whole thing would make a fine scene for the book—especially the part about the telegram—even if nothing ever came from it. "For reasons never divulged, Mr. Johnson was slow to capitalize on Barger's offer," Thompson wrote afterward, "and the Angels never went to Vietnam."

## The Ones Who Have Gone Over

Hunter Thompson's initial deadline for the book was December 1. But by the start of November he'd only managed to complete a total of forty or so polished pages. Not that he was short on substance. Since June he'd spent most of his time following the Angels throughout the Bay Area; he'd also accompanied them to rallies and parties up and down the state, in places like Bass Lake, Sacramento, and the Sierras.

The most immediate issue was organizational: how to arrange the material he'd gathered into a streamlined form that he could then render with the keen physicality of his prose. He had a structure in mind: the book would start from a fairly objective viewpoint on the motorcycle gang and then transition to more of a first-person, subjective narration. But none of this could actually happen until he changed gears and started *writing* again—a more difficult task than you might think.

For Thompson, living alongside the Angels had been a strain on his marriage and on his personal health. In their orbit he'd often felt terrified. And rightly so. But the months of reporting had also been exhilarating: he never knew who he might meet or where the night might go next. And at places like the El Adobe bar in Oakland and Ken Kesey's house in La Honda, there was, in addition to danger, a genuine sense of possibility.

Now, to actually finish the book, he'd need to spend his evenings in an entirely different environment: the solitude of his writing desk at 318 Parnassus.

Still, he refused to modify his vampiric schedule. He didn't stop drinking. Recently he'd bought the motorcycle he'd been eyeing since he signed the contract with Ballantine—the BSA 650 Lightning—which he especially loved to ride late at night, during the time he'd set aside for working. He continued to take Dexedrine—a drug that certainly improved his productivity but was no magic bullet. It helped him stay seated and focused for longer amounts of time—in the genuine hope that *anything* might start to appear on the blank page—but it couldn't create worthwhile ideas out of thin air.

And in San Francisco during the autumn months of 1965— a city in the midst of a cultural change so extreme as to make everything else feel, in retrospect, unparalleled—the distractions were uniform. At night the members of the Hell's Angels still occasionally stopped by Thompson's apartment for drinks. So did neighbors and friends. And after a year on Parnassus, he'd become familiar with the dive bars and music venues of the lively Haight–Ashbury district. He found himself in the crowd during the debut concert of the Jefferson Airplane, which took place at the Matrix, a recently converted pizza parlor on Fillmore Street. To him the Airplane captured the sound that *was* 1960s San Francisco: an electric, cacophonous wave.

For Sandy it all added up to a disturbing pattern. Thompson, after spending so much time away from his family to report on the book—not to mention the multiple occasions on which he'd brought the dangerous gang members back to their apartment— now found himself struggling to hold up his part of the bargain and complete the manuscript. "He wasn't making any changes in his behavior so that he could be a father," she would later say about their time on Parnassus. "Mostly, he was asleep, or he was at the bar, or he was out of town."

In the past—living in the quietude of places like Sonoma and Colorado—they appeared to have forged a sense of balance, something they shared and benefited from. Now, in the fall of 1965, the city was like an endless horn. How do you describe its sound when it continues to assault *everyone,* at each passing moment, with the unceasing immediacy of its blare?

Throughout that autumn Hunter Thompson did what he could to adjust again to the task of writing. But as the deadline approached, it became clear that there was no way he'd be able to turn in a manuscript by December. Instead he changed the due date to March 1. In the process he came to understand that if he didn't meet this deadline he'd miss his publishing window and might even be forced to forfeit his advance.

All up through Christmas and New Year's he isolated himself at his Parnassus desk, the twin summits of the Golden Gate blinking at him from the darkness beyond. A matter of simple arithmetic: time was running out. He had outlines and fragments—he could recognize the direction in which he was heading—but how to summon the stamina necessary and arrange the material into a cohesive narrative?

During the final week of February 1966, he reached a breaking point. The closer the deadline came the more paralyzed he felt—a degree of panic that made it impossible to get anything done. So in a fit of sheer desperation, and with his Dexedrine and typewriter and bourbon in tow, he said goodbye to Sandy and Juan, climbed into the Rambler, and drove out of San Francisco, down Highway 101. Past Gilroy, Morgan Hill, Salinas, and Watsonville. A late February journey. The coastline obscured with winter. Fog rolling in from the Pacific. It was as if he were crossing a limitless bridge, the land around him dulled by the steadiness of his passage. He didn't have the slightest idea where he was going.

Eventually, on the road near Monterey, he came upon an indistinct motel. He checked into a room. Pulled out his Selectric. The deadline was now four days away. And whether it was the inevitability of the situation or the change of environment or something else entirely, he began to experience a sense of clarity—the sort that a gambler feels, at the end of a very long night, when he realizes he has only one card left to play.

Suddenly there was just the book itself: its beginning; the undone sections of the second half; and the large portion of unconstructed material. Everything he could possibly need was scattered now on the table in front of him.

Thompson's plan was to work straight through without sleep. In the morning he walked across the street to a McDonald's, where he bought hamburgers, his only source of sustenance. Other than that he stayed in the room. An old radio provided a steady crackle of music. The cars beyond his window hissed by with varying frequency. It was the tail end of Northern California's rainy season. A marine dimness across the state. Sunset in the afternoon. He couldn't have asked for a more secluded setting.

Thompson knew what he needed to say. "To see the Hell's Angels as caretakers of the old 'individualist' tradition 'that made this country great,'" he articulated, "is only a painless way to get around seeing them for what they really are—not some romantic leftover, but the first wave of a future that nothing in our history has prepared us to cope with."

He described the Angels as a "destructive cult"; as "prototypes"; and as part of "a fast growing legion of young unemployables" who subscribed to "the same kind of retrograde patriotism that motivates the John Birch Society, the Ku Klux Klan and the American Nazi party." Any power they asserted was inherently undemocratic, the result of a violent group's desperate disregard for everyone else.

Over the course of four straight days, in the low-decked light of his anonymous Monterey motel, he fleshed out his notes and outlines into a series of set pieces that depicted a rally at Bass Lake; that awful party at La Honda; the march to the Berkeley border; and, finally, a funeral procession from Oakland to Sacramento in honor of "Mother Miles," an unfortunate Angel who'd been broadsided and killed that January by a truck in Berkeley.

When all was said and done he offered a chilling insight: "The Angels' collective viewpoint has always been fascistic." He even went so far as to cap things off with a quotation by Heinrich Himmler, the infamous Nazi SS commander, that he'd seen written out on the wall at one of the Angels' parties:

As you were, I was
As I am, you will be.

And after one hundred hours of continuous work, he collected everything into a bundle and sent it away, via US postage, to New York City. It was dawn, March 1. The draft was finished.

In retrospect, it's fair to say that such an outcome wouldn't have been possible without a drug like Dexedrine, which can be especially effective when it comes to *sustaining* momentum—to extending your output well beyond what anyone in a similar situation might reasonably expect to achieve. But there's no way to generate such effort without paying for it later. And in this way, I think it's impossible to consider Hunter Thompson's insights into the Hell's Angels and America and the dangerous direction our society appeared to be heading without also pointing out just how much *he* was sacrificing, personally, in service of this articulation.

Already, with alcohol, he was hastening an eventual mental and physical decline. The Dexedrine only accelerated the damage. And manic, days-long sessions were especially catastrophic: instead of heeding his body's natural limitations and allowing it to recover, he simply kept going—burning up, in the process, material that from that point forward would no longer be available. Really what we're talking about is a sort of Faustian bargain: in this Monterey hotel room, subsisting on bourbon and amphetamine and cheap McDonald's hamburgers, Hunter Thompson was quickening his progression toward death.

Did he know it at the time? *Could* he? How do you convince anyone—let alone a twenty-eight-year-old writer desperate to finish his very first book—what it *actually* means to cash in the only real currency you've ever been given: your future? Years later, after the broader consequences of this bargain had manifested, Thompson would begin the author's note to his collected works with a quote from Joseph Conrad: "Art is long and life is short, and success is very far off."

*

On the first of March Hunter Thompson drove back to San Francisco. But instead of resting or spending time with Sandy and Juan, whom he'd hardly seen during the previous months, he spent the next three weeks on a bender, a spiral of escalating drunkenness that was no doubt related to the stress and process of the book's completion but that couldn't be explained by any one factor—apart from the habits his life in San Francisco had taken on—and that, considering its intensity, ran the not-inconsiderable risk of consuming him altogether.

Instead there was a fight. And while the specifics of what actually happened remain unresolved to this day—it's a story that's been told multiple times, from varying points of view—the version you're about to read is the one that feels, at least in my reconciliation of the various biased accounts of it, the closest to what I imagine to be the truth:

On a March evening, returning to Parnassus after drinking at venues like the Matrix, Thompson grabbed a garbage can and rolled it down the hill, a fantastic clatter tearing the street awake. In their apartment Sandy was waiting for him. They argued. Juan, whose crib was in the other room, began screaming. Thompson grabbed the object closest to him—a boot—and he flung it at the back of the apartment, toward the bay window, the one that held in its plated glass the uppermost lights of the Golden Gate Bridge.

The window shattered. Shards everywhere. Sandy was shaking. In the next moment Hunter Thompson slapped her—hard. She reeled. Gathered herself. Suddenly she charged him. Reached for his face. She was clawing his cheek; in the skin beneath his eye her nails came down, drawing blood.

Thompson stopped struggling. He stepped back. And in the next moment he bolted from the apartment, jumped on his BSA, and roared off.

Afterward Sandy was frantic; she was worried he'd crash his motorcycle. She called the Geigers in Sonoma to see if he'd gone there. Bob Geiger was actually down in San Francisco at the time, and she got in contact with him through his answering service. He came over immediately. She told him what had happened. Already a bruise was showing at the spot where Thompson had hit her.

In response, Bob Geiger went from bar to bar in the Haight-Ashbury district until, at the back of a local dive, he finally found him.

Together they had it out. At first Thompson tried to argue. But Geiger shouted him down. "You can't ever do that!" he told his younger friend. It was completely unacceptable. Was this the kind of person he wanted to be—someone who, instead of caring for Sandy, *abused* her? Did Thompson understand that if he continued to carry on in this manner he would lose his wife and son—that his actions weren't just detrimental to himself but also to the people who loved him most? That his behavior, regardless of the desolation or pain or exhaustion that might be motivating it, was *selfish*? That at a certain point you can exhaust everyone in your life, including your wife and your friends—and that, even if you're lucky enough to eventually realize how badly you've fucked up, the damage is irreversible, and no amount of good work will ever make up for the harm you've inflicted?

Hunter Thompson stopped arguing and listened. Eventually he told Geiger that he agreed; he was sorry; he felt ashamed. Horrified. He went home to Parnassus. Apologized to Sandy. Said he would try to make things work. Promised to cut down on his drinking and to stop going out so much. He admitted that he was out of control.

On a subsequent evening—perhaps this was in the days just after their fight, though it could've been weeks later—he waited until past midnight, and, with his wife and son sound asleep, he walked outside to the curb, where he jumped on his motorcycle. At 3:00 a.m. the city was a stadium of silent avenues. Thompson descended the short distance down from Parnassus to Golden Gate Park, his engine booming. He sped through the first long turns. Shadow of eucalyptus. The biting Pacific air. In the distance, the hills and their lamps sat like islands against the deep western curve of the night.

At the end of the park he took Lincoln Way and then turned, at last, onto the Coast Highway: a seventy-mile stretch of unbroken road running the length of the peninsula. On his right lay the ocean and its cold beaches. He passed the zoo and ducked into another long curve, on the lookout for sand drifts, a deadly hazard. He kicked it up to third gear, the needle approaching 80 mph, the wind scouring the moisture from his eyes. He could barely see. Instead he found himself imagining the very thing he appeared to be approaching: a lonely, untimely death.

On a motorcycle traveling at over 100 mph, all it takes is one wrong move. Thompson's high-speed burst down that last long hill to Pacifica is perhaps best understood as an act of measurement: he was weighing his life against his ability to articulate *anything* ever again. How close can you get to the border between the living and the dead and still retain a human voice? Is it ever possible to make such an approach without disfiguring yourself in the process? And if, in the end, you *do* cross over—if the rampant emotion you're feeling is extinguished with the same abrupt finality as your life—can you really go so far as to call it anything other than a willful act?

That night, just as he passed the lights of Pacifica, Hunter Thompson let up on the throttle. At some point near Rockaway Beach he turned around. And he rode all the way back to Parnassus—its familiar heights.

When he arrived home it must've been close to dawn. He went to his writing desk. Sat down at the shattered window. In the absence of its glass the twin summits of the Golden Gate couldn't possibly flash in the same way they once had; now there'd be no reflection; the image of himself in the glass, looking out—looking back—would've been replaced, instead, by a new darkness. And out there in it, spaced as symmetrically as eyes, the lights of the bridge would be flashing as if for the very first time: a red, inhuman gaze.

Thompson's face was frozen and cracked. Tears crusted his cheeks. And for the next twenty minutes, as his vision cleared and the feeling in his forehead and chin slowly returned, he wrote out the details of the ride he'd just completed, an act of comprehension. By describing what he'd just experienced he began to recognize, at last, the direction in which he'd been heading:

> The Edge . . . There is no honest way to explain it because the only people who really know where it is are the ones who have gone over. The others—the living—are those who pushed their control as far as they felt they could handle it, and then pulled back, or slowed down, or did whatever they had to when it came time to choose between Now and Later.

\*

By the start of the summer of 1966, Hunter Thompson knew it was time to leave San Francisco. With Sandy and Juan he needed to find a quieter, more secluded place to live. Not that he was also willing to quit drinking or stop taking Dexedrine. Instead, from here on out, such trade-offs would often be about making it from one moment to the next. He understood he couldn't do that— keep surviving—if he stayed in Haight-Ashbury much longer.

In the meantime, he threw himself into the process of preparing the book for publication. Random House had recently picked up the hardcover rights—their edition would come out six months before the paperback—and the project had been handed over to a new editor, Jim Silberman. That June, Silberman flew out to San Francisco to go over the first draft. He liked what he was seeing; still, the manuscript needed to be tightened up and revised.

Bob Geiger came down from Sonoma a few nights a week and read sections of it for him, helping with the edits. The release date was pushed back until January of the next year. At the end of August, Thompson received a mock-up of the cover design—and was horrified by how crass it looked. So, in search of a new photo, he decided to join the Hell's Angels for one last outing: their annual Labor Day run to the Squaw Creek campground near Cloverdale, a town about seventy miles north of the city.

It'd been months since he'd reported on the group. Most of the members he met that afternoon were new; they had no idea who he was or why he kept snapping pictures of them with his camera. Later in the day, he was talking to an unfamiliar gang member when, from behind, he was violently struck in the head.

At first he thought it was an accident. But immediately, the other Angels joined in. He fell to the ground, surrounded. With their heavy boots they kicked him in the head and ribs. He couldn't understand why it was happening. From the corner of his rapidly blurring vision he caught a glimpse of Tiny, the enormous Angel who the year before had led the charge against the VDC protestors in Berkeley.

"That's enough," Tiny said to his fellow members. And at a lull in the action he got him on his feet and hustled him to his car.

Thompson drove to the Santa Rosa emergency room, where he called Sandy to tell her what had happened. "Listen," he said. "I'm

in the hospital. I'm okay. I've been beaten up by the Angels, but
I'm okay." Later, after he'd finally made it back to San Francisco, he
took a moment to snap a self-portrait of the damage: a black-and-
white photo from the chin up, framed by his rectangular bathroom
mirror: an image in reverse. In it his left eye is filled with blood,
blackened like grease. His right cheekbone bulges, the skin across
it tight and shining. One nostril of his clearly broken nose has been
reduced to a dot, swelling shut; the other, in comparison, appears
to flare wildly. His head lists downward—as if the ugly bruise at
the bottom of his mouth is heavy with blood, inclining his expression—so that the sum effect is that of a man peering, as if for the
very first time, into the distorted brightness of his reflection.

It's a gaze of disbelief. Of fascination. Of recognition. Should
it matter if the wounds in the mirror will eventually heal? At last
there's no looking away. The disfigurement is personal—a mask
he's spent these past two years in San Francisco growing his face
to fit.

## CHAPTER THREE

# A HAIRY ANIMAL CALLED NIXON

## 1967–1968

## Will the Real Hunter Thompson
## Please Stand Up?

The Thompsons finally left San Francisco toward the end of 1966. They moved back to Colorado—to Woody Creek, not far from the small cabin they'd rented five years earlier. At the time, Aspen's population was about 2,500. Many of the streets had yet to be paved. The airport consisted of a single narrow runway that could only accommodate the smallest planes.

Thompson was still waiting for *Hell's Angels* to come out; after months of maddening delays, the release date had been pushed back, again, to early 1967. The lawyers in the legal department kept flagging it, and to streamline the process Jim Silberman had brought in a copy editor, Margaret Harrell, who was tasked with overseeing all aspects of the project, from editing to fact-checking to working with legal to make sure everyone kept their heads.

As a copy editor, Harrell possessed a natural ability to recognize and retain the unique rhythm of Thompson's sentences—even as she worked to sharpen and shorten the manuscript as a whole—and from the beginning she seemed to ascertain that the prose of the book was, for him, a sort of signature. With each new carefully chosen clause and sentence and paragraph, Hunter Thompson was taking the risk to express his sincere, hard-won perspective on the world.

She got the manuscript in July, presumably, returning it to him copyedited for the first time at the end of August. They worked together through the autumn to iron out the issues, corresponding frequently by post and on the phone. Thompson assumed that Harrell was middle-aged—a woman in her fifties who had been shepherding first-time authors like himself for years—and it wasn't until they were months into the editing process that he realized he'd been wrong.

Margaret Harrell was twenty-six years old. She'd earned her MA in literature from Columbia—her thesis was titled *Marking Time with William Faulkner*—and she'd recently spent time in Europe and North Africa. She was an avid dancer, studying in the Martha Graham / Jose Limon modern style. Her hair was red and wavy. She'd done her undergraduate work at Duke University, in history, graduating magna cum laude. When she spoke it was with a mild Southern accent, a product of her Carolina childhood. She enjoyed reading novelists such as Kafka, Proust, and Robert Musil, philosophers in the vein of Kierkegaard, as well as poets like the French symbolists Rimbaud and Verlaine. For months she'd refrained from correcting Thompson's misconceptions of her true identity.

That November, after a long phone conversation—the first since he had learned that she was, in fact, only two years separated from him in age—he admitted that the truth had made him self-conscious: "Part of my nervousness was the sudden, general electricity," he wrote her. "I realized I was looking for an excuse to keep from hanging up. Which is a bad state for an impressionable hillbilly to come to."

Finally, in early-1967, *Hell's Angels: The Strange and Terrible Saga of the Outlaw Motorcycle Gangs* was released. The advance reviews—in *Publisher's Weekly,* the *New York Times Review of Books,* and the *New Yorker*—were spectacular. And the initial sales exceeded all expectations: already the first printing had sold out.

That February, Thompson was flown out to New York for a publicity tour, and on an afternoon at the Random House offices he had a chance to meet Harrell for the first time. He arrived at her desk and, without a word, he pulled out two Ballantine Ales from his knapsack—one for her, one for him. Neither of them spoke; already, each knew the other's perspective, an intimacy that can only be earned through the daily output of time and effort they'd been exchanging, with no ulterior motive beyond that of the book's completion, for so many months.

Together they drank from the cans. Eventually Thompson invited her to accompany him to a television appearance that had been lined up for later in the day. He was slated to go on *To Tell the Truth,* a national game show broadcast weekly on CBS, and he was anxious; knowing she was on the set, he told her, would help with his nerves.

Harrell watched from backstage. The show's setup was based on deception: a panel of four celebrity judges were read a short bio at the start—a description of the main guest's true identity—and afterward three participants, two of them imposters, sat at a table together answering the panelists' interrogations. Each professed to *be* the person in question. Only one was telling the truth.

Bud Collyer, the show's host, read out the contestant's prewritten statement: "I Hunter Thompson am a writer. Recently I spent over a year living in close contact with the notorious California motorcycle gang called Hell's Angels. I found the Hell's Angels to be an elite organization of outlaws and hoodlums whose philosophy is violence."

The other two contestants wore leather and boots, their hair greased foppishly. Thompson sat between them, in a T-shirt and a soft sheepherder's vest, his shoulders angled forward. At each question addressed to him—"number 2, who is the author that sort of leads the LSD sect out there in San Francisco?"; "number 2, how many members do the Hell's Angels have?"—his eyes sunk to the left, and for the briefest instant he paused, as if cycling through every possible response, so that when he answered it was in a quiet, careful voice.

Harrell followed the action from backstage. She was dazzled by what she saw; suddenly the intelligence behind the manuscript she'd spent so many months refining had been brought physically to life.

At the end of the show, after the celebrity panelists had cast their guesses as to the true identity of the guest in question, Bud Collyer tallied the votes and, in an emphatic voice, spoke the show's signature line: "Will the real Hunter Thompson please stand up?"

At his sides the contestants fidgeted. Finally Thompson looked down. He arched his back. Glanced at the greasy versions of himself to his right and left. In the next moment he raised his chin. And, cocking his head, he let out an enormous, unguarded smile.

The audience cheered. The celebrity panelists laughed and clapped. "Oh, I knew he was honest," one of them intoned. As the segment ended Bud Collyer said to him, "Much success with your book."

To celebrate, he and Harrell went to dinner in Greenwich Village with his publicist, Selma Shapiro, as well as his old friend Gene McGarr, who was in town at the time. Afterward they all went back to Margaret Harrell's Bleecker Street apartment. Another of Thompson's friends, William Kennedy, stopped by. Together they listened to the Jefferson Airplane's new album, *Surrealistic Pillow.*

Suddenly it was getting late. As if on cue, everyone started to leave. William Kennedy, the very last guest, looked at his friend and the young woman sitting alongside. *Lucky Hunter,* he thought to himself, departing. At last Thompson and Harrell were alone. It was obvious that he wanted to stay the night. Harrell had one condition: she asked him to sleep on the floor, in the space in front of her bed, in the small studio apartment. He agreed. "I feel like a dirty old man," he mumbled. Down there on the ground—after such an overwhelming day—he stretched out his arms and legs, struggling to fit his body into the slim trough of space.

Margaret Harrell laughed. From the perch of her mattress she could see that he'd resigned himself. "All right," she told him. "Come get into the bed."

And he did.

\*

For Hunter Thompson, the move to Woody Creek had been, in a certain sense, an act of personal partition. Now, living outside Aspen, on an alpine ridge overlooking the secluded Roaring Fork River Valley, he could divide up his life in a way that hadn't been possible on Parnassus. Home with Sandy and Juan, he was one person—a father and a husband living in a small local community who, through his work as a national journalist, supported his family. And when he was on the road, reporting and writing, he could become someone else altogether.

That April, after their time together in New York, he and Margaret Harrell spent a weekend at the Continental Hyatt House on the Sunset Strip in Los Angeles. This was during the last leg of his publicity tour; she flew out to be with him. She'd been told by a West Coast author she trusted that Thompson was in an "open marriage," which was not, she'd find out many years later, actually the case.

A week of sun and media events and poolside drinks: although neither of them could know it then, Harrell wouldn't be his editor much longer—in August of the next year she'd leave Random House to become a writer herself, move to Europe, and eventually marry the Belgian poet Jan Mensaert. But over the subsequent three decades, she and Thompson would keep in touch, the memory of the moments they'd spent together remaining in the way a letter or photograph might: something that reflects both the instant of its creation as well as the years that have passed since. It was a friendship that would last the rest of their lives. At the time they were caught up, a rush of affection that Thompson, returning home, tried to keep separate.

Decades later, Sandy professed never to have known about this affair.

*

In the spring of 1967, with the success of the book and in the wake of their transition to the Rockies, Sandy and Hunter Thompson made the decision to have another baby. She got pregnant again immediately. Initially things appeared to be going well. But then there was a complication; she was told that she would very likely miscarry. The only option was bed rest—with no guarantee that it might make a difference.

Thompson took over day-to-day operations of his family. He canceled all his travel and forfeited his current assignments. He could still head into town to shop or write or grab a drink with friends—in the afternoons he'd hired someone to help out with Juan and the housekeeping—but he needed to be near a phone at all times, able to get home at a moment's notice should Sandy's condition change.

By now the results were in: *Hell's Angels* was a resounding success—a national bestseller. But the financial return for Thompson kept falling well short of what he'd expected; his initial contract for the book had been hastily negotiated by his literary agent, Scott Meredith, and many of the terms favored the publisher—especially in the case of such strong initial sales.

Thompson was livid. He cut ties with Meredith's agency on May 19, calling the contract with Random House "a wretched, predatory document." He planned to switch to a new agent, Lynn Nesbit, who was currently representing Tom Wolfe, but he'd already signed on with Meredith through December 15 . . . which meant that he'd have to wait until the end of the year before the negotiations with Random House on his *next* project could begin.

In the meantime, his life took on a domestic rhythm. He decorated and refurbished their cabin. He cared for Sandy, spent time with Juan. He got to know the other residents of the valley, more than a few of whom had also arrived in Aspen to escape the increasingly hectic West Coast counterculture scene.

In the emptiness of his new surroundings—the cabin they were renting was located on 130 acres of unbroken alpine wilderness—he trapped skunks and shot his .44 Magnum at targets he'd made from gas cans and explored the nearby ravines and hillsides. To the few critics who'd panned *Hell's Angels* in print, he wrote scornful, sardonic letters that concluded with statements like: "I look for-ward to reviewing *your* next book." He even went back through his second unpublished novel, *The Rum Diary,* the rights to which he hoped to include in his next deal. A summer of restless, unac-customed solitude. All he could do the next few months was be patient—a virtue that, all things considered, he'd never had much reason to suspect himself of harboring.

Sandy had been told by her doctor that, despite bed rest, she was likely to lose the baby. That summer, six months into her preg-nancy, she did.

By now they'd been married for almost half a decade. Juan was three years old. Together, they planned to try again. Years later, she would say, "I wanted a child mostly because I wanted another Hunter. I wanted more of that energy on this planet."

## Enter the Brown Buffalo

In the summer of 1967, the bar at the Jerome Hotel, one of Aspen's oldest landmarks, featured on its walls an African-themed décor: spears and shields and faded leopard prints. The original floor plan consisted of two segmented areas, poorly lit. "You could ski to it right down the streets from the bottom of the mountain," James Salter wrote, "and from the closing of the lifts until past midnight everyone was there or had been." Aspen had only two seasons then—winter and summer—and the Jerome, in its crowded half-light, stood at the center of both. "The plumbing was question-able," Salter added. "People have been known to ride through the door on horses."

Early that July, on a cool alpine evening just before the hol-iday weekend, Hunter Thompson was grabbing a drink at the Jerome with some friends when he noticed movement near the entrance; someone he didn't know was walking up to the bar. This stranger was large: over six feet tall weighing at least 250 pounds. He had curly hair, A broad, expressive brow. His eyes were small and pointed—alert. He introduced himself: Oscar Acosta. "I'm the trouble you've been waiting for," he added wryly.

That week, riots had swept through the city of Buffalo. Newark and Detroit would be next. *The long hot summer of 1967*—a wave of urban rebellion all across the Atlantic and Midwest. By this point the United States had sent nearly half a million soldiers to Southeast Asia: 75,000 wounded and 14,624 dead. These losses were not uniform; the national draft, which had been recently accelerated to meet the deployment numbers that the escalating campaign demanded, drew disproportionately on demographics that lacked the personal, economic, and legal means to avoid procurement. As a result, persons of color were more than twice as likely to end up in Vietnam than their white counterparts.

Thompson and Acosta struck up a conversation. They talked about the Bay Area, where they'd both lived, about friends they had in common. At first Thompson assumed he was speaking to just another newly arrived San Francisco dropout: an idealist. But then the conversation turned to politics. And this was when Hunter Thompson suddenly found himself on the defensive.

Oscar Acosta was thirty-two years old. A few days earlier, he'd quit his job as an attorney in Oakland, where he'd been working as public defender at a local Legal Aid Clinic—part of LBJ's Great Society initiative to fight inner-city poverty—and, with only a few hundred dollars to his name, he lit out from the coast for parts unknown. He was born near the Texas-Mexico border, but he'd grown up in California's Central Valley, in Riverbank, near Modesto, on the segregated west side of town. In high school he'd been a football star and junior-class president, not to mention a standout clarinetist. By his senior year he'd fallen in love with a white girl named Alice—but the local police chief, acting on a tip from the girl's affluent parents, broke up the relationship and threatened to imprison Acosta if he ever went near her again.

So after graduation he joined the Air Force. Months later, in the boiler room of his squadron's barracks, he experienced a moment of divine revelation, was born again in the light of the Holy Spirit, and converted to the Baptist faith on the spot. Afterward, due in no small part to his musical talent, he was posted to the American base in Panama, where he served as lead clarinetist. And for the next two years, whenever he had free time, he secluded himself among a local indigenous group, serving as their minister; enthusiastically he preached his own fire-and-brimstone interpretation of the New Testament. This was in the northeast part of the country, just off the coast, a region known then as the San Blas Islands. Two years passed. At the very end of his tour—just before he was about to be shipped home—he underwent a *second* epiphany, and with the same lightning-strike logic of his initial conversion he now renounced his faith altogether.

He moved back to California. Enrolled at San Francisco State. Studied creative writing and mathematics. Submitted himself to years of Freudian analysis. Worked an assortment of day jobs. Suffered from stomach ulcers. Wrote short stories. Wrote a novel. Was married and had a son and got divorced. Eventually, while taking night classes, he earned his law degree. He passed the California Bar Exam in 1965.

Now, on a cool 1967 July evening, in the midst of his latest peripatetic journey toward self-discovery, he'd arrived out of the blue at the Jerome. He was in his glory: capable and charismatic and ruthlessly brilliant, the rarest of intellectual forces—a true believer and a pragmatist, a literal exaggerator, a self-aware absolute. Over the course of his life he'd managed to adapt himself, with innate alacrity, from one state of certainty to the next, all the while maneuvering the merciless, unjust maze of the society into which he'd been born—a society that forced him to participate, whether he wanted to or not, in a game that was rigged from the start to reward certain Americans and at the same time inhibit the upward mobility of so-many-million others.

Thompson listened. He ordered more whiskey. It wasn't just what Acosta was saying, the rigor with which he interrogated each new assumption or generality. There was something else, too: his *attention*, its physicality. Like a raucous vice he seemed to reshape his body to the quality of your logic, and as the conversation intensified—as his shoulders hunched and his head sunk low and his eyes flashed repeatedly at your own—there was the feeling that he'd already managed to predict and dismiss a position you hadn't even realized you'd committed yourself to taking. He forced you, almost by sheer will, to grasp the stakes of what he had to say.

At some point in the night their conversation turned to the nature of the American system itself: What was the most effective way to combat institutional injustice? Would it be better to work within the democratic mechanisms of the Republic and effect change from the inside out? Or had we finally reached the point where the only real way forward would be to rip up the atrophied pretense of our equal-powers governance and start over again?

Thompson, in his writing, had sought to expose corruption and greed among the powerful, in the hopes that telling the truth would inform, and change, the electorate. But Acosta was more cynical. Through personal experience, he'd seen an ostensible republic that could at the same time legally segregate, imprison, and, for good measure, publicly execute its minority citizens through state-sanctioned violence like lynching and police riots. In other words, he knew a reality in which there was no such thing as the *truth*—where all that ever mattered was the narrative you'd been forced to accept.

"I'm past my puppy-love trip with the law," he told Thompson that night. After spending the last two years working himself sick to effect change within the existing system—defending in court the poorest members of our society, the addicts and outcasts and victims of abuse whose lives LBJ's Great Society was supposed to improve—he'd started looking for something more radical: "The politics of confrontation," he called it. It was an approach that, in addition to exposing injustice, sought to challenge the moral validity of the American government.

Oscar Acosta wasn't sure how long he'd stay in Aspen—here he was, at an Old West bar decorated with the sort of colonial African bullshit that anyone who wasn't a cowboy or a hippie would've seen through immediately, what he'd later call "the wrong place . . . white man's turf"—but a few days later he wrecked his car. So he picked up an assortment of odd jobs while he tried to save up for bus/plane fare and figure out where he might go next.

Thompson, for his part, was disgusted by the recent influx of hippies to Aspen—by their obliviousness. But until Acosta's arrival he hadn't yet taken a more detailed look at what *his* presence in this valley meant: the possibility that, through circumstances of geography and identity, he was in fact just as implicated, politically, as the out-of-touch people around him.

Acosta would end up sticking around town for the next few months, over which time he and Thompson would continue, in fits and starts, the conversation they'd begun that night. Eventually he decided to continue on to El Paso, the city of his birth. This was toward the end of the year. Thompson gave him a ride to Glenwood Springs, where the Greyhound depot was located, and they had a drink at a small bar as they waited for the next scheduled departure.

Just before it was time to go, Acosta reached into his suitcase. He pulled out a small parcel. It was bundled up in layers of fabric, which he carefully unwrapped. Then he handed it to Thompson.

At first glance it seemed to be a crude figurine, of durable mahogany, that had been carved in the approximate shape of a person. But upon closer inspection certain key details seemed to be missing. It was faceless, free of eyes and a mouth. At its groin, in the hollow between the legs, the wood was smooth: an androgynous sweep. And its shoulders were strung with small fangs, ornaments that, taken at some point in the not-so-recent past from a slaughtered boar, had been cleaned and patterned and meticulously threaded together: a necklace of loose, yellowed teeth.

Thompson lifted it carefully, in the way you would a plant to the sun. "Where'd you get him?"

"Off the coast of Panama. I've had him over ten years." Acosta explained how, just as his tour in the Air Force was drawing to a close—only a few days after his *second* epiphany—an elder from the San Blas tribe had presented this offering to him in parting. "It's a real god," he said.

He meant it. According to Acosta, this wasn't just some idol, at least in the classic sense; unlike a rosary or crucifix or reliquary of polished bones, the gift that Hunter Thompson had been given *was* the deity it represented. For once, the image and object were the same.

"What's he supposed to do?" Thompson finally asked.

"Keep the evil spirits away."

At last the bus was arriving, a huge, silver-sided Greyhound. "Just remember," Acosta told him. "It's the only San Blas god in captivity."

It could've been seen as a trivial statement, but Thompson knew better: at this small-town Greyhound station on an afternoon in Colorado, Oscar Acosta wasn't trying to argue with his new friend about whether or not such deities *exist*. That was beside the point. What mattered was the willingness to look.

"Like I said," Acosta added, "he's a real god. Maybe you can use him."

### With the Integrity of a Hyena

Hunter Thompson's contract with the Meredith Agency finally ran out at the end of 1967. Afterward he flew to New York, and, over the course of a dinner hosted by executives from Random House and Ballantine, he was offered a new, lucrative multibook deal, the specifics of which included:

1) A hardcover work of narrative nonfiction on a topic that, thematically, gestured toward a much broader subject: "The Death of the American Dream." His initial idea was to write about Lyndon Johnson's Joint Chiefs of Staff—about the outsized influence

these little-known military men had begun to wield on American foreign policy—and go from there. The manuscript wouldn't be due for another year and a half: summer, 1969.

2) A more immediate account of LBJ's upcoming reelection campaign—either in the "impressionistic journalism" style he'd used for *Hell's Angels* or, conversely, in the form of an flat-out satirical novel that could be released in paperback just as the summer conventions were kicking off.

All in all, the plan was to spend 1968 reporting on politics. Random House had included in the new contract a travel account, and the writing he did on these trips could be applied to the two books and also published, beforehand, in magazines. With his recent success he'd broken through to the top of the journalism market; finally he could write the high-paying features he'd always wanted to do.

The first of these assignments, for the monthly magazine *Pageant*—basically a more liberal version of the *Saturday Evening Post*—would focus on the Republican frontrunner for the nomination, Richard Milhous Nixon, who had emerged again at the age of fifty-five to take what everyone knew would be a final shot at the American presidency.

On Sunday, February 11, Thompson arrived in New Hampshire to cover the primary campaign. He was staying at the Manchester Holiday Inn, Nixon's headquarters: a concrete hotel with Formica furniture and harsh halogen lighting. While checking in, Thompson couldn't help but notice *who* he'd be spending the week alongside: all around the lobby, fleshy middle-aged men sat socializing; with their buzz-cuts and gin-flushed faces and shark-skin suits they looked like dead ringers for the sort of real-estate broker / car salesman / senior loan agent you'd be likely to find, with only a few variations, at an Elks Lodge bar in Atlanta or Omaha or Dallas.

Even before he made it up to his room he was stopped and questioned: a young man—his bulk hidden behind the long dark sweep of his overcoat—demanded to know exactly what Thompson thought he was doing in these *damn* headquarters without any *damn* credentials . . . This was Pat Buchanan, Richard Nixon's jack-of-all-trades advisor, a twenty-nine-year-old graduate from the Columbia School of Journalism with established connections to the party's more conservative factions who'd been brought on to avoid the mistakes of the 1960 campaign. Buchanan was flanked on his left by an especially grim version of the lobby's sharkskin handlers: a middle aged, heavy-set politico from Chicago who until recently had spent his professional life selling gears and sprockets. His name was Henry J. Hyde.

"I'm with *Pageant*," Thompson said. "You can call them."

Hyde immediately stomped away to do exactly that. In the meantime, Buchanan had a question: What sort of journalist went around dressed in *damn* Levi's and a *damn* ski jacket? At Nixon headquarters, it amounted to a deliberate provocation. A few minutes later, however, everything got straightened out. *Pageant* had booked his room and arranged for access ahead of time, and despite its liberal bent, the magazine enjoyed enough status to help stave off additional confrontations. Buchanan relented, and Hyde begrudgingly backed off.

Shortly afterward Hunter Thompson found himself talking to another young Nixon staffer: Nick Ruwe, the advance man for New Hampshire. Together they sat down for a drink. Ruwe, an Ivy Leaguer from Detroit, was happy to go into detail about the nature of his position—one that, Thompson soon began to realize, played an integral and often overlooked role in any candidate's attempt to capture a primary. As an advance man, Ruwe didn't just scout out locations; he also prepared Nixon for the many unexpected variables that might develop, all the while making sure not to upset his boss in a manner that might negatively influence how things would unfold next. In this sense, a *great* advance man was like an elite horse trainer or fight manager: a tactician and spiritual guide and ceaseless motivator all rolled into one.

Ruwe was honest and relaxed—not easily offended. They talked in depth. Eventually Thompson asked him about the choice of the Holiday Inn: why go with a hotel that gave off such a Soviet-barracks feel as opposed to, say, the more alluring Wayfarer, which was located on the outskirts of Manchester?

Ruwe smiled. "We left that for Romney when we found out that it's owned by one of the most prominent political operators in the state—a Democrat." Romney was at that time Nixon's chief primary opponent. "George really stepped into that one."

Thompson was fascinated; most people had never even *heard* of an advance man, and it was a position that the press rarely wrote about, which made sense: for someone like Nick Ruwe, things were at their best when no one stopped to notice the part he'd played in how it all turned out.

Eventually, Ruwe mentioned a get-together for some journalists and Nixon staffers in the suite of *Newsweek*'s Jane Brumley; Thompson should stop by, he said. It was an amazing opportunity, especially for a newcomer like Thompson: the chance to drink privately with a group of campaign insiders.

Later that night, when Thompson arrived at Brumley's room—an enormous jug of Old Crow whiskey tucked under his arm—one of the first people he saw was the very same aide who'd challenged him in the lobby: the young Pat Buchanan.

What could he do? He walked over and offered to share his whiskey. Buchanan, as it turned out, was an Old Crow fan himself; he happily accepted. At the time he happened to be enjoying his very first date with another Nixon staffer, Shelley Scarney—his future wife—and together the three of them struck up a conversation.

Buchanan had worked for the editorial department at the *St. Louis Globe-Democrat* before entering politics. His current role amounted to a combination of policy advisor / speech writer / press secretary. In the run-up to New Hampshire he'd been one of the main architects behind the "New Nixon" approach: a strategy that, with the help of Madison Avenue veterans and a talk-show producer named Roger Ailes (then only twenty-eight years old), sought to counter the candidate's existing image by manipulating, in Nixon's favor, the television camera's inherent capacity for distortion. The goal was to create, via controlled shorts and regional ad spots and pre-edited news segments, the *illusion* of a mellow, forward-looking, unselfish patriot eager to offer the country the stability it so desperately needed—someone who (in Buchanan's words) was actually "enjoying the hell out of this campaign." Which led to the second aspect of this strategy: "I would right now lock into only the minimum necessary appearances in N.H.," Buchanan wrote in an internal memo.

The crowd in that Holiday Inn suite was surprisingly dynamic. In addition to staffers there were also beat reporters and bureau chiefs. As the night wore on, the conversation turned to the question of what it *really* felt like to participate in a major political campaign—the adrenaline rush that both journalists and staffers had come to know well.

"It makes everything else I've done seem pretty dull," Nick Ruwe admitted.

Thompson could understand. After all, the various people in this room weren't necessarily *that* different (their moral/societal views aside): they'd simply been more effective at manipulating their access to the political mechanism that shaped the world around them. Which prompted another question: what role might *he* play, as a journalistic insider, to affect the course of the electoral process he was now participating in for the first time from a backstage perspective?

At the end of the evening, after everyone else had gone to bed, Hunter Thompson and Pat Buchanan continued to drink from the enormous jug of whiskey. They stayed up arguing about communism; about Vietnam; and about the best manner in which to respond to what both political parties saw as America's one true *enemy:* the Union of Soviet Socialist Republics.

At this point, the Tet Offensive—a massive countrywide surprise attack by the North Vietnamese—had been raging for two weeks. Buchanan toed the establishment line: once a domino like Vietnam went down the rest would shortly fall, which meant that the only option, besides a preemptive nuclear strike, was containment. You had to win the war in Southeast Asia and then do your best to avoid getting drawn into the next one.

For Thompson, the real threat to the United States wasn't the Soviet Union; it was the extent to which we appeared all too willing to sacrifice our inalienable rights to support a foolish and clearly doomed militaristic enterprise—a war that, in the upcoming election, both parties would use to their benefit at the cost of more and more American lives.

Each spoke passionately. Each saw through the other's rhetoric. Each could predict the next line of attack—the facts and gestures and corollaries that were, to anyone who cared about the issue, well known. Still, Thompson was struck by the honesty with which Buchanan employed and defended and recalibrated his shitty containment argument: this young Republican staffer believed the line of reasoning he kept spouting because it was what he *needed to believe* if Nixon had a shot at winning.

Not that this kept them from bolstering their arguments with shouts and the occasional insult. To quote Fitzgerald: each disapproved of the other from beginning to end. As the sun came up on the bare New Hampshire morning they were still talking heatedly.

Many years later, reflecting at different points on his relationship with Pat Buchanan, Hunter Thompson would say: "If nothing else, he's absolutely honest in his lunacy—and I've found, during my admittedly limited experience in political reporting, that power & honesty rarely coincide." From the night they'd first met he'd learn an important lesson: "You can deal with the system a lot easier if you use their rules—by understanding their rules, by using their rules against them."

✳

Thompson had arrived in Manchester that February ready to write the article his editors expected: a brutal takedown of the politician he judged to be the worst in recent American history, a man who, for the last *two* decades, had revealed again and again his willingness to sacrifice his ideals in order to gain the most power possible. "Richard Nixon has never been one of my favorite people," he'd state in his eventual *Pageant* feature. "For years I've regarded his very existence as a monument to all the rancid genes and broken chromosomes that corrupt the possibilities of the American Dream; he was a foul caricature of himself, a man with no soul, no inner convictions, with the integrity of a hyena and the style of a poison toad." However, during his week at the Manchester Holiday Inn, Thompson couldn't help but notice the behind-the-scenes effort of Nixon's staff—"the backstage, mechanical, seemingly trivial stuff, the silent (or at least unpublicized) mechanics of the campaign"— to sell such historic foulness under a fresh, rebranded premise.

He continued to have run-ins with Henry Hyde, that beefy former gear-and-sprocket salesman from Chicago. At an afternoon taping session at a Manchester television station—Nixon was there to make a series of commercials—Hyde stared menacingly at Thompson the entire time. At another point Hyde let himself into Thompson's hotel room and read through his typed-up notes. And when Thompson asked about the candidate's *image*—Had Nixon hired a public relations firm for the primary?—Hyde flat-out lied: "That's not his style. Mr. Nixon runs his own campaigns."

Thompson also interviewed Ray Price, the campaign's principal speech writer. Together they talked about the candidate's Vietnam strategy, which seemed "straight out of the Johnson-Rusk handbook"—though with the additional caveat that Nixon shouldn't be expected to say what he really feels because any such honest declaration would undermine his ability to bargain, down the road, for what the campaign liked to call "peace with honor."

To Thompson it was clear from the start: Richard Nixon's position on Vietnam was to articulate whatever position he believed would win the election. Which wasn't really a surprise: after all, it was Price who'd written, in an internal campaign memo dated November 28, 1967: "It's not what's there that counts, it's what's projected . . . It's not the man we have to change, but rather the received impression. And this impression often depends more on the medium and its use than it does on the candidate himself." Price had then copied out passages from Marshall McLuhan's *Understanding Media* and sent them to the staff.

Throughout that week in New Hampshire, Richard Nixon rarely mingled with the reporters who'd gathered there to follow him. Occasionally—at a speech on the campus of the University of New Hampshire, or at a town-hall VFW stump—the candidate flickered into view, but at best he was a purposeful shadow; his presence evoked, with the ghost-flat physicality of a dream narrative, the idealized sort of character that his television and print advertisements were in the process of making real.

Instead, Thompson continued to strike up relationships with members of the press and staff. He caught up with the *New York Times'* Bob Semple, whom he'd known from his *National Observer* days, and he was introduced to the *Boston Globe's* Bill Cardoso for the first time. He also headed across town, to the Wayfarer, and took stock of the Democratic primary—Senator Eugene McCarthy's antiwar challenge to Lyndon Johnson's all-but-assured nomination. At night he drank whiskey with Nick Ruwe and Pat Buchanan. Eventually he went so far as to inquire about the possibility of speaking directly with the candidate, an especially difficult proposition: Richard Nixon, in addition to his general dislike of the press, was wary of freelancers who blew into town for only a week at a time.

But Ruwe and Buchanan and Thompson appeared to genuinely enjoy these late-night drinking sessions—together they'd exchanged a rare currency: self-awareness from across an ideological divide—and by the end of the week, Buchanan said he'd do his best to arrange some face time with "The Boss." Not that Thompson's article depended on an interview; already he'd begun to structure his narrative around the behind-the-scenes strategy that had dictated the candidate's carefully choreographed *lack* of a presence.

That Friday, February 16, Richard Nixon gave a speech at the Nashua Chamber of Commerce, his final engagement of the week. Afterward he planned to jet off to Florida with senior staff for a short campaign break. As the event was winding down Ray Price approached Thompson. "You've been wanting to talk to the boss?" he said. "Okay. Come on."

Suddenly they were all piling into a large yellow Mercury sedan. Up front, next to Ray Price and Pat Buchanan, a plainclothes cop was driving (it was still too early for a Secret Service detail). The back seat, fortunately, was much roomier. And it was there—on a dim private bench of leather—that Hunter Thompson found himself, for the first and only time in his life, sitting alongside Richard Milhous Nixon.

The trip from Nashua to the Manchester airport wouldn't have taken more than thirty minutes. Thompson lit a cigarette. Through the smoke-blue darkness he peered at the figure alongside. What did he see? A nose in profile. Shoulders, their boneless hunch. Cheeks and chin and fleshy jowls. And on top of it all, the famous widow's peak, its solitary head-high thatch. This was the same person who, fifteen years earlier, had looked straight into the television camera and said, "We did get something, a gift, after the election . . . You know what it was? It was a little cocker spaniel dog . . . and our little girl Tricia, the six-year-old, named it Checkers . . . " Who on the final night of the 1960 Republican Convention had the gall to claim: "Yes . . . Yes, I want to say that whatever abilities I have, I got from my mother . . . and my father . . . and my school and my church." Who'd dragged America through the televised tantrum of what he assured us all would be his very last press conference. Who'd then, two years later in San Francisco, donned his butcher's-son cloak of humility and introduced Barry Goldwater. Who'd somehow managed to survive into the late 1960s like the last mutated member of some long-extinct species, adapting just enough while everything around him fell magically into place: a long ribbon of evil luck spanning John F. Kennedy's assassination to Goldwater's thumping to LBJ's Vietnam blunders to the recent riots—spanning even now, in the deep-snow darkness of 1968 New Hampshire, where against all odds the first primary of the Republican season turned out to lack any real heavyweight challengers.

Thompson, after a week in Buchanan's presence, could've probably guessed at Nixon's answers to the usual policy questions; The Boss was nothing if not prepared. Instead, as the windows of the Mercury flickered with New Hampshire's landscape—its slick, lightless hills—he decided on another approach. Earlier that night, during the speech in Nashua, Richard Nixon had offhandedly mentioned the recent Super Bowl matchup between the Green Bay Packers and Oakland Raiders—he'd expected the Raiders to win, he'd told the audience—and now in the speeding car Thompson broke the silence between them with what amounted to a follow-up question: *Why bet on AFL Champion Oakland instead of Green Bay, the overwhelming favorite?*

Nixon replied immediately—without any of the caution that marked his public responses: he'd liked the Raiders because of what Packers' coach Vince Lombardi had confided in him up in Green Bay. In the next breath he added: "The AFL is much stronger than the sports-writers claim."

For the briefest instant Thompson felt as if he'd been knocked off balance; a few years earlier, during a similar conversation about football, he'd been told the very same thing by Bob Geiger. At the time he and Geiger were arguing over which league was better, and long story short, Geiger, a former college quarterback, insisted that AFL teams were more dynamic offensively—"They actually pass!"—and to prove his point, he and Thompson drove out to Frank Youell Field, where they watched Oakland take on San Diego in their last home game of the year. It was the first time Hunter Thompson had ever seen pro football live: Sunday,

December 21, 1964. After three quarters of back-and-fourth drives and balletic catches, the Raiders quarterback Tom Flores fired a last-second pass down the middle, just to the left of the goalpost, that receiver Art Powell somehow corralled for the game-winning touchdown. In the next moment, as the fans streamed onto the field in celebration, Thompson turned to Geiger. The excitement was genuine—he was willing to admit, at last, that the AFL was just as captivating as its more popular rival.

And now here he was, four years later, sitting in the back of a giant yellow Mercury sedan somewhere between Nashua and Manchester as Richard Nixon talked about football with the un-questioned confidence of an *insider* . . . "Oakland didn't fold up," Nixon added, referring to the Super Bowl. "That second-half drive had Lombardi worried."

Thompson knew exactly what he meant—a series of downs that culminated in a twenty-yard pump-fake TD pass to little-known receiver Bill Miller—and, not quite knowing what to say next, he described the play itself in detail: the dual beauty of its design and execution.

Nixon hesitated. For an instant he seemed preoccupied. Then he smiled. And, reaching across the leathery darkness of the Mercury's huge back seat, he tapped Hunter Thompson on the knee. "That's right," he said, laughing. "The Miami boy." Richard Nixon had not only recognized the exact play correctly; he'd actually gone so far as to identify the obscure twenty-seven-year-old receiver's college of origin.

What followed was an easy, freewheeling conversation; soon their short ride together was nearly up. In Manchester they pulled onto the tarmac of the small airport, where the Learjet was still fueling. They talked for a bit longer—about sportswriting; about the success of this recent swing through New Hampshire; even about what it felt like to run for president.

"You know," Nixon added. "The worst thing about campaigning, for me, is that it ruins my whole football season."

Thompson lit a cigarette. It had been a week of no sleep, of Dex-edrine and Old Crow and unexpected complexity. From behind the scenes, the American political process appeared to have more in common with a Madison Avenue Coca-Cola campaign than the bare-knuckled tide that had swept through the delegates, four years earlier, on the floor of the San Francisco Cow Palace . . . And now it was all coming to an end in the wake of a short surreal car ride through the New Hampshire night—a moment that would, in retrospect, represent the only time in Hunter Thompson's life he would feel comfortable claiming, without a doubt, that the words coming out of Richard Nixon's mouth were true.

Finally the jet was ready for takeoff. Pat Buchanan and Ray Price would be heading to Florida, too, the rest of the campaign staff remaining here. Thompson had been leaning on the wing of the plane, and as he straightened up to offer his goodbyes he sud-denly found himself face-to-face with advance man Nick Ruwe—with Ruwe's *expression:* a glance that might be best described as a cross between terror and bewilderment and overwhelming panic. Immediately Thompson became aware of the fuel tank located only a few feet from where he was standing; of the Zippo lighter he was holding in his hand; and of the cigarette that, like a fuse, had been dangling between his lips the entire time.

Afterward—after Richard Nixon had been lifted into the night for a weekend of tropical relaxation with his young staffers—Hunter Thompson and Nick Ruwe drove back to the Holiday Inn for a final drink.

"You almost blew up the plane!" Ruwe said. Together they laughed. But for an advance man like Ruwe the whole thing was disconcerting. "What worries me is that nobody else noticed it," he added. "My God, what a nightmare . . . "

"I'm sorry," Thompson told him. "I didn't realize I was smoking."

✳

Throughout his week at the Holiday Inn Hunter Thompson had been fascinated by the degree to which a presidential campaign's talented staff could influence, through skill and planning, the public perception of a candidate—of *this* candidate, specifically. In the end the question he'd arrived in New Hampshire to answer—had Richard Nixon *changed?*—suddenly seemed beside the point.

Not that his editors at *Pageant* saw it this way; they'd expected a surface-level hatchet job, and they had no qualms about chopping up his draft, going so far as to cut fifteen of the first twenty pages. Still, the final product—"Presenting: The Richard Nixon Doll (Overhauled 1968 Model)"—would retain clear traces of Thompson's critique: that Nixon's identity is inherently shapeless.

My assignment was to find the man behind all these masks, or maybe to find that there was no mask at all—that Richard Milhous Nixon, at age 55, was neither more nor less than what he appeared to be—a plastic man in a plastic bag, surrounded by hired wizards so cautious as to seem almost plastic themselves . . . These political handlers were chosen this time for their coolness and skill for only one job: to see that Richard Nixon is the next President of the United States.

In this sense, should it matter if the truest aspect of the candidate's character was that he liked football? The whole "nice guy" routine from the car ride only seemed to further reinforce a deeply unsettling implication: What were the limits to a well-organized, behind-the-scenes rehabilitation campaign when the thing being rehabilitated lacked any pretense of conventional—one might even go so far as to say *moral*—substance? If the electorate found the "old" version of Richard Nixon to be unappealing and craven and self-serving, was it possible to use these specific flaws in a manner that advantageously facilitated the rebranding effort?

Really what we're talking about is utility. But in what sense? Would the cumulative efforts of staff members like Price and Buchanan and Ruwe and Roger Ailes eventually amount to something so effectively novel as to provide the opportunity for pretty much any candidate, no matter how unlovely, to take the presidency? Or, conversely, did this specific Madison Avenue approach uniquely play upon the crassest and most venal aspects of *Richard Nixon's* character—unchaining, in the manner of a nuclear reaction, the terrible potential that in retrospect had always resided at the dark-star heart of this singular American politician?

At the end of his *Pageant* article, Hunter Thompson offered a pair of anecdotes. He explained how, during a speech at the University of New Hampshire, Nixon had said, "I'm not a good actor, I can't be phony about it," and then in his next breath had told the students that, after so many years, *his inability to pretend* remained one of his biggest political obstacles. "I still refuse to wear makeup," he'd added. This was on Wednesday, February 14.

"Three weeks later," Thompson wrote, "this same man, after winning the New Hampshire primary, laughingly attributed his victory to the *new makeup he'd been wearing*. He thought he was being funny—at least on one level—but on another level he was telling the absolute truth."

\*

When Richard Nixon first announced his candidacy for the 1968 nomination on February 2, during an afternoon press conference in the dreary meeting room of the Manchester Holiday Inn, he was still considered a long shot to defeat a sitting president like Lyndon Johnson.

The Tet Offensive was only two days old then. That morning, a photograph showing an a enemy prisoner in mid-execution—his head distending like a poorly fired vase as the bullet broke from one temple to the next—ran on the front page of the *New York Times*. On February 5 Lyndon Johnson called up Jack Horner of the *Washington Star,* complaining: "Your press is lyin' like drunken sailors every day." On February 27, Walter Cronkite, back in the United States after a recent trip to Vietnam, declared: "To say that we are mired in stalemate seems the only realistic if unsatisfactory conclusion. But it is increasingly clear to this reporter that the only rational way out then will be to negotiate not as victors but as an honorable people who lived up to their pledge to defend democracy and did the best they could." That same month, an unidentified American major, responding to questions about a massive ordinance strike on the city Bien Tre, was quoted as saying: "It became necessary to destroy the town to save it."

On March 10 the Joint Chiefs recommended an additional call-up of two hundred thousand troops. On March 11 Eugene McCarthy, the patrician fifty-one-year-old antiwar senator from Minnesota who alone among his party had challenged the president, nearly won the New Hampshire Democratic primary, gaining 42 percent of the vote. On March 13 Robert Kennedy announced his candidacy. On March 30 a new Gallup Poll revealed that most Americans—63 percent—disapproved of the way the war was being handled. On March 31, a Sunday evening, Lyndon Baines Johnson addressed the nation about the war: "Tonight I want to speak to you of peace in Vietnam and Southeast Asia." The thirty-minute speech concluded with a shocking announcement: "I shall not seek, and I will not accept, the nomination of my party for another term as your president."

Hunter Thompson, home in Woody Creek at the time, was incensed. "I really hated to see him quit," he wrote to his brother Jim afterward, "he deserved to be destroyed on his feet." Suddenly the second book in his contract with Random House was off the table—which meant that, as a result of the surprise news, he'd lost a $10,000 advance. Of course he also recognized the victory. "It was like driving an evil King off the throne," he'd later write. "The next President would be either Gene McCarthy or Bobby Kennedy, and The War would be over by Christmas."

Four days later, on the balcony of the Lorraine Motel in Memphis, Tennessee, Martin Luther King Jr. was shot through the head and killed. Riots broke out across American cities. In Washington, DC, entire neighborhoods burned. In Baltimore more than three thousand people were arrested. Chicago mayor Richard M. Daley put into place a "shoot to kill" order—authorizing his officers to murder rioters in the streets.

From out in California, Oscar Acosta—practicing law again, now in East Los Angeles, as an attorney for the burgeoning Chicano rights movement—wrote to Thompson:"Once upon a time I was a liberal, yesterday I was a militant, today I am a revolutionary, trying like hell not to become uptight . . . It is not inconceivable that this largest of cities could be on fire before this letter reaches you. I'm scared shitless because the anger within me looks forward to seeing the fear in their faces . . . and the burning . . . "

Over the next two months, as Nixon continued to dominate the Republican ticket and Kennedy and McCarthy traded victories, Hubert Humphrey, Johnson's vice president, worked to shore up his own candidacy, avoiding the primaries altogether while steadily gathering a large number of unpledged delegates.

On June 4, the night of the pivotal California primary, Robert Kennedy defeated McCarthy by a slim margin—46 to 42 percent. Just before midnight Pacific Time he descended in an elevator from his suite at the Ambassador Hotel to address his supporters, who'd gathered in the ballroom. "I want to express gratitude to my dog Freckles, who's been maligned," he said to raucous laughter, before adding, "I'm not doing this in the order of importance, but I also want to thank my wife Ethel . . . " He went on to acknowledge his campaign staffers in the crowd. "And it's on to Chicago," he concluded, "and let's win this!" Then he ducked into a service exit, taking a shortcut through the kitchen corridor to another ballroom, where reporters were waiting to interview him for what was to be the final press conference of the night.

Along the way he was repeatedly stopped and congratulated. Near the ice machine in the kitchen, he shook hands with Juan Romero, a young busboy. Just then Sirhan Bishara Sirhan, a twenty-four-year-old of Palestinian descent who'd been infuriated by Kennedy's support for Israel, emerged from the clutter along the wall and fired multiple shots from a .22-caliber Iver Johnson Cadet revolver. Robert Kennedy was hit at point-blank range behind the right ear.

The damage was immediate; with its fluid tail of bone the first bullet had drawn an irreversible path through his head. Still, for a few miraculous moments, he remained conscious. After the people at his side immobilized the assassin—the writer George Plimpton was there, along with two former professional athletes—he was able to ask, with startling lucidity, if anyone else had been hurt. "Everything's going to be okay," he said. A few minutes later, as he was being moved to a stretcher, he whispered in pain, "Oh, no, no. Don't." Then he lost consciousness.

At the time Hunter Thompson was driving home in Woody Creek—he'd been watching the night's events at the house of his friend Peggy Clifford, a columnist for the *Aspen Times*—when he heard on the radio what had happened.

That spring, in a speech at Vanderbilt University, Robert Kennedy had stated, "Our country is in danger. Not from foreign enemies so much, but above all from our misguided policies." He quoted Sophocles: "All men make mistakes, but a good man yields when he knows his course is wrong and then he repairs the error. The only sin is pride." Regarding his possible opponent in the general election—the current Republican frontrunner—he added: "Richard Nixon represents the dark side of the American spirit."

Thompson loved this characterization. That March, he wrote a letter to Ted Sorensen, Kennedy's informal counselor, and offered his services to the campaign. "All I really want to do is get that evil pigfucker out of the White House and not let Nixon in . . . and the only real hope I see right now is your friend Robert. So maybe I can write something for you; that's the only thing I do better than most people, so I guess that's what I should offer."

On the road to Woody Creek that June night, Thompson turned around and headed back to Clifford's. There, with other Aspen residents, he watched the coverage on ABC. "We've heard an alarming report that Robert Kennedy was shot," news anchor Howard Smith said. "A very loud noise like a clap of thunder was heard, a small explosion . . . " By dawn there was still nothing definitive to report. "It won't be like the last time," Thompson told Clifford.

But it was happening all over again. A day later Robert Kennedy was dead. And in the face of this latest assassination—the second that spring—Hunter Thompson experienced a fresh surge of the terror that'd been visited upon him and so many others a half decade earlier. Except now, as opposed to the urgency that had hit him in the wake of JFK's murder, he felt, in a word, *helpless:* if so much had happened already what could possibly be next?

## The Battle of Michigan Avenue

Imagine for a moment—as if from above, from the lake, its surface like a great mineral disc—the Midwest's one true twentieth-century metropolis: Chicago, late summer 1968, a city in all its broken jawbone glory.

Wednesday, August 28: After a week of violent skirmishes, the Democratic National Convention had been reduced to a grid of north-south checkpoints: Lincoln Park, Grant Park, the hotels at the Loop; and then four straight miles of Michigan Avenue before a final hard jog west, to Halsted and the International Amphitheatre, an old rib-roofed arena with a nine-thousand-seat capacity standing like a shipwreck against the dirty Stockyards beyond.

Already the convention was in its third day. That afternoon, Hunter Thompson was on his way back from the delegate-filled amphitheater, where he'd just watched the crushing conclusion to the party's debate over its official position on the war in Vietnam. The minority viewpoint—a resolution sponsored by Senator Eugene McCarthy and former presidential speechwriter Richard Goodwin—received spirited defenses from former members of the Kennedy campaign. "We are not outside the mainstream of the Democratic Party," Ted Sorensen implored. "We agree with the voters of every Democratic primary. Stop the war!" Speechwriter Pierre Salinger went so far as to invoke his murdered boss's name: "If Senator Robert Kennedy were alive he would be on this platform speaking for the minority." But the hawks—their position advocated by the likes of Maine senator Ed Muskie—managed to carry the final delegate vote. By 3:00 p.m. it was over; the "Humphrey-Johnson" resolution won out.

For months Hubert Humphrey had been relying on the full support of the party machine to secure delegates. In 1968 many states still didn't hold primaries, and those that did weren't always required to pledge them to the winners, which meant that, under the rules at the time, a candidate pretty much needed to sweep the entire run-up to the convention if they hoped to avoid a backroom challenge. But the vigorous McCarthy-Kennedy matchup had split the antiwar wing. In the wake of June's unthinkable assassination— amid calls for stability and order—Humphrey quickly outflanked Eugene McCarthy to secure the nomination. He was, after all, the nation's vice president, LBJ's right-hand man and chosen successor. He was also deeply distrusted by the party's antiwar crowd; everyone knew there was no way he'd go *against* the Vietnam policy of an outgoing leader whose support had done so much to secure him his position in the first place.

Thompson had left the amphitheater to attend a rally in Grant Park, a narrow stretch of waterside grass that was divided from Michigan Avenue—and the convention's main hotels—by a sunken channel of railroad tracks; to get there you had to cross a street bridge connecting the Loop and the lakefront. It was just after 4:00 p.m. He was on foot. His destination, the park's band shell, was the gathering point for the rally, which was shaping up to be the largest of the week.

But on the Balbo Street bridge he suddenly found himself face-to-face with a row of Chicago police officers. He reached for the press pass at his neck, a document that he'd worked with Jim Silberman at Random House throughout the summer to acquire, and he was walking in mid-stride when he showed it to them. He was grabbed from behind. "That's not a press pass," a cop snarled.

Thompson, struggling, showed the document again: "What the hell do you think it is?"

For an instant he was free . . . no longer being held. Then he felt himself violently struck in the gut, just above the belt. He fell to the ground. The cop had speared him with a billy club—using both hands—as if to drive his stomach out between the lowest knuckles of his spine.

He got back on his feet and retreated to his hotel—the Sheraton-Blackstone, located alongside the Hilton a few blocks away, at the intersection of Michigan and Balbo—where, trying to catch his breath, he changed into running shoes. He also grabbed his motorcycle helmet.

At Grant Park, the fifteen-thousand-person rally Thompson had hoped to reach was already coming undone. That week, the protests had been coordinated by two central groups—the non-violence-advocating National Mobilization Committee to End the War in Vietnam (MOBE); and the more confrontational Yippies—and for the event at the band shell, they'd obtained a legal permit. But Mayor Richard Daley adamantly refused to allow a *march*—the permit was only for Grant Park—and earlier in the day, he'd assigned six hundred cops to the band shell area to keep everyone there in place.

At first things went smoothly; a series of notable speakers addressed the audience, which, in addition to the thousands of young men and women who'd come from all over the country to speak out against Vietnam, also included an older, more mainstream contingent. But there was an incident near the flagpole—a teenager spontaneously decided to climb up it—and a phalanx of police, seeing this, charged and split the crowd, clubbing everyone in their way. During the confusion that ensued, the gathering was declared an illegal assembly, and the cops moved in to clear the entire park.

The thousands of protestors tried to flee. But to their horror, they realized they were trapped. Earlier in the afternoon, the National Guard, summoned by Daley, had taken up positions at the park's exits; with machine guns and rifles and bayonets they blocked the limited number of bridges spanning the railroad tracks to Michigan Avenue, and now, in the chaos, they fired repeated volleys of CN tear gas from their powerful, Army-issued launchers. In desperation the protestors, beaten and bloodied, surged toward these choke points. Eventually the guardsmen and police fell back, overwhelmed.

Around that time Hunter Thompson had reemerged from his hotel; he was standing near the entrance to the Hilton. A few blocks to his north, the mass of fleeing protestors regrouped at Michigan Avenue. Together they began to make their way south, toward the Stockyards. But their general progression was extremely slow; it took almost an hour to cross just a few blocks. In the meantime, the cops reformed at Michigan and Balbo—where the two main conference hotels were located—and to the south and west and east they established a deep perimeter; they planned to stop the march there, before it had a chance to get anywhere near the International Amphitheatre, located four miles to the south.

So the situation was this: over the next hour, seven thousand protestors slowly penned themselves into this four-way urban intersection, onto which the lake-view suites of both the Sheraton-Blackstone and the twenty-nine-story Conrad Hilton looked down—rooms inhabited at the time by the Democratic Party's most prominent leaders. The crowd stood shoulder to shoulder, singing songs and chanting slogans. HELL NO, WE WON'T GO! and: STOP THE WAR, STOP THE WAR! and DUMP THE HUMP! and: FUCK YOU LBJ! And, to the cops: SIEG HEIL! From across the city evening was coming on—a late summer twilight, arid and clear, the Chicago skyline throwing its long tusks of shadow toward the lake.

Thompson, his motorcycle helmet stowed in the large blue kit bag at his shoulder, had taken up a position against the windows of the Hilton's ground-level restaurant, the Haymarket Inn, where, from behind a row of yellow police barricades, he and other journalists stood alongside a number of Democratic staffers and delegates who'd come down from their rooms with their spouses to see what was going on.

Just before 8:00 p.m., Deputy Superintendent James Rochford, the on-site commander in charge of convention security, received word that additional reinforcements had begun to arrive—along with a contingent of paddy wagons to transport prisoners—and, to the officers gathered around and off the perimeter, he gave the order: *Clear the intersection.*

The Chicago police approached from both ends of Michigan and Balbo in tight military formation. Then they broke into a full run, charging into the crowd, attacking everyone; they swung their billy clubs with overhand strokes, in the way you would through lumber, releasing their weapons down onto the heads of their targets. They were wearing sky-blue helmets with thick, black chinstraps. For the most part they were young men from Irish and Polish and German and Italian families. Before the assault they'd taken off their badges and nameplates; they knew that the order to attack had been delayed over half an hour—deliberated upon—and once the word came down through the chain of command, arriving like a small sum of money or an equally modest fine, there could be no doubting that it represented the *official* position of Chicago's highest civilian authorities.

A new round of tear gas volleys shrouded the intersection. In the burning fog you could hear clubs striking bone. Panicked footsteps. And the screams, their orchestral pain. A breeze came up from the lake. It was night. A new wave of cops arrived. Together they chanted "Kill! Kill! Kill!"—an incantation—as they approached the intersection.

The protestors tried to flee. "Hey," a young man with a mustache said. "*Goddamn.*" A cop had doubled him over with a club to the gut and was tossing him into one of the paddy wagons. At that moment a television cameraman was filming these wagons, and now this cop turned and attacked him, too. A doctor in a white coat and Red Cross armband ran to help and was knocked to the ground by pairs of police, who kept beating him as he tried to crawl away.

There were plainclothes cops. White-shirted cops. Some had antennas at their backs to relay radio instructions. Others wore long black jackets with chevrons at the shoulders. A few were on three-wheeled motorcycles—one of whom could be heard, as he ran people over, shouting, "*WAHOO!*"

Desperate for cover a young man—at most seventeen—sprinted for the Hilton's side entrance; four cops followed closely at his heels. From under the hotel awning, Fred Dutton—a former presidential advisor who, until June, had directed Robert Kennedy's campaign—placed himself between the kid and the police. "He's my guest in this hotel," Dutton said. The police threw the young man down and began clubbing him.

Fred Dutton was forty-five years old; he'd worked as senior aid in John F. Kennedy's administration and written speeches for Lyndon Johnson. In World War II he'd been a prisoner of the Germans and was awarded a Bronze Star and Purple Heart after being wounded during the Battle of the Bulge. Two months earlier, he'd been standing in the kitchen of the Ambassador Hotel when the shots rang out; on the way to the hospital he'd ridden beside Ethel

Kennedy in the back of the ambulance, the two of them watching helplessly as Bobby, unconscious after so much loss of blood, struggled to breathe, his pulse fading.

Dutton shouted at the Chicago police to stop. He demanded their names and badge numbers. One of the cops broke off and charged at him.

He was knocked down and grabbed and pulled out into the street; the cop dragged him toward the paddy wagon. It wasn't until a reporter for the *Washington Post* ran out and explained just who it was being carried off that this cop finally let go . . . and melted away back into the violence. "Sadism and brutality!" Dutton screamed after him. To the journalists standing nearby he implored, "Report all this . . . "

Richard Goodwin—the RFK aide who, that afternoon, had cosponsored the convention's defeated peace platform—appeared beside him, and together they helped direct the wounded into the hotel lobby. "This is just the beginning," Goodwin said.

On the fourth floor of the Sheraton-Blackstone, South Dakota senator George McGovern, the party's most consistent critic of the war, watched from his window. A year earlier, in a speech republished by the *New York Times,* he'd proclaimed: "Our deepening involvement in Vietnam represents the most tragic and diplomatic moral failure in our national experience." Now he turned furiously to the others in his suite: "Do you see what those sons of bitches are doing to those kids down there?" As he and his staff looked on, a volunteer for their campaign—a young woman who had earlier been asked to deliver some files to the Hilton—crossed the intersection and was attacked by a cop; McGovern watched helplessly as the baton struck her directly in the face, shattering her teeth, her mouth filling with blood.

On the fifteenth floor of the Hilton Eugene McCarthy set up an emergency medical station to treat the injured protestors who were streaming into the lobby. Many of his young antiwar supporters and staffers had been in the park and on Michigan Avenue.

On the nineteenth floor, Pat Buchanan—in Chicago to act as Nixon's "eyes and ears"—stood at the window alongside two unexpected guests; a short while earlier, he'd been alone in his suite when through the doorway Norman Mailer suddenly appeared, looking for a drink. Mailer was accompanied by the boxer Jose Torres, former light heavyweight champion, and the three had just sat down to cocktails—"I'm more of a left conservative," Mailer was in the process of explaining—when they heard a loud bang from the street below. Now, standing side by side, they watched it all. "Sons of bitches! Sons of bitches!" Torres shouted at the cops. Mailer took it in silently. Later he'd write: "The military spine of a great liberal party had finally separated itself from its skin . . . it opened the specter of what it might mean for the police to take over society."

Buchanan also didn't speak. Instantly he understood what the violence meant; his boss had just become the odds-on favorite to win the presidency of the United States.

Three weeks earlier, during the Republican convention in Miami, Richard Nixon had played it perfectly.

*On violence:* "As we look at America, we see cities enveloped in smoke and flame. We hear sirens in the night. We see Americans dying on distant battlefields abroad. We see Americans hating each other; fighting each other; killing each other at home . . . Did we come all this way for this?"

*On stability:* "Listen to the answer . . . it is another voice. It is the quiet voice in the tumult and the shouting. It is the voice of the great majority of Americans, the forgotten Americans—the non-shouters; the non-demonstrators."

*And on his signature theme:* "The first civil right of every American is to be free from domestic violence . . . And to those who say that law and order is the code word for racism, and here is a reply: Our goal is justice for every American."

Buchanan wouldn't balk at manipulating what was happening on the street, even if he knew that such a line of attack contradicted the reality he was witnessing. Afterward his report to Nixon would be unequivocal: "We belonged on the side of Mayor Daley and the Chicago cops. That was where our future interests lay. It was where the *politics* of the day pointed us." Now they had their attack line for the general election: Humphrey was nothing more than an out-of-touch party hack who couldn't even unite the Democrats, let alone the country.

Six more floors up, at the top of the Conrad Hilton—in 2525A, an enormous suite packed with red flowers and multiple color televisions and plates of his favorite cheese sandwiches—Hubert Horatio Humphrey had gathered with his staff. But unlike everyone else he'd only glanced at the violence, choosing instead to work in another room on his acceptance speech. Suddenly his nose started itching. It was the faintest whiff of tear gas, sucked in from the air-conditioning vents. After another quick glance at the window—the Battle of Michigan Avenue had been raging now for fifteen unbelievable minutes—he retreated to the suite's bathroom, where he took a shower.

The entire time Hunter Thompson had been standing behind the yellow barricades with his back to Hilton's ground-floor restaurant, watching it all up close.

Throughout the week he'd seen the violence spread. Each night in Lincoln Park the police had attacked the protestors sleeping there, and afterward the surrounding streets had filled with running skirmishes. On the convention floor CBS correspondent Dan Rather had been punched and thrown to the ground by security guards—during a live broadcast—when he tried to speak with an antiwar delegate. Late Tuesday night, Daley had called in the National Guard. The city had also put into place multiple undercover officers, dressed like hippies, who would throw bottles or bricks toward the cops, which then gave the police the justification to respond with overwhelming force.

Thompson and the other journalists were still surrounded by older party officials and their wives; from the start it had been the safest spot. Initially there'd even been chants of "THE WHOLE WORLD IS WATCHING!" But now they were silent. The cops, taking control of the intersection, were preparing a new assault.

On Michigan Avenue—from both the north and the south— two fresh lines of police were advancing. They came together at the Hilton, a classic pincer formation, and the street's remaining protestors, perhaps five hundred, suddenly had nowhere to go. The cops kept pressing them back—in the direction of the hotel, its floor-level restaurant: the exact spot where Thompson and the others were standing.

Now the officers *charged*. They sprayed mace from handheld cans and came in fast behind the wet fogging bursts. The protestors surged back over the barricade. Thompson was forced against the Hilton. "Stay together! Stay together!" some of them were shouting. A few tried to break through the line in groups but they were quickly separated and beaten. The cordon was complete; half a thousand people were pinned against the plate-glass windows of the Conrad Hilton Hotel. The police gathered again and blitzed: their final assault.

Thompson reached frantically for the motorcycle helmet in his bag. He slipped it on just as the cops got to him. Bodies at his back and at his feet. And then the overhand blow—the billy club coming down on his motorcycle helmet, a plastic-and-leather dome that would've amplified into his ears the deafening bang. At the same time it had protected his skull and brain. Which meant that, unlike the other concussed men and women lying around him, he could still register with all his faculties intact the unmistakable message: the civic authorities were using indiscriminate violence to silence their legitimate political opposition and journalistic observers. Thompson knew immediately that if they were willing do this—if on national television the rights inherent to the Constitution of the United States could be completely and unequivocally discarded—then they could do *anything*.

From behind, he heard a new crash. Now the crowd was being forced through the Haymarket's plate-glass window, which loudly shattered; men and women tumbled helplessly down into the restaurant. The police followed them in, leaping, clubs drawn.

Thompson was a few feet away. Around him the cops shoved past. What was happening to the people who only minutes before were standing next to him? Were they down there now on the ruthless glass-strewn floor of the Haymarket? Who was dying and who was safe? Was it only a matter of time until he'd be next? Suddenly he was sure he was about to be hit by a hail of bullets—fired from above, from the rooftop—the shot exploding in his chest before he'd even heard its report. There was nothing he could do.

"I have never been caught in an earthquake," he'd say about this moment, "but I'm sure the feeling would be just about the same. Total panic and disbelief—with no escape." Something was coming that he couldn't see, speeding toward him from the menace of the night. At that instant, pinned against the shattered wall of the Haymarket, he was overcome with the terror and paralysis and regret of what it means to be hit and then, as if in a nightmare, go down.

It was the sort of fear Bobby Kennedy had been made to feel, two months earlier, during those waning minutes on the Ambassador kitchen's concrete floor when he could still ask if everyone else was okay, aware that his life was leaving him but helpless to do anything but watch it go. We're talking about the saddest moment of all—the one in which you finally realize you're beyond everyone else's reach.

Inside the Hilton, a protestor with a severed neck artery was slumped against the wall. Another, his legs paralyzed, crawled on his elbows. The cops beat them anyway—beating the diners who'd been sitting in the Haymarket, too. Then they moved on to the lobby. "Clear the floor!" one of them shouted. By now they didn't care about arresting people. The intersection was secure.

Just then Hunter Thompson saw an opening; through the remaining crowd of police and wounded protestors he sprinted to the Blackstone, about sixty feet away, where the cops near the entrance clubbed him back. "I live here goddamnit!" he screamed. "I'm paying fifty dollars a day!" He was shoved into the door. He pulled out his room key and waved it overhead until finally someone let him push through into the lobby.

In his room he locked and chained his door. His eyes burned. His clothes stank with chemicals. His gut ached. But he was unharmed. He wet a cloth and held it carefully to his face to soak out the tear gas. Then he sat on the bed, his legs crossed. His entire body was shaking. He couldn't write. None of it made sense. The whole week the police had *known* that he was a member of the press; that the men and women they'd forced through the Haymarket window were political officials; that a number of the nonviolent young protestors worked as campaign staffers for Democratic candidates. But then, that was the horrific point. Years later, looking back on this moment, he'd write: "These bastards knew my position, and they wanted to beat me anyway . . . they were powerful enough to break anybody who even thought about getting in their way . . . What I learned, in Chicago, was that the police arm of the United States government was capable of hiring vengeful thugs to break the very rules we all thought we were operating under."

The violence he'd just witnessed was clearly state-sanctioned. Political. Fascistic. And it had originated within the core electoral processes of the democratic system it now threatened. In this sense, *we* were its authors and performers and intended audience. All along this violence had been with us—was us: a song for America we'd been singing from the start.

It was just after 9:00 p.m. Down at the amphitheater the balloting for the nomination was about to begin. Thompson still had his press pass—it'd been around his neck the entire time—and he planned to put it to use, now, for something other than an invitation to a beating.

\*

In 1968 the Chicago International Amphitheatre was like an old
Roman grandstand that for millennia had somehow managed to
escape the fire. Its balconies hung right over the floor. Its lower
gallery could only be accessed through a maze of narrow tunnels.
Its carpets were red. Its speaker's podium employed the same sky-
blue theme as the Chicago Police Department. PROMISES KEPT, the
façade read. Here, for an entire week, the Democrats had sat on top
of one another arguing over the nature of their shipwrecked fate,
and now, on Wednesday night, *nominating* night, they were ready
for an all-out fight.

In retrospect, one of Mayor Daley's most effective tactics had
been preemptive: before the convention he'd helped orchestrate an
electrical-workers strike, which had the cumulative effect of pre-
venting the networks from broadcasting live at any Chicago locations other than the amphitheater. As a result, the cameras on hand
for the police riot at Michigan and Balbo all contained film, which
meant they still needed to be developed and cut—a time-intensive
process—and for an hour and a half, the footage remained unseen.

At nine thirty David Brinkley interrupted the nominating process to say: "The tape you're about to see was made thirty or forty
minutes ago." Throughout the floor, many of the delegates and
aides and congressional leaders who'd been at the amphitheater all
evening were learning about the violence for the first time.

By this point Hunter Thompson had made his way to the press
balcony, its precipitous apron, where, wild-eyed and stinking—the
tear gas still in his skin—he watched the proceedings. When the
Alabama delegation, led by infamous seventy-one-year-old Bir-
mingham segregationist Bull Connor, nominated the football
coach Bear Bryant for president, Thompson started bellowing
down at them, "MARTIN BORMANN!"—the name of Adolf
Hitler's personal secretary and Nazi Party *Obergruppenführer* who for
years had been rumored to have escaped to Argentina. *"MARTIN
BORMANN! MARTIN BORMANN! MARTIN BORMANN!*

*MARTIN BORMANN!"* he screamed at the delegates—many of them close enough to hear. In a letter a few weeks later he'd describe the moment: "The Jesuit priest sitting next to me kept me from hurling my binoculars . . . and Daley's thugs, sitting all around me, luckily didn't know who Martin Bormann is/was."

Down on the floor the convention chair, Carl Albert—an old little Oklahoman with a very big gavel—kept trying to move things along. But by now word of the Battle of Michigan Avenue had spread through the delegates.

A few rows back, Mayor Richard Daley was sitting with the Illinois delegation. He was approaching seventy, balding and fleshy, his purple lips locked tightly together: a man who'd spent his entire adult life in politics; who in 1960 had helped Jack Kennedy take Illinois and with it the presidency; who'd opened the convention on Monday by saying, "As long as I am mayor of this city, there is going to be law and order in Chicago"; who'd supported Hubert Humphrey since the spring over the likes of Bobby Kennedy because, Vietnam aside, this year it was the vice president's turn. He was the last unquestioned party boss the Democrats would see: powerful enough, under the current allocation system, to swing the delegates loyal to him in such a way as to determine the future of the country itself. That night, as news of the violence spread, Lyndon Johnson, watching from the White House, got in touch with Daley: if the current president were to board Air Force One and fly to Chicago at that instant, would there be enough support to give him the nomination he'd declined to pursue four months earlier? Daley said *yes;* he promised Johnson he could get the delegates. But just as the president was considering such a dramatic turn of events, his Secret Service detail told him it wouldn't be possible: there was no way they could ensure his safe passage to the amphitheater. In the end Johnson decided against it. The possibility of yet another disastrous assassination—his own—would be too much for the country to handle.

At around 10:00 p.m. Senator Abraham Ribicoff, the former governor of Connecticut, approached the podium. He was fifty-seven years old. He wore a slim black tie and dark suit; when he spoke, the pointer finger of his right hand chopped down at the air in front of him. That week he'd written a nominating speech for George McGovern—the South Dakotan had been a late, antiwar entry into the race—but after what had happened at the Hilton he couldn't stay silent. "As I look to the confusion in this hall," he said, "and watch on television the turmoil and violence that is competing with this great convention for the attention of the American people, there is something else in my heart tonight, and not the speech that I prepared to give."

Daley watched in disbelief—a lidless, fish-eye glare.

"And with George McGovern as president of the United States," Ribicoff continued, "We wouldn't have to have Gestapo tactics in the streets of Chicago . . . With George McGovern we wouldn't have the National Guard."

The crowd erupted. Chairman Albert smacked his gavel. Richard Daley, standing up straight now, cupped his hand to his mouth like a megaphone. "Fuck you!" he screamed toward the podium. "You Jew son of a bitch! You lousy motherfucker! Go home!"

Everyone in the vicinity could hear, including Ribicoff, who nodded slowly. "How hard it is," he said. "How hard it is . . . How hard it is to accept the truth."

Thompson watched from the balcony. When the convention was over he'd write in a letter to Ribicoff (whom he'd never met): "Everything you did that night seemed to rest on a bedrock of human decency . . . There was an awesome dignity in your handling of Daley and his thugs, and for a moment that whole evil scene was redeemed—but only for a moment."

It was unprecedented: a senator had just accused the head of his party's elaborate machine, on national television, of using government-directed violence to silence dissent, punish rivals, and prevent the press from publicizing what was really going on. Rib-icoff had called out Daley's tactics for what they were. During the convention you had a hodgepodge of local and federal authorities loosely associated around a single issue, the country's militaristic campaign in Vietnam, and when one of these factions had turned out to be willing to go so far as to beat the antiwar opponents they at the time all shared, the others—including the current president of the United States, his chosen successor, and the recently nom-inated Republican rival—justified this violence by explaining it away with hollow catchalls like nationalism and patriotism and weakness, as in: these protestors were really just a bunch of plotting communist outsiders who deserved what they got because they were too contemptibly weak to back up their chants and speeches in the street fight they'd brought on themselves. "The city of Chi-cago and the people of Chicago didn't do a thing that was wrong," Hubert Humphrey said afterward. "There are certain people in the United States who feel that all you have to do is riot and you can get your way. I have not time for that."

That night, just after 11:00 p.m., it became official. With Penn-sylvania, Humphrey's delegate count finally broke the threshold. The nomination was his on the first ballot. He'd represent the Democratic Party against Richard Nixon in the general election. The next day, during his acceptance speech, he'd find it appropri-ate to quote Saint Francis of Assisi: "Where there is hatred let me sow love."

Afterward—now it was Thursday afternoon, the last of the con-vention—Hunter Thompson was kicked out of the amphitheater by Mayor Daley's security agents, who appeared to be escorting away any and all members of the press, regardless of their behavior or political bent, without explanation. He spent the rest of the night wandering the city, drinking and writing, unable to sleep; whenever he tried to explain what he'd seen he broke down crying. At sunrise on Friday morning, on his way back from a *Ramparts* magazine party, he was crossing to his hotel from Grant Park when out in front of the Hilton he came upon Blair Clark, Senator Gene McCarthy's campaign manager (and the former vice president of CBS News). Clark was pacing up and down the sidewalk. His eyes, Thompson noticed, were shining with tears.

Inside the lobby, people were running and screaming and holding on to one another. Some appeared to be bleeding profusely. Thompson tried to find out what had happened.

Only a few minutes earlier, dozens of police, accompanied by members of the National Guard, had stormed the operations suite of the McCarthy campaign on the fifteenth floor, and with their billy clubs they'd beat the young staffers who'd been volunteering for the campaign since New Hampshire. The police would later claim they were pelted by debris thrown from McCarthy's headquarters, but that was impossible; the windows to the suite had been shut and locked for hours. Richard Goodwin happened to be in the room when the violence broke out—he'd stopped to say goodbye—and as everyone was being herded downstairs in the lobby for arrest, he sent a message to McCarthy to gather up his Secret Service detail and come immediately. The senator promptly arrived with his suit-wearing agents and demanded to know who was in charge. But the cops and guardsmen shrugged; together they melted away, back out onto the street. "Just what I thought!" McCarthy called out after them. "Nobody's in charge."

By now the sun was coming up over the lake. It was Friday morning, August 30: the tail end of the very worst political convention in American history. Hunter Thompson stood there in the Hilton lobby watching its final bloody act—the curtain falling as a recent presidential candidate and his Secret Service detail faced off against the combined members of the National Guard and Chicago police, whose victims lay wailing and bleeding on the lobby floor. How could America continue to exist in the manner it was once conceived if its mechanisms could be appropriated so easily in the name of everything the Republic was meant to stand against?

"It was the ultimate horror," Thompson described afterward in a letter to a friend. "The final groin-shot that only a beast like Daley would stoop to deliver. It was an LBJ-style trick: no rest for the losers, keep them on the run and if they fall, kick the shit out of them."

## CHAPTER FOUR

# FREAK KINGDOM IN THE ROCKIES

## 1969–1970

## A King-Hell Bummer in Almost Every Way

On Monday, January 20, 1969, beneath a low Atlantic sky the color of wet concrete, Richard Milhous Nixon descended the steps at the Capitol's East Portico and repeated back the oath administered to him by Chief Justice Earl Warren, taking office as the thirty-seventh president of the United States.

"The greatest honor history can bestow is the title of peacemaker," he proclaimed in his address. "When we listen to 'the better angels of our nature,' we find that they celebrate the simple things, the basic things—such as goodness, decency, love, kindness."

Hunter Thompson had made the trip east from Colorado to cover the inauguration; Bill Cardoso, whom he'd met during the New Hampshire primary, was now an editor for the *Boston Globe*'s weekend magazine, and he'd commissioned Thompson to write a freewheeling feature on the festivities, going so far as to secure a press pass from the newspaper's political bureau.

"The peace we seek to win is not victory over any other people but the peace that comes with healing in its wings," Nixon said now. "As our eyes catch the dimness of the first rays of dawn, let us not curse the remaining dark. Let us gather the light."

Immediately Thompson recognized the source of the overwrought rhetoric: Ray Price, the administration's chief speechwriter who'd helped spearhead, during the campaign, the rebranding effort that had sought to repackage Nixon as the patriotic, stabilizing unifier America so desperately needed. Not that such a feat would've been possible without this specific candidate's unique mutability. Still, in victory, Richard Nixon had proven that he could become *anything*—including, against all odds, the unquestioned leader of the free world. "I went to Washington for his Inauguration," Thompson would write, "hoping for a terrible shitrain that would pound the White House to splinters. But it didn't happen; no shitrain, no justice . . . and Nixon was finally in charge."

In retrospect, however, the true extent of Richard Nixon's amorality would turn out to be far more drastic than anyone at the time could prove—something that's only recently come to light, almost half a century later.

In the months that followed the August convention in Chicago, Richard Nixon had enjoyed a double-digit lead over his Democratic rival, Hubert Horatio Humphrey. But on October 31, 1968, just a week before the election, Lyndon Johnson went on national television and announced a halt to the bombing of North Vietnam, effective immediately, as a final attempt to secure a negotiated peace with the communist regime in Hanoi. All the involved parties, including the Soviets, appeared to be on board: the settlement would establish a coalition government between the South Vietnamese and the Vietcong in Saigon, an approach that both Robert Kennedy and Eugene McCarthy had advocated and that Johnson was only now willing to embrace, for a variety of reasons, not least of which was the increasingly likely defeat of Humphrey's candidacy. "We have the best deal we now can get," Johnson's national security advisor Walt Rostow informed him, "vastly better than any we thought we could get in 1961."

Nixon, tipped off to the development by a sympathetic participant in the negotiating process, knew that such a settlement might cost him the election. "Events could cut down a lead as big as ours," he'd said about a possible end to the war in Vietnam. He wasn't wrong; overnight Humphrey's poll numbers shot up. Suddenly Nixon was faced with the very real prospect of defeat. In response, with the help of senior campaign advisors John Mitchell and H. R. Haldeman, he orchestrated a backchannel message to the current leader of the regime in Saigon, president Nguyen Thieu, communicating through intermediaries that it would be in the South's best interests if *he* won the election: with a stout anti-communist Republican like Nixon in the White House to drive a harder bargain at the negotiating table, Saigon would get a much better deal in future peace talks.

This was, at the very least, a felony offense; private citizens are forbidden by federal law to interfere with negotiations between governments. But in reality the consequences were much starker: he'd betrayed the interests of his country in order to serve his own.

And it had worked. Thieu delayed, refusing at the last moment to commit to the talks. Lyndon Johnson was incensed. Already he'd discovered the real reason for Thieu's astonishing recalcitrance: through information gathered from a CIA listening device that had been placed in the South Vietnamese presidential office, as well as an FBI wiretap on Saigon's phone lines to their embassy in Washington, Johnson could prove that the Nixon campaign was attempting to sabotage the peace talks. "This is treason," he told senate minority leader Everett Dirksen, an old friend, on November 2. "They're contacting a foreign power in the middle of a war!"

The next day, Nixon, who'd by now caught wind of the fallout—Johnson was considering going public with the information—decided it was time to give LBJ a call.

"Ah, Mr. President, this is Dick Nixon," he said.

"Yes, Dick."

Nixon stammered. "Any rumblings about, uh, *someone* trying to sabotage the Saigon government's attitude certainly has no . . . has absolutely no credibility as far as I'm concerned."

"I'm very happy to hear that, Dick," Johnson replied—knowing full well that what he'd just heard was a lie. "Because that *is* taking place."

"My God!" Nixon exclaimed, his words breathy and melodramatic. "I would *never* do anything to, ah, to *encourage* Saigon not to come to the table."

What could Lyndon Johnson do? After years of telling the public the opposite of what was actually going on in Southeast Asia he'd lost all credibility; if he accused Nixon he'd have to reveal the methods by which he'd gathered the information—spying on American citizens and on an allied government. In the end he decided it would be too risky.

The peace process never got back on track for Johnson. Over the next two days Nixon's campaign wrote off the bombing halt as a desperate last-ditch effort to save Humphrey. And on November 5 Nixon took the Electoral College, pulling out the popular vote by half a percent. He had committed treason in a desperate attempt to secure the presidency . . . and no one had stopped him. At last he'd *won*.

From the moment he began his term he was unthinkably compromised, and the only way to protect himself from exposure would be to rely on the same crooked impulses that had gotten him into this situation in the first place. Which meant that, from here on out, the shape-shifting capacity that had carried him so unbelievably far—his greatest political skill—would be unavailable to him. He was locked into place, once and for all, by the extreme actions he'd pushed himself to take. To survive the next eight years, this latest mutation—into a traitorous, treasonous beast of man— would have to be his last. It was the version that Hunter Thompson had sensed from the start.

Thirty-five thousand Americans had already died in the war Nixon had just interfered to extend. More than twenty thousand would perish in the next seven years, a number that gets at the real horror of what it means for someone so deeply self-serving to assume control of the American government: because of the nature of the presidency in the context of the postwar world, Richard Nixon now held the power of life and death over every single one of his citizens—a human currency he was clearly willing to cash in if it might personally benefit him.

"For its part," Nixon said at the end of his address, "government will listen. We will strive to listen in new ways." And then he got into his enormous bulletproof Lincoln limousine and kicked off the day's inaugural parade, which, in its route from the Capitol to the White House, would take him within a literal stone's throw of the thousands of protestors who now lined the city's winter streets.

Hunter Thompson, thanks to his press credentials, was able to stake out a prime spot at the end of the parade route—the corner of Pennsylvania and Fifteenth Street, across from the large stand of bleachers—the intersection where the president's vanguard would make its penultimate turn before passing into the vast security cordon of the White House.

It was early afternoon. The wind had come down from the northeast, freezing and brittle, knocking at everyone's hats and handbills and high-collared coats. Nixon's motorcade advanced directly into its teeth, up the city's long angled corridor—Pennsylvania Avenue—a diagonal that connected one seat of American power to another. The procession was led by a wedge of thirty police motorcycles. Secret Service agents trotted alongside.

The protestors had posted up along the parade route at three main locations. Throughout the weekend, they'd been gathering for what was being called the "Counter-Inaugural," a multiday event organized by the same activists from the Democratic National Convention, including MOBE leader David Dellinger and Yippie founder Jerry Rubin, who together, on account of Mayor Daley's wrath, were facing five-year prison sentences in Illinois on trumped-up "conspiracy to riot" charges.

After Chicago, the mood of the general antiwar movement had soured. "Violence and confrontation are the themes now," Thompson would write in his *Globe* feature, which would be published three days later. "Vicious dissidence is the style."

As the motorcade approached the intersection of Twelfth Street and Pennsylvania—the site of the Old Post Office and Clock Tower—the first small group was waiting. They were flanked front and back by navy-jacketed DC police and National Guardsmen, as well as an additional unarmed contingent from the Army's 82nd Airborne Division. Not that it mattered; as soon as the limousine appeared they unleashed a dense hail of rocks and sticks. Members of the Secret Service, walking alongside, struggled to bat down the projectiles. Someone lofted a softball-sized wad of tinfoil that, in its precipitous arc, appeared to be falling directly toward the vehicle carrying Mr. and Mrs. Nixon—which accelerated, jolting its occupants and forcing the agents on the street into an accompanying run.

The next set of protestors—the largest—had gathered at Fourteenth Street near the National Theatre, on the north side of Pennsylvania: the parade route's widest spot. Here, more than a thousand young men and women chanted slogans at the motorcade: "FOUR MORE YEARS OF DEATH!" "HO, HO, HO CHI MINH. N.L.F. IS GONNA WIN!" "TWO. FOUR. SIX. EIGHT. ORGANIZE TO SMASH THE STATE!" And: "ONE. TWO. THREE. FOUR. WE DON'T WANT YOUR FUCKING WAR!" From the crowd came a new barrage. A paint-filled Christmas ornament shattered against the pavement. A smoking can was tossed just ahead of the presidential limousine, rolling underneath. National Guardsmen and DC police surged against the crowd, reaching for the assailants. But the protestors grabbed and beat anyone from law enforcement unlucky enough to venture too far into their midst—one cop, after charging into the crowd, had been nearly stripped naked—and as a result, the hail kept coming down. They threw stones, bottles, cans, firecrackers, and smoke bombs; they threw pennies and pebbles; they threw table forks and a spoon; they threw tomatoes; they threw manure; they lit on fire the miniature American flags that the Boy Scouts had been passing out and threw them as hard as they could in the general direction of the new president.

It was 2:45 p.m. Hunter Thompson was still in his spot at Pennsylvania and Fifteenth Street. Across the avenue, in the white-plank bleachers—where MOBE leaders had legitimately purchased 200 tickets—protestors were holding up signs with messages like STOP THE WAR AGAINST BLACK AMERICA and NIXON IS THE ONE—THE #1 WAR CRIMINAL! They waved Vietcong banners. They passed around a blotchy dark sack they kept calling "The Black Flag of Anarchy."

Someone threw a half-gallon jug of wine. Standing alongside Thompson, a newscaster from CBS announced into his microphone, "Here comes the president . . . "

From around the corner the limousine appeared: "A sort of huge, hollowed-out cannonball on wheels," Thompson would write. "A very nasty looking armored car . . . There was a stench of bedrock finality about it."

It had been a year of assassinations and police riots and internecine defeats that had led, in the end, to the most unthinkable outcome of all: Richard Nixon's victory march to the White House lawn.

"The whole concept of 'peaceful protest' died at the Democratic Convention," Thompson wrote that night for his *Boston Globe* piece. Up until Chicago there'd been the assumption, however far-fetched, that the politicians running the country were capable of perceiving a mass demonstration on something like the war in Vietnam within the context of America's general political reality; that they were *listening*—were willing to play by the same set of guidelines the Republic had agreed upon almost two centuries earlier—even if they vehemently disagreed with what they heard.

"The 1960s were full of examples of good, powerful men changing their minds on heavy issues," Thompson would write years later—the pinnacle being Lyndon Johnson's shocking decision to recognize his failure in Vietnam and preemptively forgo a second term. Which was why the current reality felt so devastating: "With Agnew and Nixon and Mitchell coming into power," he'd explain, "there was simply no point in yelling at the fuckers. They were born deaf and stupid."

He'd realized that it no longer mattered how effectively you conducted a demonstration: the people you were hoping to reach were incapable of hearing what you had to say.

The presidential limousine continued past Thompson. He watched it turn from Fifteenth Street to the White House and then disappear behind a wall of black leafless trees. The temperature was dropping. The sky thickened and dimmed. Now the protestors were fighting among themselves. Police rode by on horseback. The wind lifted and let fall the parade's long ribbon of debris. Overhead, an enormous helicopter beat the air. The city smelled the way it always does in winter, like dust and freezing rain and shallow, stagnant water. Thompson zipped up his ski jacket and walked south, toward the Mall. Around him the white-sand statues and memorials revealed themselves as if haphazardly—like relics—their individual meaning suddenly subsumed beneath the thing the city had become: *Mr. Nixon's City*. A monument to the office he'd finally won—to *him*.

From the Mall he could see Arlington National Cemetery, its vast hillside landscaped evenly with more graves than he could count. That was part of the monument, too, the worst part: across the gray river, Bobby Kennedy lay closed in a coffin only a few feet off from that of his older brother, both of them forced now to adorn, in death—in *silence*—the sinister spectacle of the present.

"The only thing necessary for the triumph of evil is for good men to do nothing," Bobby said just before he was assassinated, a quote his brother had attributed to Edmund Burke. Thompson would never forget hearing this line—he'd hold it dear for the rest of his life—though on a day as haunted as this one, such wisdom could be heard to mean something different: it's only after the very best of us are driven into silence that the most destructive characteristics in our nature find the means to flourish.

And suddenly Hunter Thompson felt disgusted and bone-chilled and at a loss. Overhead the sky was about to break. He walked back to his hotel in the wind. "What a fantastic monument to all the best instincts of the human race this country might have been," he'd later write, "if we could have kept it out of the hands of greedy little hustlers like Richard Nixon."

\*

A few weeks after the inauguration, Thompson traveled to Edwards Air Force Base in California to write about its test-pilot program for *Pageant:* a lucrative assignment. Afterward—after peppering career officers with questions on Vietnam as he watched SR-71 reconnaissance jets scream across the desert sky—he checked in to the Hyatt Continental Hotel, on LA's Sunset Strip, where he planned to finish a draft of the article.

Each day, he also drove out to East Los Angeles, and in the company of Oscar Acosta he was offered a glimpse into the dynamic Chicano movement, a subject he was considering for his "Death of the American Dream" project. By this point Acosta had been practicing law in Southern California for just over a year; already he'd become one of the most well-known attorneys in the state. For his first major case he'd defended a group of high school students and teachers who'd organized a citywide walkout to protest the underfunded educational system in East LA. The police had physically attacked these students and then charged them afterward with conspiracy, a felony, even though the thing they were accused of plotting—disturbing the peace—was only a misdemeanor. It was an outrageous escalation on law enforcement's behalf; if convicted, the defendants faced up to forty years in prison. But Acosta would get all the charges against them dismissed; to do so he employed a three-pronged argument, claiming 1) a lack of evidence, 2) the violation of the defendants' First Amendment right to freedom of speech, and 3) discrimination, under the equal protection clause of the Fourteenth Amendment, based on the fact that the grand jury used to indict them lacked representation from the Mexican-American community.

Since joining the movement Acosta had come to understand that, in the face of widespread institutional racism, *everything* is political, and in the courtroom he refused to separate his partisan arguments from his legal ones, as he'd been taught to do in law school. As a result, his unorthodox tactics were shining a huge amount of unwanted attention on police practices. At press conferences in front of the courthouse, he'd recount the stories of Chicano youths who'd died without explanation in police custody. He was regularly held in contempt and jailed for days at a time. Once, in court proceedings, he took an unloaded gun from the evidence display and waved it at members of the jury, ordering everyone to get on the ground—and then he proceeded to ask them, in a normal tone of voice, if under such intimidation they should be expected to give an accurate testimony of events, in the way his *own* clients were.

But his real activism was only getting started: for his next move, he was preparing to attack the legal validity of the grand jury system itself. At that time, in LA County, grand juries were appointed by circuit court magistrates, who were almost always white. Acosta's plan was to subpoena *all* the judges in the area and interrogate them as to their relationships with and prejudices toward members of the Mexican-American community.

During his first few nights in town—when Thompson was supposed to be writing the *Pageant* article—he and Acosta hit the Sunset Strip. Over drinks they continued the political discussion they'd started in Aspen: whether it was still possible, in the context of a year like 1968, to improve the American system from within; or if it was finally time to tear the whole thing down and start again. Acosta's recent legal success had exposed him to the full scrutiny of his very powerful enemies. "Not only are my telephones bugged," he'd recently confided, "but the District Attorney, here in Los Angeles, is out to get me." Like Thompson he also took a large daily dosage of amphetamine—his chosen variety was Benzedrine—and that February, along the West Hollywood street's famous rainy rise, they closed out Whisky a Go Go and worked their way back to the Hyatt Continental, the day coming up behind its cycle of low, winter storms.

Needless to say, by the end of the week Hunter Thompson's article on the Air Force's test-pilot program wasn't finished. (It would eventually take him another month to complete a draft for submission.) What's more: eight hours before his flight back to Aspen he found himself completely out of Dexedrine. "Getting toward dawn now," he wrote in his notebook, "very foggy in the head . . . For the first time in at least five years I am out of my little energy bombs." All he had left were five Ritalin pills—"useless at this point . . . not strong enough"—and a giant homemade capsule Acosta had given him that was equal parts amphetamine and mescaline.

It's not as if a sudden burst of Dexedrine would've made much of a difference now. In the two years since *Hell's Angels* he'd written hundreds of polished pages—some of his very best work—but almost all of it was on subjects that he found deeply compelling. When it came to an article he was only doing for the money, no amount of adrenaline and hard deadlines and Dexedrine could make up for his lack of personal attachment. "There is something perverse and even suicidal about speed," he'd written in his journal the year before. "Like 'The Devil and Daniel Webster': buy high and sell low . . . ignoring that inevitable day when there's no more high except maybe a final freakout with cocaine . . . the certain knowledge of burning out a lot sooner than if I played it healthy."

Now he was trapped in his Los Angeles hotel room with a limited number of hours until he needed to send off the article and check out. He felt panicked. And at that moment, what he wanted more than anything was to be free from these failures and deadlines and responsibilities altogether—or, failing that, to make them somehow irrelevant.

"Well, I just swallowed the bugger," he wrote. "In this dead-tired, run-down condition . . . any reaction will be extreme. I've never had mescaline."

Instead of working on the test-pilot article, he spent the next eight hours documenting, on his typewriter, his experiences. "The physical end of the thing is like the first half-hour on acid," he wrote, "a sort of buzzing all over." And: "A sense of very pleasant physical paralysis." And: "The ball on this typewriter now appears to be made of arterial blood." And: "The cloud is off the sun again, for real this time, incredible light in the room, white blaze on the walls, glittering typewriter keys."

As his departure time approached he felt desperate for Aspen—for safety, for home. Finally he called Acosta, who came by the hotel and helped him to the airport.

"The drug is gone now," Thompson wrote from the plane, "failing energy, disconnected thoughts . . . smelling of booze in this cabin, nobody speaks, fear and loathing, dizzy, flying and bouncing through the clouds. No more hole cards. Drained."

\*

During the fall and winter months that followed the Democratic Convention, Thompson couldn't talk to Sandy about what he'd seen there without sobbing. "Hunter was a patriot," she'd later say. "He cared so much. He knew the Constitution . . . And then there he was, in Chicago, and it's all being destroyed."

Afterward, returning to Colorado, he began to look at Aspen and its local political system in a fresh way: how might this western valley be employed as a buffer against the mob-style violence he'd experienced? There was the region's natural isolation and also its small population: two factors that, in the context of his evolving perspective on activism—*Politics is the art of controlling your environment,* he realized after the police riot—spoke favorably to enacting change on a smaller scale, which at the moment looked a lot more viable than trying to get someone like Richard Nixon to acknowledge the legitimacy of your grievances.

As such, it wasn't enough anymore to seclude himself here for most of the year with his family and then travel, when necessary, to report on the American political system; he also needed to make Aspen *safe.*

In 1969, he and Peggy Clifford, now the top columnist for the *Aspen Times,* attended meetings for a neighborhood advocacy organization, the Citizens for Community Action (CCA), which, with its anti-sprawl and pro-environmental platform, was preparing to contest the key city and county positions up for election in the fall. He was introduced to James Salter, ten years his senior: a novelist and screenwriter with a lyric style who, after purchasing a house on the west side of town, had helped found the CCA.

This valley was, after all, Thompson's home, the place where he and Sandy planned to spend the rest of their lives together. That winter, she was pregnant again. This time there weren't any complications. Juan was five. They were renting a large property on Little Woody Creek Road—it included a main house and another for guests, where their close friends Billy and Anne Noonan lived for a time—and in the aftermath of 1968 Thompson was ready to refocus his political effort toward the more immediate aspects of his life.

That April, he received a welcome surprise in the mail from Bernard Shir-Cliff at Random House: $15,000 in royalties from *Hell's Angels* sales. He quickly worked out an arrangement with George Stranahan, his current landlord and friend, to purchase the houses he was renting, along with twenty five acres of surrounding land: for the first time he and Sandy would own their own place. He also sent money back to Louisville so his younger brother Jim, who was draft-eligible, could make his tuition payments at the University of Kentucky.

Sandy was due in mid-July. At the end of the spring Thompson stopped traveling and returned to the seclusion of Owl Farm—the name he'd bestowed on the property—where, preparing for the baby, he could turn his attention to the "Death of the American Dream" book. Somehow he hoped to put together a draft from the vivid fragments of political reporting he'd written over the last year, the latest being a commissioned piece for *Esquire* on the gun lobby: after Bobby Kennedy and Martin Luther King Jr.'s murders, he'd found himself reevaluating his affinity for guns. The problem was that this latest feature had already ballooned to 140 pages—*four times* longer than what the magazine expected—with no clear end in sight.

It was the same when it came to the Random House manuscript: "I'm sitting here staring at about 400 pages of disconnected bullshit that may or may not boil into a book," he wrote Shir-Cliff in May. To Jim Silberman he added: "Actually, I've been writing like a bastard the past six months." Which was true: the issue wasn't so much one of output but organization. He still hadn't found the vehicle upon which he might lash his firsthand reportage on the shocking series of events that had unfolded across America the previous year. By June it was clear: he'd miss his deadline; the material was in need of a more viable, self-contained structure.

Still, 1969 was shaping up to be an enormous improvement over the year before. Even if he'd failed to meet his target date, he had a pile of pages waiting to be arranged. In Woody Creek his new property was coming alive: a blooming, alpine hillside. At any moment the baby would arrive. The house cat and the family's new Doberman were also pregnant. "I feel like Johnny Appleseed," Thompson wrote to Selma Shapiro. "Dogs, cats, children, trees, grass, huge wooden structures, pottery, metal sculptures; I have a euphoric sense of building a dynasty of some kind. So maybe I should grow a beard, along with all the rest."

"It was beautiful at Owl Farm," Sandy would later say. "It was summertime and there were lots of flowers. Everything just could not have been happier or more fertile and growing. Hunter was happy and Juan was just this little tiger of a kid in a cowboy hat and cowboy boots and he wore a little pistol."

## Before the Bomb and After

During the third week of July, amid the global drama of the Apollo 11 moonshot, Sandy went into labor. She and Thompson drove to Aspen Valley Hospital, located on the west side of town. It was a bright morning, rich and deeply green. Things progressed quickly. Thompson was in the delivery room with her when she gave birth. Suddenly: a baby girl. *Sara*.

Afterward there was a terrible silence. The baby's face was blue. Now the doctor was whisking her away.

Sandy refused to look; in the absence of the expected cries and congratulations she couldn't bear to see what was happening. Thompson tried to reassure her: "She's as big as a football player," he said. Outside, through the hospital's wide window, the broad west-Aspen meadow was carpeted with wildflowers, a great inland sea of them.

After Juan was born, the Thompsons had been told that, because of their blood types' conflicting Rh factors—Sandy was Rh-negative, the rarer of the two—the antibodies she'd naturally develop during subsequent births could result in hemolytic anemia, a condition in which the baby's red blood cells would be destroyed more quickly than they could be replicated.

This was why their daughter's skin was blue: the antibodies that during the delivery had been transferred over were now disrupting her oxygen supply. At the time the only effective treatment involved a transfusion of Rh immunoglobulin, which would target and destroy these antibodies. But in 1969, the Aspen Valley Hospital didn't carry the amount of blood necessary for the procedure. There was nothing they could do.

The doctor came in. As soon as Sandy saw his face she knew: their daughter was dead. It was as if an enormous gate had been closed on her. "I could just walk out of here," she said to her husband. She was watching the meadow through the window, its deep, wildflower sea. "Just walk out there and then nothing is real. And if it's not real, then my baby didn't die."

With his gaze Hunter Thompson worked to draw his wife's eyes back to his own. "Sandy," he said. "If you need to do that . . . if you need to go away, then you do that. But I just want you to know that Juan and I need you and that we'll be glad when you come back."

At last she turned and looked. Suddenly she could see him seeing her—his gaze like a well-thrown anchor. "I just switched," she'd later say. "I came back. And to me that was one of the most beautiful things Hunter has ever done."

Afterward—as Sandy rested—Hunter Thompson screamed at the doctors and staff. What had they done with his daughter's body? Finally he was told that it would be disposed of according to hospital regulations.

Outside, against the hood of a car, he placed his head in his hands and wept. And then, with the help of his friend Billy Noonan he went back into the hospital; together they located Sara's body. He and Noonan drove down-valley, to a secluded bank of the Roaring Fork River. They dug a grave. And they buried the baby in a plot overlooking the water. For the rest of his life Thompson would decline to discuss, let alone write about, what had happened.

*

Nearly a month later—at 3:00 p.m. on September 10, 1969—the Austral Oil Company, working with the Atomic Energy Commission in a joint effort to explore previously untapped reserves of natural gas, detonated a forty-kiloton fission bomb inside the Battlement Mesa near the small town of Rulison: just forty miles due west of Aspen.

About fifty protestors, many of them members of the local CCA—Hunter Thompson included—traveled to the blast site's observation post on the day of the explosion. Tom Benton, a talented Los Angeles artist who'd recently moved to the region, designed silkscreen posters for everyone to carry; each featured a vivid, concentric target accompanied by the text:

STOP THE BLAST

NO CONTAMINATION WITHOUT REPRESENTATION

The bomb was lowered 8,442 feet underground; upon ignition, it shattered the deep, gas-rich reef of sandstone and shale at the range's western base. The resulting shockwave lifted the surface of the mountain. The protestors, standing with the crowd of Austral Oil workers, AEC representatives, and local dignitaries, swayed as if at sea. In the distance the mesa's bluffs crumbled and smoked, a series of rockslides sending up dense gusts of dirt. Enormous boulders broke free, taking off topsoil and trees as they tumbled toward the Colorado River. Telephone cables were severed. Chimneys collapsed. In nearby Grand Valley, bricks fell out from the walls of the post office. Across the region the sound of the bomb resonated like a jet's—sonic and stark, a distinct, human-made thunder.

"The oil companies and these fucking death bombs . . . ," Thompson wrote afterward. He and the protestors returned to Aspen, where they gathered that evening for a CCA event at the town's famous Humanistic Institute. The topic of discussion turned to the upcoming local elections.

At the time there were three pressing community issues: development, civil liberties, and the environment. Each opened onto the other. The local moguls who in the 1950s had bought up large tracts of land—back when Aspen was still a secluded former mining town—were hell-bent on developing the area into an elite resort; already they were looking to sell their properties and erect new hotels and condominiums.

As a result, the town's less affluent residents—a number of whom had ended up here from San Francisco's Haight-Ashbury district—were deemed inimical to development; the council and magistrate enacted strict vagrancy laws, urging the sheriff, a humorless Oklahoman named Carrol Whitmire, to charge and imprison the "hippies" flooding the town.

What's more, the resort development had outpaced the community's environmental concerns; questions of sustainability and growth and transportation and pollution and land use were dismissed by the members of the city council—a three-person board that basically ran things—in fear of hurting investment.

At the end of the proceedings, CCA cofounder Robin Molny, a local architect who'd studied under Frank Lloyd Wright, claimed that, in regards to the upcoming election, it would be better to "forge a confederacy of neighborhood groups" that could then "impose their collective wills on elected representatives"—as opposed to *fielding* their own candidates. Molny's excuse? "There is not enough time."

Hunter Thompson was enraged: afterward, in an op-ed for the *Aspen Illustrated News,* he wrote that the CCA "will wither into history as a bad joke unless they can muster a slate from their own ranks to run for mayor and city council." It wasn't enough anymore, "in this evil Nixon autumn," to carry signs and stage sit-ins; to him the Rulison demonstration was just another "bad echo of the doomed 'Protest Tradition.'" He also didn't hesitate to call out the town's prominent developers and businessmen by name—labeling them "greedy, plastic bastards" and "cheap, carny hustlers." He was willing to run for office himself, he added, but as a resident of Woody Creek he was only eligible for county, as opposed to city, positions. "What we do need," he concluded in the op-ed, "is a decent thinking candidate for mayor, and a slate of potential councilmen he can work with."

\*

After the death of his daughter, Hunter Thompson wrote to Tom Wolfe: "I find myself watching the horizon and hoping to see flames."

To William Kennedy: "Well, I said I would write, but I'm damned if I have the stomach for it. Everything that could possibly go wrong here, has."

To his maternal aunt in Louisville, with whom he'd always been close: "Thank you for the birthday present and the nice note to

Sandy—which won't be answered, since I've told her to forget any references or replies to that situation. She appreciated your note, but under the circumstances I think she'll be better off forgetting the whole thing."

To Joe Benti, an anchor at CBS whose newscast he'd found lacking: "You people are in fact a gang of cowardly, self-censoring swine . . . Your coverage of the [Chicago DNC] conspiracy trial is a cheap cop-out . . . Fuck this action; I have better things to do."

To Jim Silberman: "My need for a focus is beyond critical; it borders on paralysis and desperation."

"Years later," Sandy would say, reflecting on that summer's tragedy, "I was with Hunter and another person and I said something about losing 'my' children. And Hunter looked at me and very gently he said, 'Sandy, they were my children, too.'"

When they lost their daughter, the Thompsons had retreated to Owl Farm, situating themselves on the land they'd purchased in expectation of their new family member. But that September, after the CCA meeting, and seeing so clearly the environmental and political threats to their home, Hunter Thompson felt angry enough about the state of things to write the op-ed for the *Aspen Illustrated News*. It was published at the end of September. Suddenly Thompson found himself, to his surprise, publicly and privately attacked by the rich developers he'd called out; they were far more outraged than he'd imagined possible.

A few days later he sat down with James Salter and Peggy Clifford to consider possible last-minute candidates for the mayoral race, which was now only a month away. The best option appeared to be a twenty-nine-year-old local attorney named Joe Edwards who, the year before, had successfully challenged the city in district court over its discriminatory vagrancy policies. As an original member of the CCA Edwards had also spoken out against overdevelopment. With his Clark Gable mustache and talent for motorcycle racing he cut an alluring figure: someone the hippie crowd *and* the long-established liberal residents might rally around.

On the spur of the moment Thompson decided to give Edwards a call. The two had never met. It was after midnight and the conversation started awkwardly; Edwards, it soon became clear, had been asleep.

"We need to straighten out this town," Thompson told him. "We need to organize all the bartenders and ski bums, the kids working the ski lifts and in the restaurants and bars. We have the numbers; if we can just get them registered and get them interested and get them to participate, we'll have the political power to change the town."

Edwards was intrigued. "Running for mayor . . . ," he finally said. "Fuck it. Why not?"

And like that it was happening. With Thompson serving as the de facto campaign manager—and with the help of Clifford and Salter and mutual friends like Tom Benton, Billy Noonan, and Michael Solheim, a local bartender and house painter—the Edwards campaign set off on a manic, monthlong drive to convince enough residents that it was in their best interests to elect this young, anti-expansion, pro-environment candidate.

Thompson devised a two-step plan of action. The first part focused on voter registration. Over the next ten days, they worked to find and bring into the fray the hundreds of hippies who'd arrived in Aspen during the last few years. Which wasn't easy: one of the reasons for fleeing to the Rockies in the first place was to try and escape what they perceived as the rigged nature of American life. Later, looking back on this phase of the campaign, Thompson would write: "Somewhere in the nightmare of failure that gripped America between 1965 and 1970, the old Berkeley-born notion of beating The System by fighting it gave way to a sort of numb conviction that it made more sense in the long run to Flee, or even to simply hide, than to fight the bastards on anything even vaguely resembling their own terms."

It was a consuming process, into which Thompson threw himself. With the campaign he could work from home and in town—close to his grieving, devastated wife—while also distracting himself with something besides the despair-heavy solitude that, after the death of his daughter, infused everything, including the writing process. From Owl Farm and other locations they made phone calls, checked registries, and personally canvassed different districts of the city.

There were perhaps 1,600 possible votes at stake, and with a three-person race—in addition to the town's pro-business candidate (a nondescript attorney named Leonard Oates), the local Republicans were running a longtime party socialite, Eve Homeyer, who portrayed herself as embodying Aspen's Platonic ideal of a "den mother"—a few late registrations could make all the difference.

The second phase, beginning in mid-October, consisted of a multiplatform advertising campaign. Peggy Clifford crafted newspaper ads. "Joe Edwards will work with residents and planners to develop a long-range plan for orderly growth and preservation of our resources," she wrote. They took out a series of radio spots. Tom Benton designed new silkscreen posters; each featured a fist with two fingers raised in the peace sign. IF YOU DON'T GIVE A DAMN DON'T REGISTER TO VOTE, some read. Others: SELL ASPEN OR SAVE IT THERE'S STILL TIME. They all included the line at the bottom: JOE EDWARDS FOR MAYOR.

Edwards's platform had five parts: 1) move all telephone and electrical utilities underground, 2) set aside mandatory green spaces, 3) reroute traffic from the city center and create a pedestrian mall in place of the busiest blocks of street, 4) enact an ordinance to preserve and update historic buildings, and 5) hire an ecologist-planner to estimate the valley's current resources and the extent of its overall capacity for growth.

By November the town's pro-business faction—identified by Thompson as "the sub-dividers, ski-pimps and city-based land-developers who had come like a plague of poison roaches to buy

and sell the whole valley out from under the people who still val-
ued it as a good place to live, not just a good investment"—was
nervous. For them, Aspen, with its rising lift ticket and restaurant
and lodging prices, represented "a king-hell gold-mine with no
end in sight . . . the showpiece/ money-hub of a gold rush that
has made millionaires." And they weren't about to give up their
political influence—and, in turn, their *profits*—without a fight. By
election day the race appeared to be a toss-up. It would all depend
on the November 4 turnout.

At the polls that Tuesday, the two leaders of the pro-
development faction opposing Edwards—the town's outgoing
mayor, Dr. Robert "Bugsy" Barnard, and Guido Meyer, a ma-
niacal hippie-hating Swiss-born resort owner—had threatened
to challenge and disqualify the newly registered voters. So that
morning, Thompson sent a group of poll watchers, led by Tom
Benton, to the polling section at Ward 1—located at Cresthaus
Lodge, which was owned and operated by Guido Meyer—armed
with a tape recorder and microphone and copies of the state
election statutes. Bugsy Barnard arrived in his Porsche just after
dawn. Guido came out to the parking lot to watch. But as the
outgoing mayor pulled to a stop, the Edwards voters he'd come
to challenge descended on him. "You're fucked, Bugsy!" one of
them yelled. Another: "Your whole act is doomed." Another:
"We're going to beat your ass like a gong!" Bugsy sprinted inside,
where Benton was waiting: "The reason I have this little black
machine," he said to him, "is that I want to tape every word you
say when you start committing felonies by harassing our voters."
And when the two pro-business leaders tried to challenge one
of the first voters, a kid who looked at most eighteen, the young
man replied: "Go fuck yourself Bugsy! You figure out how old
I am. I know the goddam law. I don't have to show you proof
of anything!"

Which was how things would pretty much go all throughout the rest of the day. Just before the polls closed, the campaign

double-checked its lists with notes from the poll watchers. They commandeered a bank of telephones to remind unaccounted-for supporters that it was their last chance to make a difference. It appeared as if they might actually win: the turnout had been much greater than expected. Bugsy and Guido's candidate, diminutive lawyer Lennie Oates, had been blown out of the water. The only question was whether Eve Homeyer, the Republican Party's self-proclaimed den mother, would draw enough support.

It was 5:00 p.m. The voting was over. There was nothing more Thompson could do; the high-speed burn of the last month's effort was finally at an end. He was exhausted. Surprised. Bemused. Most of all he was elated: "The campaign was a straight exercise in Jeffersonian Democracy," he'd write; in the wake of Chicago it had been "imperative to get a grip on those who had somehow slipped into power and caused the thing to happen," and with the Edwards campaign he'd come at them directly, at the "cartel of local businessmen who instructed the cops to do whatever was 'necessary' to protect the town's image." With someone like Richard Milhous Nixon setting the general tone in Washington, regional crooks like Bugsy and Guido would only grow more powerful if left unchallenged.

That night, the election turned into a toss-up. Eventually it came down to absentee ballots. At last it appeared that Joe Edwards had lost by six votes—a margin that, when all was said and done, would grow as slim as *one*. The campaign staff talked about mounting a legal challenge, but it would've been too costly; instead they decided to try again, the next November, when a new slate of key positions would be up for grabs.

"What emerged from the Joe Edwards campaign," he'd write, "was a very real blueprint for stomping the Agnew mentality by its own rules—with the vote, instead of the bomb: by seizing their power machinery and using it, instead of merely destroying it." He called it the Aspen Technique: "Neither opting out of the system, nor working within it . . . but calling its bluff, by using its strength to turn it back on itself . . . and by always assuming that the people in power are not smart."

Afterward, faced again with the reality of his everyday life—its grief and demands—Hunter Thompson arranged for Juan to visit his grandmother in Florida, and he took Sandy to Los Angeles, where they enjoyed what he'd call "a ten year delayed honeymoon." They stayed in style at the Hyatt Continental, and at night, with Oscar Acosta and his new wife Socorro Aguiniga, a student at UCLA, they hit the town. During the day they sat by the rooftop pool. The Thompsons were grieving together. At one point they launched honeydew rinds from the twelfth floor down at the cars on the Sunset Strip below, laughing and hiding as if they were decades younger.

They got back to Aspen in early December with a maxed-out Diners Club card right around the time the Rolling Stones' *Let It Bleed* was released, an album that Hunter Thompson would remain particularly attached to for the rest of his life. On December 6, the Stones held a free concert at the Altamont Speedway, and as Mick Jagger belted out "Under My Thumb," a drunken posse of Hell's Angels, serving as the venue's security force (in exchange for free beer), stabbed to death eighteen-year-old Meredith Hunter at the base of the stage.

It was an echo of what Thompson had seen four years earlier at the Oakland-Berkeley border, when the fledgling antiwar movement had been so naïve as to think a group as fascistic as the Angels would join their cause. Now, on a familiar note of violence, the 1960s drew to a close. Not that Thompson was surprised; for him the spirit of hope and change that had defined so much of the decade had been crushed more than a year earlier, on the corner of Michigan and Balbo; this was just the final act. "The orgy of violence at Altamont merely *dramatized* the problem," he'd write. "The realities were already fixed; the illness was understood to be terminal, and the energies of The Movement were long since aggressively dissipated."

## Light Years

During the final week of April 1970—in the midst of a storm that pressed Aspen with a surprising, late-season snow—Hunter and Sandy Thompson drove to dinner at the house of the writer James Salter and his wife, Ann. An elegant meal, continental in style: they sat together for hours. Salter had been coming to Aspen since 1959; like the Thompsons he knew the town before its recent transition into a resort. His two-bedroom house was located on the west end, near the Meadows.

Salter preferred to spend time with Thompson in these sorts of settings, private and contained . . . uncrowded. Somewhere they could talk without distraction. A couples dinner was ideal; in the cozy dining room, these two very different men were able to enjoy one another's company. They'd become friends the previous fall, working together on the Edwards campaign.

After the meal was done they sat together in front of the living room fire. They talked about writing. Eventually Thompson went into his struggles. His "The Death of the American Dream" book was long overdue, but he *had* to finish it; there was no way he could ever pay back the advance (once again his money situation was dire). His experience running the Edwards campaign had offered a possible fix: by telling the story of his efforts in small-town participatory democracy, he might be able to provide a through-line on the disparate set pieces documenting recent national disasters. But for that to work, he told Salter, he'd need to see the process through—in the upcoming November elections he'd decided to run for sheriff of Pitkin County—which would only delay the book further. In the meantime he was desperate for well-paying journalistic assignments. He had a new magazine in mind: *Scanlan's Monthly,* which was run by his friend Warren Hinckle. The problem was finding the ideal topic to write about next.

James Salter listened attentively. He was forty-four, hale and unassuming and without haste. Across from Thompson he held himself with the posture of an elite athlete—that of a rock climber, or a swimmer—his carriage a carryover from his previous career in the Air Force, during the course of which he'd flown more than one hundred combat missions. In Korea he'd been a member of the 335th Squadron, damaging one enemy jet and shooting down another. While still on active duty he'd published a novel about the war, *The Hunters,* that became such a critical and financial success that he gave up his commission to write full time. Over the course of his literary career he'd enjoyed a series of successes and also stinging failures, and he understood the despair and frustration and desire for recognition—for greatness—that his younger friend was talking about: the idea that your work, in a certain sense, *was* you.

On the whole, James Salter enjoyed Thompson's writing. At the end of the night he had a suggestion: "What about going back to Louisville and doing something on the Kentucky Derby?"

The notion hadn't occurred to Hunter Thompson. But it made sense. Later, back at Owl Farm, he called up Hinckle in San Francisco, who quickly got on board. And just like that it was happening: the magazine could pay $1,500, plus $500 for expenses, including plane tickets that Hinckle FedExed the next day to Woody Creek. The deadline to meet the June issue was fast approaching; everything would have to be finished the week after the race. Hinckle also agreed to send out an illustrator to provide artwork for the feature, a political sketch artist for the London-based magazine *Private Eye:* Ralph Steadman.

"The story, as I see it," Thompson said after the dinner at Salter's, "is mainly in the vicious-drunk Southern bourbon horseshit mentality that surrounds the Derby [rather] than in the Derby itself."

He arrived in Louisville on Thursday around midnight, April 30. A few hours earlier, Richard Nixon had gone on national television to explain a startling escalation in the Vietnam War: the US-backed offensive into Cambodia. "I have concluded that the time has come for action," Nixon said. "My fellow Americans, we live in an age of anarchy, both abroad and at home." Nobody

had expected it—only ten days earlier the president had announced a drawdown of 150,000 troops—and a wave of protests
broke out at colleges across the country.

Finding himself in his hometown of Louisville again under such
circumstances—a weekend featuring both the Derby *and* mass turmoil over the continuing war in Southeast Asia—Thompson was
appalled. Everywhere he looked—at the airport, at his hotel, at
Churchill Downs and its riotous Paddock Bar—he saw people who
physically embodied the nation's Nixon/Agnew mentality: the sort
of Americans who on the whole thought the *protestors* at the DNC
had gone too far; who couldn't understand why certain groups
in our society felt so disadvantaged; who, in their incuriousness
and acquiescence, gave voice to the percentage of the population
willing to, without any sense of hypocrisy, support felony charges
for something like marijuana possession as they proceeded to drink
and gamble themselves into a lifelong stupor of mainstream vices;
and who, when it came to the national unrest over the war, didn't
hesitate to blame the violence on the victims of the attacks. In
short: what Thompson had seen in Chicago was just the latest expression of the injustice he'd grown up with here during the 1940s
and '50s, in Jim Crow–era Louisville—what he called "the mask of
the whiskey gentry . . . a pretentious mix of booze, failed dreams
and a terminal identity crisis."

As a senior in high school fifteen years earlier, he'd barely escaped this city, enlisting in the Air Force as a way out. And this was
only after he'd spent thirty days in the county lockup: he and two
other friends had been accused of robbing four teenagers—this
was during a confrontation at one of the bluffs overlooking the
river—but his friends, the sons of wealthy attorneys, had connections to the judge. In the end Thompson was the only one who
actually went to jail. "Returning to the scenes of my youth," he'd
write to Hinckle after the race, "was not, all in all, an exceptionally
wise idea."

The next day—Friday, May 1, still twenty-four hours from the start of the race—he headed to the track so he could meet his fellow *Scanlan's* correspondent, Ralph Steadman. They finally found each other in the Derby's press box. "This is a weird place," Thompson said to him. "Why don't we grab a few beers and maybe talk things over."

Steadman was a talented thirty-three-year-old Welsh illustrator whose general aesthetic was one of comic exaggeration. With his tweed jacket and thick beard, he'd been struggling ever since he landed in Kentucky to acclimate himself. Which fit well with Thompson's own rage-tinged discombobulation at returning home. And for the next three days, as America undid itself with a final paroxysm of Vietnam War protests and dissent and lethal violence, these two interlopers—in tandem with thousands of Southern celebrants—got uproariously drunk.

They spent Saturday at Churchill Downs. They toured the infield and its madness. They drank for free in the press section. At race time they took up their allotted positions just beneath the governor's box—Barry Goldwater and other prominent politicians were there, along with local dignitaries like Colonel Sanders—and during the race itself, which only lasted two minutes, they watched everyone in the grandstand watching the horses. "We'd come there to watch the real beasts perform," Thompson would write.

Later that night, they hit up the Pendennis Club, an old Southern venue, but almost immediately they were kicked out; Steadman had gotten too friendly with one of the members' wives. Sunday it was the same: a human sea of mud and alcohol and revulsion and anger as they hopped from bar to bar. At one point a can of Mace may have been used.

By Monday, as the university protests continued to escalate, Ralph Steadman finally left Louisville. Thompson stayed another night; while still back in his hometown he heard, disbelievingly, about the massacre that had occurred that afternoon on the campus of Kent State University: four students had been murdered by National Guardsmen, who'd fired repeatedly into the unarmed crowd of five hundred antiwar protestors.

Afterward he flew up to New York, where, at the Royalton Hotel—located near Times Square, a block from *Scanlan's* East Coast office—he hunkered down in his dilapidated suite and began the process of transforming his notes into the article. He stayed in the city until Sunday: his deadline.

That week, Richard Nixon said, "When dissent turns to violence it invites tragedy." Spiro Agnew, the administration's attack dog for all matters concerning civil liberties, antiwar demonstrations, and press freedom, referred to the protestors as "exhibitionists who provoke more derision than fear" and suggested that they'd incited the tragedy, which he called "predictable and avoidable." A day later both the president and vice president were reprimanded by their own secretary of the interior in an astonishing open letter that concluded, "Youth in its protest must be heard." Hundreds of campuses were closed. In Iowa City, students broke into the Old Capitol building and set fires. In Madison, Wisconsin, homemade bombs were thrown into empty classrooms. The National Guard used tear gas at Southern Illinois and Kentucky and West Virginia. In all, four million students went on strike to protest the war. On Friday, at Broad and Wall Street—about six miles from Hunter Thompson's Manhattan suite—hundreds of construction workers, chanting "ALL THE WAY, USA!," attacked a crowd of antiwar demonstrators; afterward they marched to city hall where they forcibly raised the American flag, which had been lowered to half-staff in honor of the Kent State victims. On May 14, at Jackson State in Mississippi, guardsmen would open fire again, killing two more students.

Working in his suite, Thompson was initially able to construct set pieces from his collected notes. But by the end of the week—as New York City was hit by a startling heat wave, and as the country deteriorated into all-out conflict over the war—he retreated to the Royalton's bathtub, where, with a quart of scotch and his usual supply of Dexedrine, he resorted to finishing the article by hand. In the end the timing got so tight that he found himself inserting his original notes directly into the draft. On Sunday night he and managing editor Don Goddard were able to compile a chronological draft and then cut four thousand additional words—digressions on the deeply Nixon/Agnew-esque character of Louisville society and on his own experience growing up there—and then they sent their draft of the feature to Hinckle in San Francisco, who, after cutting a few more pages and inserting a series of organizational headers ("The View from Thompson's Head," "A Huge Outdoor Loony Bin," etc.) delivered it with Ralph Steadman's artwork to the printer—just hours before the deadline.

"The Kentucky Derby Is Decadent and Depraved" came out in June. For Hunter Thompson, the whole thing felt like a compromise, an unfinished draft—a failure. "I wish there'd been time to do it better," he wrote to Hinckle when he saw the galleys. "With another week I might have honed it down to a finer, meatier edge." To Steadman: "The article is useless, except for the flashes of style & tone it captures—but I suspect you & I are the only ones who can really appreciate it." To Bill Cardoso: "It's a shitty article, a classic of irresponsible journalism . . . Horrible way to write anything."

But as soon as the issue came out Thompson started getting phone calls and letters from friends and colleagues. Tom Wolfe said that it was the funniest thing he'd ever read. William Kennedy told him it was a formal breakthrough—part reportage, part memoir, part exaggeration/fiction. And Cardoso sent a note of encouragement: "Hunter, I don't know what the fuck you're doing, but you've changed everything. It's totally gonzo."

At the start of the piece, Thompson alluded to the new wave of unrest while he flipped through the *Courier Journal* at an airport newsstand, and in the final scene the first reports of the massacre at Kent State were coming over through the car radio, but all of the direct cultural analysis was cut out of the final draft.

Instead, the scenes themselves would serve to make his political point; by focusing on the experiences that he and Steadman endured over the course of the weekend (instead of the actual race) he managed to indict the perspectives of the people around him by taking on their behavior as his own, which allowed him to criticize them by criticizing *himself*—a much more effective line of attack. "My eyes had finally opened enough for me to look in the mirror across the room," he wrote in the last section, "and I was stunned at the shock of recognition . . . There he was, by god, a puffy, drink-ravaged, disease-ridden caricature . . . like an awful cartoon version . . . It was the face we'd been looking for—and it was, of course, my own."

By the final paragraph the transformation was complete: Thompson had turned himself into a cartoonish version of the cops who'd beaten and Maced him in Chicago:

The journalist rams the big car through traffic and into a spot in front of the terminal, then he reaches over to open the door on the passenger's side and shoves the Englishman out, snarling: "Bug off, you worthless faggot! You twisted pig-fucker! [Crazed laughter.] If I weren't sick I'd kick your ass all the way to Bowling Green—you scumsucking foreign geek. Mace is too good for you . . . We can do without your kind in Kentucky."

In the end, the article itself, composed in a New York bathtub as America descended into a horrific replay of the last decade's conflict, worked like a grotesque mirror on a country willing to beat and shoot and send off to war—to sacrifice—its own children: "a symbol of the whole doomed atavistic culture."

The original June 1970 issue of *Scanlan's* ended on a short author's note: "Hunter Thompson has gone back home to rest in Aspen, Colorado, where he edits the Aspen Wallposter and is threatening to become a candidate for sheriff of that community."

## All Their Foul Hopes and
## Greedy Fascist Dreams

That fall, for the first debate in the 1970 race for sheriff of Pitkin County, Hunter S. Thompson appeared at Snowmass's Opticon Theater wearing a multicolored L.L. Bean shooting jacket and dark Levi's jeans. He was smoking a Dunhill cigarette from his plastic Tar-Guard mouthpiece. Around his neck hung a silver Aztec medallion, a recent gift from Oscar Acosta (once again it was meant as a talisman). On his head he sported a floppy, white-brimmed tennis hat; earlier in the day, with the help of Billy Noonan, he'd shaved his scalp, a move that now allowed him the opportunity to describe the other person up onstage—the county's current sheriff, clean-cut Carrol Whitmire—as "my long-haired opponent."

It was Monday, October 12. Over three hundred people had turned out, a packed house. Things kicked off with the flip of a coin: each candidate would give a short presentation and then the proceedings would turn to the floor—to the audience members, who'd prepared written questions.

Whitmire won the toss. He chose to go second. Thompson, sitting next to him, leaned into the microphone. "The power of the office," he said, "could be used to good effect to help improve quality of life, to help slow development, fight pollution and check on consumer fraud." But to do so, he explained, it was imperative "to change county government for those of us who want to live here . . . to keep the place from being sold out from under us."

Which got at the central issue of his campaign: for Aspen to retain its identity it would need to embrace a *public* discourse—the politics of openness and transparency—as opposed to what he'd been referring to throughout his campaign as "private politics (the Old Politics): those of secrecy and deals made behind closed doors for the interests of the few."

Old Politics only benefited the valley's powerful developers: the "greedheads" and "land rapers" who'd sell out the town until there was nothing left to take. Across the country it was the same. The recent triumph of Old Politics in Chicago and Washington, DC, threatened the very premise of the American system: "on every side, from coast to coast, on the TV news and a thousand daily newspapers, we have blown it: that fantastic possibility that Abe Lincoln called 'The Last, Best Hope of Man.'"

New Politics, as Thompson had recently explained in his campaign newsletters, was premised on accountability: "The essence of democracy is that *the people are the power base* of their government." His own interpretation of this approach was called Freak Power, a concept he'd been exploring since the first issue of his wallposters:

> This is the real point: That we are not really freaks at all—not in the literal sense—but the twisted realities of the world we are trying to live in have somehow combined to make us feel like freaks.
>
> We argue, we protest, we petition—nothing changes. So now, with the rest of the nation erupting in a firestorm of bombings and political killings, a handful of "freaks" are running a final, perhaps atavistic experiment with the idea of forcing change by voting . . . and if that has to be called *Freak Power,* well . . . whatever's right.

That autumn afternoon at the Opticon, to conclude his opening statement, Hunter Thompson said, "I'm here to prove to the disenchanted—the freaks—that the political processes still work."

Sitting alongside, Carrol Whitmire glanced out at the enormous crowd, his eyes glistening with disbelief. He was thirty-eight years old, dressed in a dark suit and patterned tie. When he finally spoke it was in a drawl: "I know about writing citations," he explained during his opening statement, "about accidents in the middle of the night, accidents in the mountains." He swallowed loudly. "I want the job real bad."

The general format for both sheriff debates that October centered around a straightforward question-and-answer format. The race was actually a three-way affair, but the Republican candidate, Glenn Ricks, had skipped the first event. "Due to the fact that this meeting has apparently been turned into a three ring circus," he'd announced, "I cannot condone it with my appearance."

The general consensus in town was that Thompson would put on a show; that he was unserious; and that the whole thing was a publicity stunt. He'd suggested as much himself: "I'd really prefer not to win," he'd told the *Los Angeles Times* at the start of the month. "In the end, I may make my program so outrageous that I won't get any votes."

But once the debates kicked off it was clear that Hunter Thompson planned to run a serious, thoughtful, well-prepared campaign. Which shouldn't have come as all that much of a shock to people who knew him well. As Peggy Clifford would later remark about his candidacy: "He had never had any talent for remaining aloof."

In his response to one of the earliest questions—when challenged to enumerate on the duties that a position like sheriff should entail— he pulled out and read from a copy of the Colorado Revised Statutes. Moments later, Carrol Whitmire was asked if lawmen should carry a gun. "I have only pulled my gun one time in nine years," the incumbent replied, "but when I need a gun I want it there."

Immediately Thompson turned this statement around: if a law enforcement officer had only needed to draw his firearm once a decade, wasn't that proof in itself that the opposite was true? "I see a sheriff as a person who can help people as well as bring people to justice," he explained. "Not arming police would be a worthwhile experiment and worth trying. If it didn't work officers could be armed again."

All in all, he responded in detail to the questions posed to him over the course of the two debates, which were held that October on the twelfth and twenty-fourth:

MODERATOR: *Why are you running for sheriff?*

HUNTER S. THOMPSON: We either have a participating democracy or a police state . . . The only power we have is the vote. This is the last time perhaps where freaks may obtain control. Democracy is not working in the rest of the country . . . the war goes on, no progress on civil rights . . . but we can make it work here.

M: *What will you do about users of hard narcotics?*

HST: Junkies are bad people to deal with, they make all our lives harder . . . I don't like needle-injected drugs. I'm dead against them . . . Any heroine and speed dealers will be advised by this community that they must quit or get out of town.

M: *Do you think mere possession of marijuana (1st offense) should be a felony?*

HST: Absolutely not. The current laws were passed in 1935 during a time of mass hysteria and total ignorance about marijuana. The single law has made felons out of an entire generation of people and has widened the generation gap to a chasm . . . It's time that we either bridge that chasm with some kind of realistic law enforcement or else I don't think it's going to be bridged in this country . . . we're going to get a revolution.

M: *Where do you plan to put your major effort if elected?*

HST: I plan to expand the scope of the sheriff's office to encompass the prevention and elimination of the causes of crime as well as merely dealing with the effects of it after the fact. I intend to hire a competent undersheriff to handle the job of sheriff as it has been conventionally regarded. I have an identifiable communication with the kids that no ordinary law enforcement officer would have. As mentioned before, the younger generation regards the police as the enemy. I would use this line of communication to be a sociologist-type ombudsman.

M: *What is a "freak"?*

HST: The way things are going in this country today, it's a very honorable designation, and I'm proud of it. To be abnormal—to deviate from the style of government that I deplore in America today—is not only wise but necessary.

\*

Following the debates—in the wake of a new voter-registration push that appeared to net an additional seven hundred possible supporters for the Freak Power ticket—the residents of Aspen who stood to lose the most from a Hunter Thompson victory started to panic.

"If he was elected sheriff," Whitmire said to a British film crew in town to cover the election, "it would actually destroy Aspen."

Carrol Denver Whitmire had been born in 1931 in Stillwater, Oklahoma. Afterward, in the wake of economic and ecological catastrophe—the Great Depression, the Dust Bowl—his family moved to western Colorado. Before he could finish the ninth grade he dropped out of school; he never went back. Fifteen years later he showed up in Aspen, where he took a position in the sheriff's department and was promoted to deputy. Eventually he challenged and defeated the county's elderly incumbent, Lorraine Herwick.

"Real lawmen are in the business because they like it," he said during the debates, "not for the money." From the voice-over to his 1970 campaign ad: "The American sheriff's job was carved out of the rugged West. It was a desperately needed position of few words, much action, little praise, and little glory . . . It takes a man who knows his people and their laws and *wants* to be a sheriff of Pitkin county." For Carrol D. Whitmire—someone whose family had migrated west along with millions of others in search of reprieve—getting elected head constable was, by all accounts, a lifetime achievement.

He'd become sheriff in 1966, and his first term happened to coincide with a fresh influx of migration to the county seat—a bracing wave of countercultural young men and women from California that nothing in Whitmire's personal and professional experience had prepared him to handle. For his entire adult life he'd worked in and around the Continental Divide. He had eight children. He lived with his family in the basement of the Aspen courthouse. His wife was also named Carol. At local parades he would often be seen riding a horse. He once deputized John Wayne, a frequent guest at the Jerome. And in response to the cultural upheaval that since the Summer of Love had continued to spread throughout the Roaring Fork River Valley, Carrol Whitmire felt, in a word, besieged.

Back at the start of the summer, he'd claimed at a conference in Denver that he'd been receiving a series of alarming reports from the Colorado Bureau of Investigation: outside agitators were plotting to attack the valley in the run-up to the election. What's more, such provocateurs were already here, posing as locals to overtake the town's institutions and attack its leaders—a list of targets on which he himself had been included. Not that these reports ever appeared to have any basis in fact. Still, after everything he'd seen in the past four years, both nationally and at the local level, they must've made a certain amount of unpleasant sense. *Something* was happening, and for him the best way to explain it was with the same logic that national law enforcement entities like the FBI had been relying on for years: America was being infiltrated by its foreign adversaries—their ideas, matériel, and manpower—by ruthless, unceasing enemies whose ultimate goal was to burrow into the deepest ranks of preexisting leftist organizations to destroy the fabric of society itself.

Hunter Thompson had learned about Whitmire's growing paranoia from a friend in the state's Democratic caucus, and that June, he headlined his Wallposter no. 4 with the article, "Aspen, Summer of Hate, 1970 . . . Will the Sheriff Be Killed?" "The plot, according to Whitmire," Thompson wrote, "was for a full-scale invasion of the town. Several thousand drug crazed motorcycle thugs, led by the Hell's Angels would make a twin-pincer frontal assault . . . while, at the same moment, the town would be blasted and terrorized . . . by well-trained demo-teams of Black Panthers and Weathermen."

It was satirical, the same rhetorical device he'd employed in his essay on the Derby; he exaggerated the threat against the sheriff to punctuate the absurdity of the logic. Beneath the article a Tom Benton graphic read: TODAY'S PIG IS TOMORROW'S BACON. In the final paragraph Thompson concluded: "With his job on the line and his public image sagging, a crisis atmosphere might be just the gimmick he needs to get back in the limelight . . . keep in mind that 1970 is an election year."

The thing about satire, however, is that by using it effectively you're pretty much setting yourself up for a fight no matter what: the people against you who *get* it—who understand what you're calling them out on—also recognize how successful the tool can be when it comes to exposing the true nature of their intentions . . . which usually causes them to then raise the stakes. On the flipside, the remaining opponents—the simplest of your adversaries, those officials over whose heads the whole sardonic gesture is bound to fly—now tend to react, in turn, with an unabashed degree of horror and terror and ruthless self-defense; they can't help but perceive at face value the threats you'd simply meant as comic exaggerations.

In this sense, Carrol Whitmire, the region's predictable basement-dwelling lawman, was at best a tool—a dangerous one, to be sure—who from the start was being manipulated by the people who had the most to gain from the town's continued mass development.

There was Guido Meyer, the monomaniacal Swiss hotelier who hated hippies so much, he'd actually packed his children off to boarding school in Europe; it was only after Richard Nixon had finally won the presidency—restoring his faith in the viability of the country's future—that he allowed his son and daughter to return to America.

Also: Dr. J. Sterling Baxter, "a crude local version of Lyndon Johnson" who fellow Freak Power candidate Ned Vare was challenging for the county commissioner position. And recently elected mayor Eve Homeyer, who earlier that spring told the *Denver Post:*

"Aspen is going to become a place for a second vacation rather than a way of life."

To counter, Hunter Thompson had put together his own group of talented local citizens. His campaign manager was Michael Solheim, the owner of the Invisible Line, an interior decorating outfit that specialized in Victorian painting and wallpapering. Ed Bastian, a former University of Iowa basketball player—and staff member on the Nelson Rockefeller and George Romney 1968 presidential bids—served as the main event and strategy coordinator. In her column for the *Aspen Times* Peggy Clifford wrote just before the election: "Old-style Big Daddy politics have not worked in Pitkin County. I think it's time we try something else." And James Salter produced and narrated the main radio advertisement, which was set against the jazz flute overture of Herbie Mann's "The Battle Hymn of the Republic":

> Hunter Thompson is a moralist posing as an immoralist. Nixon is an immoralist disguised as a moralist. This is James Salter. There'll be thieves and auto wrecks in Aspen whoever gets elected. But Hunter represents something wholly alien to the other candidates for sheriff: ideas. And sympathy towards the young, generous, grass-oriented society which is making the only serious effort to face the technological nightmare we have created. The only thing against him is that he is a visionary. He wants too pure a world.

Thirteen days before the election, on a Wednesday afternoon in downtown Aspen, a man wearing a motorcycle jacket with what appeared to be the insignia of a winged death's-head on the back walked into the bar located beneath the Wheeler Opera House. He introduced himself as Jim Bromley. He was in his twenties, bearded, and muscular. "I'll take a double bourbon," he said. When it arrived he pulled out a switchblade; flicking open the knife, he slowly stirred his drink. "I'm a friend of Hunter Thompson. Anyone know where I can find him?"

A few hours later, Bromley roared up Woody Creek Road on his bike and peeled to a stop in front of Owl Farm. To Thompson he shouted that he'd been sent by Sonny Barger. He was in town to deliver a message. "Your fucking house will be blown up and you'll be fucking killed if you win the election." And then he turned around and sped off.

The first thing Thompson had noticed was Bromley's motorcycle. It was a Harley-Davidson, but no genuine outlaw biker would ever be caught dead on it—a bike that didn't bear any resemblance to the classic Angels "chopped hog" style. If this stranger had been for real his Harley would've been stripped down to its essentials. Which meant that Bromley was most likely an undercover agent or some other sort of provocateur. Thompson didn't consider dropping out of the race. Three days later, just after the second debate— in which Carrol Whitmire's most coherent statements all had to do with how badly he wanted the job—Jim Bromley showed up at Thompson's campaign headquarters, located in Parlor B of the Jerome Hotel. He claimed that he'd talked to Sonny again. Now things had changed: Bromley wanted to *help* the campaign in any way he could. He offered to make copies and send out mass mailers. He asked if he could join on as Thompson's bodyguard—at no cost to the candidate. And then, to a clearly uncomfortable audience that included Bastian and Solheim and also Oscar Zeta Acosta—in town on his way back from Denver, where he'd been representing the Chicano activist Rodolfo "Corky" Gonzales—Bromley suggested that the best thing for them to do was gather a posse together and kick the shit out of Sheriff Whitmire and anyone else stupid enough to get in the way of their Freak Power ticket. "We'll kill them," he said. "There will blood on the streets up to our ankles." At one point he even mentioned that he happened to be selling, at a decent price, guns and explosives. Thompson's campaign had already contacted the district attorney and filed a formal complaint, but so far they hadn't heard back.

That Sunday night, Acosta, who earlier in the summer had also run for sheriff—of Los Angeles County, coming in second—sat down with Bastian and Thompson at the Jerome bar for an hours-long strategy session. Afterward they were walking out of the hotel when a friend on the Aspen police force—Rick Crabtree, a former English major at Columbia—stopped them and said, "Hey, you guys should know—that guy that's been hanging around your office? Well, we found a car on Main Street parked in a place it shouldn't have been and we towed it in and opened up the trunk and found a trunkload of automatic weapons. We found out where the guy is staying and went to his motel and brought him in for questioning, at which point he showed us his identification as an ATF agent and says, 'You can't arrest me. I'm here on federal business.'" Crabtree had taken as evidence a pump-action 20-gauge sawed-off shotgun, but a deputy from the sheriff's department had summarily returned it to Bromley.

So on Monday afternoon, October 26—the election just over a week away—Thompson and Solheim scheduled a meeting in Joe Edwards's law office with the sheriff and his campaign manager. The assistant DA was there, too.

Hunter Thompson jumped right in; he told his opponent he knew what was going on. Bromley was an undercover federal agent who'd threatened to kill political candidates. What's more, he'd been brought out to Aspen by the town's current sheriff to interfere in the democratic process. By now Thompson had learned and reviewed every line and section and statute of Colorado voting law—which Whitmire had clearly just violated.

Suddenly Carrol Whitmire panicked. He admitted it; he'd hired Jim Bromley and brought him to Aspen to investigate recent "incidents" in town: from a hitchhiker and an ambulance driver he'd heard about a suspicious plot involving the town's dynamite supply, and he'd also been told by his informants in the Colorado Bureau of Investigation that federal fugitive Katherine Anne Power, a wanted member of the radical Weathermen faction of Students for a Democratic Society (SDS), was hiding in the area. He swore that he never gave the order for Thompson to be contacted *directly*. But he did admit that he'd known about Bromley's Saturday visit to the Jerome, which he'd discussed afterward with his campaign manager.

Thompson turned to the assistant district attorney. "This is felony conspiracy," he said. But the DA's office refused to get involved.

Later that day, APD officer Rick Crabtree received a phone call from the manager at the Applejack Inn: a maid had just found a terrifying-looking sawed-off shotgun in the room of one of their guests: a certain James Bromley, who'd been staying with them since Saturday. Crabtree drove down Main Street and from Bromley's empty room he confiscated for the second time in two days the illegal weapon. Thompson called the DA and told him that things had gone too far; certain members of his campaign were so fed up, they were rallying together at that very moment to storm the Applejack hotel and make a citizen's arrest.

A half hour later Bromley snuck onto the impound lot and without filing any paperwork retrieved his car. That night he drove back to Boulder—but not before he'd apparently found the time to raid the ski corporation's dynamite hold. In place of the stolen case of explosives he'd left a note:

This will only be used on Hunter Thompson if he is elected sheriff.

   —SDS

"Only a cop's brain could have churned up that mix of silly bullshit," Thompson would write afterward, "and although we never doubted that, we also understood that the same warped mentality might also be capable of running that kind of twisted act all the way out to its brutally illogical extreme."

On Wednesday night, with the election less than a week away, Thompson sent Sandy and Juan to stay at Michael Solheim's house, and with a half-dozen friends, he set up patrols on the grounds of Owl Farm, each of them armed to the teeth. He knew that people like J. Sterling Baxter had millions of dollars in future developments and investments riding on the outcome of the election, and that they were willing to do *anything* to protect and preserve, in Thompson's words, "all their foul hopes and greedy fascist dreams."

For Carrol Whitmire the stakes were just as high; if he lost the election he'd also lose his family's sole source of income *and* his place of residence; with his eight children and wife he'd be forced to move out of the county courthouse basement in which he'd lived for the last four years.

The next day the *Aspen Times* published a detailed account of the whole Bromley affair—"Towed Car Reveals Election Scandal," the article was titled—along with the sidebar "Case of Dynamite Stolen Recently From Ski Corp." The editorial board endorsed Thompson: "We can not condone the flagrant disregard for the democratic process that the presence of an informant-agent-provocateur in his political opponent's headquarters demonstrates."

The following evening Thompson opened his mail to find a polaroid photograph. It pictured James Bromley—a self-portrait. In it, Bromley was posing in front of an enormous Nazi flag. A poster in the background depicted a maniacally grinning skeleton. GOD IS DEAD, this poster declared. The skeleton was wearing Nazi headgear. In each hand it appeared to be holding a long-nosed revolver. Bromley, sitting just to the left of the flag, had on sunglasses and a Nazi officer's visor. A swastika pendant the size of a milk saucer hung from a chain around his neck. "TO HUNTER THOMPSON FROM JIM," he'd written on the back of the photo. "SEE YOU SOON."

\*

That autumn, *Rolling Stone*—a biweekly San Francisco music magazine published by then twenty-four-year-old Jann Wenner—featured

Hunter Thompson's work for the first time: "The Battle of Aspen," an account of the Joe Edwards mayoral campaign that also included passages of political speculation on the nature of small-town politics. "An underground candidate who really wanted to win," Thompson wrote, "could assume, from the start, a working nut of about 40 percent of the electorate—with his chances of victory riding almost entirely on the Backlash Potential."

His opponents took note. The weekend before the election, after failing in a variety of ways to head off the Freak Power ticket, the town's two major parties made a deal: the democrats would drop out of the county commissioner race, giving the edge to J. Sterling Baxter over Ned Vare, and Republican Glen Ricks would concede the sheriff's race, transferring his voters to Whitmire. A subsequent telephone / chain letter campaign managed to contact every single resident in town multiple times. One man reported receiving more than a dozen calls.

On election night—to the packed crowd at the Jerome Hotel, which included reporters for national newspapers and from magazines like *Life, Harper's,* and *Look,* as well as two documentary film crews—the results went from bad to worse. In the end Thompson lost to Whitmire 1,533 to 1,065. And Vare went down to Baxter by a margin of 197 votes.

For his concession speech, Hunter Thompson, an American flag draped over his shoulders and a blond wig cocked awkwardly on his scalp, announced: "Ladies and Gentlemen, this is my last press conference. You won't have Hunter Thompson to kick around anymore."

In truth, he was relieved. He was a writer—a political one, but still, an *artist* . . . not a rural county sheriff. In the wake of Chicago he'd fought back, and it gave him hope. "It might still be possible to alter the fascist drift of this nation," he wrote afterward, "without burning it down in the process."

In Aspen the changes he'd fought for were already beginning to take hold. The recent election had been a county-wide affair, but they'd won the city itself by a large margin. In the 1972 elections they'd finally take over the city and county governing councils with CCA representatives Ned Vare and Joe Edwards. And a few years after that, Carrol Whitmire, caught red-handed redirecting funds for personal benefit, would resign in disgrace.

That autumn, Thompson, reflecting on where he'd been and what he might do next, wrote to his aunt in Louisville: "The net result of this last incredible campaign seems to be that I'm now plunged heavily into national politics—but on some very odd level that doesn't seem to fit with anybody's idea of Left or Right or Center or anything else. And that's just about the way it should be, I think."

## CHAPTER FIVE

# SOME DREAMERS OF THE GOLDEN DREAM

## 1971

## The Pink Palace

On Friday, March 19, 1971, Hunter Thompson climbed into his rental car, a Ford Pinto, and drove west on Whittier Boulevard. He was headed to Oscar Acosta's place, which was located near the Ramona Gardens housing projects, about four miles away. For the past week he'd been staying at a boardinghouse in East Los Angeles to report on the Chicano movement for *Rolling Stone*.

It was early afternoon: across the four-lane street only a few thin bars of shade remained, the smog brightening the sky. He passed beneath the Long Beach Freeway. Suddenly on his left was Laguna Park, a grassy expanse of softball fields and picnic tables that, six months earlier—during a twenty-thousand-person march organized by the National Chicano Moratorium Committee to protest the Vietnam War—had been the site of a deadly police riot. Driving by it, he would've been hard-pressed to look in the direction of its chain-link backstops without picturing, if only for a moment, the same widespread violence sparking up again.

In the last year, Whittier Boulevard had been the scene of upheaval—violent conflagrations that descended as if from a ridge to engulf the surrounding neighborhood. The way things were going now, all it would take was another protest—followed by a rock or two—and the police response would materialize in a way Thompson knew all too well: the volleys of tear gas, great billows of it, and then a mass of people desperately fleeing the Los Angeles sheriff's department, its officers advancing like an ancient phalanx down the full breadth of the avenue. Cautiously. Meticulously. Side-by-side in white helmets and khaki shirts, the gas masks distorting their faces.

That was exactly how things had played out during the August 29, 1970, Chicano Moratorium demonstration in East LA: a Chicago-style police riot that had left three people dead and caused millions of dollars in damages.

The temperature was in the low sixties. The sun was a high bright pane in the smog. Thompson steered the Pinto in his usual fashion—with skill and nerve—accelerating into the spaces between his car and the next as block after block of Whittier Boulevard slid past.

He'd spent the past week alongside Acosta in the company of the Brown Berets, who'd made it a point to let Thompson know they didn't trust him. And why should they? The movement then was rife with suspicion and dissent. Anyone who wasn't from East Los Angeles was seen as an outsider. The night before, Thompson had been hanging back in the kitchen of Acosta's place near Ramona Gardens when, from the other room, he'd heard someone shout, "What the hell is this goddamn *gabacho* pig writer doing here? Are we fuckin' *crazy* to be letting him hear all this shit? Jesus, he's heard enough to put every one of us away for five years!"

*Longer than that,* was Thompson's first thought. In his presence, the Brown Berets had repeatedly talked about combating police brutality with organized violence of their own, and throughout the week they'd suggested that it would be in his best interest to stay away altogether. On his previous trips to East LA there'd been moments of tension and awkwardness, but nothing like this. Now there was no way around it; he was a stranger who didn't belong.

Thompson had been considering writing an article on the movement since 1968, but the catalyst to his current trip was the murder, during the August 29 Moratorium march, of the Mexican-American journalist Ruben Salazar—a brilliant, well-known columnist and television host who, at the time of his death, also happened to be Los Angeles law enforcement's most prominent critic.

Six months earlier, on that hot afternoon in August, Salazar had been covering the rally when the police, on the pretense of

responding to an alleged theft at a local corner store, declared the
crowd of twenty thousand in Laguna Park an unlawful gathering and moved in to clear it. They'd attacked with tear gas and
clubs, striking children and elderly family members and anyone
else who'd been sitting on the grass and listening to the notable
roster of speakers, which included Rodolfo "Corky" Gonzales, a
poet and former boxer who'd founded the Denver-based Crusade
for Justice.

Desperately the protestors had fled eastward, toward Whittier
Boulevard, and in an attempt to stay ahead of the violence, Ruben
Salazar and a colleague ducked into the Silver Dollar Lounge, a
yellow tavern with a red-curtained entrance located at 4045 Whittier. Together they were sitting at the bar hoping to wait things out
when, unbeknownst to them, a team of sheriff's deputies, acting on
what they'd later claim to be an anonymous tip, surrounded the Silver Dollar and sealed off the premises—and then proceeded to fire
high-powered canisters of tear gas through the curtained entrance.
One struck Salazar in the temple, killing him instantly.

Thompson's current article was centered on the question everyone in East LA had been asking: Was Salazar *assassinated?* The answer,
he knew, could represent an irreversible escalation. "When the cops
declare open season on journalists," he'd write, "when they feel free
to declare any scene of 'unlawful protest' a free fire zone, that will be
a very ugly day—and not just for journalists."

But was that actually the case? If Salazar had been the target
of a high-level conspiracy to silence dissent, where was the evidence? "It was difficult, even for me, to believe that the cops had
killed him deliberately," he'd explain. "I knew they were capable
of it, but I was not quite ready to believe they had actually done
it . . . because once I believed that, I also had to accept the idea
that they are prepared to kill anybody who seemed to be annoying
them. Even me."

All week, he'd been trying to get to the bottom of it. He'd
stayed up until dawn drinking with Acosta and the movement's

leaders. He'd interviewed sheriff's deputies and spokesmen. He'd forced himself to read through the 2,025-page coroner's inquest into Salazar's death. He'd walked up and down Whittier Boulevard as the conversations around him switched immediately to Spanish. No one on either side trusted him. What Thompson needed was perspective: the context to arrange Ruben Salazar's death within the broader narrative of the Chicano movement and rampant police brutality.

By Friday he was seriously considering giving up on the piece, which would've been a disastrous development. In the last few months he'd found himself in terrible credit card debt after Warren Hinkle's magazine, *Scanlan's,* had gone bankrupt before it could pay his fees and reimburse him for his expenses from multiple assignments—five thousand dollars' worth—and as a result, his American Express and Diners Club accounts had been frozen. He was worried his Carte Blanche card would be next. He'd just received a "Final Notice Before Seizure" letter from the IRS stating that he owed three thousand dollars in back taxes. He still hadn't sent Jim Silberman a coherent draft of the "Death of the American Dream" book—it would need a much a more drastic restructuring than he'd initially realized—and he couldn't count on Random House for immediate cash. He *had* to get this article done for *Rolling Stone.* Jann Wenner liked his work, and already there'd been talk about a possible staff writer gig, which would mean a steady paycheck.

But he was running out of time . . . in more ways than one. After a week of hardly any sleep—of all-night drinking bouts with Acosta and the Brown Berets and frightening daytime interactions with police officials—his Dexedrine usage, which in the face of such constant danger had increased to previously uncharted levels, was beginning to double back on him, a rebound effect of panic and fear that was amplified with each new pill he swallowed. At this point the ups-and-downs were *physical:* when the drug wore off he could feel its passage, receding like a tide from the blue depths of his veins.

Which would perhaps help to explain why he was willing to go out on a limb, now, and show up unannounced at Acosta's place: a last-ditch attempt to secure the information on which his article depended.

He turned right on Soto Street. Headed north. At a small bungalow he pulled over and parked. Then he walked up to Acosta's porch and knocked loudly on the door. A shadow across the tiny eyewindow. Voices beyond. In the next moment he stepped into a midsized living room filled with a dozen young members of the East Los Angeles Brown Berets. During the recent riots a fifteen-year-old Brown Beret had been shot and killed by law enforcement. Others were currently on trial for arson, accused (falsely) of starting fires on the upper floors of the Biltmore Hotel during a 1969 speech by Governor Ronald Reagan. Together these young militants had christened Acosta's house *El Pueblo* and declared it an independent territory from the city and its police. In their possession they had guns and knives, as well as a substantial amount of gasoline, soap, and oil—the necessary ingredients for a large cache of homemade firebombs. Thompson stepped around them; he needed to see his friend.

Oscar Acosta was standing near the kitchen, and with everyone else he watched this *gabacho* reporter walk toward him alone and unannounced.

It had been six months since Thompson had last visited Southern California, a period in which the political atmosphere of East Los Angeles had changed dramatically. Now, whenever Acosta went anywhere, he was accompanied without fail by his three bodyguards. At all times he kept at his side a leather attaché case packed with blank legal pads, an enormous amount of marijuana, a .357 Magnum Colt Python handgun, and a box of bullets. Lately he'd been saying things like, "How long do they expect us to keep coming down to their goddamn courthouse and begging for justice?" And: "This legal bullshit ain't makin' it." And: "The day of blood will come." The FBI had opened multiple files on him. LA law enforcement kept this house and his activities under near-constant surveillance.

In court that week, Acosta was representing Corky Gonzales. During the August 29 police riot, Gonzales had fled with family and friends alongside thousands of others once the cops descended, was pursued by a helicopter, pulled over, and arrested on trumped-up charges of robbery and weapons possession. Acosta had also set into motion his legal assault on the grand jury selection system; representing the Brown Berets accused of arson—the Biltmore Six, as they'd become known—he'd subpoenaed and, under oath, interrogated every single Los Angeles County Superior Court judge, 109 in all, as to the logic by which they chose their candidates for the grand juries. The blowback had been enormous; by both friends and enemies alike he'd been told, repeatedly, that he'd crossed the line. Did he really expect to get away with humiliating the most powerful figures in Los Angeles?

That afternoon, Thompson didn't plan on staying. Instead, he asked Acosta to join him for a moment on the porch. At *El Pueblo* he and Acosta were never alone—surrounded, as always, by teenage militants—and over the past week they hadn't had a single moment to speak privately.

Finally the young militants were out of earshot. Acosta was still accompanied by his three bodyguards, but Thompson knew these men well enough to understand that their uneasiness at his presence had less to do with revolutionary ideology than common sense: a story in *Rolling Stone* might put added pressure on the LA sheriff's department and highlight the issue of Chicano rights to a national audience, but other activists would see Acosta's cooperation as grandstanding—selling out—and besides, the movement had already tried the journalism route, and the only thing that came out of it, in their opinion, was a tear gas canister to Salazar's head. In other words: the article was all risk and no reward, and they were worried for Acosta's safety.

The front yard was dusty and dry. In its lack of shade everything seemed to shine at once—a blinding, saturated light. Acosta was within a few feet of the rented Pinto. It was the moment Thompson had driven to the house to engineer. "I can't stand it anymore!" he finally said. "I can't even talk to you . . . " They needed to speak together privately, he suggested, *now*. He asked his friend to get in the car with him.

All week Acosta had been on edge. He hadn't had a quiet moment in ages. He was tired of looking over his shoulder. In the last few months he'd become convinced that the police were out to silence him in the same way they silenced Salazar, who on the whole was far less oppositional. How many of the young militants were in reality paid informants for the sheriff's department? How long would it be until deputies appeared in the middle of the night and fired tear gas canisters at point-blank range through the windows and walls of *El Pueblo*'s crowded living room? "The cops never lose," he'd recently told Thompson. "I think maybe the real shit is about to come down." It could happen at any time.

And perhaps this was why, in the next instant, without further discussion, Acosta followed Thompson to the street and climbed into the Pinto's front seat. There was nothing that the bodyguards could do; he'd made the decision himself.

Together they drove across the viaduct and merged onto the Hollywood Freeway, heading for hills beyond. Thompson already had a destination in mind.

∗

In 1971, the Polo Lounge at the Beverly Hills Hotel was the ideal place to enjoy a few quiet afternoon drinks: throughout its terraced patio—beneath its great sunstruck canopy—there was enough shade and obscurity to last a lifetime.

At a price, of course. This was the same venue that Mia Farrow had supposedly been banned from for having the gall to arrive in a pair of slacks. Zsa Zsa Gabor signed her first movie contract here.

Joan Didion, a frequent lunchtime guest, lived just up the road. And the patio had recently become the preferred meeting place on western swings for high-ranking officials in the Nixon administration's Committee to Re-Elect the President. With its bougainvillea and trellises and arid pools of shade, the Polo Lounge was West Coast elegance at its best, a secluded refuge for the rich and famous that was far less likely to subject its patrons to the degree of public scrutiny they'd come to expect elsewhere.

On the patio they were shown a table near the palm trees. They ordered gin cocktails—Singapore Slings—with mescal on the side. They ordered coffee. They ordered beer and extra ice. *Rolling Stone* would cover the expenses, Thompson insisted, once the article was finished.

After a while a grand piano struck up. The wind caught in the high green sails of the palms. Along the flowered terraces of the patio section the sense of privacy was immense. No one at the Polo Lounge wanted to be overhead—it's why people came here, to do business—and while it would've been abundantly clear to anyone looking on that Hunter Thompson and Oscar Acosta were not what you'd expect in the usual Friday afternoon crowd at the Beverly Hills Hotel, they'd managed to take advantage of the seclusion that the Hollywood scene, itself eccentric, demanded.

At last Thompson could talk privately with Acosta about Salazar's death: "I'm starting to get a bit wiggy from all this pressure," he admitted. He explained how difficult things had been, this past week in East LA, caught between the Brown Berets and the police. It was like standing onstage all the time. Like finding yourself in the middle of a prison riot. It'd been impossible to tell who was lying and who was telling the truth. From every direction the weasels were closing in.

Acosta drank and listened. No doubt he'd already thought up rebuttals to his friend's complaints—to these metaphors that betrayed the blind spots of Thompson's position. After all, a stage actor gets to go home once the performance is done. In a prison

riot it's the interlopers—the guards—who find their freedom revoked. How could someone who spends all his time in an alpine
valley possibly understand what it was like to live under the threats
of LA law enforcement . . . let alone imagine, in the face of such
odds, the courage it takes to fight back? Besides, what precisely did
he mean by "weasels"?

But Acosta could also see Thompson's general point: the article
was something they'd settled on together, out of mutual trust and
respect, to expose the corruption and brutality of the Los Angeles
police and sheriff's departments to a larger audience, and by refusing to talk about the Salazar case honestly with Thompson this
past week, he'd gone back on his word—the one currency that had
sustained their relationship from the beginning.

"I agree," Acosta finally replied. He explained that the real
problem was *El Pueblo*—his leadership status there—which as of
late had made it impossible for them to be seen as friends. A year
earlier—running for LA County sheriff in the summer of 1970—
Oscar Acosta's political battles in East Los Angeles had still included
a recognizable approach. Of course he never expected to win the
election, and from the start the whole thing had been a publicity
stunt, a way for him to get his voice heard. But he'd been willing to
work within the existing system to achieve this publicity. And in the
end the campaign had brought him an enormous amount of attention. Celebrities like Anthony Quinn came out to support him. He
did television and radio interviews and was featured prominently in
the *Los Angeles Times*. More than a hundred thousand residents had
cast their votes for him.

But in the process he'd also drawn the undivided attention of
one of postwar America's most formidable institutions: Law Angeles
law enforcement, at the height of its twentieth-century glory. Now
Acosta was convinced they were out to get him. And in the last six
months, after the riots and murders and a series of courtroom set-
backs, he'd become so desperate and disillusioned that he'd resorted
to more extreme measures.

By all accounts he'd recently begun to participate in a clandestine bombing campaign against civic and financial targets. He used homemade dynamite with timers. He threw Molotov cocktails from his car. With the most radical Brown Berets he'd formed a new group—the Chicano Liberation Front, operating out of *El Pueblo*—and after each attack one of the teenagers would call in from a pay phone and claim responsibility. Most of these bombings took place late at night—the targets were unoccupied federal buildings, schools, and banks—but during one, in a bathroom at the Hall of Justice on January 29, an innocent bystander had been killed.

This turn had come about only recently, in the months since he'd last seen Thompson in Aspen. It was something they hadn't yet had a chance to discuss—the worry at all times about the possibility of surveillance. But at that moment in their lives few people knew Acosta better than Thompson, and to anyone who was looking closely, the activities at *El Pueblo* over the past week would've implied more than enough. Which was perhaps the main reason the *Rolling Stone* article was falling apart. Thompson could sense the extremes to which his friend had gone, but because they hadn't been able to talk about it privately, he couldn't yet understand *why;* he was desperate to hear the story behind Acosta's turn to violence.

Across Los Angeles the sun was descending west. Now the patio section was draped entirely in shade. You'd be far more likely to find J. Edgar Hoover here than one of his countless informants, but for all its privacy and elegance, the Polo Lounge still fell within the reach of law enforcement's surveillance capabilities, and both Thompson and Acosta understood that it was no place to openly discuss the specifics of a bombing campaign.

"How would you feel about getting out of town for the weekend?" Thompson suddenly asked.

Acosta was intrigued. He told Thompson as much. What were their options?

"How about an all-expenses-paid trip to Las Vegas?"

Earlier that week, Thompson had received an unexpected offer from Tom Vanderschmidt, a senior editor at *Sports Illustrated,* to write a few hundred words of copy to go along with a photo essay on the Mint 400 motorcycle race, scheduled to be run in two days—on Sunday, March 21—in Las Vegas. A cushy assignment: Vanderschmidt and Thompson had worked together at the *National Observer,* where they'd become friends. But when the offer was made he'd hesitated; this was before the Salazar article started falling apart, and he'd been worried about overcommitting himself.

*Sports Illustrated* was willing to pay $300 up front. They'd also cover the hotel and travel expenses. It really was the perfect solution: in addition to their politics, Thompson and Acosta had always had in common an almost preternatural instinct for a night on the town, and in a setting like Las Vegas, the sky would be the limit.

Acosta didn't have to be back in court until Monday. Besides, the hardest part—getting away from *El Pueblo*—was already done. He agreed to the trip.

Thompson motioned for a waiter and ordered a pink telephone, one of the Polo Lounge's famous perks. He called New York to accept the gig.

But across the continent, Vanderschmidt had already left the *Sports Illustrated* offices. The message would be forwarded; who knew when he'd return the call. In the meantime there was nothing to do now but wait. It was 3:00 p.m., then 5:30. More mescal and gin. Fresh ice. The empty glasses were cleared. The leaves scattered what was left of the sun. Thompson understood that, at some point, after so many days of drinking and amphetamine and no sleep, a crash was coming. It always did. This time it'd be especially bad; already, in his desire to uncover whether or not the Los Angeles sheriff's department had begun executing journalists, he'd pushed himself farther than he'd gone before.

By 6:00 p.m. the dinner crowd was starting to arrive. The sky was sleek and empty and the new patrons were dressed more formally, as if to match the piano in the lobby. Couples lingered near the bar. The patio was a cool blue shadow against the evening. From the glass doors a waiter appeared; he was carrying the iconic pink telephone. "This must be the call you've been waiting for," he said to them.

Thompson reached for it. Held it to his ear. The conversation that followed was brief: on the other end it was all formalities. Afterward he turned to Acosta. Vanderschmidt had come through. "Let's get the hell out of town," he said.

The next few hours were spent in preparation. The most essential order of business was to procure a new rental car. It was imperative that they find a convertible. The whole reason Thompson had taken the assignment was so they could finally talk freely about Salazar's murder—and its effect on the Chicano movement, on *Acosta*—without anyone else listening in, and if you're looking for real privacy, there's nothing quite like the boom of a high-speed interstate with the top down.

At a rental agency on the Sunset Strip they exchanged the Pinto for a large red Chevrolet convertible. Thompson paid with his credit card; he assured Acosta that he'd be reimbursed by the very deep pockets of *SI*'s parent company, Time Inc. In their possession they had the marijuana from the attaché case and a decent supply of stimulants—Dexedrine and Benzedrine, respectively. That was it. The plan was to leave first thing in the morning.

Later that night, Thompson spotted a hitchhiker on the nighttime road. He slowed up. "What the hell?" he said to Acosta.

It was a young man, tall and graceless. He appeared to have been stranded for a while. His smile was enormous.

"Hop in," Thompson said.

"Damn," the kid exclaimed. "I never rode in a convertible before."

The comment caught Hunter Thompson off guard. He was struck by the naked optimism. And suddenly it was as if he'd been the one stranded along the dark California roadside, waiting endlessly as car after car streamed by—a young man who would've given anything for a chance to squeeze into the back seat of the remarkable convertible he now found himself piloting. "You're in the right place," he said.

## Like a Waterless Canal

From LA to Las Vegas it's just under three hundred miles. Thompson and Acosta hit the road after breakfast. They took the Hollywood Freeway, passing Santa Anita and San Bernardino before bearing north at the Cajon Pass, where the San Gabriel Mountains fell away and Interstate 15, completed in 1968, cut like a waterless canal through the repeating basins and ranges of the Mojave Desert.

In a convertible at good speed the wind becomes your canopy—a roaring, translucent barrier. For the first time since the sheriff's campaign in Aspen they could say what was on their minds—about the Chicano movement, about Ruben Salazar, and about the tactics Acosta had recently resorted to in his battle with the police. It was an extension of the same conversation they'd been having since the very first night they'd met, in the bar of the Jerome Hotel on a cool Aspen summer evening, back before assassinations and police riots and the brutal reality of a Nixon-Agnew administration had come to pass: How do you overcome institutional injustice? From their letters around that time:

ACOSTA: You remind me of the hippie and the militant. The former wants to be left alone and the latter, to destroy, so he can be left alone.

THOMPSON: I want to have a place where I can live like a human being when I get tired of all the screaming bullshit that comes with trying to change a nation of vicious assholes.

ACOSTA: Mankind is doomed. Period.

THOMPSON: True—and all the more reason for trying to save at least a small chunk, instead of insisting on the destruction of the whole thing because they won't give you credit for saving it all.

ACOSTA: The struggle is just as much yours as it is mine. But still you sit on your ass and look forward to football on TV.

THOMPSON: You've got yourself so wired up with that Jesus-complex that you cause more problems than you cure.

ACOSTA: In fact, I am superior to Christ.

THOMPSON: One of these days you'll realize that the fuckers you're up against don't care if you live or die; they'd just as soon deport you, or—failing that—kill you. So the only way to deal with them is to scare them; find a weak link and focus on that, instead of fighting the whole chain.

ACOSTA: You dumb motherfucker . . . Do you think my vision is so limited?

In 1968, when Acosta first joined the movement, the goal had been to expose discrimination through nonviolent protest: the boycotts against the Los Angeles City School System for its contin-ued neglect of Mexican-American communities. But the sheriff's department's response was so violently disproportionate, everyone involved was caught by surprise. The Brown Berets formed in the wake of these boycotts. As a group they emphasized community defense: now the goal was to protect the population from police assaults and also to publicize, through a weekly periodical like *La Causa,* the rigged and biased nature of the system in which they lived. They conceptualized their struggle through the emerging concept of "Aztlan," a term that identifies the territory in the American Southwest that had once been part of Mexico before it was seized, a century earlier, during the US-Mexican War. Aztlan had become a rallying point: a fresh way to articulate, as a source of pride and strength, the identity of millions of marginalized Amer-ican citizens.

Not that law enforcement saw it this way. In 1968 the Los An-geles Police Department created a secret intelligence group—titled, amazingly enough, the Special Operations for Conspiracy—that worked to infiltrate the movement. Its undercover agents were given multiple directives. They gathered information. They also sought to disrupt the Brown Berets from within, undermining their leadership and promoting suspicion. They even went so far as to incite violence. On multiple occasions and without the consent of the actual militants, these infiltrators attacked the police, providing law enforcement the rationale they needed to use deadly force. At the same time, J. Edgar Hoover had initiated his own separate investigation, demanding "continuous and aggressive investigative attention" of the Chicano activists; to him they were all communist subversives, and in a signed memo he'd personally deemed them "a threat to the national security of the United States."

Oscar Acosta would never learn the full extent of this surveillance and infiltration, but at the time he could sense it everywhere. Which was why the front seat of a very fast convertible had become the one place he could sit back and relax.

On the road between Los Angeles and Las Vegas, he finally explained all this to Thompson, as well as the reasoning behind his recent turn toward violence: law enforcement officials were clearly willing to do far worse to *him*—and were winning, as a result. The movement was being torn apart by infighting and constant harassment. Everything he'd struggled for would be lost. And the knockout punch, it appeared now, was Salazar's murder.

It's difficult to overstate just how prominent a journalist Ruben Salazar had become. When he started at the *Los Angeles Times* he was the only Mexican-American in a newsroom of more than a hundred people. In 1965 he was promoted to international correspondent, reporting from Vietnam and later Mexico City. He interviewed Dwight Eisenhower. He was a friend of Bobby Kennedy's. In 1968, when he was recalled stateside and assigned the domestic beat in Los Angeles, what he saw shocked him. He began documenting police brutality, writing about the routine deaths of minority citizens at the hands of an institution that flat-out refused to examine its tactics or question its policies or, for that matter, acknowledge that it was even capable of making a mistake. In 1970, as his popularity continued to grow, the local Spanish-language television station KMEX made him a generous offer to become its news director. That summer he was repeatedly warned by senior law enforcement officials to tone down his coverage. He responded with a fresh exposé on police intimidation. He was probably the only person with the authority and visibility to expose the biggest players in the city's power structure for the state-sponsored violence they'd spent years facilitating. And then he was shot in the head with a tear gas canister, at 5:30 p.m. in a windowless bar on Whittier Boulevard, by a young blond sheriff's deputy named Tom Wilson.

For Hunter Thompson, this was the precise point where the story had started to fall apart. Wilson had testified that, just before the shooting, he'd panicked and mistakenly loaded the wrong type of tear gas canister into his bazooka—a deadly ten-inch projectile meant for piercing barricades that never should've been used. He'd arrived at the riot late, along with other reinforcements from the Montrose Station. He claimed that he had no idea who Ruben Salazar was, or even what he looked like.

Not that Thompson thought for a moment that anyone in the sheriff's department was telling the truth. From the beginning the police had given contradictory explanations of Salazar's death. First they blamed errant gunfire, then street snipers, and finally communist infiltrators, even though photographic evidence and eyewitness testimony clearly proved otherwise: that Wilson had been the one to fire the shot.

But now that Thompson and Acosta had the chance to go through all these details together in depth, it really was beginning to seem that, despite the discrepancies, the evidence alone didn't suggest *premeditation,* at least in the standard sense of a single assassin stalking and eliminating a high-profile target. Instead, something more complex appeared to be going on.

At last Hunter Thompson was getting down to the heart of the matter: if Ruben Salazar hadn't been directly assassinated, how did you explain his death within the context of law enforcement's frightening escalations?

Both the FBI and the Los Angeles police saw the Brown Berets as an existential threat to American society. In a conflict like this, the state held an enormous material advantage, but with a significant limitation: they couldn't deploy their resources against American citizens in the fashion they'd like—militarily—without some sort of lawful pretext. Which is exactly what the sheriff's department had fabricated on that afternoon in August when Ruben Salazar was killed: the police deemed the nonviolent antiwar rally unlawful, donned riot gear to clear out the protestors, and any resistance was met with deadly escalation. If not an antiwar rally, something else would've come up to justify the offensive; the undercover agents would've seen to it. Really, what happened on August 29 would be best described as a *premeditated* police riot: thousands of heavily armed cops flooded East Los Angeles in the culmination of extensive and longstanding preparation by both federal and local law enforcement to unleash the most formidable weapon in their arsenal—massed, lethal force—in a legally justifiable manner. As such, officers like Tom Wilson were technically incapable of a targeted assassination because the violence they'd been tasked with enacting was inherently indiscriminate, which was also what made the tactic so effective—it communicated the irrefutable truth that to be Chicano in East LA in 1971 was to risk your life. Ruben Salazar died because he was sitting in a bar on Whittier Boulevard. It could have been the person next to him. That was the point. In the end the police had been willing to blow off *someone's* head to show to everyone in the barrio just how easily it could be done.

This was the realization that Hunter Thompson arrived at over the course of their long drive through the desert: there *was* a conspiracy, just not of the sort that included a singular, preplanned assassination. Instead, the whole thing was more generalized and brutal. The LAPD's Special Operations for Conspiracy had been plotting for years to incite the sort of unrest that allowed the cops on the ground to use deadly force—an astonishingly effective tactic, in retrospect.

Thompson had kept himself awake for days on end to try and understand it: the murder, the movement, and the specific context of East Los Angeles and its terrifying sheriff's department. At last he had what he needed to finish the article. It had been a matter of recognition: now the puzzle pieces fit together, but in a surprising way. Of course there was no way he could've gotten to this point without Acosta's help. At the same time, he also recognized just how insanely dangerous things had gotten in the life of the friend sitting next to him.

Suddenly Acosta's bombing campaign no longer fit into their political conversation—whether to work within the system or tear it down. Acts of violence committed in the name of the Chicano movement were exactly what law enforcement had been conspiring to instigate. Which meant that the bombs Acosta had been making would never be mechanisms for change. Instead, they'd become an expression of hopelessness against absolute authority. With each new explosion Acosta was hastening the awful police-state trap that Salazar's death had confirmed to be out there all along, lying in wait.

They'd been talking for hours. Interstate 15 passed through Barstow and Baker before jogging north to Nevada, where the mountains around Las Vegas hung like smoke in the fine blue distance. The city was ahead. Only a few miles left to go.

It was Saturday, March 20, early in the afternoon. The motorcycle race wasn't scheduled to start until the next day. Together they took the turnoff for the Mint Hotel, located just north of the strip. *Sports Illustrated* had reserved their room. They still needed to tie up a few loose ends—arrange the press credentials; check in with the photographer; and scope out the venue itself, just beyond the city limits, near the border of Floyd Lamb State Park—and soon it was dusk, the sun sinking behind the mountains. The temperature dropped. From the east: a cool desert wind.

Thompson and Acosta didn't have specific plans. For a while they cruised the Strip in their fireapple-red convertible. They stopped at the Desert Inn for a drink, where Debbie Reynolds and Harry James were performing to a packed house. At the Circus Circus they caught up with the musician Bruce Innes, a friend of Thompson's from Aspen whose band, the Original Caste, had recently notched a top 40 hit with their song "One Tin Soldier." Afterward they headed back to the Mint Hotel's first-floor bar—charging everything to their room. It wasn't entirely clear if *Sports Illustrated* had agreed to cover *all* the expenses, but for the first time on the trip Thompson's money problems weren't on his mind; he was happy to just sit and relax without having to glance every few moments over his shoulder. For Acosta it was the same. Finally there was nothing to keep track of. And while in the long run not all that much had really changed, at least there was the feeling, with each new cocktail they ordered, of betting house money. Together they stayed up the entire night. It was like old times.

The next morning, Thompson drove out to Floyd Lamb State Park at sunrise—Acosta remained back at the hotel—and in the lead-up to the motorcycle race, which was scheduled to begin at 9:00 a.m., he found himself in the makeshift pressroom at the Mint Gun Club, huddling alongside the many other journalists covering the event. He drank and gambled. Took notes. With *Life* magazine's West Coast bureau chief he talked about the sorry financial state of the journalism market. Eventually they all walked over to the dirt track to watch the first bikers speed off into the desert. This was how it would go for the rest of the day—the race was staggered, with a new group heading out every few minutes—and soon an enormous cloud of dust descended on everything, reducing visibility to zero. There was nothing more to see. He spent a few hours jotting down lengthy, digressive descriptions for his *SI* assignment. Then he headed back to the hotel.

Oscar Acosta needed to return to Los Angeles that night; he had to be in court Monday morning for the Biltmore Six trial. Thompson gave him a ride to the airport. Afterward, as Acosta's plane ascended west and disappeared, he glanced at the passenger seat. To his horror, he realized that Acosta had left behind the attaché case he never went anywhere without.

Thompson reached over. Picked it up. Felt the weight of what it contained. And immediately understood the nature of the items that had been left behind in his care.

Back in the privacy of his suite he inventoried its contents: a Colt .357 Magnum. Its box of bullets. And an enormous bag of marijuana. In the next moment, seeing these items as if for the very first time, he was hit by paranoia and agitation that pulsed through him in relentless succession, like waves. Racing thoughts. Terrible sweats. As if he were sinking like a stone—an honest-to-god panic attack. The crash had finally come.

There was the biological aspect: days without sleep, his last-ditch burst to get a handle on the Salazar case. He'd reached the point of physical collapse, a deficit in basic human well-being that no drug could mask. After nearly a decade of taking Dexedrine daily—not to mention a lifetime's worth of drinking—he'd still never found himself up against a breakdown like *this*. There was also the environmental factor. In his campaign for sheriff he'd re-searched the legal statutes on marijuana in states throughout the West, and none offered stiffer penalties than Nevada. If he were to be pulled over in a red convertible with the attaché case in his lap—and without a brilliant criminal lawyer in the passenger seat to protect him—he could easily end up in prison for the next ten years. To say nothing of the handgun.

He didn't have much cash on him. His credit card could be canceled at any moment, especially in light of the bill he'd run up the past few days. It still wasn't entirely clear *who* was paying for the room at the Mint—if the reservation had been handled by *SI* or if he was supposed to pick up the tab himself and then get re-imbursed . . . which could very well spell the end of his credit line.

Here he was, alone and broke on a cool Sunday evening in a Las Vegas hotel room: whatever agency and ambition had carried him to this moment would now be useless to help him escape it.

Of course this was the price he'd agreed to pay all along. If he'd learned anything in his years taking Dexedrine it was that the drug, at its core, amounts to a zero-sum game: whenever something is given, something is also lost. The breakdown that hit him at that moment wasn't just expected; it represented the currency upon which he'd been trading his passage to the moment he found himself in now.

What could he do? In his present state of mind only one thing made sense: *Flee.* But his checkout time wasn't until noon the next day. If he left he worried he'd draw too much attention to himself. He needed to find a way to pass the hours until dawn, to lessen the waves of emotion he could no longer control.

He called room service. Ordered milk, coffee, rum, and two club sandwiches. Plugged in his tape machine. Put on the only album in his possession, *Get Yer Ya-Ya's Out!,* a live recording of the Rolling Stones. Took more Dexedrine. And he forced himself to write exactly what he was feeling at that moment: the essence of his panic, the overwhelming crush.

He was listening to "Jumpin' Jack Flash," "Carol," "Stray Cat Blues," "Love in Vain," "Midnight Rambler," and a seven-minute version of "Sympathy for the Devil." A terrifying, exhilarating experience. He filled his notebook with descriptions of the panic that had hit him, of the motorcycle race through the desert, and of the city itself. In doing so he found a way to circle the thing felt—a movement on the page that mirrored his own vortical logic—which in turn had provided just enough of a buffer to keep things together.

Now it was 5:00 a.m. Time to take the escalator to the lobby. Find the valet. Tip him five dollars. And wait for the enormous red convertible to be brought around to the entrance. He'd already packed up most of his luggage in the trunk. All that was left was his tape player and notebook—and Oscar Acosta's attaché case. With these items he walked across the casino floor, where, at a spot near the poker tables, he forced himself to read the early morning

edition of the *Las Vegas Sun. You are not guilty,* he told himself—
repeating these four words like a mantra.

Around him, the casino was vibrant. Gamblers crowded the
early-morning poker and craps tables. At that time the Mint
Hotel—and Las Vegas in general—attracted an older clientele. They
were dressed cheaply, gaudily, men and their wives who'd come of
age during the Depression, who tomorrow would be flying back
to their suburban homes in Dallas and Denver and Milwaukee and
St. Louis. And here they were gambling until sunrise—while an
equally nonviolent vice like marijuana, of which the attaché case
was packed full, was punishable by a lengthy prison sentence.

Suddenly Hunter Thompson felt as if he'd seen these gamblers
before. *All* of them. Why? It was their faces, he realized—in each
and every one of them he couldn't help but recognize the same
meaty mask that had been haunting him for years: In San Francisco, in 1964, on the Cow Palace floor during the terrifying climax to Goldwater's speech. In New Hampshire, at the Holiday Inn,
when he couldn't even make it through the lobby without getting
stopped and harassed. In Chicago, in Louisville, in Los Angeles, too.
Almost a decade had passed and still this face—its blueprint—hadn't
changed. It was the face of Mayor Daley. Lyndon Johnson. Spiro
Agnew. Flesh and stubble and fetters and jowls and big greed-blind
eyes. *Richard Milhous Nixon.*

In the next moment Thompson was overcome by a degree of
outrage that rivaled his panic. The hypocrisy! Las Vegas, with its
anodyne, state-sponsored vice, was exactly the sort of place that
kept so many people from stopping to question why things have
had to be the way they were—and *how* the structure of American
society restricted everyone's upward mobility. At least these white
early-morning gamblers could tell themselves they might still get
rich if they played their cards right—that the opportunity for personal and financial improvement continued to exist—and now
with a better shortcut than ever: *Fly out to the desert and you, too,
can be a millionaire!* Which was their reward for refusing to examine

the system in which they were complicit; as long as they didn't interfere directly they were more than welcome to book a trip to Nevada and spend their savings on the incredibly slim shot of leaping, in a single bound, all the way to the very top. In the meantime the Constitution could be shredded and habeas corpus suspended and millions could be beaten and jailed and killed but in this crowd nothing would really change: they'd be back at these tables the next weekend, and the weekend after that. For them this *was* America. Its future. Las Vegas was what the entire country would look like after our democratic ideals had long since been cast aside.

Thompson noticed all of this in passing. In the end the whole thing constituted a singular image—a grotesque tableau of middle-aged men hunkered down in the stale blue smoke of a Vegas casino at sunrise. Still, he immediately recognized the value of what he'd seen. Despite his lack of sleep and preoccupation with the Salazar story—not to mention his ongoing breakdown—Hunter Thompson understood that he'd just been granted a glimpse of the very thing he'd been looking for everywhere: a distilled, dramatic example of the death of the American Dream.

It was Monday morning, March 22, 1971. At last his enormous convertible swooped down from the parking ramp and pulled to a stop at the Mint Hotel's front curb. Thompson handed over his valet tag, packed his remaining luggage, and then he drove off without a hassle.

How many fireapple-red Chevrolet convertibles would you expect to see, on a spring weekday in the desert, crossing Interstate 15 between Las Vegas and Los Angeles? Thompson was positive that his was the only one. Now he'd entered the bargaining phase of his breakdown: he would give *anything* for just a few more hours of safety. After all, hadn't he worked hard? Didn't he deserve, at the very least, the opportunity to expose the police-state mentality and rampant institutional injustice that had led to Ruben Salazar's murder?

Was that really too much to ask? Suddenly he saw himself as the victim of his own personal tragedy: he'd finally gotten what he'd been searching for—just as the hammer was about to come down.

The only thing that helped was the same remedy as before: filling his notebook with descriptions of the trip itself. But at the wheel of a convertible in the middle of the desert this was no easy task. What could he do? Between Stateline and Barstow, Thompson kept pulling over—at rest stops, gas stations, and strange honky-tonk restaurants—so he could dramatize, in vivid bursts, the world around him. He described both real and hypothetical scenes. What mattered was the inspiration: he was channeling the unfiltered light of the moment in a way that captured his subjective experience in its purest form—a style of instant reportage he'd begun to call Gonzo Journalism.

In this context, his concept of "truth" is perhaps best understood in terms of composition: in his notebook he could narrate an imagined encounter with a California Highway Patrolman or he could describe at-length his panic attack, but as long as these passages were written *immediately,* while he was on the assignment, then one was as "true" as the other since they both represent his unique experience in as honest a manner as possible. The real issue, for him, was authenticity: a trip like this couldn't be faked because included in his recounting of it was the price he'd paid, personally, to pull the whole thing off.

Soon he was passing through Barstow. For the first time in days the sky was overcast. He approached San Bernardino. Descended the mountains. And at last he was speeding along the Hollywood Freeway, surrounded by thousands of other motorists. He'd reached the anonymity only a very large city can offer.

This time Thompson wouldn't be staying at the boardinghouse on Whittier Boulevard. Instead, he drove to Pasadena. With his last reserves he checked into a two-story motel just across from the Santa Anita Racetrack, where, for the next five days, he'd sleep late and write until sunrise, allowing himself the chance to recover from the breakdown he'd just endured.

At this time of year the motel was packed to capacity with a vast entourage of horse people and their associates: owners, trainers, gamblers, jockeys, and what appeared to be very tall women. The 1971 spring racing season was in full swing. For Thompson, this setting amounted to an unexpected gift, a chance to feel lost in a crowd of people stranger than himself. In his possession he had whiskey, Dexedrine, a large black Selectric typewriter, the marijuana from Acosta's attaché case, and of course the revolver. For the next five days, in a room paid for by the magazine, he worked without distractions.

The resulting article, "Strange Rumblings in Aztlan," would appear in *Rolling Stone* no. 81 the following month. From the start Thompson didn't pull any punches. He compared law enforcement's approach to the military in My Lai: if everyone in the community is considered an enemy, the use of *indiscriminate* force becomes inevitable. He examined the Salazar case from multiple angles. In the end he arrived at the conclusion he and Acosta had worked out together during their car ride across the desert:

> The malignant reality of Ruben Salazar's death is that he was murdered by angry cops for no reason at all ... It is a local variation on the standard Mitchell-Agnew theme: Don't fuck around, boy—and if you want to hang around with people who do, don't be surprised when the bill comes due—whistling in through the curtains of some darkened barroom on a sunny afternoon when the cops decide to make an example of somebody.

Thompson concluded "Strange Rumblings" with a description of a dynamite attack on the downstairs restroom of City Hall—part of a bombing campaign perpetrated on behalf of the Chicano Liberation Front. And even though he in no way revealed the person behind this violence, his ending, in retrospect, felt a lot like *doom*, its intimation, as if, by lamenting one last time on the way things had turned out, he might somehow convince his old friend to avoid the direction in which he appeared to be headed next.

## Vegas, Part II

Hunter Thompson and Jann Wenner had met for the first time the year before, in July 1970, at *Rolling Stone*'s San Francisco headquarters. Despite differences in age and background—Thompson was nearly a decade older than the well-off New York–born editor—they'd both been living in the Bay Area in the 1960s, where Wenner, before dropping out of Berkeley, had reported on Mario Savio and the free-speech movement. And in the magazine business they'd worked with many of the same people, including Ralph Gleason, the iconic *San Francisco Chronicle* music critic who'd cofounded *Rolling Stone*. Thompson had come out to pitch his article about local Aspen politics, and during their meeting he laid it on heavily, smoking and shouting and gesticulating as he finished a six-pack of Coors without bothering to detach the cans from their plastic rings—a purposeful show, meant to keep the young editor intrigued and off-balance.

It worked. Wenner was excited by the Freak Power concept, especially within the context of *Rolling Stone* and its target demographic. He also recognized his luck; if *Scanlan's* hadn't gone belly-up—leaving its authors holding all the bills—Thompson would still be writing for Warren Hinckle. Immediately Wenner signed on to publish the Aspen article and future ones, too, including the investigation into Ruben Salazar's murder. He also suggested that the two of them collaborate together on a national level. "Your story in R.S. should be part of the larger effort to get everyone to register in 1972," he said.

He was talking about a recent proposal to lower the voting age to eighteen (*Rolling Stone*'s ideal audience) that would soon be better known as the Twenty-Sixth Amendment to the Constitution. This historic work of legislation, as it happened, would be approved by the House of Representatives and forwarded to the states for ratification on Tuesday, March 23, 1971—the same afternoon that Hunter Thompson had finally settled into his motel at Santa Anita after escaping across the desert.

The Salazar article, it turned out, wasn't the only thing Thompson had been working on over the course of his secluded stay in Pasadena. Each morning, as the sun came up—as the thin-walled rooms resonated and shook with the presence of so many different people preparing to make their way to the racetrack—he spent an hour or so typing up his recent notes: the dozens of handwritten pages that he'd composed, in and around Las Vegas, to shape the emotion that'd been closing in on him.

It was a *story*, he started to realize, one that was being related in the form of a hallucinatory road narrative. But the theme, it soon became clear, was the same: the limits of individual social mobility in the face of widespread injustice. For Thompson, the concept of the American Dream was always at its heart a matter of agency: if you could just pull yourself up by your bootstraps and work harder than everyone else, you'd succeed. The only engine you needed to move forward across a truly level playing field was effort . . . a situation that existed in this specific society because of the freedoms and ideals that were initially enshrined in its political system.

In this sense, the American Dream was indistinguishable from the American Ideal: both were premised on our capacity for improvement, and the death of one signaled the concomitant destruction of the other, a loss of all political and personal flexibility.

At the end of his week in Pasadena, Thompson showed the beginnings of this story to David Felton—the editor *Rolling Stone* had assigned him for the Salazar piece—who told him to see it through. "You're really on to something," he said. "Keep it up."

*The Vegas Book,* he was calling it now. That April he sent the first pages to Jann Wenner and Jim Silberman, both of whom responded with encouragement. But as April wore on, he felt his momentum waning, and he was looking for a way to re-create the rush that had set in motion the initial pages when, by chance, the perfect opportunity presented itself: in his mail he discovered an invitation to attend The National District Attorneys Association's Third National Institute on Narcotics and Dangerous Drugs (it'd been sent his way, no doubt, on account of his campaign the year before to become sheriff of Aspen), which was scheduled to take place from Monday April 26 to Thursday April 29 at the Dunes Hotel. *Rolling Stone* would let him cover it—and put him up at the Flamingo. Oscar Zeta Acosta agreed join him again. And so, just thirty-five days after his initial trip to Nevada, he took a Sunday flight back to Las Vegas, immersing himself, again, in a desert city so unapologetically false, it's not all that much of a stretch to imagine what it might look like thousands of years from now, miraculously unchanged, still pumping out its meritorious version of America to a population that no longer exists.

This time around, knowing in advance that he'd be there for *The Vegas Book,* he brought with him a portable, state-of-the-art recording system, which he would use to collect more than a hundred minutes of dialogue and interactions and reflections from that long ago weekend in April.

∗

"It's Monday afternoon," Hunter Thompson said into the microphone. "We have a white convertible." In the background Oscar Acosta could be heard playing a flute: the distinctive opening to "Taps."

That morning they'd attended the drug conference's first session. "Having to walk that fucking lobby . . . ," Acosta said. "People mistake me for a bellboy and want me to take their baggage for them. I get tired of that shit."

He and Hunter Thompson were standing at the window to their room at the Flamingo—room 1224, building 9, a $23-a-night suite—and gazing down at the hotel's kidney-shaped pool, where their fellow conference-goers were lounging.

"Look at that bald-headed fat son of a bitch by the tree," Acosta said. "He looks like you."

"Me?" Thompson exclaimed. "I don't look like that. He looks like a waterhead. Hydrocephalic. He looks dangerous."

A woman was jogging around a small grove of palms. Olive trees ringed the pool.

"I saw some of the biggest fucking DAs of my life this morning," Acosta said. "God there were some huge Texas-looking bastards . . . I already feel weird without any weapons, except this little goddamn knife." He was talking about his pocket knife, a Gerber Mini-Magnum. On his flute he started playing "When Johnny Comes Marching Home," an old Civil War ballad.

"I must have a haircut," Thompson said. "I must get my shoes shined."

"I don't feel good without a gun anymore," Acosta said. "I really don't."

In their possession on this trip they had marijuana, a bottle of Chivas Regal, a single red capsule of Seconal—"for when things get really unbearable," Acosta said—and a dwindling supply of amphetamine: twelve Benzedrine pills and ten Dexedrines. Once again they hadn't brought any psychedelic substances like LSD or mescaline.

The night before, they ended up at Caesars Palace, where, at three in the morning, they'd run into the wandering casino photographer and posed together for a picture. In it, they're sitting at a small circular table. Thompson is wearing Levi's, a striped shirt, and his bird-shooting jacket, to which he's attached a large sheriff's badge. At the brim of his tennis cap he's sporting another pin, thumbnail-sized and square: a shiny metallic American flag. He's got on lightly tinted aviators. His right foot is propped on a chair, revealing, in part, the treads of a Converse shoe. His left hand grips his chin, the band of his wedding ring catching the flash: for the camera he's mugging it up. And so is Acosta: dressed exquisitely in a suit coat and patterned tie and rich wool slacks, he's also got his thumb to his chin . . . except that, unlike Thompson, he's wearing a single, black-felt glove. His posture is perfect. His eyes are knowing and intent. Neither man is smiling. Instead their lips are pursed in the style of a nineteenth-century daguerreotype—as if, in an effort to be seen clearly, they've spent the last five minutes in perfect repose, allowing the light around them to filter naturally.

On his flute that Monday afternoon, Acosta started playing the first notes to "Oh! How I Hate to Get Up in the Morning." The convention's evening session was about to start, but he wanted to skip it. He hated the pall of silence and judgment that descended on the room when they'd walked in, the crowd of one thousand cops watching their every move. He and Thompson had arrived at the conference dressed for the part—that morning he wore his expensive courtroom suit—but it was clear by now that they'd never fit in. How could they? The opening session had unnerved Acosta so badly he'd walked out of it, drawing the room's attention. "That's two thousand eyes," he told Thompson. "Two thousand ears listening to our footsteps. One thousand noses. Five thousand fingers reaching out towards our necks . . . "

"We've already missed half the workshops," he replied. "We better zap over there."

Together they headed down to the Dunes. For Acosta it was even worse than before; the mostly Middle-American police officers—men from Alabama and Texas and Georgia and Oklahoma— all looked like cheap knockoffs of Bull Connor and George Wallace. What's more, he was sure that someone from East LA was going to see him here, evidence at last of what his rivals in the movement believed to be his true identity: an opportunist looking to infiltrate and betray his comrades.

Afterward they walked over to Caesars Palace and found a seat near the bar. Thompson wanted to purchase the photograph they'd posed for the night before. But when the server appeared—a middle-aged woman wired uncomfortably into a tight toga, the casino's theme outfit—Oscar Acosta asked for someone named "Dusty" instead.

"I don't know her," their server replied. "Do you want drinks or what?"

"Yes," Thompson said quickly. "We'll have—"

"Wait a fucking minute!" Acosta screamed at the woman. "What do you mean you don't *know* her?"

The server darted off. She was talking to the captain of security. Clearly they were getting ready to walk over. Thompson pulled his tennis cap low. "We need to get up and go," he said to his friend. "Flee!"

A horrible scene—they hustled away, barely making it outside before the casino goons could stop them. Acosta was still livid— about the waitress, about the conference, about life in general.

Back at the Flamingo, Thompson tried to contact a friend at the *Free Press*. He was hoping to score some mescaline, a way to cut Acosta's amphetamine/alcohol stupor, which, in a town suddenly filled with thousands of white Southern-looking cops, didn't bode well for the rest of their week. But they couldn't get in touch with anyone.

The next day—Tuesday April 27—Thompson and Acosta skipped the morning session of the conference and drove around in the white Cadillac. "It's now 11:30 a.m.," Acosta said into the microphone. "Moby Dick is pulling away from Building Nine. We are going out again in search of the American Dream. We've yet to find it. We don't think it's at the District Attorney's convention. Nothing's happening there. They're all a bunch of lily-colored liverworts. Dodging all the significant issues of the day. They're spending millions and billions of dollars on rehabilitating persons that they'd obviously like to kill."

Acosta told Thompson that it was time to take matters into their own hands. "I think we should seriously get to it and *look* for the American Dream. We should just start interviewing people, like, 'Where is the American Dream and what is it?' You know, sidewalk interviews . . . "

Thompson wasn't so sure. They started to argue.

ACOSTA: I'm getting tired of giving you advice you're not taking. I'm working without a fee, you know.

THOMPSON: The trouble is obvious.

ACOSTA: Yeah, you're lazy.

THOMPSON: No! Last time it came out accidentally. I was actually making an attempt to cover the Mint 400.

ACOSTA, PAUSING: The story that you did in between is what's affected you. You did *Salazar,* and now you're trying to do a continuation of the Mint.

THOMPSON: No, we're just trying to act the story. That's why.

ACOSTA: Yeah. But I'm not being paid very well for it.

THOMPSON: What do you want, all the rest of my money?

ACOSTA: All the rest of your money . . . How much money you got?

THOMPSON, LAUGHING: A hundred dollars.

ACOSTA, LAUGHING, TOO: You must have a really low opinion of me.

*

They drove out of the city. They passed a water pumping station. They arrived at a subdivision called Via Bonita. "Yes, yes," Acosta said. "They certainly like to use our language. Gives it all a romantic flavor."

Across Boulder Highway they spotted a place called Terry's Taco Stand USA and pulled over for coffee. At the drive-through Acosta said to the waitress, "We're looking for the American Dream, and we were told it was somewhere in this area."

She took his comment literally. She asked her boss if he knew where they could find the place. After an extended discussion, she gave them directions—"It's called the Psychiatrist's Club now," she said—to a gas station near the Tropicana.

They headed that way, asking other people they met the same question. Most didn't know what they were talking about, or thought they were looking for some sort of brothel—"The Dream Ranch, out in the valley?"—or simply humored them by rephrasing the question back in their direction. At a music store, as Thompson was trying to bargain over the price of a clarinet, the attendant said he knew the place they were looking for, the American Dream: it burned down three years ago. He gave them the location. They drove over to see for themselves. All that was left was a base of charred concrete and weeds.

"It struck me what's going on here," Acosta said. "Anybody that is in search of the American Dream needs a lawyer and a doctor and a bodyguard because there's no other way to look for it without that sort of counseling."

"And a credit card," Thompson said.

Afterward they ended up at a bar across the street from the blackened lot. The Fog Cutter. A tiki lounge. "Sort of Polynesian," Oscar Acosta said. He was beginning to slur his words. With thirty dollars he worked out a deal with the management for a variety of goods: coconuts, grapefruit, wooden bowls, and a hammer. "That hammer . . . ," he said. "That'll outlast everything. That hammer will be here, somewhere, on this earth . . . "

They made it back to the hotel for dinner, and afterward they headed down to the evening session, a screening of the movie *Know Your Dope Fiend*. By now Acosta had changed out of his suit and tie. Instead, he was wearing a tight yellow fishnet shirt, his hairy chest spilling from its many gaps. At his hip, sheathed in a leather belt, he was carrying his pocket knife, the Gerber Mini-Magnum. "You see," he told Thompson, "it's not concealed. The shirt makes it legal. It shows through the net."

When they walked into the conference room it was dark. The movie was already showing. Acosta grabbed a chair and dragged it past the projector, all the way to the front. With his back to the screen, he stared balefully at the crowd of cops, who—watching the movie—had no choice but to watch him, too: a very large Chicano man in a lurid see-through top burning his eyes into them all, a knife strapped to his belly.

Thompson backed slowly out of the room. A few minutes later Acosta exited, too; now he was deeply agitated—wild with paranoia. *Those racist pigs!* He was sure they were coming—that the whole room was about to empty out after him. Thompson tried to calm him down. They got in the Cadillac, drove away from the Dunes, and cruised down the strip. Suddenly Acosta started vomiting everywhere, in his seat, on the dashboard, and over the side of the car; it was his stomach, his ulcer, flaring terribly after so much scotch.

They headed back to the suite. But Acosta couldn't calm down. In the eyes of all those cops he'd seen the same thing he'd been up against these past three years in Los Angeles: pure, unrelenting hatred; they wanted him *dead*. And they had the power to make it happen—that was the most fucked up part—they could murder him like they did Salazar and get away with it.

He grabbed the hammer they'd bought at the Polynesian bar. He started smashing the coconuts. He pounded the table itself. Then he got up and shattered the lamps by the bed and the mirrors on the wall and in the bathroom. He was breaking everything. When there was nothing left he took out his pocket knife. Grabbed a grapefruit. And proceeded to slash it into smaller and smaller portions, until all that remained, afterward, was the pulp.

Thompson watched. He was waiting for his friend to calm down so he could offer him some Seconal. Which was what happened—eventually Acosta relented. He told Thompson this was it; he was leaving on the next flight. This whole fucking town was full of cops, *Jesus Christ!*

At dawn the next morning they headed to the airport. It should've been a short drive. But they were nearly at the California line when they realized they'd missed the turn. Thompson threw the Cadillac into a screeching U-turn; he plummeted across the central gulley of dirt and weeds—the interstate's median—and gunned the enormous car up the other bank, emerging on the roadway again with a sickening flop. Now he was speeding back toward the terminal. At the Western Airlines counter he pulled to a stop. Suddenly they were saying goodbye. "Don't take any guff from these swine," Thompson said. Acosta waved. It was not clear when they'd have a chance to see each other again.

Thompson drove back to the Dunes, where the morning session was about to start. There was a panel on the international supply chains for illegal drugs, but the Nixon administration official leading the discussion kept going on and on about organized crime syndicates and shipping lines originating in France—in Marseille—without ever once acknowledging what everyone knew to be the real source: Vietnam and Laos.

Thompson had seen enough. He was done with the cops and attorneys and their unendurable conference. He got in the convertible and started driving. "Half-Crazy on Booze + Speed," he scrawled in his notebook. In three days he'd slept at most a few hours.

He headed toward Lake Mead, where he hoped to find a quiet place to do some work. But at an intersection near the water he passed in front of a cop car. He panicked. He pitched the half-full beer he had in his lap and turned down a random access road, which eventually dead-ended at a desolate, forsaken rise of earth. The cop didn't follow. "What the hell is this?" he said into the tape recorder, trying to read the signs. *"Blasting signals? All clear?"* Suddenly he understood: he'd pulled onto a test range, part of a munitions factory he saw now on a nearby hill. "Turn the radio off!" he shouted to himself. "If it's part of a shot I'll hear a series of blasts . . ."

The sky was cloudless and blue, the first clear day of the trip. Thompson spent the rest of the afternoon driving in loops through the hills and ranges that marked the terrain east of Las Vegas. At the Colorado River he crossed into Arizona. He saw the Hoover

Dam. He ascended a steep mesa. A sign read: WATCH FOR MOUNTAIN SHEEP. Another advertised an indoor reptile exhibit—KING COBRAS! Near the town of Henderson he was almost run off the road by a tanker truck.

Later that night, back at the Circus Circus, Bruce Innes was scheduled to play his usual set, and before he went on he and Thompson grabbed a drink by the main stage. They talked about the flight from Las Vegas to Denver—how, even in the face of the drunkest passengers, the stewardesses always seemed to remain preternaturally calm and accommodating. "I bet you could take an ape on that plane and they still wouldn't say anything," Thompson offered. "Can you imagine? 'This is my son, if you could be kind enough to avoid calling any extra attention to his infirmities . . . he's very sensitive.' They wouldn't say a thing!"

Overhead, the Flying Wallendas were performing their famous trapeze act—the Circus Circus was actually an enormous four-story-high tented structure with nets and posts and tightropes set up above the gambling floor—and after a while the topic of their conversation turned to its owner, Jay Sarno, a vain, eccentric, unscrupulous real-estate developer known for attacking anyone who got in the way of what he did best: taking his customers' money by convincing them they really are winners . . . or at least could be, as long as they kept coming back. Thompson had been trying to arrange an interview, but Sarno hated reporters; for him the free press was the very worst thing about America. Not that Sarno seemed to care about the type of music he was paying Innes and his band to play. They could choose whatever songs they wanted, so long as the lyrics were loud and the tempo was upbeat and people were spending money at the bar.

That night, Thompson stuck around to catch the first part of the set. He was watching the action on the floor—distracted by the flurry of acrobatics above—when the band broke into "Chicago," the Crosby, Stills, Nash & Young hit that begins, "This is a song for Mayor Daley." At that moment it was as if Bruce Innes, from a stage at the very center of Las Vegas's all-consuming blare—its endless, carnival heart—was singing to Thompson alone. *We can change the world / Rearrange the world / Is dying / To get better.*

"The Circus-Circus is what the whole hep world would be doing on Saturday night if the Nazis had won the war," Thompson wrote afterward. "This is the Sixth Reich." By now he'd seen enough. "After five days in Vegas you feel like you've been here for five years. Some people say they like it—but then some people like Nixon, too. He would have made a perfect Mayor for this town."

## This Doomstruck Era

That April, Oscar Acosta's most high-profile client, Corky Gonzales, was convicted on a trumped-up misdemeanor weapons charge stemming from the August 29 police riot and sentenced to over a month behind bars. Two days later, the legal challenge to the impartiality of the Los Angeles County grand jury system—a case Acosta had spent a year meticulously building—was thrown out by Daniel Alarcon, one of only four Mexican-American jurists on the superior court's 134-judge bench. The Biltmore Six trial went forward, with Alarcon upbraiding Acosta for failing to carry himself "in a consistent and lawyerlike manner." Over the course of the proceedings this judge would also call him "rude, insolent, and contemptuous"; describe his behavior as "improper and disruptive"; and at one point he'd send Acosta to jail for seven days on charges of contempt. That spring it was revealed that an original defendant in the case, Fernando Sumaya, was in reality a police officer working as a provocateur for the Special Operations for Conspiracy division.

In May, a week after the second trip to Vegas, Acosta heard a loud knock at the door to *El Pueblo.* Six of the movement's leaders demanded to see him. They were carrying guns. "You said too much," they told him. They were talking about the information he'd given Hunter Thompson for "Strange Rumblings in Aztlan," which they saw as a betrayal of their cause to an outsider, a journalist whom Acosta had gone so far as to personally vouch for. "It's time for you to go." They threatened to kill him if he didn't leave East Los Angeles.

He spent part of the summer in the Bay Area working on his writing, and with Thompson's help, he finally found a publisher: the newly formed Straight Arrow Press, a division of *Rolling Stone*. Alan Rinzler would be his editor. He was given a $2,500 advance. *Autobiography of a Brown Buffalo*, he titled the book. When he returned to Los Angeles for the Biltmore trial, the uproar over "Strange Rumblings" appeared to be dying down.

On August 28, Acosta was driving back from the courtroom to his house near Ramona Gardens when two unmarked LAPD sedans surged from the freeway exit and jammed his car off the road. Undercover officers rushed out with their shotguns drawn; they threw him and his bodyguards facedown on the pavement. One of the cops held up a crumpled cigarette case filled with Benzedrine tablets. It was Acosta's, the police would later claim; they'd seen him toss it away. Most likely these *were* his pills—he'd been taking amphetamine regularly since law school, but unlike Thompson he didn't have a prescription and purchased his supply illegally instead—but that afternoon the drugs had been in the possession of his bodyguard, as to avoid a situation like the one he was experiencing now.

It didn't matter. The DA charged him with felony possession. The papers reported his arrest as a "high-speed drug bust." Bail was set at $1,250. The leaders in the Chicano movement, already incensed over his literary activities—by Thompson's article and also by his recent book contract—abandoned him entirely. He was dropped from the Biltmore case. He was evicted from *El Pueblo*. His car was repossessed. He and Socorro were getting divorced. He had to move back in with his parents in Modesto. Eventually his case would go to a jury trial, and even though he'd be acquitted on all counts, his career in Los Angeles as a lawyer—and Chicano activist—was finished.

*

Hunter Thompson spent the summer of 1971 working intensely on the Vegas Book, which had morphed into a fictionalized account of his real experiences—one that streamlined the Mint 400 and drug-convention trips into a single, surreal weeklong narrative.

With his family he situated himself at Owl Farm, setting aside his usual freelance travel assignments, and kept to a schedule: each night, from dusk until dawn, he wrote nonstop in the basement den of their mountain home, a large room with redwood paneling and a plush carpet. He and Sandy fell into a familiar rhythm. For months their relationship was stable; things weren't getting worse.

For once, the project he was working on—its voice and energy—didn't feel like a chore. "It was fun to write," he'd explain afterward. "I've always considered writing the most hateful kind of work. I suspect it's a bit like fucking, which is only fun for amateurs. Old whores don't do much giggling. Nothing is fun when you have to do it—over & over, again & again—or else you'll be evicted, and that gets old."

In the Vegas Book he'd found a new way to write about a subject he'd been pursuing from the start: whether or not it's actually possible to change the nature of the world in which you live. "San Francisco in the middle sixties was a very special time and place to be a part of," he'd write that summer. "Every now and then the energy of a whole generation comes to a head in a long fine flash, for reasons that nobody really understands at the time—and which never explain, in retrospect, what actually happened."

But for him the fatal flaw in the previous decade's mass-protest and cultural movements had been clear from the start. "There was a fantastic universal sense that whatever we were doing was *right*, that we were winning . . . our energy would simply prevail."

The problem with consciousness expansion as a political concept, Thompson wrote, was that it dismissed "the grim meat-hook realities lying in wait," and, in doing so, exposed the countercultural activists to opponents who, in places like Chicago, treated the conflict like what it was: a matter of life and death. In the end the war continued. Richard Nixon became president. And the movement fractured into "a generation of permanent cripples, failed seekers, who never understood the essential old-mystic fallacy of the Acid Culture: the desperate assumption that some-body—or at least some *force*—is tending that Light at the end of the tunnel."

To Thompson, 1971 Las Vegas embodied the victors' nihilism. If the only limits on American society are greed and power, you'll inevitably arrive at exactly this sort of desert city: a place where the very few take everything they can from the people who keep com-ing back—all the while providing endlessly diabolical entertain-ment as to numb and distract from the repeated pain of loss. And it would only get worse, Thompson concluded, "in this doomstruck era of Nixon."

Jann Wenner had loved the energy of the Vegas Book from the start; after seeing only a few pages he'd offered to publish it in *Rolling Stone*. The plan was to put the whole thing out in two parts, in the sort of issue-sized format that magazines like the *New Yorker* had employed to spotlight unique, necessary work.

Thompson was also looking to bring in his editor Jim Silber-man. At first he hoped to use this new manuscript as a way to fulfill his longstanding "Death of the American Dream" project—a guiding force to the Vegas narrative from the start—but Silberman, after reading a selection, decided that it should be its own book, independent of the hundreds of other pages Thompson had com-posed over the last four years.

Thompson was elated. Random House authorized a $12,500 advance—for a manuscript that, unlike all the others, was pretty much finished. In September he turned in a draft to *Rolling Stone*. The edits were light. Suddenly it was done: that fall, parts one and two of *Fear and Loathing in Las Vegas: A Savage Journey into the Heart of the American Dream* appeared in the magazine.

At the end of the summer Jann Wenner and Hunter Thompson sought to plan out what to focus on next. There'd been talk of an assignment to Vietnam, but instead, Wenner proposed what he'd come to realize would be the biggest story of the upcoming year: the 1972 presidential election.

It wouldn't be a *journalistic* assignment, at least not in the classic sense: that year, Wenner had become close with Max Palevsky, a forty-seven-year-old tech investor who'd sold his computer company to Xerox for nearly a billion dollars. Palevsky had helped shore up *Rolling Stone*'s finances, becoming a part owner, and as an ardent supporter of the Democratic Party, he was looking to finance the upcoming national campaign of George McGovern, the progressive senator from South Dakota who'd gathered together many former members of the Bobby Kennedy team to make a run at the nomination. The plan was for Hunter Thompson to be granted insider access to the entire McGovern operation. *Rolling Stone*, with its youthful demographic, could help carry the candidate's message to the millions of new voters from eighteen to twenty who were now eligible thanks to the Twenty-Sixth Amendment.

What's more, under this specific framework Thompson would retain his independence. Unlike the other writers who usually followed the national election—who'd spent their careers working their way up to the top of their profession and who, as a result, tended to play it safe, avoiding the stories that might jeopardize their access to the candidates or open their publishers to libel suits—he could call it as he saw it. In his cutting literary style that played best with younger readers, he'd be free to savage the hypocrisy and double-talk of the Democratic challengers, two of whom—Hubert Humphrey and Ed Muskie—he still blamed for the catastrophic 1968 Democratic National Convention.

All things considered, McGovern really was the only viable candidate capable of sustaining Thompson's ruthlessly satirical approach. As opposed to nearly everyone else in the ambitious, dissembling field of challengers, the congressman from South Dakota couldn't be unmasked: he was, as Bobby Kennedy had once said, "the most decent man in the Senate." Really it was the perfect fit:

there was no one better to articulate George McGovern's appeal to the jaded youth vote than Hunter Thompson.

To pull all this off, Thompson would need to travel with the pack of beat reporters throughout the primaries and general election, an assignment famous for its brutal, nonstop schedule. He would be away from Sandy and Juan for many weeks at a time. His general approach would be three-part: characterize McGovern's strengths to the new subset of voters, expose the unforgiveable weaknesses of the competition, and—should things work out—take aim at the target he'd been after for nearly a decade, a first-term president looking to win the last election of his life, Richard Milhous Nixon. Really it wasn't all that dissimilar to his previous Freak Power approach—an attempt to bring into the fold a significant number of marginalized, disillusioned outsiders—except that this time the effort would be on a national scale.

*Rolling Stone* made Thompson a salaried writer—$17,000 a year, an enormous amount—and Wenner paid to move Sandy and Juan to Washington for the primaries, relocating them into a large house on Rock Creek Park. With his family Hunter Thompson was moving to the nation's capital; for the next year he'd actually have the opportunity, as both a writer and activist, to influence the direction in which the country might be headed next.

\*

That October, Oscar Acosta wrote to Hunter Thompson, "You dumb cocksucker . . . Your arrogance has gone to your head. Could it be it's because you're becoming successful?" He actually wasn't upset about the Salazar article. "I have no regrets," he said about its ramifications, "you came through like a champ."

It was the galleys to *Fear and Loathing in Las Vegas* that had set him off. "Did you even so much as ask me if I minded your writing & printing the Vegas piece? Not even the fucking courtesy to show me the motherfucker . . . as a friend who has *already* suffered the pangs of purgatory because of your first piece, one would think my old buddy would say, Here it is, what do you think, and do you mind?"

Acosta said that the narrative unfairly depicted him in the role of "some fucking native, a noble savage . . . discovered in the woods." He also thought that the participatory nature of the piece ought to be acknowledged upfront and with financial compensation. "My God!" he'd write to Alan Rinzler, "Hunter has stolen my soul. He's taken my best lines and has used me. He has wrung me dry for material." He threatened to sue for libel. Random House, worried about the legal challenge, delayed the publication date.

"You stupid fuck," Thompson wrote him. "You've managed to turn a possible best seller into a 'spooked property' that nobody wants to be a part of . . . I assume you had some excellent, long-stewing reason for doing this cheap, acid-crippled paranoid fuckaround." He begged his friend to sign the release so the book could go to press. He explained that he'd specifically avoided using any identifiable details as to protect Acosta from disbarment and other attacks from enemies like the LAPD who were looking to use anything they could get their hands on as leverage. Finally they had it out over the phone.

"What kind of journalist are you?" Acosta shouted. "Don't you have any respect for the truth? I can sink that whole publishing house for defaming me." The real issue, he said, had to do with Thompson's depiction of him as a three-hundred-pound Samoan as opposed to a Chicano attorney and civil rights activist whose anger in Las Vegas was directly proportional to the nature of the very real threats weighing down his life.

Thompson agreed to set the record straight. But by now it was too late in the publication process to change the text itself, so instead they struck a compromise: the back of the book would feature that early morning photograph from their second trip to the desert—Thompson with his aviators and sheriff's badge, Acosta dapper and demure and sporting a single black glove—along with the caption: "The author, shown here in the Baccarat Lounge of

Caesars Palace, Las Vegas . . . with Oscar Zeta Acosta, who insists on being identified as Dr. Gonzo." With that Acosta signed the release.

A half-decade later, reflecting on this moment, Thompson would write about his old friend:

> He had a lawyer's cynical view of the Truth—which he felt was not nearly as important to other people as it was to him; and he was never more savage and dangerous than when he felt he was being lied to . . . His formula for survival in a world full of rich Gabaucho fascists was a kind of circle that began at the top with the idea that truth would bring him power, which would buy freedom . . . which would naturally put him even closer to more and finer truths . . . indeed, the full circle.

## CHAPTER SIX

# HE SPEAKS
# FOR THE WEREWOLF

## 1972–1974

## The Raven Is Calling Your Name

The 1972 primary contest to determine the Democratic presidential nominee reached unbearable proportions, for Hunter Thompson, on the afternoon of Friday, February 18—weeks before a single vote had even been cast.

At the time he was riding on Senator Ed Muskie's "Sunshine Special": a two-day whistle-stop tour from Jacksonville to Miami along the Seaboard Coast Line Railroad, a trip that Muskie, the frontrunner in the contest to secure Florida's eighty-one-delegate primary prize, had paid an enormous amount of money to charter. At each destination the scene repeated itself: there was a crowd of uninterested, bussed-in supporters; staged camera shots; and, to cap things off, a speech that ended again and again on the same cringeworthy line: "It's time for the *good* people of America to get together behind somebody they can trust—namely me."

The first major primary tests in New Hampshire and Florida would be held at the beginning of March, and Ed Muskie, the tall, imperious fifty-eight-year-old congressman from Maine, had come into the election year as the candidate who, according to the party leaders and national press, stood the best shot of beating Richard Nixon in the fall. In recent Gallup polls he'd opened up a five-point lead on his nearest opponent. But everything would depend on the upcoming primaries; after the disastrous election cycle four years earlier, in which Hubert Humphrey had clawed his way to the nomination without entering a single contest, the Democratic primary system had been reworked to better reflect the will of the electorate. Now delegates would be bound to the actual winners.

However, for "Big Ed" (as Thompson had taken to calling him), things on the ground weren't going nearly as well as the polls suggested. His staff seemed to be playing it as conservatively as possible, hoping to run out the clock until the general election. In terms of policy, his speeches were gallingly neutral, devoid of any real content. And his series of elaborate campaign events fell consistently flat: if the Sunshine Special was awkward for its audiences of bussed-in crowds, it was sheer torture for the members of the national press, all of them forced, as if in a bad dream, to witness the candidate's same wooden "Namely me" line again and again. What's more, Muskie himself, in the last few weeks, had become strikingly unpredictable, locking himself away from his supporters and staff day and night . . . except for a few moment of inexplicable, towering anger, during which he'd emerge to berate anyone in his vicinity. "It was a very oppressive atmosphere," Thompson wrote from Florida, "very tense and guarded," and by the end of that Friday afternoon most of the writers on the chartered train had taken to drinking heavily from the free bar.

"These people act like goddamned Republicans!" someone said. Another called the whole spectacle "disgracefully bad." The scene felt even more artificial, to Thompson, than the one he'd experienced exactly four years earlier at the Manchester Holiday Inn: "It came as a definitive shock to find that hanging around Florida with Ed Muskie was even duller and more depressing than traveling with Evil Dick himself."

Just before the train pulled into West Palm Beach for the night, the passengers—including a dozen or so "Muskie girls" who, in the style of cheerleaders, wore hot pants and leotards with buttons that read TRUST MUSKIE, BELIEVE MUSKIE, MUSKIE TALKS STRAIGHT— were all directed toward the dining car, where one of the younger staff members led a sing-along to the lyrics of the candidate's new campaign song: "He's got the whole state of Florida . . . In his hands . . ." Afterward Thompson said to a friend from the *New York*

218 FREAK KINGDOM

*Times,* "That was one of the most degrading political experiences I've ever been subjected to."

Much later that night, around 2:00 a.m. at the Palm Beach Ramada Inn's lobby, Hunter Thompson was heading out in search of food with a fellow captive from the Sunshine Special—University of Florida student-reporter Monty Chitty—when they came upon an enormous young man. He was blond, at least six and a half feet tall, over 250 pounds. At the night clerk he was bellowing: "All these pansies around here keep trying to suck up to Muskie!"

His name was Peter Sheridan. He was wearing Levi's and a Cuban work shirt and an old, flattened Panama hat. He'd grown up in Chevy Chase, Maryland, but recently he'd been living in the Bay Area, where he'd become friends with bikers from the Oakland chapter of Hell's Angels—as well as the members of the Grateful Dead. He was one of Jerry Garcia's favorite people. He was close with Timothy Leary. As a prank he'd once laced the doorknobs of a local police station with LSD. His nickname in California was "Craze." He'd recently been ordained as a bona-fide clergyman—a "BooHoo"—in the Original Kleptonian Neo-American Church, an offspring of the psychedelic movement that challenged existing drug laws by claiming LSD as a sacrament. That Friday, he'd just gotten out of jail (vagrancy) and after learning that Big Ed was in town he'd stopped by the hotel to check in with an old friend, Richie Evans, who happened to be working as the campaign's advance man. But Evans, it turned out, was not available.

"I listened for a moment," Thompson would write in his *Rolling Stone* dispatch, "and then I recognized the Neal Cassady speed-booze-acid rap—a wild combination of menace, madness, genius, and fragmented coherence that wreaks havoc on the mind of any listener." He invited Sheridan to join him and Chitty.

"Don't mind if I do," the Neo-American BooHoo responded. "At this hour of the night I'll fuck around with just about anybody."

They spent the next four hours floating from one pool hall to the next, at each of which their new friend managed to cause a scene, and just after sunrise, as they made their way back to the hotel, Sheridan mentioned that his plans for the next day were to hitchhike down to Miami.

"To hell with that,"Thompson said."Take the train with *us*." He offered to let Sheridan use his press pass for the Sunshine Special.

Sheridan grinned. "I think you're right," he said. Together they went to the elevator. Thompson rode up to his room. Then he placed his orange press badge in the empty carriage and sent it back down to the lobby, where Peter Sheridan could grab it once the doors opened, as if the badge had accidentally been dropped onto the floor. Of course the Muskie campaign would still let Thompson board the next day, even if only a few of the staffers actually knew him; he was, after all, the political correspondent for a major American magazine.

But two hours later, the train departed without him. He was still sleeping in his room at the time, and the staffers saw no reason to wake him up. "There is a certain amount of poetic justice in the results of that decision," Thompson would write. "By leaving me behind, they unwittingly cut the only person on the train who could've kept the BooHoo under control."

A blue Atlantic morning, the wind gusting from the west: at 8:00 a.m. the Sunshine Special started chugging south toward Miami Beach. Sheridan—wearing a HUNTER S. THOMPSON, ROLLING STONE press badge—burst into the lounge car. "Triple Gin Bucks," he ordered from the bartender, "without the Buck."

Over the next three hours, as the train continued toward its final stop in Miami, Peter Sheridan downed at least a dozen martinis. When the bartenders stopped serving him he grabbed a bottle of gin and careened up and down the private cars. He called R. W. Apple Jr., the senior correspondent for the *New York Times,* "an ugly little wop." He accused a *Washington Post* reporter of being "a Communist buttfucker" and threatened to throw him out the window at the next bridge. Eventually word of what was going on filtered back to car no. 300—Muskie's private sanctuary—that a certain Hunter Thompson, apparently under the influence of some sort of psychopharmacological substance, was causing a violent scene. The senator thought about forcibly restraining this Thompson, but he figured that any reaction on his part would only draw the sort of negative press that would overshadow the expensively orchestrated trip.

Sheridan spent the rest of the ride chasing the Muskie cheerleaders throughout the compartments, shouting, "Now I gotcha, you little beauty!" At the station in Miami he stumbled off the train—down onto the tracks—before anyone could stop him (it was still too early for Secret Service protection).

It was around then that Big Ed Muskie finally emerged from his private compartment. He headed out on the elevated caboose platform at the back of the Sunshine Special, where he planned to deliver his climactic whistle-stop address. Down below him the cameras were all set up. The members of the press were waiting with their notebooks. The whole point of the two-day trip had been to orchestrate a moment like this one now.

But as soon as he started speaking, the activist Jerry Rubin—a founding member of the Yippies and current Chicago Seven defendant who happened to be in South Florida at the time—suddenly emerged from the crowd. He interrupted the speech, demanding that the candidate explain his previous support for the Vietnam War; this *was* Ed Muskie, after all, the man who'd spoken in favor of the majority stance at the 1968 Democratic Convention and supported Mayor Daley while Rubin and so many others were being beaten in the streets.

"Shut up young man," Muskie barked. "I'm talking."

"You're not a damn bit different from Nixon!" Rubin shouted back.

Just then, Muskie felt something at his leg. He looked down. Through the bars of the elevated caboose he glimpsed a dark, preternatural figure:

Peter Sheridan—holding an empty gin bottle and standing directly beneath him—was reaching up with his free hand to claw at the senator's pants. In horror Muskie tried to shake him off. But Sheridan was very tall. "Get your lying ass back inside," the BooHoo bellowed up at the candidate, "and make me another drink!"

It went on like this for a bit longer—Rubin kept yelling about the war as Sheridan reached up through the bars, demanding more gin and saying things like "You worthless old fart!"—when at last Ed Muskie seemed to reel backward, toward the door of the caboose, a stumble that everyone could clearly see . . .

Which was when Big Ed finally decided to give up and, according to reporters from the *Washington Star* and *Women's Wear Daily,* "cut short his remarks."

Afterward Peter Sheridan dragged himself toward the city and its tropical streets, disappearing just as suddenly as he'd arrived. About him Thompson would write: "[He] was in fact an excellent person, with a rare sense of humor . . . an obvious aristocrat of the Freak Kingdom."

\*

Thompson's account of Ed Muskie's Sunshine Special appeared as part of his political coverage in *Rolling Stone* no. 106. It immediately became a hit with his fellow correspondents, whose own publications would never allow them to chronicle the campaign in such a way.

In retrospect, the train narrative was a great way to characterize, to *Rolling Stone*'s youthful demographic, a candidate like Muskie: that consummate party hack who wasn't all that different from his Republican counterparts. To anyone covering the campaign at that time—back during January and February, when Muskie's poll numbers showed him ahead of Nixon in a possible general election face-off—it was clear that the frontrunner was, in reality, imploding. Which drove Thompson crazy; these reporters, hoping to retain access to the candidate (and worried about the scrutiny and pressure their editors might face), played it safe, rarely revealing to the electorate what was really going on. Thompson didn't have to worry about any of that. From the start he and Wenner had conceived his literary/advocacy gig as a one-off thing.

About Muskie, Thompson would write: "He talked like a farmer with terminal cancer trying to borrow money on next year's crop." And: "Working for Big Ed was something like being locked in a rolling boxcar with a vicious 200-pound water rat. Some of his top staff people considered him dangerously unstable." And: "Sending Muskie against Nixon would have been like sending a three-toed sloth out to seize turf from a wolverine . . . it was stone madness from the start to ever think about exposing him to the kind of bloodthirsty thugs that Nixon and John Mitchell would sic on him. They would have him screeching on his knees by sundown on Labor Day."

He wrote this passage three months before the Watergate break-in—*long* before the full extent of Richard Nixon's astonishing criminality had come to light—but then that was the point: to anyone who, like Hunter Thompson, had been watching Nixon carefully these last ten years, a "dirty trick" in the vein of breaking into your rival's headquarters wasn't a revelation. Of course the thirty-seventh president would do this and more to keep his hold on power. The real question: just how deep did it all go?

In the summer of 1971, after RAND employee Daniel Ellsberg blew the whistle on the top-secret Pentagon Papers, the administration had created and funded a secret unit within the existing Committee for the Re-Election of the President—"Plumbers," they were called—to surveil, sabotage, and blackmail critics. They broke into the office of Ellsberg's psychiatrist. They plotted a robbery/bombing of the Brookings Institution, where Nixon was worried that evidence of his treasonous interference in the 1968 election had been housed. "I want it implemented on a thievery basis!" the president had said to H. R. Haldeman, his chief of staff. That September he'd had White House counsel John Dean draw up an enemies' list. And in January, when the senator from Maine emerged as the frontrunner, senior operative Donald Segretti cooked up what would later be called "the Canuck Letter": a forged account that accused Muskie, among other things, of slurring Canadians, who happened to represent a sizable voting bloc in the state of New Hampshire.

Big Ed suddenly found himself the target of multiple unflattering attacks by conservative outlets like the Manchester *Union Leader*—"America's worst newspaper," Hunter Thompson called it—and on February 26, a week after his experience with Peter Sheridan and Jerry Rubin in Miami and ten days before the first primary of the year, Muskie called a noon press conference. From a flatbed truck in the middle of a snowstorm, he rebutted the accusations—appearing, at one point, to break down weeping.

Finally the other campaign trail reporters felt confident reporting on Muskie's instability—and they did, tanking the senator's candidacy in the process. The real source of the Canuck Letter wouldn't be revealed until many months later, at which point there'd be a great deal of retrospective hand-wringing: had the press unwittingly aided and abetted in Richard Nixon's destruction of an opponent?

For Thompson, such second-guessing was beside the point. "Muskie is a bonehead who steals his best lines from Nixon speeches," he wrote in February. He'd never forgiven Big Ed for supporting Mayor Daley and Hubert Humphrey in Chicago four years earlier—nor for the violence that resulted. And as the Muskie camp tried and failed to stagger back from the fallout associated with their infamous snowstorm press conference—in the wake of devastating primary losses in Florida on March 14, Wisconsin on April 4, and Pennsylvania and Massachusetts on April 25—Hunter Thompson would offer his own stylistic coda on the senator's outlandish behavior. "It had long been whispered that Muskie was into something very heavy," he wrote in the May

11 issue of *Rolling Stone* (two weeks after Big Ed had suspended his campaign); he then claimed to have finally heard *what* it was: a psychedelic compound derived from the Iboga plant used in West African ceremonies. "The Man from Maine had turned to massive doses of Ibogaine as a last resort." It was a satirical explanation of the senator's very real behavior the last few months: "Muskie's tearful breakdown on the flatbed truck in New Hampshire, the delusions and altered thinking that characterized his campaign in Florida, and finally the condition of 'total rage' that gripped him in Wisconsin."

Thompson assumed that the humor of it all would be clear from the start. But the defeated Muskie campaign missed the joke; they saw it as another calculated falsehood. And even though Thompson explained that such exaggerations were part of his sub-jective style—"[besides], I never said it was true," he'd clarify, "I said there was a rumor to that effect. I made up the rumor"—months later Thompson would find himself accused, to congressional in-vestigators, of working as an agent for Richard Nixon's notorious Committee for the Re-Election of the President, a turn of events even more absurd than the incident from which it stemmed. "The accusation came as a welcome flash of humor," he'd write in a footnote to the Peter Sheridan incident. "This also reinforced my contempt for the waterheads who ran Big Ed's campaign like a gang of junkies trying to send a rocket to the moon to check on rumors that the craters were full of smack."

*

Hunter Thompson's campaign articles first appeared in the winter of 1972, and for the next eleven months—to meet his twice-a-month deadlines—he'd write hundreds of pages on the Demo-cratic primaries and general election.

That winter Sandy was pregnant again—their last try, they'd decided. The doctor told her that the odds of carrying the baby to term would be about twenty-five percent.

The house they were renting on Rock Creek Park in DC was large and beautiful, a three-story red-brick colonial, but Thompson was rarely there. And while in retrospect much about their relationship during this period remains unclear—Thompson had to abandon his usually prodigious letter-writing habit while covering the campaign—Sandy's later reflections on their time in Washington suggest that whatever balance they'd managed to strike during the previous half decade in Woody Creek was rapidly deteriorating under the stress of the move and the campaign and her pregnancy.

"He was taking a lot of speed," she'd say years later. "He was wired. He didn't have any recovery time . . . Hunter was just so much in his own thing, in his own world . . . I remember myself smoking—I had taken up smoking!—and drinking a lot. Here I am, pregnant, right? . . . He didn't know that every single night I was drunk."

Had he ever pushed himself as hard as he did during this winter and spring of that long-ago election season? He was thirty-four years old. The past decade he'd been working his way toward the point he'd arrived at now: a position from which, through his dual roles as an artist and de facto advisor, he'd finally earned the opportunity to have a say in the direction the Republic might be headed next. In other words: for Hunter Thompson, because of the very real possibility of a personal and familial breakdown, the stakes had never been higher.

George McGovern's win-or-go-home moment would be the Wisconsin primary, the fourth of the season. That was how the campaign staff had planned it out all along, a blueprint they'd shared ahead of time with Thompson. They'd skipped certain states like Florida and Illinois and instead marshaled their resources in a grassroots campaign that would carry them to victory in Wisconsin, which would open up a path to winning Massachusetts and Nebraska and—with its 271 winner-take-all delegates—California.

To everyone's surprise, this strategy appeared to be working. At their Milwaukee headquarters on April 4 word came through that they'd won a stunning, seven-point upset. Three weeks later, in Massachusetts, they crushed Muskie so badly he dropped out of the race.

In Big Ed's place, two candidates looked to fill the power vacuum and contest McGovern. The first was none other than Hubert Horatio Humphrey, that perennial agent of the establishment who'd somehow managed to elbow his way back into the race.

And the other was fifty-two-year-old Alabama governor George Wallace, the incendiary segregationist who'd run as an independent in 1968. Wallace had decided at the last minute to seek the Democratic nomination. In Florida, during the same weekend that Muskie had paid thousands of dollars to charter the Sunshine Special, he'd showed up at the Daytona 500, where he had a chance to speak directly to the one hundred thousand fans in attendance. His central issue—opposition to mandatory school busing, which the Supreme Court had held up the year before as a necessary antisegregation tool—was for many white voters in the South and throughout "Middle America" the most important.

Hunter Thompson watched Wallace's demagogic ascent with morbid fascination. Most of the Democratic establishment dismissed the Alabama governor's campaign as the latest incarnation of the hate-fueled populism he'd been spewing for years, but after seeing him live in Milwaukee's Serb Hall Thompson understood that the appeal went far deeper than most people would care to admit: "The air was electric even before he started talking, and by the time he was five or six minutes into his spiel I had a sense that the bastard had somehow levitated himself and was hovering over us . . . It was a flat-out fire & brimstone *performance* . . . He campaigns like a rock star."

Wallace was tapping into the anger and dissatisfaction of people who felt they'd been left behind by all the technological and cultural changes that were sweeping the country—Americans from both sides of the traditional political spectrums—and in his raucous rhetoric he offered what Thompson called a "thundering, gut-level appeal to rise up and smash all the 'pointy-headed bureaucrats in Washington' who'd been fucking them over for so long."

To be sure: From the start he saw George Wallace for what he was . . . an unapologetic charlatan. "The ugly truth is that Wallace had never even bothered to *understand* the problems," he'd write, "much less come up with honest solutions." But the vengeful emotional outlet the campaign provided was what mattered most, and in retrospect, with his general strategy of cashing in on the frustration and resentment of white Americans, George Wallace was racking up delegates—a legitimate contender for the nomination who at the very least could scramble the electoral map in November.

But that all changed at a May 15 campaign rally in Laurel, Maryland, when, walking through the crowd, Wallace was shot four times at point-blank range by Arthur Bremer, a delusional twenty-one-year-old whose motivation didn't have anything to do with ideology; he just wanted to see his name in the paper. One of the bullets clipped Wallace's spinal cord, and although he'd survive, for the rest of his life he'd be confined to a wheelchair.

The shooting had taken place only a half-hour's drive from Hunter Thompson's house on Rock Creek Park, but at the time he was up in New York, a guest speaker at the Columbia School of Journalism, and instead, Timothy Crouse, his young partner at *Rolling Stone,* would be the one to cover the story.

That afternoon, Chris Lydon, the bow-tie-wearing *New York Times* reporter who, along with the rest of the campaign press corps, had recently made it a habit to read each new "Fear and Loathing on the Campaign Trail" dispatch, said regretfully to Crouse, "Hunter Thompson should be here to record this, for history."

\*

At the end of May, as the decisive California primary approached— after Big Ed Muskie's collapse and with the horrific assassination attempt on Wallace—there was only one candidate left who still had any chance at stopping George McGovern's improbable rise to the nomination: Hubert Humphrey, the former vice president who, after losing to Nixon in 1968, had returned to Minnesota, where he'd won back his old senate seat. He was sixty-two years old—desperate to snatch what he sensed would be his last shot at the presidency.

Humphrey and George McGovern descended on California that May for what was becoming the perfect finale to the primary season's evolving narrative: Old Politics vs. New. In one corner you had Hubert Horatio, the candidate of Mayor Daley and Big Labor—the very people whose hold on power, after the recent rule changes to the delegate system that McGovern had spearheaded, was seriously threatened. And now, with McGovern way ahead in the polls (a win in California would allow him to secure the nomination on the first ballot), they were willing to do whatever it took to make sure they retained a veto over who represented *their* interests . . . even if it meant crippling the party in November.

In California Humphrey went with a scorched-earth approach, accusing his senate colleague (and old friend) of harboring support for The Three A's: Acid, Amnesty, and Abortion. He also spread falsehoods about drug legalization and appeasement and defense spending and the US position on Israel. Which was regrettable—dirty—but not at all out of line, in retrospect, with the way that politics as usual had been conducted in this country for centuries.

The same couldn't be said, however, for the other approach Humphrey and his backers were prepared to take: should they lose California, they planned to rewrite the new primary rules with a procedural challenge on the floor of the convention, freeing up delegates from the vote totals they'd been bound to in a last-minute plot to steal the nomination from McGovern.

To Hunter Thompson, Old Hubert's deceit was clear, and he wasn't about to let anyone forget it. That spring he'd call the former vice president "a treacherous, gutless old ward-heeler who should be put in a goddamn bottle and sent out with the Japanese

Current"; "a shallow, contemptible, and hopelessly dishonest old hack"; a "rabid skunk"; a "brain-damaged old vulture"; and (with the exception of Richard Nixon), "the purest and most disgusting example of a Political Animal in American politics today."

In the other corner was George McGovern. To Thompson, the senator from South Dakota was and always had been, in both life and politics, an honorable, reasonable, straight-shooting believer in the American system's potential to represent its forgotten and overlooked citizens. "He is probably the most honest big-time politician in America," Thompson would write. McGovern had been the driving force behind the new delegate selection process, and with his grassroots campaign he was hoping to mobilize the same coalition that had come together for Bobby Kennedy, "a weird mix of peace freaks and hardhats, farmers and film stars, along with urban blacks, rural Chicanos, the 'youth vote' . . . a coalition that could elect almost anybody." He'd picked up many of RFK's talented former staffers, including Frank Mankiewicz, his campaign director, and Fred Dutton, who like Thompson had been attacked by police in front of the Chicago Hilton four years earlier.

For Hunter Thompson, McGovern was the perfect candidate to support *and* write about. Because of his honesty he was the only challenger who could survive Thompson's blistering critiques: someone whose very real faults—his lack of charisma, his refusal to break completely the Democratic old guard, his naiveté when it came to dirty politics—in the end made him a *more* favorable option, especially in contrast to his opponents. He was the candidate the country had been deprived of during the last cycle: a genuine alternative to Richard Milhous Nixon.

That May, in the middle of the primary contest, Sandy went into labor. She was not yet at full term, just seven and a half months into her pregnancy. Thompson, back in DC, drove her north—they'd chosen Johns Hopkins Hospital in Baltimore, which had the necessary resources to facilitate the complex procedure necessary for the expected Rh-factor complications—and after a successful delivery and immediate blood transfusion, the baby, a boy, was doing well. When Sandy saw him she was amazed (considering how much she'd been drinking and smoking).

But a few hours later his breathing became labored. He'd developed infant respiratory distress syndrome, a condition that occurs in premature births: the surface of the lungs becomes coated in a glassy, crystalline membrane. At the time it was called hyaline membrane disease. An effective treatment—a predelivery injection—wasn't yet widely available.

The baby died later that day. Thompson, devastated, returned to Washington and buried himself in work, and Sandy stayed at the hospital so they could monitor her health. Decades later, she'd say, "When I was ready to come home, I called Hunter and told him that he didn't need to come and get me . . . I told him I could take a taxi. And for years after that, I was hurt and angry that he had not said to me, 'No, no, no. Don't take a taxi.'"

What could they do? It had happened again—terribly—in the same unaccountable fashion. Thompson fell back on the response he'd relied on in 1969; together they spent a few days in California—at this point the primary was only ten days away—at billionaire Max Palevsky's Bel Air home (Jann Wenner helped arrange for them to stay there), where they sat in the sun by the pool. This six-bedroom house was tucked against the western end of the Sunset Strip. It had been designed in 1929 by George Washington Smith: a tree-shadowed Spanish mansion in the style of the Beverly Hills Hotel, as if the Polo Lounge had been replicated and rearranged in the privacy of an old friend's backyard.

But it was not just the two of them. That weekend, Palevsky's house was central to McGovern's California operations: a base of isolation and solitude that the candidate and his aides could use as a private shield against the sudden media crush that had accompanied their new frontrunner status. Hunter Thompson and Sandy orbited the mansion within this new crowd. Among them,

Thompson didn't permit himself the chance to grieve. Instead he focused on the campaign, its energy.

On Monday afternoon, while he and Sandy were staying together at the Palevskys', George McGovern arrived with his Secret Service agents. The senator was hoping to spend a few quiet hours away from the insanity of the campaign; he couldn't yet know that only a few days earlier, on May 28, Richard Nixon had planted listening devices at the Democratic National Committee's Watergate office, or that the Plumbers, led by G. Gordon Liddy and Howard Hunt, had tried to bug the McGovern campaign headquarters on Capitol Hill. Or that Nixon had demanded that the IRS flag and audit major donors like Max Palevsky.

It was a cool, cloudy day. George McGovern immediately stripped to a bathing suit and, in the fern-shadowed pool behind the house, began swimming laps. Hunter Thompson got in the pool, too. Together the two of them moved through the water at the same pace, talking privately. They discussed strategy—against Hubert Humphrey, against the Democratic machine in general, against Nixon. Should McGovern reach out to his defeated primary opponents and the establishment wing of the party in a show of unity, or was it possible to win the general election on his own terms—as the outsider he'd been from the start? To Thompson the best course was clear—the latter—but he also understood that on every major issue of the last decade, from civil rights to the war in Vietnam to presidential excess, this forty-nine-year-old senator from South Dakota, a minister's son and war hero who'd been a civics professor before entering politics, had been on the correct side of history.

They talked like this, swimming together, for a rare uninterrupted stretch. Afterward—as the sun finally broke through and the day revealed itself for what it was, a late-spring burst of light and heat and wind-cleared sky—they sat casually by the pool, their conversation continuing. The rest of the national press corps had

been relegated to the street out in front of Palevsky's mansion, and
as Thompson and the senator spoke they were all left waiting, infuriated, for the chance to shout the questions they needed answered
in order to file their daily stories.

McGovern would go on to win California, despite Hubert
Humphrey's desperate procedural challenge. By then it was clear:
the nomination would be McGovern's. Against all odds he'd beaten
his opponents: the same men who, in 1968, had stood by as the old
party bosses used violence to silence and suppress legitimate dissent—men Hunter Thompson would *never* forgive, let alone forget.
That spring he'd write:

> Remember me, Hubert? I'm the one who got smacked in the
> stomach by a billy club at the corner of Michigan and Balboa on
> that evil Wednesday night four years ago in Chicago . . . while
> you looked down from your suite on the twenty-fifth floor of
> the Hilton, and wept with a snout full of tear gas drifting up
> from Grant Park.
>
> I have never been one to hold a grudge any longer than ab-
> solutely necessary, Hubert, and I get the feeling that we're about
> to write this one off. Big Ed was first . . . then you . . . and after
> that—the Other One. Nothing personal. But it's time to bal-
> ance the books. The Raven is calling your name . . .

## FOUR MORE YEARS!

Just before 10:00 p.m. on June 17, 1972, Hunter Thompson was
swimming laps in the Watergate Hotel's indoor pool—located at
that time deep within the structure's basement—while, about a
hundred yards away, the political crime of the century was in the
process of being perpetrated.

Thompson had bluffed his way into the pool, a skill he prided
himself on: whether through an arrangement with a security guard
or an old guest pass, he preferred to swim during the off-hour

stretches of the day, when pools like the one he found himself in now were closed and empty.

A low ceiling. The smell of chlorine. Wet linoleum. A blue subaqueous timbre to the light. The hotel was newly built, and for Thompson, after six months of nonstop campaigning and deadlines and domestic tragedy and sleeplessness and sickness and dreadful Midwestern motor lodges, the opportunity for a late-night swim—to comb privately through the water of this great empty basement—represented a chance for solitude and self-possession that was becoming rarer and rarer to achieve. In the pool that evening he was submersed in a rhythm of movement and muted sound. Nearby, the world itself—*history*—was changing. How could he know? How could anyone?

His second book, *Fear and Loathing in Las Vegas,* had just been published by Random House. "To Bob Geiger," he'd dedicated it, "for reasons that need not be explained here." The reviews were excellent, especially in the *New York Times,* but because of the delay over Acosta's threatened suit he'd failed to capitalize on the momentum from the earlier *Rolling Stone* two-part publication, and the sales weren't as strong as he'd hoped.

He and Sandy and Juan were in the process of moving back to Woody Creek. He was about to turn thirty-five, a self-described "speed freak with half his hair burned off from overindulgence." For two decades he'd been a serious alcoholic. At last he'd arrived at the heights he'd been seeking since he'd first moved from Colorado to California in 1964: literary success *and* the chance to influence the Republic's political direction. However, considering the rate at which he was going, how much longer could he really expect to keep it all up?

Thompson had driven down to the Watergate through Rock Creek Park (about a twenty-minute trip) to meet a friend, the Washington *Daily News* sportswriter Tom Quinn. Together—sitting at the bar after his late-night swim—they talked until last call about life and politics and professional football. High above them, on the sixth floor of the building, five mercenaries for Richard Nixon's Committee for the Re-Election of the President were photographing documents and wiring surveillance devices into telephone receivers.

That spring, Nixon had found himself surprised, along with the rest of the American political elite, by the emergence of George McGovern. In May his Plumbers had tried to bug McGovern's campaign headquarters on Capitol Hill *four* different times, to no avail . . . though not before a certain G. Gordon Liddy, the most dead-eyed of the president's many glass-faced henchmen, had shot out more than a dozen streetlights with his handgun.

Instead, the Plumbers, desperate for results—hundreds of thousands of dollars had been illegally funneled their way—chose the Democratic National Headquarters at the Watergate as a target; on May 28, they'd broken into and wiretapped the main phone lines to the office of Larry O'Brien, the party chairman. Their goal was to unearth damaging information, a standard Nixonian tactic: when accused of misbehavior, the administration often held up a comparable Democratic offense and loudly lamented the liberal media's egregious double-standard.

But in the wake of this first break-in, one of the listening devices malfunctioned. So Liddy was forced to call back his gang of burglars: a group of anti–Fidel Castro former intelligence officers. And on the third Friday in June, they broke into the Watergate through its parking garage, taping the locks to its below-ground series of doors—taping them horizontally, for anyone to see—and then they made their way to the DNC's sixth-floor headquarters to replace the bug and gather new evidence. Afterward, the plan was to continue on to McGovern's office on Capitol Hill, where they intended to install listening devices for the first time.

That never happened. As Hunter Thompson and Tom Quinn were finishing their tequilas, undercover DC police officers dressed as disheveled, drug-dealing hippies—in bellbottoms—came upon five suit-wearing burglars in the stultifying darkness of 2600

Virginia Avenue Northwest. They seized the men and everything they were carrying, which included advanced surveillance equipment, latex gloves, multiple rolls of crisp $100 bills, and a small spiral pad with a note about the *White House* written in it. The next morning, Liddy, in a panic, contacted on an unsecure line his contact in Nixon's inner circle, Jeb Magruder; across the county, Magruder was sitting at the breakfast table on the outdoor patio of the Beverly Hills Hotel's Polo Lounge, and he was brought on a platter that pink telephone—linking, for all of time, the hatchet-job burglary with the administration that had ordered it.

At the Watergate that night Hunter Thompson and Tom Quinn paid for their tequilas and walked to their cars. The parking lot was quiet. They didn't notice anything unusual. It was a balmy Chesapeake evening, their armpits stained with sweat, the night like a hot breath of air that's been swallowed much too quickly.

Afterward Thompson drove home, taking the parkway up through Rock Creek as if it were any other night, which in a certain sense it was.

\*

That summer, both the Democratic and the Republican conventions were held in Miami Beach, a month and a half apart, and as the first gave way to the second, the run-up to the general election suddenly seemed to be taking on the air of a classical farce: one in which Richard Nixon, despite increasing evidence of his crimes, was growing stronger in the polls.

It was a development that could be explained in part by the president's deeply cynical maneuvering on Vietnam: back in 1968, Nixon had promised the country that he had a "secret plan" to get out of Southeast Asia—a move that now, four years later, had at last begun to play out: "The plan was to end the war *just in time* to get himself re-elected in 1972," Thompson wrote bitterly. Nixon and Kissinger knew from the start that the conflict couldn't be won, and they were looking to withdraw, but they didn't want

Saigon to collapse *before* he went up for his second term, which was why they'd stalled the peace talks. In the meantime thirty thousand more American young men had died violently.

But the deadliest blows to the McGovern campaign were, in retrospect, self-inflicted. The slide started in early July, at the Democratic convention, when, in an effort to fight off a last-ditch technical challenge by Hubert Humphrey on how the California delegation should be counted, they neglected to pay enough attention to their consideration of a vice presidential candidate—assuming, wrongly, that Ted Kennedy would take the slot.

Back then, the winning nominee needed to choose a running mate by 4:00 p.m. on the Thursday of the convention week, or else the decision would go to the delegates on the floor, who could then select *whoever* they wanted. So in desperation McGovern went with Thomas Eagleton, a young Catholic senator from Missouri. It was a terrible decision from the start, in Thompson's opinion, because it signaled McGovern's willingness to move to a more centrist stance, an overture to the Old Politics figures he'd won his candidacy contesting.

But the deeper issue wouldn't emerge for another two weeks: Eagleton, it turned out, had lied to McGovern about his medical background, which included extended hospitalizations for severe depression, as well as electroshock therapy.

Initially McGovern had stood by his pick, but after consulting with psychiatric experts and with Eagleton's doctors, he was told that a relapse of such a severe illness, should Eagleton become president—subjected to the unparalleled stress of the White House—would endanger the country. So at the end of July the congressman from Missouri was replaced by Sargent Shriver, a milquetoast member of the extended Kennedy family.

By then the damage was done; McGovern emerged from the incident looking erratic—*untrustworthy,* especially in the eyes of voters who, after the tumult of the 1960s, had begun to prize stability above all else (Nixon's "silent majority"). In August his poll numbers went into an absolute free fall, which would in turn provide a nervous overreactive candidate like Richard Nixon the greatest gift of all: a large lead, which allowed the president to abandon the campaign trail completely and hide out in DC for much of the fall, cutting off even the semblance of openness and press access.

There were other factors that went against McGovern, such as the lingering accusation of radicalism (the "Acid, Abortion, Amnesty" attack line), the absence of George Wallace from the general election to split the conservative vote, and a galling lack of support from Big Labor. But the Eagleton selection was the disaster that made everything else about the senator's candidacy suddenly seem suspect—amateurish and unprofessional—and by the end of the summer, as the Republicans gathered in Miami to support their Nixon-Agnew "Law and Order" ticket, the president enjoyed an unprecedented *twenty-point* advantage over his Democratic counterpart.

Hunter Thompson arrived back in South Beach bewildered and exhausted and generally disgusted by everything and everyone. Both of the 1972 conventions would avoid the riotous violence that had characterized Chicago in 1968. During the Republican one, many of the wealthy delegates actually camped out on yachts in the hope of glimpsing a confrontation:

Every time the Fontainebleau lobby started buzzing with rumors about another crowd of demonstrators bearing down on the hotel from the direction of Flamingo Park, the boats across Collins Avenue would fill up with laughing Republican delegates wearing striped blazers and cocktail dresses. There was no better place, they said, for watching the street action. As the demonstrators approached the front entrance to the hotel, they found themselves walking a gauntlet of riot-equipped police on one side, and martini-sipping GOP delegates on the other.

The convention itself was ruthlessly stage-managed—a secret GOP schedule of events (sent by mistake to members of the media) included the exact times and locations for multiple "spontaneous" floor demonstrations—and after his first day at the center of it all Thompson felt an overwhelming desire to flee. On Tuesday afternoon—August 22—he was driving in his rented Impala convertible south to Key Biscayne, where he planned to find an empty stretch of beach and float in the water for a few hours, a brief reprieve of sun and solitude, when he suddenly glimpsed what appeared to be a vast column of people advancing up Collins Avenue.

He pulled over and parked his car at a meter. It was a spontaneous march by the members of the Vietnam Veterans Against the War (VVAW); more than twelve hundred young men were proceeding in a silent, solemn battalion from their campground at Flamingo Park. They were headed to the Fontainebleau Hotel, the headquarters for the Republican Party in Miami Beach, and for the next twelve blocks, Thompson shadowed their procession. They were wearing fatigues and helmets, the sun beating down. A few swung themselves forward on crutches. At the vanguard, ex-marine sergeant Ron Kovic was being pushed along the avenue in his wheelchair, his hands linked with those of the paralyzed veterans on his left and right. The six-lane street was bordered on its west side by Indian Creek, a saltwater causeway fashioned with multiple docks and piers, and on the east by massive condominium complexes, where the residents (mostly senior citizens) had come out to watch. The only sounds were those of thudding feet. Of horns. Of the dull rhythmic rotor-beat from distant helicopters. The battalion coordinated its movements with hand signals. Kovic drank from a canteen, slumping in the humidity, the VVAW flag draped behind him.

For the convention the Fontainebleau had been cordoned off with walls of temporary fencing, in front of which more than five hundred police guarded the entrances, wearing plastic riot visors and white shirts. Ron Kovic and the Last Patrol approached them in silence. The hotel guests, police, and even the delegates watching from their yachts were suddenly quiet.

The VVAW members gathered in the street at the hotel entrance. One of the leaders shouted through a bullhorn: "We want to come inside!"

Someone gasped. Thompson could see the horror in the plastic-shielded eyes of the state troopers: were they really prepared to attack over a thousand unarmed American veterans in order to defend a hotel-full of martini-sipping yacht-faring political operatives?

Without thinking Thompson tucked his notebook into his belt and took off his watch. "The first thing to go in a street fight is always your watch," he'd write, "and once you've lost a few, you develop a certain instinct that lets you know when it's time to get the thing off your wrist and in a safe pocket."

Just then, at a gap in the chain-link wall, Pete McCloskey—an antiwar Republican representative from California who, as a colonel in Korea, had been awarded two Purple Hearts—demanded that the police let him speak with the demonstrators.

"You can't get in through here!" a young cop said to him.

"Don't give me that *crap*," McCloskey shouted. "I'm a member of the Congress of the United States and if you think you're gonna stop me from going in there . . . " He was sure, like Thompson, that violence was imminent. Finally he flashed his ID at the police and walked quickly to the VVAW vanguard. To the veterans and their spokesman he said, "You've got a reaction by a government that fears you, you gotta believe that." Later he spoke with Kovic, who told him a story about being dumped out of his wheelchair and dragged to jail for protesting in front of Nixon's Los Angeles headquarters.

With McCloskey's arrival things finally calmed down. "We don't even *want* to go in," the spokesman admitted. "We just want to make them turn us away in front of network TV cameras."

Afterward Thompson wrote, "I have been covering anti-war demonstrations with depressing regularity since the winter of

1964 . . . and I have never seen cops so intimidated by demonstrators as they were in front of the Fontainebleau Hotel on that hot Tuesday afternoon in Miami Beach." It was an expertly executed protest, poignant and haunting and honorable. However, with the current administration it didn't even register. "If God himself had showed up in Miami and denounced Nixon from the podium," Thompson added, "hired gunsels from the Committee for the Re-Election of the President would have quickly had him arrested for disturbing the peace."

∗

Later that night, Hunter Thompson spent a few hours roaming the floor of the convention center, his *Rolling Stone* press pass granting him extensive access. Not that there was all that much to see. "The Nixon celebration was an ugly, low-level trip," he'd write, "that hovered somewhere in that indefinable limbo between dullness and obscenity, like a bad pornographic film." The Republicans were mad at Walter Cronkite for not standing during the national anthem. There was a brief controversy over Representative McCloskey and his antiwar platform, but it was quickly silenced . . . and without any of the fireworks that had characterized Nelson Rockefeller's appearance, eight years earlier, in San Francisco.

Thompson didn't plan to stick around for the main event—the roll call that signaled Nixon's official nomination—and around 9:00 p.m. he ducked into a backstage hallway, hoping to stop in for a few free drinks at the Railroad Lounge, a temporary bar, when he realized he'd taken a wrong turn.

The hallways were a merciless maze. The rooms were uniform and bright. Eventually he found himself in a bleak unrecognizable corridor. From the opposite direction, people were approaching. A great number of them. Suddenly he was beset upon by nearly two thousand college-aged individuals. They wore red-white-and-blue straw boaters and carried signs that read NIXON IS THE ONE. Together they were singing "Nixon Now," the campaign's theme song: "Reaching out / to find a way / To make tomorrow / a brighter day / Making dreams / reality / More than ever / Nixon now / for you and me / Nixon now! / Nixon now! / He's made the difference / He's shown us how."

Thompson knew he'd never make it past them; instead, turning in the opposite direction, he let himself be carried by this young boisterous crowd.

They arrived at an enormous "Ready Room," where dozens of handlers began barking orders about the "spontaneous" demonstration—scheduled for 10:33 p.m., the moment of the roll call's climax—that all these young men and women would surge enthusiastically out onto the floor to enact.

By this point Thompson figured he might as well see the whole thing through and join the participants—"Nixon Youth," he'd dubbed them—in their planned spontaneity. And for the next few minutes he positioned himself demurely against the back wall, careful to hide his *Rolling Stone* badge. To his surprise, everyone seemed to be leaving him alone.

But there was a commotion; from the main entrance Ron Rosenbaum, the talented twenty-five-year-old *Village Voice* journalist—attempting to infiltrate the Nixon Youth crowd so he could write about it himself—burst through the handlers who'd discovered him and fled toward the far end of the room. "No press allowed!" they screamed after him. "You can't stay!"

Just then Rosenbaum spied Thompson hiding by the wall. He dashed over—they'd become friends on the campaign trail—and pleaded, "They're trying to kick me out!"

Hunter Thompson jumped to his feet. "You crazy bastard!" he said to Rosenbaum. "You fingered *me*! Look what you've done!"

The Nixon Youth handlers saw Thompson's press badge. They started shouting at *both* of them to leave.

Thompson turned on Rosenbaum. "That's right!" he snarled. And then, to the Nixon Youth handlers: "Get that bastard out of here! No press allowed!"

Rosenbaum, aghast, fled back into the crowd.

In the next moment, Thompson tried to explain to these very upset Republicans that he wasn't really a *journalist* so much as a political observer planning out a future candidacy. "Have *you* ever run for office?" he quickly asked them.

"What?" one replied. "What about you—what office did *you* run for?"

Hunter Thompson smiled at this young man. "Sheriff, my friend. I ran for Sheriff, out in Colorado—and I lost by just a hair. Because the *liberals* put the screws to me." Which was, in a certain sense, true.

After that things seemed to go much better. Begrudgingly, they agreed to let him stay—until suddenly someone else pointed out the large blue-and-white McGovern button Thompson had pinned at his chest. The argument started up again, and long story short—in the wake of another quick-footed parry—they worked out a bargain: Thompson didn't have to leave, so long as he was willing to fit in with everyone else by donning a straw-boat hat and carrying a sign. Which he was. They gave him a hat and some cardboard and pens. GARBAGE MEN DEMAND EQUAL TIME, he wrote on the blank white square of paper.

Soon it was time: from the rough-voiced handlers a countdown started up. The two thousand demonstrators were organized into four groups, many of whom were supplied with bags of balloons. Together they were funneled onto the floor—this was just after ten thirty—and as the balloons fell from the ceiling, signaling Nixon's renomination, they paraded past the delegates to release their own rising helium versions. When Hunter Thompson finally stepped out onto the scene he was momentarily blinded by the trans-vertical cascade of bright balloons.

Along with everyone else he circled the speaking podium, shouting a few ironic insults at his old CBS friends in the booth above—John Chancellor, notably—but just then a new set of chants started up. FOUR MORE YEARS!, the thousands of organized

Nixon Youth were screaming in unison, many of them shoving their way toward the television cameras to curse the biased, unpatriotic members of the media.

The chant was growing louder. It wasn't just the Nixon Youth. The delegates shouted feverishly, too. FOUR MORE YEARS! A terrifying crescendo. Thompson quickly fled back through the screaming crowd, covering the McGovern button with his elbow, but when he reached the press exit he was suddenly overcome by an intense wave of déjà vu—the uncanny realization that, at another time in his life, he'd found himself crushed beneath the same inexplicable weight of sound bearing down upon him now. But when? He stood at the rim of the arena, trying to figure it out . . .

> Then it came to me. Yes. In 1964, at the Goldwater convention in San Francisco, when poor Barry unloaded that fateful line about "Extremism in the defense of liberty is no vice, etc. . . . " I was on the floor of the Cow Palace when he laid that one on the crowd, and I remember feeling genuinely frightened at the violent reaction it provoked. The Goldwater delegates went completely amok for fifteen or twenty minutes. He hadn't even finished the sentence before they were on their feet, cheering wildly. Then, as the human thunder kept building, they mounted their metal chairs and began howling, shaking their fists at Huntley and Brinkley up in the NBC booth—and finally they began picking up those chairs with both hands and bashing them against chairs other delegates were still standing on.

✳

What does it mean to spend a decade trying to fight back against injustice, to work within the democratic system's existing means (its electoral contests, nonviolent opportunities for protest, and investigative possibilities of its free press) only to end up being thoroughly pummeled by Richard Milhous Nixon and his un-abashedly corrupt inner circle? What can one make of a defeat at the hands of a gang of political criminals whose main advantage was that they never bothered to acknowledge limitations like the Constitution and its Bill of Rights, the moral fabric on which the country they're looking to control had been founded?

That fall, after a few recuperative weeks in Aspen, Hunter Thompson hit the campaign trail again. It was his ninth month in a row of daily engagement, a schedule as extreme as those of the candidates themselves. During the last week of September, the plan was to cover the Republican side of the contest. Thanks to some pulled strings by Pat Buchanan and by Bob Semple, his old friend who'd become the top political reporter for the *New York Times,* Thompson was finally granted a White House press pass.

It happened unexpectedly. He was back in DC when he found out—told by the deputy press secretary Gerald Warren to make his way to Edwards Air Force Base—and suddenly he was flying out to California to cover a rare Nixon campaign swing.

In Oakland, along with all the other reporters, he was corralled into a small roped-off press area two hundred yards from the run-way; and it was from such a remove that he witnessed the stunning choreography of Nixon's emergence from the front ramp of the blue-topped Air Force One. He recognized every gesture: the bussed-in youth-brigade cheerleaders, the awful lyrics to "Nixon Now," the signs and the TV cameras and the president's ghoulish two-handed wave—all of it culminating with the campaign's signature chant: FOUR MORE YEARS!

Later, at a ribbon-cutting ceremony for the new BART subway system, he was herded into a hallway, where a loudspeaker had been set up for the press to listen to the president's speech.

"Jesus," he said to another reporter. "Is it always like this?"

His colleague laughed. "This is accessible," he replied.

Afterward they traveled to Los Angeles. That night, at the Century Plaza, Nixon hosted a $1,000 a plate dinner—emceed by Bob Hope—that the press was once again forced to watch on a closed-circuit television feed. Outside the hotel, thousands of antiwar protestors had gathered, including representatives for the VVAW, who'd arranged themselves beneath an upside-down version of the American flag.

Thompson glared balefully at the TV sets. To Bob Semple, standing next to him now, he said, "They're like slugs on a snail farm." He was talking about the national press. In the face of Nixon's draconian tactics—the lack of basic line-of-sight access—he was disgusted; all presidents battled with the people tasked to report on them, but only someone with truly devastating secrets would seek to limit access to such an absurd extent.

Just then Ron Ziegler, the administration's press secretary— "an arrogant thirty-three-year-old punk who trained for his current job by working as a PR man for Disneyland," Thompson called him—appeared in the hallway, walking quickly.

Thompson tried to ask him about a misguided McGovern attack on Nixon regarding collective bargaining—a softball question, simply meant to start a dialogue—but Ziegler never broke stride. "NO!" he shouted without looking up.

Afterward Thompson turned to Semple. "Does he ever talk like that to you?"

"Yes," the *New York Times'* chief political correspondent said. "Excuse me," Semple added. "I have to get a martini."

Later, Hunter Thompson was smoking near one of the hotel's indoor palm trees when Terry McDonell, a young reporter who'd spoken to Thompson for the first time that evening—and who, years later, would become his close friend—walked up to him.

"Fucking sheep," Thompson exclaimed. "We're all sheep." He was wearing sunglasses, the cigarette shifting in his mouth, and to McDonell he suddenly looked strikingly—unaccountably—sad.

For Thompson, the night was shaping up to be another example of the journalistic profession's inherent inadequacy when it came to covering a figure as powerful and ruthless and duplicitous as the current president. More than a hundred reporters were in attendance for the campaign event at the Century Plaza, and nearly all of them would arrange the paltry amount of information they'd been granted into insipid, next-day write-ups. They all knew, in real time, that they were being fed a false narrative, but none of them seemed to have the time or capacity of insight to take it apart. As a result, they found themselves reinforcing the administration's stage-managed reality. In this sense, the Nixon administration, by manipulating the press's brutal deadline-schedule dependence on information—on *news*—had found an absurdly effective way to promulgate meretriciousness to the general electorate.

At the start of October Nixon's lead had increased to twenty-two points. For Hunter Thompson, a single week of being tethered to the current president was more than enough. Before switching back to report on the McGovern campaign—its doomed final act—he'd write:

This may be the year when we finally come face to face with ourselves; finally just lay back and say it—that we are really just a nation of 220 million used car salesmen with all the money we need to buy guns, and no qualms at all about killing anybody else in the world who tries to make us uncomfortable . . .

McGovern made some stupid mistakes, but in context they seem almost frivolous compared to the things Richard Nixon does every day of his life, on purpose, as a matter of policy and a perfect expression of everything he stands for . . .

That is the one grim truth of this election most likely to come back and haunt us: The options were clearly defined . . . And it is Nixon himself who represents that dark, venal, and incurably violent side of the American character almost every other country in the world has learned to fear and despise. Our Barbie doll President, with his Barbie doll wife and his box-full of Barbie doll children is also America's answer to the monstrous Mr. Hyde. He speaks for the Werewolf in us.

*

As the election approached, Thompson pleaded with Jann Wenner to offer the McGovern campaign free full-page advertisements in the upcoming issues of *Rolling Stone,* but Wenner refused; each one would've used up $2,000 worth of revenue space. He spent the first part of October hanging around the new McGovern headquarters on K Street, offering advice and watching Nixon's lead continue to grow. Then he went back out on the campaign trail so he could follow the last act to the candidacy of George McGovern, someone who—after their year together trying to unseat an incumbent they both saw as a singular threat to our constitutional democracy—Thompson would consider for the rest of his lifetime a close friend.

But by the start of November Hunter Thompson had all but given up. He endured the final week of the campaign on the "Zoo Plane," the chartered United Airlines 727 that ferried the overflow press and network technicians to events. The candidate himself, his staff, and the main reporters rode on the main 727—"The Dakota Queen II"—and on this auxiliary one, the usual rules associated with airplane flight were disregarded. There was unlimited booze. The Rolling Stones blared over the intercom speakers. During landings as many people as possible crammed into the cockpit, watching as the ground rushed up at them through the windows. At takeoff the network cameramen would unspool their excess film, letting it flow like streamers down through the cabin during the forty-five-degree ascent. There was dancing and drugs and sex in the restrooms and silly-string duels that left the seats crusted with neon filament. Onto the overhead racks the passengers had taped more than seven hundred room keys from hotels across the country.

In such a setting Thompson faced the coming election by drinking himself to the point of physical and spiritual collapse. "I no longer even have the energy to grind my own teeth," he wrote. "My brain has gone numb from this madness." On the road for nearly a year, barely seeing his wife and son, he'd sacrificed so much. And for what? To watch firsthand as one of the most honorable candidates in presidential history shouted as if into a void about Richard Nixon's unfitness and corruption—about Watergate, a scandal that CBS had brought to national attention in October but that most of the country still continued to write off as just another example of politics as usual? For Thompson it was nothing short of an American tragedy, one to which there seemed to be no end.

Then, on Tuesday, November 7, George McGovern lost the presidency in the largest landslide in modern history, by 503 electoral and 17,995,488 overall votes: a margin of 23 percentage points. Afterward, Hunter Thompson, with his deadline for the book version of his campaign dispatches looming, was suddenly faced with what seemed an impossible task: trying to *explain* such an outcome.

He did one last piece of reporting, an interview in December with McGovern. They talked about all the things that'd come to pass—about Hubert Humphrey and George Wallace and the Eagleton debacle and the shocking November 7 loss, the sheer size of it . . . about *how* it could've possibly happened. Thompson, more than once, broke down in tears. At the end of their discussion, when the tape recorder was turned off, he said something that McGovern would never forget: "Did the American people know you? Did they know Nixon as you two really were and decide they wanted Nixon? If they really knew him and really knew you and made that judgment, to hell with this book. I don't think it's even worth publishing . . . But if they didn't know you as you really were and didn't know Nixon as he really was, then there's some hope for the future."

Afterward, Thompson holed himself up in San Francisco at the Seal Rock Inn, which overlooked the Pacific, to put the book together—and provide a postmortem on the loss.

He couldn't do it. After days of revision and retrospective footnotes he gave up on trying to hammer out that last burst of analysis; instead, he sat down with his editor from *Rolling Stone*'s Straight Arrow Books, Alan Rinzler, and filled the final section with audio conversations. Rinzler asked the political questions that still needed to be addressed and Thompson, speaking aloud, replied as best he could. The resulting transcript was placed at the end of the narrative, a capstone to the year he'd just endured.

"I was determined," he'd go on to explain in the introduction, "to write about [a presidential campaign] the same way I'd write about anything else—as close to the bone as I could get, and to hell with the consequences." On the whole the book would stand as his best example of impressionistic journalism—of *Gonzo,* as he called it now—a record of calamity in which the effort he exerted to construct it made his statements all the more authentic: he'd done the work of a beat writer but with the insight of a cultural essayist. It was a combination that, when all was said and done, gave the book an elegiac feel: he was watching the Republic fail and there was nothing he could ultimately do but offer his own fragmented testament to its ruin.

In doing so, he also found himself in a unique position to critique the specifically insidious way the Nixon administration had continually manipulated reality to win a second term. By calling them out on their stage management and duplicity and inaccessibility in a manner that the other reporters on the campaign trail each day couldn't or wouldn't do—and by highlighting his own subjectivity from the start—he broke ground as a journalist, as someone whose goal was to evaluate and hold accountable the people in power . . . a task that, when all was said and done, he took as seriously as democracy itself.

In his audio recordings with Rinzler he concluded:

When you vote for President today you're talking about giving
a man dictatorial power for four years. I think it might be better
to have the real business of the presidency conducted by a City
Manager–type, a Prime Minister, somebody who's directly an-
swerable to Congress, rather than a person who moves all his
friends into the White House and does whatever he wants for
four years. The whole framework of the presidency is getting
out of hand. It's come to the point where you almost can't run
unless you can cause people to salivate and whip on each other
with big sticks. You almost have to be a rock star to get the kind
of fever you need to survive in American politics.

## Trading Time Now for Time Later

The Watergate burglary as we've come to understand it today—
part of a far-reaching conspiracy perpetrated by the executive
branch against its perceived enemies—wouldn't emerge as a full-
blown scandal until nearly a year after the botched break-in had
taken place.

On March 24, 1973, District Court judge John Sirica, during
what was supposed to be a sentencing hearing for James McCord
(one of the five burglars who'd been arrested at the scene) instead
read aloud to the audience in the courtroom a letter he'd received,
one in which McCord claimed that the defendants had all been
pressured to keep silent; that the operation involved previously
undisclosed individuals; that it wasn't a CIA gig as had previously
been suspected; and that, now that he was speaking out, he feared
for his safety: "I do believe that retaliatory measures will be taken
against me, my family, and my friends."

Over the next two months a series of similar revelations suggested the conspiracy's astonishing reach. On April 27, the head of
the FBI, L. Patrick Gray, quit after it came out that he'd destroyed

evidence. Three days later, four of Nixon's senior aides—chief of Staff H. R. Haldeman, domestic affairs advisor John Ehrlichman, Attorney General Richard Kleindienst, and White House counsel John Dean—all resigned. In response, the Justice Department appointed a special prosecutor, Archibald Cox, to conduct an independent investigation. On May 17 the Senate Watergate Committee, chaired by North Carolina's Sam Ervin—"Just an ol' country lawyer," as he liked to call himself—began its nationally televised investigation into the scandal.

In Woody Creek, Hunter Thompson spent the start of the summer in front of the television; each morning, he'd drag his color set out onto the porch to watch the daily five-hour broadcast.

He was still trying to recover from the extremes of the campaign trail. Since the fall he and Jann Wenner had been fighting over money—each felt that the other had taken advantage—and that spring, as they negotiated new terms, he explained to Wenner that he was out of gas: "To push it any further, I think, would be coming pretty close to trying to squeeze blood out of last year's corpse." Thompson could sense that something drastic was happening—to his body, to his self-identification as a literary writer. Most of all: to his relationship with the world and the people he cared about.

But he also knew that this was part of the price he'd agreed to pay from the start: the outcome of his hard-living bargain that, for the past decade—via Dexedrine and alcohol—he'd embraced. "At the moment I feel like I've pushed myself—& been pushed—just about as far as I can stretch for the time being," he wrote to Wenner, adding: "One of the central tenets of my concept of chemical 'speed' is that it is not energy in itself, but merely enables the brain & the body to tap latent natural energy resources, which amounts to willfully trading—on a two or three to one basis—time Now for time Later."

In response, he was trying to come up with a more manageable schedule for his life; the plan was to travel less and to take fewer

journalistic assignments, which meant breaking his existing contract with *Rolling Stone* so he could freelance again for lucrative
venues like *Playboy*. He also wanted to focus on book revenues
and advances, as opposed to a steady gig of well-paying reporting
assignments. Recently he'd been looking to plan a conference on
New Politics with all the major Democratic Party heavies, which
*Rolling Stone* would eventually host in (of all places) Elko, Nevada.
There'd also been talk of making a national political run—for Colorado's open senate seat—but he knew better than anyone that a
campaign like that would probably finish him off completely. "I
look forward to as many months as possible of sloth & unemployment," he wrote his mother in April.

*Fear and Loathing: On the Campaign Trail '72* was rush-published
that spring with a first run of ten thousand. But Wenner's printer,
which was based out of Reno, improperly inked the copies, and
only about five hundred were legible, almost all of which were sent
out to newspapers and magazines.

As a result, the reviews started coming in before the books
themselves were available for purchase—a serious marketing
fuck-up, especially in this case, considering the reception. "The
best account yet published of what it feels like to be out there in
the middle of the American political process," Tom Seligson wrote
in a glowing full-page review in the Sunday *New York Times,* arguing that Thompson—as opposed to Norman Mailer or Theodore
White—represented the perfect marriage of in-depth journalism
and a subjectively novelistic style, especially when it came to covering the Nixon administration: "'Fear and Loathing' lets us understand why the men we elect to the presidency may have needle
tracks on their identity."

Across the country—in the *Washington Post,* the *Chicago Tribune,*
the *Los Angeles Times,* and the *New York Post*—it was the same: a
resounding wave of critical recognition that surpassed anything
he'd previously experienced with *Hell's Angels* or *Fear and Loathing
in Las Vegas.*

But for Hunter Thompson it represented another missed opportunity: once again his effort and skill had failed to translate into money. And as the sales sagged due to printing and distribution issues, his resentment toward *Rolling Stone* and Jann Wenner deepened.

Wenner wanted him to go back to Washington to cover the hearings, but that May and June, he hunkered down at Owl Farm and watched the events unfold on TV. Each morning some new incendiary detail came to light—on the very first day there were stories about stolen files and perjury—and it was becoming clear that, sooner or later, proof was bound to emerge linking the president himself to the scandal.

On June 25, John Wesley Dean III entered the Caucus Room of the Senate Office Building, just north of the Capitol, to testify before the committee. He was thirty-four. A Midwesterner, he'd graduated from Georgetown Law School and was close with the Goldwater family, who'd helped him get a job during the Johnson administration as minority counsel on the House Judiciary Committee. In 1970 he was brought on to Nixon's staff, and over the next three years, as the president used the apparatus of the state to attack and silence his critics, he'd been the point man between the Haldeman/Ehrlichman bloc of the executive branch and departments like the IRS and FBI. However, two months earlier, facing the prospect of extensive jail time, Dean had agreed to cooperate with US attorneys and reveal everything he knew.

For his testimony that day he'd cut his blond hair short. He was wearing a pair of tortoiseshell glasses to make himself look older. Thompson, watching in Woody Creek, wrote, "Dean radiates a certain very narrow kind of authority—nothing personal, but the kind of nasal blank-hearted authority you feel in the presence of the taxman or a very polite FBI agent." The former White House counsel spoke with a deliberative cadence, his clauses accruing in an eerily Nabokovian fashion: "To one who was in the White

House and became somewhat familiar with its inner-workings," he said in his opening statement, "the Watergate matter was an inevitable outgrowth of a climate of excessive concern over the political impact of demonstrators, excessive concern over leaks, an insatiable appetite for political intelligence, all coupled with a do-it-yourself White House staff regardless of the law." He referred to a "covert intelligence operation" run by multiple operatives. He shed light on the Ellsberg and Brookings Institution plots. A full transcript of his testimony was published in the *New York Times*. His appearance before the senate committee would stretch out across five days; at one point he described a recent March meeting in which he tried to warn Nixon of the criminal nature of their actions: "I began by telling the president that there was a cancer growing on the presidency, and if the cancer was not removed, the president himself would be killed by it."

Afterward Thompson wrote, "If the Ervin committee lets even half of Dean's testimony stand, Richard Nixon won't be able to give away dollar bills in Times Square on the Fourth of July."

Throughout the hearings, the central issue could be boiled down to a question that Senator Howard Baker repeatedly posed: "What did the president know, and when did he know it?" John Dean was the first inner-circle witness to step up and answer unequivocally: *Nixon knew it all, and he fucking knew it all along.*

✳

"Everything Richard Milhous Nixon ever stood for," Hunter Thompson wrote while watching Dean's testimony, "was going up in smoke right in front of our eyes." He set aside his issues with Jann Wenner; he knew he needed to get to Washington as soon as possible.

He arrived in mid-July, the city a steaming basin of thick mid-Atlantic air that never seemed to clear. *Rolling Stone* got him a front-row press pass to the hearings. On one of his first days there—Monday, July 16—the senators called a surprise witness:

Alexander Butterfield, an assistant to Nixon. Thompson was a few feet away when Butterfield responded to a question from the minority counsel: "I was aware of listening devices, yes sir."

Thompson couldn't believe it; in his notebook he scribbled: "*Butterfield* regales room with tales of elaborate taping machine." From this moment on, the scandal would take an entirely new shape: that of a battle between the president and Congress over the possession of this amazing cache. "Nixon Wired His Phone, Offices to Record All Conversations; Senators Will Seek the Tapes," the *New York Times* proclaimed the next day.

That week he also witnessed testimony from H. R. Haldeman and John Ehrlichman. He was struck by the physicality of the hearing room, "a sense of smallness . . . unlike the vast theater it looks on TV." From his up-close vantage point, he found himself gazing for what began to feel like unnatural lengths into the eyes of the committee members. "Interesting," he wrote in his notes. "Sitting directly behind witness chair—you can look right at Ervin and catch his facial expressions—as if he was looking at *me*. Nodding— fixed stare—occasional quick notes with yellow pencil."

*Rolling Stone* had flown out Ralph Steadman from London to join him. And the photographer Annie Leibovitz, only twenty-three at the time, was also on hand for the magazine. Together the three of them crowded into the Old Senate Office Building for the show. At one point Steadman, drunk, tripped and spilled a beer all over Senator Sam Ervin, who was on his way to the bathroom. Eventually Thompson began to find the whole thing tedious; he liked to watch the proceedings on television in a nearby bar, and whenever something dramatic happened he'd bolt over and join the crowd to witness it live.

That week, Thompson drove up to George McGovern's house in Chevy Chase, where the senator was throwing a party to mark the one-year anniversary of his nomination to the Democratic ticket. Over two hundred people attended—the staffers, aides, and journalists who'd spent the previous year together covering the campaign. Thompson had been worried that the gathering would be a downer considering how the election had played out, but instead it turned into a loose and festive reunion; in the context of Watergate, McGovern's candidacy was no longer being talked about as a mistake-filled blowout. With reporters Jules Witcover, Jack Germond, Dick Stout, and others the conversation turned to trying to unpack the "dirty tricks" that Nixon had employed in the last election. "Which one of the Secret Service men assigned to protect McGovern had been reporting daily to Jeb Magruder at CREEP," Thompson wrote, "and which one of the ten or 12 journalists with access to the innards of George's strategy had been on CREEP's payroll at $1500 a month."

He and McGovern had kept in touch. Recently he'd sent the senator a copy of the book (as well as a signed copy of *Fear and Loathing in Las Vegas* for his wife, Eleanor), and in addition to the party at the senator's house they'd also scheduled a dinner together, a chance to catch up in a more intimate setting.

A few days later, McGovern picked up Thompson at the Washington Hilton on Connecticut Avenue, and they headed to a local Mexican restaurant on Seventeenth and R Streets. Eleanor joined them, along with Steadman and a few others. They talked about Watergate. About literature and marijuana laws and the mood of the country. There was a guitarist making the rounds between tables, and when Thompson saw him he turned to Steadman. "You know 'Masters of War,' right?" he said. He was insistent. "Ralph! Sing 'Masters of War' for the Senator."

Steadman borrowed the guitar and started in with the chords. Suddenly everyone at the table began to belt out Bob Dylan's protest song against Vietnam—singing it for one of the few people within the powerful chambers of the American system who'd been listening from the start.

George McGovern received the gesture graciously. That summer Thompson had written him: "Despite all the foul things I said about your pragmatism, I look back on your campaign as one of the high points in my life and one of the most honest & honorable efforts in the history of politics, including my own, I might add . . . and that's rarified air to be fixed in."

"We had entire different personalities, but we hit it off," McGovern would later say. "He used to tell me I was an honest man—and I don't think he delivered that judgment on very many people. He also said, 'You're the best of the lousy lot,' but I always took that as a compliment."

It was a reference to *The Great Gatsby*, this compliment—to a scene at the end of the book, during what would turn out to be the final exchange between the narrator, Nick Carraway, and his enigmatic friend James Gatz:

> We shook hands and I started away. Just before I reached the hedge I remembered something and turned around.
>
> "They're a rotten crowd," I shouted across the lawn. "You're worth the whole damn bunch put together."
>
> I've always been glad I said that. It was the only compliment I ever gave him, because I disapproved of him from beginning to end. First he nodded politely, and then his face broke into that radiant and understanding smile, as if we'd been in ecstatic cahoots on that fact all the time.

\*

Hunter Thompson got back to Woody Creek in the middle of August. He'd been impressed by the overall coverage of Watergate: "There was not a hell of a lot of room for a Gonzo journalist to operate in that high-tuned atmosphere. For the first time in memory, the Washington press corps was working very close to the peak of its awesome but normally dormant potential."

Instead, the role he would carve out for himself during the final year of the Nixon administration would perhaps be best described as that of an essayist: the most pertinent part of his writing on

Watergate—narratives that tended to dramatize just how difficult it'd become for him to compose *anything*—consisted of extensive ruminations on Richard Milhous Nixon's drastic turn of fortune.

"What will Nixon do?" he wrote that fall. He quoted a comment the president had recently made: "When I am attacked, it is my instinct to strike back." This was a man, Thompson explained, who'd once been so successful "for the same reason he was finally brought low. He kept pushing, pushing, pushing—and inevitably he pushed too far." Now, backed into a corner in the battle over the tapes—after October's Saturday Night Massacre, in which he fired the attorney general and his deputies for refusing to replace the independent prosecutor, Archibald Cox—was there any way out of the situation except with a constitutional crisis?

At the end of the year, the *New York Times* contacted Thompson about writing an editorial on Watergate. "Fear and Loathing in the Bunker" was published on January 1, 1974. In it he went through possible end-games, from resignation on account of "health reasons" to a preemptive nuclear strike against China, "with the full and formal support of our old ally, Russia." The best-case scenario, which he also laid out, was beginning to seem less and less likely: "All we can really ask of him, at this point, is a semblance of self-restraint until some way can be found to get rid of him gracefully. This is not a cheerful prospect . . . "

In the meantime the economy was sliding. The energy crisis—precipitated by the Yom Kippur War and subsequent oil embargo by Middle Eastern countries—continued. There'd been inflation and stock market crashes and apocalyptically long gas-station lines. "The greedy, fascistic incompetence of Richard Nixon's Presidency," he wrote at the end of his op-ed, "will leave scars on the minds and lives of a whole generation—his supporters and political allies no less than his opponents." In the end the tragedy wasn't just about Nixon, at least in the strictest sense; what was really at stake would be much bigger than the current moment. As he'd written that summer: "The slow-rising central horror of 'Watergate' is not that it might grind down to the reluctant impeachment of a vengeful thug of a president whose entire political career has been a monument to the same kind of cheap shots and treachery he finally got nailed for, but that we might somehow fail to learn something from it."

*

At the end of 1973 Oscar Acosta wrote to Hunter Thompson: "You cocksuckers have been ripping me off for a long time." Recently he'd been informed (incorrectly) that *Fear and Loathing in Las Vegas* was being optioned as a movie, and now he demanded 20 percent of the profits; the release he'd signed was only for the book, he argued. "Believe me, man—I am dead serious . . . It would be better for all if we settled it and forgot it. Besides you can afford it now." He signed the letter: "Your old ex-friend, Oscar."

Earlier that year they'd spent a weekend together in Mexico, where Acosta had been living on and off—Thompson had traveled there to write a piece on shark hunting for *Playboy*—but in the time since, Acosta's life had taken a precipitous turn. He'd moved past his Benzedrine habit; now he was mainlining methedrine. His health was faltering. Just before the holidays he wrote Thompson again—this time without the threats. Instead he tried to explain how terrible things had gotten. "I am blackballed everywhere," he lamented, "in Frisco & L.A. I've lived off food stamps and petty theft. As you know, counter-culture 'legends' don't pay off in cash . . . Despite all messages & nightmares to the contrary, I still am looking to you as my only serious white connection for the big contract." He offered to help with Thompson's proposed senate campaign. He talked about a political alliance between the Freak Power and Chicano movement. Once again he asked for his 20 percent cut of the film rights. "Deduct my loans from you to me," he added, "and wish me well, as I do you."

Thompson replied a few days later: "What in the fuck would cause you to ask me for *money*—after all the insane bullshit you've put me through for the past two years?" He wasn't in the mood for reconciliation. "The ugly truth, Oscar, is that there *never was* and as far as I know *never will be* a fucking penny for the film rights to *Vegas*." It would prove, in retrospect, to be their final exchange. "I can still make a living by *writing,* old sport—but all you seem to be able to do is burn your ex-friends." He signed the letter: "Good luck, Whitey."

At Thanksgiving Acosta saw his family for the last time. In January, hospitalized for his stomach ulcer, he wrote a long letter to his son Marco, in which he explained his plans to start a new book: *The Rise and Fall of General Z.* He also sketched out his last will and testament. When he'd regained his strength, he left California and headed back down to Mexico. Six months later—sometime in June 1974—he called Marco and said that he was about to get on a friend's sailboat. He would never be seen or heard from again.

In the years since, speculation about his fate would run rampant. There was the initial assumption that he'd been shot and thrown overboard during a drug deal that'd gone badly. Or the boat had been swept up and wrecked by a storm off the Pacific coast. Or maybe something much more sinister was at play: what if he'd been targeted and assassinated by the American intelligence agencies—they'd been following him nearly a decade, after all—for running guns to Mexican rebels? No one would ever really know for sure. This much was true: Acosta was gone.

## Your Brain to Cement

On April 30, 1974, Richard Nixon, hoping to somehow avoid the outcome that was beginning to appear inevitable, released his personal version of the transcripts of the White House recordings relevant to the Watergate break-in—as opposed to the tapes themselves, which the special counsel had subpoenaed. These redactions, featuring extensive "unintelligible" and "expletive deleted" passages, were immediately questioned and dismissed by nearly everyone, from the press to the politicians to the general public. "One of the darkest documents I ever saw," Hunter Thompson would say about these transcripts.

In response, Congress and the Justice Department simply ignored these facsimiles and kept up their pursuit of the tapes themselves. By midsummer it all appeared to be heading to a showdown at the Supreme Court; the only hope Nixon could muster was that the Democratic-controlled House would jump the gun and impeach him ahead of time, which would provide the opportunity, however slim, to peel off in the Senate the thirty-four votes necessary to avoid conviction.

Once again Thompson planned to spend part of the summer in Washington, positioning himself beneath its deepening pool of heat and stagnant skies, with the hopes of finally witnessing the downfall of the person who for more than a decade had embodied the most dour and corruptible characteristics of the Republic's centuries-old identity. Jann Wenner agreed to fund Thompson's presence there, despite their continuing disputes over money. He'd head to DC in July. In the meantime, *Rolling Stone* had another assignment for him; recently the magazine had come into possession of an advance copy of a newly released book of Sigmund Freud's writing, *The Cocaine Papers*—about the famous Viennese's hands-on studies of the drug—and David Felton, now a senior editor, mailed the book to Woody Creek . . . along with a large supply of the drug. The plan was for Thompson to write a *participatory* take on the text, as it were.

Cocaine was a substance that Hunter Thompson had in the past avoided—he saw it as an overpriced party drug for dilettantes and celebrities and rich people—and for this assignment, taking it in large quantities for the first time, he found that the only way to articulate his thoughts on the subject was through a series of audio recordings.

"It seems to induce a kind of speedy interior reaction with a very sloppy exterior reaction," he noted. "Jesus, I do seem like I've been beaten in the teeth with some kind of mush hammer." He spent more than a week burning through the supply Felton had sent, composing reels of audio in the process, the edited-down transcript of which he then sent to *Rolling Stone* (in place of a written article).

It was never published. For the rest of his life—for the next thirty years—he'd use cocaine regularly, substituting this more re-active stimulant for Dexedrine, which no longer seemed to help him function in the way it once had. "From then on," his editor David Felton would later reflect, "he wouldn't do a story unless you included cocaine with the payment. And he dried up and couldn't write. I was there when he had huge fits of screaming because he couldn't write the next sentence . . . It was very difficult for him. It turns your brain to cement."

This switch coincided with what appeared to be a new career path: that year he'd found that he could make a great deal of money on the college lecture circuit—delivering impromptu monologues and raking in $20,000 fees along the way—which allowed him to keep up the image of a lifestyle he now found himself, for all intents and purposes, trapped beneath.

His career would never be the same. Over the next three de-cades, he'd still write some fascinating short pieces, but in the wake of these two changes (cocaine and fame) he'd never again find the dedication and perspective to render the heart of the American condition—especially within a political context—in the way his more sustained work once had. Years later Sandy would say:

I do not think he was a great writer. I think he clearly had great potential, both as a writer and a leader. However, he fell, dra-matically, and a very, very long time ago. Hunter wanted to be a great writer and he had the genius, the talent, and, early on, the will and the means. He was horrified by whom he had become and ashamed—or I really should say tortured. He knew he had failed. He knew that his writing was absolutely not great. This was part of the torture. And yet, he could never climb back.

＊

After Hunter Thompson got back from the presidential campaign trail, Sandy was opening the mail—at the time he was down in Mexico working on his *Playboy* article—when, in a package from Lucian Truscott IV, the young *Village Voice* writer who'd also reported on the 1972 conventions, she found a cassette; attached to it was a note: "It may not be a good idea to let Sandy listen to this tape."

It was a recording from an afternoon in New York. Truscott's voice was on it. So was Thompson's. At one point, a young woman could be heard speaking. She said, "Shall I get you another Wild Turkey, Hunter?" Immediately from the tone Sandy knew: they were having an affair.

She confronted him, made him promise to break it off. In the end she assumed—falsely—that this was his only extramarital relationship. Both of them continued to drink heavily. And when Thompson started to use cocaine regularly, Sandy did, too; they began taking the drug together. One night, during an especially brutal comedown, she said to him, "Is this the time when there's only two ways to go? . . . More cocaine or take Thorazine? Is this it?" Thorazine (chlorpromazine) was a strong antipsychotic sedative; since the 1940s it had been used mainly to treat schizophrenia.

"That's it," Thompson said. "That's where we are."

Over the course of the next four years, the two of them would separate, get back together, break up again, and then return to Owl Farm to try and make things work one last time. In 1978, Sandy initiated divorce proceedings; with Juan, who was in his early teens, she finally left Hunter Thompson for good.

＊

In May 1974, Republican congressman Charles Wiggins, one of Nixon's staunchest supporters, tried to contextualize the mushrooming Watergate scandal: "These things go in fifty-year cycles," he said, "from Grant to Harding to Nixon."

That summer, Hunter Thompson had posted up at the Washington Hilton once again, attending morning news conferences and afternoon hearings—rarely sleeping—as the drama drew to a close. At 11:00 a.m. on July 24—a rain-gray Wednesday, unseasonably cool—Chief Justice Warren Burger revealed the Supreme Court's unanimous decision in *The United States v. Nixon*: the president was ordered to hand over all pertinent tapes.

At last Richard Nixon had no more cards left to play. If he failed to do so he'd be impeached. And if he complied, well, the truth would be confirmed.

Which was exactly what happened: on August 5, the 5:00 p.m. CBS News announced that a previously undisclosed tape, recorded six days after the break-in, proved incontrovertibly that the president had ordered the head of the FBI to stop any and all investigations into the matter. "Call Pat Gray," Nixon had been caught telling Haldeman, "and just say, 'Stay the hell out of this!'" *The smoking gun,* as it would become known.

The House Judiciary Committee worked to finalize its articles of impeachment. Barry Goldwater, seventy-three years old and still representing Arizona, paid the president a visit and explained that the Senate was prepared to convict him by a large margin. Representative Wiggins told CBS it was time to plan for "the orderly transition of power from Richard Nixon to Gerald Ford."

The next day, Hunter Thompson was jolted awake in his Washington Hilton bed around noon by a loud pounding on his door. "Wake up!" Craig Vetter, another *Rolling Stone* writer, shouted from the hallway. "The whole town's gone crazy—the son of a bitch has caved in—he's quitting!"

There were rumors that Nixon was about to address a joint session of Congress; that he was planning to give an impromptu speech on all three networks; and that he was actually set to appear, at any moment, in the briefing room alongside Ron Zeigler. The White House switchboard was completely jammed, something that had never before happened.

Thompson and Vetter decided to set up a command post at the Hilton pool, where they'd worked out a deal with a security guard to allow them after-hours access. With a portable TV set and FM radio they camped out at a table near the lifeguard stand to see out the last few hours of their summer-long death watch. Soon it was official: "I shall resign the presidency effective at noon tomorrow," Nixon announced from the Oval Office.

The next morning, Hunter Thompson headed down to the pool at dawn. The plan was for him to join up with Annie Leibovitz and document for history the impending departure. In the meantime, after setting up his portable TV, he got in and swam a few laps. Rain scattered the surface of the water. The town suddenly seemed empty—desolate. He climbed out and, exhausted, lay down in the grass. He was listening for the news. Soon it was time for him to change clothes and take a taxi down to the White House, a mile and a half away. Leibovitz was waiting for him. But he never moved.

"Hunter was back at the hotel," Leibovitz would write in her memoir. "Every reporter on the planet was at the White House, and Hunter was in the swimming pool at the Hilton with a battery-powered TV set."

Alone in the grass with his portable television, Thompson watched Nixon deliver his farewell address from the East Room.

"Always remember," the president said, sobbing openly, to his cabinet and staff. "Others may hate you, but those who hate you don't win unless you hate them—and then you destroy yourself." On a red carpet he walked to the South Lawn, where the helicopter was waiting. And then Richard Nixon was flying away. For a

moment, as Thompson sat there watching the televised departure—
the chop of distant rotors indistinguishable from the city's charac-
teristic blare—it was as if a light had gone out of the world:

> There would not be this kind of morning anymore, because
> the main ingredient for that mix was no longer available in
> Washington . . .
> No . . . even with the pool and the ale and grass and the
> portable TV set, the morning news will not be the same with-
> out the foul specter of Richard Nixon glaring out of the tube.
> But the war is over now and he lost . . . Gone but not forgot-
> ten, missed but not mourned; we will not see another one like
> him for quite a while. He was dishonest to a fault, the truth was
> not in him, and if it can be said that he resembled any other
> living animal in this world, it could only have been the hyena.

＊

Afterward, like Nixon, Hunter Thompson flew west to California;
Wenner had set aside eight pages for the article on the resignation.
Thompson camped out in the *Rolling Stone* office suite, which
was stocked with drugs and booze, in order to meet his rapidly
approaching deadline.

Which brings us now to a final, time-lapsed image, our last
glimpse of Hunter S. Thompson before we take our leave of him,
here:

Once again he's alone in a room. Next to him is a full vial of
cocaine. It's empty. It's full. It's empty again. The sun rises and sets.
There's darkness. There's light. The blue morning depth of the sky.
He hasn't typed a single word. Still he won't leave his desk. He's
been sitting at his typewriter for days. But the page remains blank.
The image doesn't change. The deadline comes and goes. He's
missed it. Remember: the worst eulogy of all is the one you never
get a chance to write for yourself.

# ACKNOWLEDGMENTS

This book would never have been completed without the help of so many talented, thoughtful individuals:

My agent, the outstanding Kathy Anderson; Ben Adams, my patient and insightful editor; the excellent crew at PublicAffairs, including Clive Priddle, Josie Urwin, Miguel Cervantes, Collin Tracy, and Jane Robbins Mize; and Angela Baggetta, publicist extraordinaire.

Early readers of the manuscript: Michelle Delgado; Nick Kowalczyk; and the great Margaret Harrell, whose effort, generosity, and insight proved invaluable.

Everyone who took the time to sit down for interviews, to answer research questions, and to engage in wide-ranging discussions on the life and times of Hunter S. Thompson: Dr. Bob Geiger; Bruce Innes; David Hamilton; Jane Click of the Aspen Historical Society; Kay Salter; Terry McDonell; Zane Kesey; Ernesto Vigil; Phillip Rodriguez; David Ventura; and the brilliant and tireless Ricardo Lopez.

All the friends and family across the country who let me stay with them while I was reporting and writing: Kathy and Brian

Duisenberg in Kirkwood; Mikey Denevi and Julia Ortinez-Hansen in San Francisco; Jim Colyar and Elena Toscano in Sonoma; Matt Karpinski in Colorado; Chris and Emily Denevi on Summit; Chris Maier and Pam Carmasine on H Street; Tom Hope in Philadelphia; Charlie Gans in New York; and Mike Brownfield in Cleveland.

The friends and family of Hunter S. Thompson in Louisville, as well as the coordinators of the amazing GonzoFest: Juan Thompson; Ron Whitehead; Lauren Hendricks and L. Kevin Tur; Chandra Gordon; Lee Remington; Art Dietz; and Jim Blanton.

The magazine and journal editors who published the essays from which this book would evolve: Jonny Diamond, Paula Whyman, Cari Romm, Jeff Gleaves, and Nate Brown, who believed in this project from the start.

My amazing colleagues and students at George Mason University; my nonfiction teammate, Kyoko Mori, whose support made it possible to somehow write a book *and* teach classes at the same time; the Little Salon crew in DC; and all the friends who offered encouragement and insight into the project, including but not limited to Andre Perry, Clay Hopper, M. Thomas Gammarino, Bella Pollen, Cutter Wood, Jen Percy, Dylan Nice, Adam Winkler, Mark Bresnan, Matt Davis, and Chris Maier.

Most of all, there's my family, both extended and immediate: Palmer and Lee, whose help made it possible to finish the book; the Denevis in Los Gatos; Chris (for the daily conversations); Katie and Ed and Penny and Teddy; Sean and Crystal; my mother and father; Sylvia; Jack, the most amazingly empathetic and thoughtful young man in the world; and Brett, who, unlike me, never doubted that this book—that being a writer—was worthwhile.

I'm also deeply indebted to previous works concerning Hunter Thompson and the 1960s/1970s political scene: *Freak Power* by Daniel Joseph Watkins; *Stories I Tell* Myself by Juan Thompson; *Chicago '68* by David Farber; *Love and Riot* by Burton Moore; *Washington Journal* by Elizabeth Drew; *To Aspen and Back* by Peggy Clifford; Margaret Harrell's *Keep This Quiet!* series; William

McKeen's *Outlaw Journalist;* and everything James Salter wrote about Aspen.

"You have to keep putting out books," Salter said during a dinner I was lucky enough to spend with him a few years ago. "They're the only thing that will last." I like to think that Hunter Thompson's astonishing career is a testament to this statement— to the difficulty and reward at the heart of the writer's endeavor. Creating a book is already a nearly impossible task, and all I can say is that without the help and generosity of so many people, what you're reading here would've never existed.

Or to quote Thompson's acknowledgement in *Hell's Angels*: "To the friends who lent me money and kept me mercifully unemployed. No writer can function without them. Again, thanks."

# NOTES

For every detail in the text, I've attempted to delineate a source. The distance between these sources and the narrative itself can vary: some are rendered more directly than others. I've tried to map this distance in the best manner possible through the use of these endnotes, a section that, for me, is about authenticity—why you, the reader, should take the time to trust and engage what it is I'm writing. My goal is for you to understand my starting point with the material *and* the manner in which I've ended up using it. As with a work of translation, a research-based biography of this sort is really one of *relation*: some meanings come across perfectly. Others demand the intercession of the translator to expand upon and render a more explicitly subjective judgment. Facts are never singular, even if Truth may very well be. In summary, I believe that it's the responsibility of someone in my position to *show* the work that went into the story's composition. Which is what I've tried to accomplish, here . . .

## Author's Note

ix     **"to pass an astonishing amount":** James Salter, in his memoir *Burning the Days*, 203, writes: "Life passes into pages if it passes into anything, and his had been written." Salter was talking about the writer Irwin Shaw, whom he'd been close to, but the sentiment is especially applicable to the life of Hunter Thompson—a neighbor of Salter's in Aspen, where they became friends in the late 1960s. Salter expanded on this sentiment in the essay "Why I Write," which was included in his 2017 collection of nonfiction *Don't Save Anything*, 7: "Within me was an insistence that whatever we did, the things that were said, the dawns, the cities, the lives, all of it had to be drawn together, made into pages, or it was in danger of not existing, of never having been. There comes a time when you realize that everything is a dream, and only those things preserved in writing have any possibility of being real."

x     **"that fantastic possibility":** Watkins, *Freak Power*, 70.

## Chapter One

2     **"startled by a knock at the door":** The details for this scene are drawn from the series of letters Thompson wrote in the aftermath of Kennedy's murder, published in his first volume of correspondence, *The Proud Highway*, 417–425.

2     **"this pioneer-family rancher wasn't the joking type":** Thompson, *Proud Highway*, 418. On the evening of Kennedy's murder Thompson would write to Paul Semonin, "Wayne Vagneur, the rancher up the road, stopped by with the news. I started to cry but figured that was not called for, so cursed instead. He is not the type for jokes, or otherwise I could not have believed it."

3     **"first televised presidential debate":** Thompson, *Proud Highway*, 234.

3     **"With a friend":** Paul Semonin, a friend from Louisville.

3     **"three years since":** In his letter to Semonin that night he wrote: "But there is no sense crying for lost hope and a dead effort that was only a foot in the door but at least the door was open as long as the foot was there" (Thompson, *Proud Highway*, 419).

4     **"gotten a foot in the door":** Decades later, looking back on the uniqueness of the Kennedy administration—in comparison to what would come after—Thompson would write:

> It seems to me that the underlying assumption of any public protest—any public disagreement with the government, "the system," or "the establishment," by any name—is that the men in charge of whatever you're protesting against are actually listening, whether they later admit it or not, and that if you run your protest Right, it will make a difference. Norman Mailer made this point a long time ago when he said that the election of JFK gave him a sense, for the

first time in his life, that he could actually communicate with the White House. (*Kingdom of Fear,* 81)

4    **"Billy Graham sermons":** Thompson, *Proud Highway,* 421.

4    **"old friend from Louisville":** Thompson, *Proud Highway,* 418.

4    **"some other communist satellite":** Thompson, *Proud Highway,* 418.

5    **"lead to nuclear war":** White, *Making of the President: 1964,* 311.

5    **"Shitrain":** Thompson, *Proud Highway,* 419–420.

5    **"This was what he imagined":** That night, he wrote to Semonin:

> "I am trying to compose a reaction to the heinous, stinking, shit-filled thing that occurred today . . . This savage unbelievable killing, this monstrous stupidity, has guaranteed that my children and yours will be born in a shitrain" (Thompson, *Proud Highway,* 419).

In another letter that night, to William Kennedy, he added, "We now enter the era of the shitrain, President Johnson, and the hardening of the arteries" (ibid., 420).

5    **"dirty itself in endless succession":** From Thompson, *On the Campaign Trail '72,* 69: "The shittrain began on November 22nd, 1963, in Dallas—when some twisted little geek blew the President's head off." (Ten years after the fact, the metaphorical *rain* of shit preempted by the Kennedy murder has become, instead, a *train*—and whether this change represents an evolution in the metaphor or simply a copyediting mistake I'm not entirely sure, though in my opinion the best explanation is most likely the former.)

6    **"cared to think":** For more on Thompson's experiences in South America, see Kenney, *Footloose American*; and Hamilton, "In an Innertube, On the Amazon."

6    **"indistinguishable from speculation":** Thompson, *Proud Highway,* 421.

6    **"'the time of the end'":** Thompson, *Proud Highway,* 424.

7    **"gutted as well":** Thompson, *Proud Highway,* 424.

7    **"the fight that was to come":** From his letter at the time: "What I have in mind is steady work, day and night, until after the '64 election, and then take stock again," he explained a week after the assassination (Thompson, *Proud Highway,* 425).

7    **"an ugly, unprecedented battle":** "My view at the time is that politics in this country for the next nine months is going to resemble nothing more or less than a Nazi cockfight" (Thompson, *Proud Highway,* 424).

7    **"keep that man Nixon out of the presidency":** He stated his opposition bluntly: "I don't mind saying that my primary motive is to keep that man Nixon out of the presidency" (Thompson, *Proud Highway,* 424).

7    **"William Kennedy, his close friend":** William Kennedy and Thompson had first met in Puerto Rico, after corresponding regarding a newspaper job; they'd be friends for the next four decades. William Kennedy would go on to win the Pulitzer Prize in 1984 for his novel *Ironweed.*

8 **"that short phrase he made famous"**: Thompson, *Proud Highway,* 419. In his introductory note to this collection of correspondence, Douglas Brinkley, Thompson's literary executor, wrote: "'Fear and loathing'—without apologies to Søren Kierkegaard—soon became Thompson's trademark phrase, his shorthand for justified contempt toward an overindulgent and dysfunctional consumer culture" (xxi).

8 **"John F. Kennedy's assassination"**: Thompson, *Proud Highway,* 439.

8 **"Sandy's mother"**: Thompson, *Proud Highway,* 381.

8 **"their relationship at the time"**: This analysis is drawn from Sandy's comments in E. Jean Carroll's biography *Hunter* (99–109); from Thompson's letters from the time period in *The Proud Highway*; and from chapters 2 and 3 in the oral history *Gonzo: The Life of Hunter Thompson*. To elaborate on their relationship a bit further: They each had a surprising ability to modulate the polarity of the other's personality—in the way Thompson's enthusiasm made Sandy feel that things mattered and could be changed for the better; in the way Sandy's eagerness allowed Thompson to feel present and substantial.

9 **"hazel eyes"**: Sandy's driver's license from that time was included in the FBI file that would eventually be opened on Hunter Thompson; for more, see Nash, "Hunter S. Thompson's Appropriately NSFW FBI File."

9 **"conservative curriculum"**: Carroll, *Hunter,* 77–78.

9 **"promised to someone else"**: Seymour and Wenner, *Gonzo,* 65.

9 **"Agar slept in the bed between them"**: Seymour and Wenner, *Gonzo,* 66–67.

9 **"Jack London had called it"**: Jack London had popularized this name of Sonoma in his 1913 novel *The Valley of the Moon.*

9 **"Only a few of the roads were paved"**: These details are from Thompson's descriptions of Glen Ellen in his letters in *Proud Highway,* 439–465.

10 **"morning in March"**: Seymour and Wenner, *Gonzo,* 66.

10 **"You could've given birth in a field"**: Seymour and Wenner, *Gonzo,* 66.

10 **"one of Thompson's favorite books"**: In Seymour and Wenner, *Gonzo,* 66, William Kennedy explains: "Hunter loved Fitzgerald, and he named his son Juan Fitzgerald Thompson after Scott and also after the other Fitz—John Fitzgerald Kennedy."

10 **"Juan had suffered a health scare"**: Loiederman, in his 2005 *Los Angeles Times* essay "The Darker Side of a Night with Hunter S. Thompson," explains that Juan received a blood transfusion just after his birth.

10 **"Hunter Thompson's typewriter"**: Thompson, *Proud Highway,* 451.

10 **"best in her life"**: Seymour and Wenner, *Gonzo,* 66.

11 **"April 7 letter"**: Thompson, *Proud Highway,* 449.

11 **"the 'deep ugly funk' he found himself in"**: Thompson, *Proud Highway,* 439.

11 **"what did Sandy think about bringing"**: This scene is based on rec-
ollections in *Gonzo,* and from details provided by Bob Geiger during our
interview in Sonoma.

11 **"South Vietnam"**: For more on Geiger's novel, published by Atheneum, see
the April 15, 1964, write-up in *Kirkus Reviews,* "Ask Me for Tomorrow."

12 **"shorter than the right"**: 3/8 of an inch, to be precise. Thompson, *Fear and
Loathing in Las Vegas,* 199.

12 **"the world around them"**: The summary of Thompson and Geiger's relationship is drawn from the April 27, 2017, interview I conducted with Geiger.

13 **"Freedom Riders"**: Seymour and Wenner, *Gonzo,* 70.

13 **"*Impressionistic Journalism*"**: Thompson, *Proud Highway,* 450.

13 **"functioning alcoholic"**: Years later Sandy would say:

> He'd been drinking for a long time. I don't know when he started,
> fourteen or something like that. He never went a day without alco-
> hol. Me either. The alcohol dulled the pain. And then what the speed
> would do for him was to sharpen his mind again so he could write, so
> he could think. And then the alcohol would take the edge off again.
> It was an incredible formula for years and years. (Carroll, *Hunter,* 100)

13 **"surprisingly well"**: During his trip through South America, notably; for
more, see Seymour and Wenner, *Gonzo,* chapter 2, "An Itinerant Professional,"
and Hamilton, "In an Innertube, On the Amazon."

13 **"the assassination would precipitate"**: On April 28, 1964, Thompson
wrote to Paul Semonin: "For the past two months I have been in a black bog
of depression, fathering a son, living among people more vicious and venal
than I ever thought existed, and bouncing from one midnight to the next in
a blaze of stupid drunkenness" (*Proud Highway,* 451).

13 **"no matter the circumstances"**: From my interview with Bob Geiger.

14 **"but he'd never taken them regularly"**: Seymour and Wenner, *Gonzo,* 56.

14 **"many thousand Americans"**: for more on cigarettes and stimulants, see
Gladwell, "Running from Ritalin."

15 **"just as he did alcohol"**: In a 1969 essay, Thompson would write: "Getting
toward dawn now, very foggy in the head . . . and no Dexedrine left. For the
first time in at least five years I am out of my little energy bombs" ("First Visit
with Mescalito," from *Songs of the Doomed,* 129).

15 **"*National Observer*"**: Thompson, *Proud Highway,* 451.

15 **"political context"**: McKeen, *Outlaw Journalist,* 87–88.

15 **"four articles"**: Here's a list of the articles he wrote on this trip:

> "What Lured Hemingway to Ketchum?" (5/25/64)
> "Whither the Old Copper Capital of the West? To Boom or Bust?"
> (6/1/64)
> "Thoughts on the Future of Butte, Montana" (6/15/64)
> "The Atmosphere Has Never Been Quite the Same" (6/15/64)

"Why Montana's 'Shanty Irishman' Corrals New Votes Year After Year" (6/22/64)

(Thompson, *Great Shark Hunt*, 593)

15 **"sense of conviction"**: Reprinted in Thompson, *Great Shark Hunt*, 375.

16 **"trophy"**: McKeen, *Outlaw Journalist*, 88.

17 **"high above the floor and the delegates there"**: Thompson, *Fear and Loathing in America*, 69; at first he had a *Wall Street Journal* badge (through the *National Observer*).

17 **"5,423 press credentials"**: Dickerson, "Never Goldwater."

17 **"Dwight Eisenhower"**: Norman Mailer, in his *Esquire* article "In the Red Light," which would eventually be published as a stand-alone book, documented the 1964 convention in extensive detail. Two of his comments help sum up what it must've been like to see Eisenhower that evening:

> He was in a private pond. He had been in one for years. Something had been dying in him for years, the proportions and magnitude of his own death no doubt, and he was going down into the cruelest of fates for an old man, he was hooked on love like an addict, not large love, but the kind of mild tolerant love which shields an old man from hatred. And so on he would go as if he were sinking very slowly and quietly into the waters of his future death which might be a year away or ten years away but was receiving him nonetheless like a marsh into which something disappeared twitch by twitch, some beating of wet wings against his fate. (Mailer, *In the Red Light*, loc. 294)

And:

> Ike usually fought a speech to a draw. It was hard to listen. (Ibid., loc. 482)

18 **"'My deep dedication to Republicanism!' he said"**: Mailer, *In the Red Light*, loc. 480.

18 **"invade Cuba"**: Mailer, *In the Red Light*, loc. 784.

18 **"the Soviet Union and its allies"**: In *The Making of the President: 1964*, Theodore White, who was also at the convention, addresses this issue: "[Goldwater's] press conferences and his quick rejoinders on a hundred occasions provided the Democrats, as they had provided Scranton and Rockefeller, with a score of choice quotes which proved that he did indeed sincerely believe that to avoid war one must first be willing to risk war" (300).

18 **"bluffs and blockades"**: Mailer, *In the Red Light*, loc. 769.

19 **"across all strata of society"**: Which got at the central rationale behind Goldwater's answer to the question of risk. In his view, for the United States to endure the coming war it would need to remain a caste-based system in which every person played his or her role accordingly: a nation of ingenious men and subservient, necessary minorities who, together, would either win the greatest conflict in human history or die trying.

20  **"they shouted"**: The descriptions here are drawn from details provided by White and Mailer. Thompson would later describe the event, eight years later, in *On the Campaign Trail '72*, 327.

20  **"he intoned"**: Rockefeller, "Remarks on Extremism at the 1964 Republican National Convention."

20  **"he hated them for it"**: A recording of Rockefeller's speech is available online at the C-SPAN video archives, "Nelson Rockefeller Addresses 1964 Convention."

20  **"five minutes"**: The quotes here are drawn from the video of Rockefeller's appearance; for more on the raucous reception he received, also see Dickerson, "Never Goldwater."

21  **"passed fully into being"**: Mailer, *In the Red Light*, loc. 526.

21  **"recaps"**: Perry, *Fear and Loathing*, 90.

21  **"provide security"**: "I got the Pinkerton badge," Thompson would explain four years later in a letter to his editor Jim Silberman, "from a mutual friend of [Kentucky Democratic senator] Thruston Morton's son, who (the friend) was hired and fired from the Goldwater palace guard within 24 hours and simply neglected to turn in his badge." He also reflected on the effectiveness of these credentials—and how differently everyone treated him when they figured he was working security, as opposed to reporting. *Fear and Loathing in America*, 69.

21  **"I can go anywhere I want"**: Perry, *Fear and Loathing*, 90.

21  **"was open"**: The details here are based on passages from Whitmer, *When the Going Gets Weird*, 140–141; and Perry, *Fear and Loathing*, 89–90.

22  **"television networks"**: Whitmer, *When the Going Gets Weird*, 140.

24  **"without stating them directly"**: For a transcript, see Goldwater, "Goldwater's 1964 Acceptance Speech," *Washington Post*. For video, see the YouTube entry, "Goldwater 1964 Acceptance Speech."

25  **"*Observer*"**: Thompson would write in an August 19, 1964, letter to his friend Don Cooke:

> I went to the Republican convention and put on a bulldrunk that scared the shit out of the Observer honchos sent out to put me to work. They got the honest fear and did me in with their reports back to D.C. (Our man in the West is a foaming anarchist, a naked boozer who never sleeps and won't work and thinks Goldwater is a nazi.) So they wrote and told me to straighten up or fuck off—and I still haven't decided which way to swing. (*Proud Highway*, 463)

25  **"would haunt him"**: Thompson, *On the Campaign Trail '72*, 336.

25  **"really clean it out"**: This was written in a letter to Paul Semonin on November 25, 1964. "Another four years of Ike would have brought on a national collapse," Thompson added, "but one year of Goldwater would have produced a revolution" (*Proud Highway*, 472).

26  **"with their wives"**: Throughout the composition of this book I've struggled with whether to refer to certain people by first or last names alone. In this instance, I really don't want to seem like I'm only using first names to refer to

women, as opposed to their husbands; it's just that, in the case of Hunter and
Sandy Thompson, I don't feel comfortable referring to Hunter Thompson
by his first name considering that I never had a chance to meet him. To call
him *Hunter*—in the manner his friends and family do—would in my opinion
imply too much intimacy. I haven't met Sandy, either, which of course under-
mines the point I've just made. And whether any of this is correct or not, I'm
not sure; I'd simply like to offer you, the reader, an explanation, when it comes
to authorial decision-making in regards to gender and language.

26    **"dry dark hillside":** The following scene is based on my interview with
      Geiger, as well as Geiger's previous account of it in Seymour and Wenner,
      *Gonzo*, 68.

27    **"needed in surgery immediately":** from my interview with Geiger.

27    **"Joan Didion":** I happen to believe that Joan Didion is the very best essay-
      ist of the last century. Nevertheless, I think it's important to point out that,
      regarding her *political* awareness circa 1964, she both supported and voted for
      Barry Goldwater; see Menand, "Out of Bethlehem."

27    **"blueprint":** In a November 15, 1964, letter to Paul Semonin, Thompson
      spoke about Mailer's influences and about "In the Red Light," saying he ad-
      mired Mailer's "depth of decency and despair" (*Proud Highway*, 470).

27    **"bribed a guard":** Mailer, *In the Red Light,* loc. 803.

27    **"different employment venue":** McKeen, *Outlaw Journalist,* 91–93.

28    **"a perfectly reasonable thing to do":** This scene is based on my April
      27, 2017, interview with Bob Geiger, and also on Geiger's account of it in
      Seymour and Wenner, *Gonzo*, 67–68.

28    **"immediately":** From my April 27, 2017, interview with Geiger, regarding
      the eviction:

      "But who's fault was it really?" I asked.
      "It was my fault," Geiger said to me.
      "Really?"
      He laughed. "It was Hunter's fault."

29    **"brief Sonoma tenure":** Details in this section are drawn from my April 27,
      2017, interview with Geiger.

29    **"by the end of the summer":** Some additional highlights from the month
      the Thompsons spent with the Geigers, as related to me by Bob Geiger during
      our April 27, 2017, interview:

      One evening at the apartment complex, while falling asleep, Bob Geiger
      heard shouting. In the living room he found Hunter Thompson watching the
      late news on a newly purchased television. Thompson had been so shocked
      and disturbed by the events he was seeing that he'd started screaming at the
      screen.
      Another time, Geiger and Thompson were sitting around with Agar and a
      small tabby kitten the Geigers had recently gotten. "Get him Agar!" Thomp-
      son said. "Get the kitten!" He was joking. But Agar's hesitation seemed to
      upset him. He kept encouraging the Doberman forward. Just then the kitten

pounced into the air and landed on the dog, its claws digging in, and as Agar careened around the condo and the kitten rode on his head Bob Geiger found himself laughing hysterically. Thompson, on the other hand, turned strangely sullen. Afterward, with an awkward sort of self-awareness, he tried to hide how he was really feeling: mad at his Doberman for being afraid of a kitten.

Throughout the summer, people were always coming and going, friends of both families. One morning as Geiger was leaving for his run he noticed, to his surprise, six women sleeping on the floor by the television. "Oh that's just Joanie," Thompson explained later—an acquaintance from his Big Sur days, Joan Baez; she was on tour. At the time Geiger had no idea who she was.

At some point during their month together Geiger began receiving cryptic notes from his messaging service—a "Doctor Thompson" kept calling. When he asked his houseguest about this, Thompson pulled out a five-dollar degree he'd ordered from the back of a magazine. HUNTER S. THOMPSON, DOCTOR OF DIVINITY, it read. From then on, to prove a point, Thompson wouldn't hesitate to add in the midst of a conversation: "Trust me: I am, after all, a doctor."

29    **"In your heart, you know he *might*":** The famous ad that articulated this stance aired only once, On September 7, 1964. It can be found on YouTube under the title "'Daisy Girl' Rare 1964 Lyndon Johnson Political Ad."

29    **"nuclear crisis":** White, *Making of the President: 1964,* 24.

30    **"America had won":** Mailer, in *In the Red Light,* wrote:

> We had had a hero. He was a young good-looking man with a beautiful wife, and he had won the biggest poker game we ever played, the only real one—we had lived for a week ready to die in a nuclear war. Whether we liked it or not. But he had won. It was our one true victory in all these years, our moment; so the young man began to inspire a subtle kind of love. His strength had proved stronger than we knew. Suddenly he was dead, and we were in grief. But then came a trial which was worse. For the assassin, or the man who had been arrested but was not the assassin—we would never know, not really—was killed before our sight. In the middle of the funeral came an explosion on the porch. Now, we were going mad. (loc. 740–744)

30    **"conflict between democracy and communism":** White articulates this point in *The Making of the President: 1964,* 24, emphasizing the détente that followed the Cuban Missile Crisis: "War and peace were to be the dominant issue of the campaign of 1964; Barry Goldwater was to be destroyed by this issue. The threat of nuclear annihilation had been removed from the American mind, as from the Russian mind, and this the Americans would not permit Goldwater to raise again."

30    **"Americans would choose Johnson":** 70,621,479 Americans voted for Johnson; 43,126,218 for Goldwater. White, *Making of the President: 1964,* 400.

30    **"three sons":** Thompson's father died of myasthenia gravis at the age of fifty-seven in 1952. McKeen, *Outlaw Journalist,* 13.

30    **"Armed Forces journalistic network":** Brinkley, in his editor's note to *The Proud Highway*, xxii, writes that Thompson was incarcerated "from May 1955 to July 1955 at the Jefferson County Jail for a robbery he didn't commit."

30    **"they were married":** Thompson, *Proud Highway*, 380.

31    **"I feel like I've been put in trust":** The dialogue here was provided by Bob Geiger during our April 27, 2017, interview.


## Chapter Two

34    **"San Francisco's rocky bayshore":** This scene is drawn from two letters in *The Proud Highway*, dated March 26, 1965, and March 27, 1965 (498–510); from the original article Thompson wrote for *The Nation*, "The Motorcycle Gangs: Losers and Outsiders," which was published May 17, 1965; from details provided in Thompson's November 1974 interview with Craig Vetter in *Playboy* (available in Anita Thompson's collection *Ancient Gonzo Wisdom*, 31–56); from the chapter "Hell's Angels: Long Nights, Ugly Days, Orgy of the Doomed" in Thompson, *Songs of the Doomed*, 113–115; and from Thompson's references to the night in *Hell's Angels*, 43–46.

34    **"machine oil":** Some of the physical details used to re-create the setting are based on my own experiences in this specific neighborhood, mostly between 2000 and 2003, when, on trips back from the college I was attending in the Midwest, I spent entire days hanging around (and writing about) the San Francisco Giants new baseball stadium, then called Pacific Bell Park, that had been built in the SoMa neighborhood of the city, which—almost forty years after Thompson's experiences there—was in the process of becoming a nearly uniform expanse of wealth and privilege stretching from Hunters Point to the Golden Gate. For the first time in my life I felt as if I had pressed my ear against the city itself; each day I would park a block or two from the former location of the DePau and then walk along the bay, often stopping at a derelict Navy ship floating in the harbor, *The Mount Washington,* where I'd sit and make notes, drinking and smoking; occasionally I'd find myself wondering what this city might someday be like—at a point say, fifty years from the moment I was living through right then . . . which was the sort of process that inherently led me to imagine, conversely (based on the material of my own past and my limited cultural experience) the shape that this bayshore had once taken, fifty years *earlier*—a past that I somehow understood to contain, along with the many moments in the city's history I'd never know, instances similar to the one from Hunter Thompson's life that you're reading about now: a fog-dark night in San Francisco's second postwar decade that, because it had happened once, could naturally never again happen in the same way . . .

34    **"there wasn't much he could do":** Thompson, *Songs of the Doomed,* 114.

35    **"his position there"**: Thompson gave different versions of his split with the *National Observer:* for more, see William McKeen's take on it, which is excellent, in *Outlaw Journalist* (93–95).

35    **"cover his rent"**: Thompson, *Fear and Loathing in America,* 142.

35    **"For the time being, at least"**: Thompson, *Proud Highway,* 498–501.

35    **"What do you want to know?"**: Thompson, *Hell's Angels,* 44.

36    **"*gotten things wrong*"**: Thompson, *Proud Highway,* 499.

36    **"day-to-day activities"**: Thompson, "Motorcycle Gangs: Losers and Outsiders."

36    **"it brings the heat down on us"**: Thompson, "Motorcycle Gangs: Losers and Outsiders."

36    **"melancholic smile"**: from Thompson, *Hell's Angels,* 43: "He would pause now and then, letting a question hang, and fix me with a sad little smile . . . an allusion to some private joke that he was sure I understood."

36    **"more action than we can handle"**: Thompson, "Motorcycle Gangs: Losers and Outsiders."

36    **"Who is this big cat?"**: Thompson, *Proud Highway,* 499. These three lines of dialogue are drawn from the March 26 letter to Charles Kuralt.

36    **"across the Bay"**: Thompson, *Hell's Angels,* 51.

36    **"*Crazies recognize each other*"**: *Playboy* interview, in Thompson, *Ancient Gonzo Wisdom,* 37.

36    **"I don't know you"**: Thompson, *Ancient Gonzo Wisdom,* 37.

36    **"he explained"**: Thompson, *Proud Highway,* 502.

36    **"Everything out there now is terrible"**: Thompson, *Proud Highway,* 499.

37    **"types like you guys"**: Thompson, *Proud Highway,* 499.

37    **"might as well cooperate"**: Thompson, *Proud Highway,* 502.

37    **"It's all bullshit"**: Thompson, *Hell's Angels,* 55.

37    **"explained the situation to Sandy"**: Thompson, *Proud Highway,* 502.

37    **"tried to calm her"**: From his March 27 letter to Clifford Ridley, in Thompson, *Proud Highway,* 502: "You can imagine how Sandy felt; she was quietly hysterical for the next five hours."

37    **"heard horrible things"**: Seymour and Wenner, *Gonzo,* 74.

37    **"notice everything"**: Juan Thompson, in *Stories I Tell Myself,* his beautiful memoir about his father, addresses the issue of attention—of how Thompson *noticed* everything—on multiple occasions, especially on page 136.

38    **"double-barreled 12-gauge shotgun"**: Thompson, *Proud Highway,* 502.

38    **"mutually assured destruction"**: On March 27 to Clifford Ridley Thompson wrote:

> After all the rape-beating publicity, you can imagine how Sandy felt when we showed up; she was quietly hysterical for five hours. Before

I let them in, I explained that I wasn't in the habit of settling my beefs with my fists, but with a double-barreled 12-gauge shotgun. Which was obvious to them upon entry. This seemed to strike a balance of terror that eventually dissolved into a very pleasant evening. (*Proud Highway,* 502)

38 **"newly opened Hilton":** Thompson, *Hell's Angels,* 55.

38 **"PAIN OF BEING A MAN":** The details of his apartment are from Loiederman, "The Darker Side of a Night with Hunter S. Thompson."

38 ***"The Freewheelin' Bob Dylan":*** Thompson, *Proud Highway,* 500.

38 **"his guests":** To Ridley he wrote: "The odd thing is that these guys are like wild children, extremely volatile, genuinely dangerous in a wrong situation, but very open, curious and even moral when they figure they're talking to a straight person" (Thompson, *Proud Highway,* 500).

38 **"resentment and bewilderment and loss":** Thompson, *Hell's Angels,* 43.

39 **"getting ready to leave":** Thompson, *Proud Highway,* 498.

39 **"he felt exhilarated":** At the end of his letter to Kuralt, Thompson exclaimed: "Christ, I haven't written a five-page letter in years. I must be boiling over" (Thompson, *Proud Highway,* 501).

39 **"coastal rain":** Thompson, *Proud Highway,* 501.

39 **"distinctly lucrative":** in the letter to Kuralt, who was a CBS news correspondent, Thompson pitched a TV news special. Thompson, *Proud Highway,* 500.

40 **"more at stake than money":** The section that follows is based on a general analysis of the night, as well as Thompson's reflection on it in *Songs of the Doomed,* 113–115.

40 **"made them up":** Thompson, *Songs of the Doomed,* 114.

40 **"in Monterey":** For more, see "Oral History Interview with Frederick S. Farr" in the California State Archives State Government Oral History Program.

40 **"sensational":** To compose the report, Lynch queried more than one hundred California law enforcement officials; he created his own elaborate questionnaire and then sent it to sheriffs, district attorneys, and police chiefs. No one from the gang itself had ever been contacted. Thompson, *Hell's Angels,* 22.

40 **"Old West–style lawlessness":** Only three days before Thompson made his initial contact with the Angels at the DePau, *Newsweek* released a 5,000-word feature—"The Wild Ones," an allusion to the 1953 Marlon Brando film of the same name—which attributed nearly all of its most outrageous allegations to Lynch's document. That same week, *Time,* sensing competition, published another take—"The Wilder Ones"—that, in its unrelenting depiction of blood and theft and prostitution, may have sold thousands of extra copies but went way beyond its source material and, in retrospect, appeared to have no real basis in fact whatsoever. Thompson, *Hell's Angels,* 23.

41 **"intelligent, charismatic, ruthless president"**: McKeen, *Outlaw Journalist*, 99.

41 **"marijuana possession"**: This biographical information on Sonny Barger is drawn from *Hell's Angels*, 10.

41 **"a final arbiter"**: Thompson, *Hell's Angels*, 10.

42 **"the response is especially troubling"**: for more on this line of thought, see the excellent 2016 essay in *The Nation* by Susan McWilliams (Carey's granddaughter), "This Political Theorist Predicted the Rise of Trumpism."

42 **"nothing else seems to offer"**: Thompson, "Motorcycle Gangs: Losers and Outsiders."

42 **"April 9"**: Thompson, *Proud Highway*, 503.

42 **"a month's worth of rent"**: Thompson, *Proud Highway*, 506, 520.

42 **"couldn't afford another"**: Thompson, *Proud Highway*, 506.

43 **"Sonoma County"**: Thompson, *Proud Highway*, 520.

43 **"in search of work"**: Thompson, *Songs of the Doomed*, 113; *Playboy* interview, in Thompson, *Ancient Gonzo Wisdom*, 36.

43 **"delivering periodicals"**: Thompson, *Songs of the Doomed*, 113–114.

43 **"just under $500"**: Thompson, *Proud Highway*, 514.

43 **"free-speech movement at Berkeley"**: This article, titled "Nonstudent Left," would be published on September 27, 1965, in *The Nation*. Thompson, *Great Shark Hunt*, 594.

44 **"April 18 letter"**: To Paul Semonin, Thompson, *Proud Highway*, 509.

44 **"you never know"**: Thompson, *The Proud Highway*, 520.

44 **"beat a hangover"**: This essay was published in full in *The Proud Highway*, 237–239; Thompson had sent it to Abe Mellinkoff, editor at the *San Francisco Chronicle*, after he hadn't heard back from an earlier job query.

44 **"time to start over"**: Thompson, *Proud Highway*, 239.

44 **"hold tight"**: Thompson, *Proud Highway*, 513.

45 **"slimmest passageway"**: To Marguerite Gifford on April 27, 1966, Thompson wrote: "From the window of my studio I can see the Golden Gate Bridge and hear the boats coming through. Foghorns always make me feel like going somewhere . . . like train whistles. This is a pleasant place to live, at least for a while" (Thompson, *Proud Highway*, 568).

45 **"lost control of his car"**: Here's the full account from *The Proud Highway*:

> The weekend before last I passed out at the wheel and ran into what they call a "bridge abutment" at 70 mph, but somehow managed to pull out of the spin without hitting anyone. The right side of the car is wiped out but the beast still moves and I have to think I was lucky beyond anything I deserve. It scared me so badly that I am still afraid to drive. (520)

46 **"the May 17 issue of *The Nation*"**: *The Nation*, a magazine that had been published weekly since 1865, was well known for its longstanding progressive

reputation and devoted readership; a number of its recent authors, including James Baldwin, had gone on to secure book deals after their work first appeared in its pages.

46    **"still disconnected"**: Thompson, *Proud Highway*, 527.

46    **"piled haphazardly on the tile"**: On April 25, 2017, while back in San Francisco to research this book, I knocked on the door of 318 Parnassus; a young man—he appeared to be on his way to some sort of adult hockey/ lacrosse practice—opened it, and we spoke for a few minutes; briefly he showed me the entryway described here—which, by all appearances, had *not* been remodeled or changed in the many years since Thompson once occupied the same space.

46    **"more money than The Nation"**: McWilliams, *Education of Carey McWilliams,* 236.

46    **"New York publishers"**: Thompson, *Proud Highway,* 522.

46    **"Alfred A. Knopf"**: Cameron's biographical info is taken from his 2002 *New York Times* obituary; see Martin, "Angus Cameron, 93, Editor Forced Out in McCarthy Era."

46    **"alienated losers and outsiders"**: This is from a previously unpublished letter, from Cameron to Hunter Thompson, dated June 7, 1965; I came across it in the Knopf archive at the Ransom Center on January 9, 2017. For more, see the collection "The Alfred A. and Blanche Knopf Library," which is housed at the Harry Ransom Center at the University of Texas, Austin.

46    **"you write well"**: Five years earlier, Cameron had been one of the few editors to respond to HST's queries about his first unpublished novel, *Prince Jellyfish.* Thompson, *Proud Highway,* 208.

46    **"and ironically"**: From a previously unpublished letter, Cameron to Thompson, June 15, 1965, Ransom Center, Knopf archives.

47    **"still to be negotiated"**: Thompson, *Proud Highway,* 527.

47    **"by today's standards"**: Almost $50,000 by present-day standards.

47    **"next two months"**: Thompson, *Proud Highway,* 538.

47    **"shotgun and camera equipment"**: Thompson, *Proud Highway,* 527.

47    **"new health insurance policy for his family"**: these details are drawn from a previously unpublished letter, from Thompson to Cameron, on June 15, 1965 (Ransom Center, Knopf archives); in this letter he mentions that he also planned to buy his brother an L.L. Bean Hudson Bay blanket that he'd promised to get him the previous Christmas.

47    **"BSA 650 Lightning"**: *Playboy* interview, in Thompson, *Ancient Gonzo Wisdom,* 37.

47    **"damn tired of being poor"**: From Thompson to Cameron, June 15, 1965, Ransom Center, Knopf archives; for this letter Thompson used letterhead that read *Whalen McArtt,* the name of an interior furnishers store on Webster Street in San Francisco—a sign of how bad things were economically.

47    **"by the time this thing is done":** Thompson to Cameron, June 15, 1965,
      Ransom Center, Knopf archives.

47    **"Junior Johnson":** cf. Tom Wolfe's "The Last American Hero Is Junior
      Johnson. Yes!," which was published in *Esquire* in 1965:

> Ten o'clock Sunday morning in the hills of North Carolina. Cars,
> miles of cars, in every direction, millions of cars, pastel cars, aqua
> green, aqua blue, aqua beige, aqua buff, aqua dawn, aqua dusk, aqua
> aqua, aqua Malacca, Malacca lacquer, Cloud lavender, Assassin pink,
> Rake-a-cheek raspberry, Nude Strand coral, Honest Thrill orange,
> and Baby Fawn Lust cream-colored cars are all going to the stock-car
> races, and that old mothering North Carolina sun keeps exploding
> off the windshields. Mother Dog!

48    **"blue ballpoint pen":** The details and quotes here are from Thompson's
      June 28, 1965, letter to Cameron, which was included in *The Proud Highway*,
      528–530; the original, located at the Ransom Center, contains the handwrit-
      ten markings and edits to which I refer here.

48    **"adding machines":** Thompson, *Proud Highway*, 529.

48    **"San Francisco's coastal range":** The details for this extended scene—the
      August 7, 1965, party at Ken Kesey's house in La Honda—are drawn from
      the following:

> Biographies: McKeen, *Outlaw Journalist*, 106–107; Perry, *Fear and Loathing*,
> 105–108; Seymour and Wenner, *Gonzo*, 81–82; and Whitmer, *When the Going
> Gets Weird*, 152–159.

> Interviews: 1974 *Playboy* interview with Craig Vetter, in Thompson, *An-
> cient Gonzo Wisdom*, 33–34; and the 2000 *Paris Review* interview with Doug-
> las Brinkley, George Plimpton, and Terry McDonell, in Thompson, *Ancient
> Gonzo Wisdom*, 262, 264–265.

> Letters: Thompson, *Proud Highway*, 536–539.

> Personal accounts: by Thompson, *Hell's Angels*, 191, 227–235; Thompson,
> *Songs of the Doomed*, 118–120; and Wolfe, *Electric Kool–Aid Acid Test*, 168–178.

> Film: see Alex Gibney's 2008 *Gonzo: The Life and Work of Dr. Hunter S.
> Thompson*.

> Audio: *Gonzo Tapes*, disc one, tracks 13–15. (I've made my own transcript
> of these recordings, which totals about twenty minutes of audio notes that
> Thompson recorded during and immediately after the party.)

> Additionally, I've cited specific moments of dialogue as they occur.

48    **"THE MERRY PRANKSTERS":** Ken Kesey had grown up in Oregon, in the
      farmlands of the Willamette Valley, the son of a dairy magnate. In college
      he'd been a standout wrestler. Later he'd attended Stanford's creative writing
      program—the reason he'd initially ended up in the Bay Area. For more, see
      Dodgson, *It's All a Kind of Magic*.

49    **"a few drinks":** From the *Paris Review* interview, in Thompson, *Ancient
      Gonzo Wisdom*, 263:

> One day I went down to the television station to do a roundtable show with other writers, like Kay Boyle, and Kesey was there. Afterwards we went across the street to a local tavern and had several beers together. I told him about the Angels, who I planned to meet later that day, and I said, "Well, why don't you come along?"

49    **"meet those guys"**: Paris Review interview, Thompson, *Ancient Gonzo Wisdom*, 263.

50    **"his wife and son"**: *Playboy* interview, Thompson, *Ancient Gonzo Wisdom*, 33.

50    **"he began to panic"**: *Playboy* interview, Thompson, *Ancient Gonzo Wisdom*, 33.

50    **"cautioned against taking it"**: Thompson, *Songs of the Doomed,* 119.

52    **"the Grateful Dead"**: The Grateful Dead were still known at the time as the Warlocks; they wouldn't change their name until December 4, 1965, in San Jose; their first show together as a group was on May 5, 1965. In retrospect, I think it's important to state that, out of the many songs I've listened to throughout the course of my youth and adulthood—having grown up, myself, near San Jose, in the 1990s—there is not another ballad more dear to me than the Dead's "Me and My Uncle," the composition of which happens to be another story altogether, one involving John Phillips of the Mamas and the Papas that you should definitely look up if you have a chance (it takes place in a 1963 hotel room also occupied by Neil Young and Stephen Stills, among others . . .).

52    **"Perry Lane"**: The biographical information here is drawn from Dodgson, *It's All a Kind of Magic,* and also from Wolfe, *Electric Kool-Aid Acid Test.*

54    **"sons of shitlovers"**: Thompson, *Hell's Angels,* 232; this was an incredibly reckless gesture on Cassady's part: once you invite the cops onto property, they have the right to legally raid the grounds.

54    **"see what was going on"**: Thompson recounted this moment in his audio notes, which can be found on *Gonzo Tapes,* tracks 13–15, "The Merry Pranksters Welcome the Hell's Angels."

55    **"make Cassady jealous"**: In the Merry Prankster–published magazine *Spit in the Ocean,* vol. 6 (1981), Anne Murphy provides a startling account of her relationship with Neal Cassady—during which she recounts the incident in question:

> Most of the time, though, sex with him was fun. It often originated from his jealous fantasies, which he used to spice up a performance, but sometimes, too, he went "over the line," and fantasy became reality and he would punish me for imaginary infidelities. Later, these fantasies of his became realities to many of his women; we found ourselves doing exactly what he accused us of at an earlier time.
>
> For instance, I was joyously "gang-banged" by the Hell's Angels right before his eyes. Well, after all, he had three girls in tow simultaneously: a gorgeous blonde Aries named June, a "closet beauty" who wore little spectacles and Buster Brown shoes; a white-skinned, long-legged,

full-bosomed, perfumed, redheaded Taurus named Sharon; and me, a flat-chested, ill-tempered, much older crazy-woman.

We three and Neal ("Cassady's Circus" we were called) ate, slept and lived together for some weeks until the Hell's Angels came to a party at Ken Kesey's La Honda ranch where everyone got high and mellow and the Angels took June and me, if not loyal Sharon. Afterward . . . Neal left for New York right away. (63)

Her entire account from the 1981 installment in the series, which was titled "Number 6: The Cassady Issue" and was edited by Ken Babbs—it also features reflections on Cassady's life from Jerry Garcia, William Burroughs, and Larry McMurtry, among others—is striking in its complicated depiction of the sexual politics Murphy describes; in fact, reading it for the first time, I was most struck by the emphasis on death that ran through both Cassady's and Murphy's lives: "I was sure I would die first. I even tried suicide because I missed my son so much, who was in his father's custody by then . . . Neal said he'd tried to kill himself several times when he was young but when he came to believe in reincarnation, he feared the penalty too much. Now he dared God to do it instead by a reckless defiance of all danger" (65). Cassady would live another three years; in February 1968 he'd die of complications from exposure in Mexico after taking downers and wandering off on his own on an especially cold desert night.

55  **"Thompson was horrified"**: "A mad, mad scene," Thompson recounted in his audio notes.

55  **"what was going on"**: Seymour and Wenner, *Gonzo*, 78–80.

55  **"what he'd seen"**: Juan Thompson briefly alludes to this moment in his outstanding memoir *Stories I Tell Myself*, 9: "At one point during the party the Hells Angels gang-raped a woman in a small cabin, an event that haunted Hunter for a long time afterward."

55  **"in the first place"**: Seymour and Wenner, *Gonzo*, 80.

56  **"on the drive home"**: Thompson, *Proud Highway*, 512.

56  **"sleeping children"**: Thompson, *Stories I Tell Myself*, 9–10.

56  **"he didn't feel violent or wild"**: *Playboy* interview, in Thompson, *Ancient Gonzo Wisdom*, 34.

56  **"found these depths empty"**: From the *Playboy* interview, in Thompson, *Ancient Gonzo Wisdom*, 34: "I went to the bottom of the well and found that there's nothing down there I have to worry about, no secret ugly things waiting for a chance to erupt."

57  **"the scene Thompson had witnessed"**: cf. James Salter, *Burning the Days*, 188: "Dreams remained. For years afterwards in nightmares stark as archive footage, I was what I had been."

58  **"Operation Rolling Thunder"**: *Vietnam War*, episode 4.

58  **"none other than LBJ"**: This letter to LBJ was dated March 11, 1965. Thompson, *Proud Highway*, 495.

59    **"trying to make"**: At the time the FBI was already keeping tabs on Hunter
      Thompson—though not for his letters to LBJ; they'd started shadowing him
      because of his subscription to the communist magazine *Worker's World*; for
      more on Thompson's FBI file, which would span a half of a decade, see Nash,
      "Hunter S. Thompson's Appropriately NSFW FBI File."

59    **"by the end of the year"**: *Vietnam War,* episode 4.

59    **"everyone in attendance"**: The details here are drawn from Thompson's
      account in *Hell's Angels* and from Wolfe's *Electric Kool-Aid Acid Test.*

60    **"second-to-last speaker"**: from Tom Wolfe's description of events:

> Kesey's fantasy for the occasion was to come upon the huge anti-war
> rally as a freaking military invasion. It was a true inspiration, this
> fantasy. They were going to rig up the bus as a rolling fortress with
> guns sticking out and all the Pranksters would dress military. Then
> they would get cars and rig them up the same way, and at the head of
> the whole convoy there would be—The Hell's Angels in a running
> formation, absolutely adangle with swastikas. It would freaking blow
> their minds, or at least give their cool a test like it never had before.
> (*Electric Kool-Aid Acid Test,* 217)

61    **"the gusts"**: Details of temperature and wind are taken from "We Shall
      March Again," a short film of the march accessed online through the Univer-
      sity of California, Berkeley, Art Museum and Pacific Rim Archive.

61    **"from the eucalyptus branches"**: cf. Maggie Nelson's opening sentence
      to *The Argonauts,* 3: "October, 2007. The Santa Ana winds are shredding the
      bark off the eucalyptus trees in long white stripes."

61    **"Tiny"**: Thompson, *Hell's Angels,* 18, 52, 179, 214.

62    **"the John Birch Society"**: Thompson, *Hell's Angels,* 244.

63    **"official bail bondsman"**: Details are taken from the film "Ralph 'Sonny'
      Barger Confronts VDC," located in the San Francisco Bay Area Television
      Archive, which is accessible through San Francisco State University.

63    **"greased and shining"**: At the beginning of this film, a reporter, so as to
      introduce the press conference, intones: "The very idea of the Hell's Angels
      holding a news conference conjures up some unusual and perhaps interesting
      ideas about social comment" (ibid.).

63    **"including Hunter Thompson"**: Harrell, *Keep This Quiet!,* loc. 1647.

63    **"best for the country"**: Here are a few more highlights from the press
      conference (as seen on the footage available from the San Francisco Bay Area
      Television Archive):

When someone asked whether the Angels planned to vacate Oakland during
the march, Barger smiled wryly and answered, "We'll do whatever we do on
a normal Saturday. Probably go the bar and drink a few suds." When another
reporter—the one female journalist in the room—wondered what the girl-
friends and wives of the members of the bikers thought about all of this, he

shot back, "They have no say about it"—which caused both the Angels and the press to erupt together in a bout of sustained, deeply menacing laughter.

64  **"never went to Vietnam":** Thompson, *Hell's Angels,* 253.

64  **"forty or so polished pages":** Thompson, *Proud Highway,* 547.

64  **"He had a structure in mind":** In an unpublished letter to Gordon Lish on September 3, 1965, Thompson explained his structural conceit: "The book will be a combination of the two"—of the "relatively objective" approach that characterized the *Nation* article with the subsequent "first-person and subjective" narration of events like the run on Bass Lake. This letter is from the Ransom Center and can be found in the archives under the Genesis West collection.

65  **"unparalleled":** San Francisco's cultural revolution in the 1960s always reminds me of this quote by Italo Calvino (from his fabulist creation-myth-of-the-universe collection *Cosmicomics,* 25: "We were peering into the darkness, criss-crossed with voices, when the change took place: the only real, great change I've ever happened to witness, and compared to it the rest is nothing."

In fact, Calvino visited San Francisco in the early 1960s and would later render it as a sort of metropolis for the future; in its webbed commerce of bridges and cables cars, it was eerily similar to the fantastical settings he would conjure in his 1974 book *Invisible Cities,* 138: "San Francisco . . . which spans the Golden Gate and the bay with long, light bridges and sends open trams climbing its steep streets, and which might blossom as a capital of the Pacific a millennium hence."

65  **"apartment for drinks":** Loiederman, "Darker Side of a Night."

65  **"Fillmore Street":** Thompson, *Proud Highway,* 542.

65  **"electric, cacophonous wave":** Thompson had been invited to the Airplane's debut by Merry Prankster Jerry Anderson, whose wife, Signe Tole Anderson, was at that time the lead singer of the group; Grace Slick was also in attendance, though not as a band member; at the time Slick was the lead singer of the Great Society; it would be another year until she joined the Airplane and became its signature vocalist—someone about whom Thompson would write:

> [She] made even the worst Matrix nights worth sitting through. Grace Slick was always my best reason for going to the Matrix. I would sit back in the corner by the projection booth and watch her do all those things that she later did with the Airplane and for LOOK magazine, but which seemed so much better then, because she was her own White Rabbit. (*Fear and Loathing in America,* 2, 8–9)

66  **"time on Parnassus":** Seymour and Wenner, *Gonzo,* 75.

66  **"out of town":** In *Gonzo* Sandy recounts:

> When Juan was an infant, Hunter was very sweet with him—in the first year or so. By the time he was two, he just wasn't there for him. Hunter told me, "Juan's your novel." He could come out and be there when he needed to be there, for someone or something. He could

rise to the occasion, and then when he didn't have to, he could sink back into the uncharming self. (Seymour and Wenner, 75)

66 **"by December"**: From the September 3, 1965, letter to Gordon Lish, Ransom Center, Genesis West collection.

66 **"reached a breaking point"**: The account of this trip to Monterey is based on Hunter Thompson's description of it in his 1974 interview in *Playboy* magazine (Thompson, *Ancient Gonzo Wisdom*, 39) and a selection from the chapter "Among the Angels" in William McKeen's *Gonzo*.

66 **"impossible to get anything done"**: Thompson, *Songs of the Doomed*, 114.

66 **"Watsonville"**: Thompson described a similar route in his book:

Between San Jose and the turnoff to Monterey, 101 rolls gracefully through the rich farming foothills of the Santa Cruz Mountains. The Hell's Angels, riding two abreast in each lane, seemed out of place in little towns like Coyote and Gilroy. People ran out of taverns and dry-goods stores to stare at these fabled big-city Huns. (*Hell's Angels,* 11–12)

67 **"on the table in front of him"**: cf. Johnson, *Jesus' Son,* 53: "The cards were scattered on the table, face up, face down, and they seemed to foretell that whatever we did to one another would be washed away by liquor or explained away by sad songs."

67 **"made this country great"**: Thompson's analysis here, that the Angels represent some aspect of the past—that old "individualist" tradition "that made this country great"—was further expanded upon by Thompson himself, in 1967, during his press tour for the book:

REPORTER: Is there any conclusion to be reached?

HST: About the Hell's Angels? Only that it represents a sort of growing menace that might or might not be called Hell's Angels. These people are breeding all over the country. And the more qualified you have to be to get a job, the more people that are going to be forced out, off the job market . . . All these people don't ride motorcycles and they don't all wear jackets saying Hell's Angels, but they're around, and there are more and more of them, and you can draw your own conclusions about what's going to happen when we get to a certain level. I'm not sure what that level will be. (The full interview, under the title "Rare 1967 Throwback: Hunter S. Thompson Interview about the Hell's Angels," can be found on YouTube.

67 **"young unemployables"**: Thompson, *Hell's Angels,* 255–257.

68 **"always been fascistic"**: Thompson, *Hell's Angels,* 245. A full definition of fascism—both in regards to the twentieth century interwar period in Europe and also, in a drastically less dominant form, in American political and social currents during the 1930s, 1940s, and the postwar era—can at times seem dauntingly multiform, but certain core tenets remain. The best explication of

these tenets has been provided, in my opinion, by Umberto Eco, in his June 22, 1995, essay "Ur-Fascism" for *The New York Review of Books*. But another good starting point can be found in this quote by Kevin Passmore, which is from his deliciously titled book *Fascism: A Very Short Introduction,* 31:

> Fascism is a set of ideologies and practices that seeks to place the nation, defined in exclusive biological, cultural, and/or historical terms, above all other sources of loyalty, and to create a mobilized national community. Fascistic nationalism is reactionary in that it entails implacable hostility to socialism and feminism, for they are seen as prioritizing class or gender rather than nation.

In other words: the Angels actually saw themselves as the *most-American* Americans out there—as opposed to a *countercultural* (and inherently anti-establishment) force, which is what Kesey et al. seemed to mistake them for—and as a result, while the biker gang's fealty to concepts like imperialism/militarism (not to mention their violent suppression of antiwar dissent) came as a shock to almost everyone in the Bay Area scene, Hunter Thompson wasn't surprised; he'd had to deal with their fascistic, uncompromising, power-in-masculine-numbers tendencies from the beginning, if simply out of regard for his own self-preservation.

68 **"you will be":** Thompson, *Hell's Angels,* 260.

68 **"a drug like Dexedrine":** For more context, see these two quotes from Thompson's 1977 interview with Rod Rosenbaum for *High Times* (in Thompson, *Ancient Gonzo Wisdom,* 86):

> 1) "I never considered speed fun. I use speed as fuel, a necessary evil."
>
> 2) "I'm really an adrenaline junkie; I never get anything done without the pressure of some impossible deadline."

68 **"appeared to be heading":** Seymour and Wenner, *Gonzo,* 80. Thompson told Bob Geiger, "These guys are really showing us where society is going."

69 **"Joseph Conrad":** Thompson, *Great Shark Hunt,* 17.

69 **"success is very far off":** Joseph Conrad's quote is from an 1897 introduction that he wrote for the new edition of his novella *Children of the Sea* (published in Britain as *The Nigger of "Narcissus"*). The full passage:

> Art is long and life is short, and success is very far off. And thus, doubtful of strength to travel so far, we talk a little about the aim—the aim of art, which, like life itself, is inspiring, difficult—obscured by mists. It is not in the clear logic of a triumphant conclusion; it is not in the unveiling of one of those heartless secrets which are called the Laws of Nature. It is not less great, but only more difficult. To arrest, for the space of a breath, the hands busy about the work of the earth, and compel men entranced by the sight of distant goals to glance for a moment at the surrounding vision of form and color, of sunshine and shadows; to make them pause for a look, for a sigh, for a smile—such is the aim, difficult and evanescent, and reserved only for a few to achieve. But sometimes, by the deserving and the

fortunate, even that task is accomplished. And when it is accomplished—behold!—all the truth of life is there: a moment of vision, a sigh, a smile—and the return to an eternal rest. (Conrad, *Narcissus and Other Stories,* 120)

In retrospect, I think it's important to note that Vladimir Nabokov, of whom Thompson was a fan, wrote the following passage in his memoir *Speak, Memory,* which gestures overtly to the previous quote from Conrad:

> Whenever in my dreams I see the dead, they always appear silent, bothered, strangely depressed, quite unlike their dear, bright selves. I am aware of them, without any astonishment, in surroundings they never visited during their earthly existence, in the house of some friend of mine they never knew. They sit apart, frowning at the floor, as if death were a dark taint, a shameful family secret. It is certainly not then—not in dreams—but when one is wide awake, at moments of robust joy and achievement, on the highest terrace of consciousness, that mortality has a chance to peer beyond its own limits, from the mast, from the past and its castle tower. And although nothing much can be seen through the mist, there is somehow the blissful feeling that one is looking in the right direction. (34)

All of which is to say: literary lineages are long and winding and not without their surprises.

69    **"any one factor":** I think it's too easy to explain this bender in a "writerly" way—to blame Thompson's drinking that March on the emotion he may have felt after finally finishing a draft of the book: the desolation and fear and powerlessness that can arrive in the wake of any artistic endeavor's completion. Instead, it's important to remember that Thompson was an alcoholic, and this sort of bender is what alcoholics do.

However, I'm reminded of a story about William Faulkner—which may or may not be apocryphal—that I first heard in a literature lecture almost two decades ago. Whenever Faulkner would finish a novel, he'd drink himself into a sickened state, pass out, and then wake up and keep drinking—a bender to silence the voices of the characters he now found himself parting with. For him, it seemed to be a means of forgetting, or at the very least, of letting go.

Once, just as he was finishing a book—at any moment the bender would commence—his daughter came to him in his study (she was perhaps ten), and said to him: "Pappy. You know tomorrow's my birthday. Please. Just this one time. Can you just this once not do it? Can you wait until after my birthday's over, at least?"

Faulkner leveled his gaze at her and, after a pause, said: "No one ever remembered Shakespeare's daughter."

69    **"consuming him altogether":** In a March 17, 1965, letter to Carey McWilliams, in *Proud Highway,* 562, Thompson wrote, "I'm now trying to get a grip on myself after three weeks of running totally out of control. Got the book off by March 1, as planned, and then went into a wild spiral up and down the coast, stuffing myself with every kind of drug and booze imaginable. Now my head feels a bit clearer and of course I'm dead broke again."

69     **"points of view":** The details here are based foremost on a fight that Bob
       Geiger related during our interview; I'm still not sure if this was the same
       fight that Sandy Thompson would relate in Seymour and Wenner, *Gonzo,* 76–
       77; and to E. Jean Carroll in *Hunter,* 99–101; and that Roberto Loiederman
       would describe in even more detail in his February 27, 2005, personal essay
       for the *LA Times,* "The Darker Side of a Night with Hunter S. Thompson."
       Both Sandy and Loiederman say that Thompson consumed LSD at one point
       in the night; however, Geiger never mentioned anything about drugs—in his
       view Thompson was just very drunk—and whether these three stories actu-
       ally recount separate instances from that terrible three-week March bender or
       in fact represent a single, drawn-out moment, I can't say; instead, I've tried to
       narrate the moment in the way that feels closest to Geiger's account while still
       including some of the visual/dramatic descriptions from the others that, in my
       opinion at least, fit with my honest attempt to express what might've actually
       happened.

69     **"the truth":** cf. Maxwell, *So Long, See You Tomorrow,* 27:

       > What we, or at any rate what I, refer to confidentially as mem-
       > ory—meaning a moment, a scene, a fact that has been subjected to a
       > fixative and thereby rescued from oblivion—is really a form of story-
       > telling that goes on continually in the mind and often changes with
       > the telling. Too many conflicting emotional interests are involved for
       > life ever to be wholly acceptable, and possibly it is the work of the
       > storyteller to rearrange things so that they conform to this end. In
       > any case, in talking about the past we lie with every breath we draw.

70     **"slapped her—hard":** This detail is from Geiger's account; in her account
       from the night Sandy described Thompson rushing at her, but she didn't clar-
       ify if he hit her. But in E. Jean Carroll's *Hunter,* Sandy did talk about physical
       abuse occurring at other times: once, at the very start of their relationship, in
       upstate New York in 1959, Thompson struck her out of what he claimed was
       jealousy; he struck her again, years later, as their relationship deteriorated:

       > There were beatings. Maybe six after the first heavy wallop when
       > we were first together. Except for the last time when I had not had
       > a drink in six months, I was always drunk. And when I'd get re-
       > ally drunk I could say things I'd never say sober. It was not pretty,
       > not sweet, and very ugly. Hunter would have been drinking too,
       > of course, but not necessarily drunk. My behavior clearly triggered
       > some very deep part of him and he would lash out with hands, fists
       > to whatever part of my body. I would whine and roll up into some
       > pathetic little ball, making him even angrier. (Carroll, *Hunter,* 192)

70     **"drawing blood":** In Carroll, *Hunter,* 102, Sandy said: "I was so scared and
       angry. I just clawed him. All that had to happen was for him to throw that
       boot and it went crash and I went wild." And from Seymour and Wenner,
       *Gonzo,* 74: "I reached up—this was a mom protecting her son—and scratched
       his face. There was blood. And it was weird, but he stopped. I guess that jolted
       him."

70    **"crash his motorcycle"**: Thompson had already crashed his motorcycle once, months earlier, injuring a friend riding with him:

> One night in the winter of 1965 I took my own bike—and a passenger—over the high side on a rain-slick road just north of Oakland. I went into an obviously dangerous curve at about seventy, the top of my second gear. The wet road prevented leaning it over enough to compensate for the tremendous inertia, and somewhere in the middle of the curve I realized that the rear wheel was no longer following the front one. The bike was going sideways toward a bank of railroad tracks and there was nothing I could do except hang on . . . There is nothing romantic about a bad crash, and the only solace is the deadening shock that comes with most injuries. My passenger left the bike in a long arc that ended on the railroad tracks and splintered his thigh bone, driving the sharp edges through muscle and flesh and all the way out to the wet gravel. In the hospital they had to wash the dirt off the bone ends before they put his leg back together . . . but he said it didn't hurt until the next day, not even when he was lying in the rain and wondering if anybody on the road would call an ambulance to pick us up. (Thompson, *Hell's Angels,* 96)

70    **"answering service"**: The details in this scene are from my interview with Bob Geiger.

71    **"out of control"**: On March 17, 1966, Thompson wrote to Carey McWilliams: "I'm now trying to get a grip on myself after three weeks of running totally out of control. Got the book off by March 1, as planned, and then went into a wild spiral up and down the coast, stuffing myself with every kind of drug and booze imaginable" (Thompson, *Proud Highway,* 562).

71    **"weeks later"**: Thompson's BSA had been wrecked during a crash that winter; it was only in the spring that he'd gotten it fixed and could ride it again. Thompson, *Hell's Angels,* 269.

71    **"he jumped on his motorcycle"**: It's hard not to read in Thompson's concept of the "Edge" another Joseph Conrad passage—this time from *Heart of Darkness,* a book that Thompson quoted throughout *Hell's Angels*—in which Conrad describes the narrator's near-death experience:

> I have wrestled with death. It is the most unexciting contest you can imagine. It takes place in an impalpable greyness, with nothing underfoot, with nothing around, without spectators, without clamour, without glory, without the great desire of victory, without the great fear of defeat, in a sickly atmosphere of tepid skepticism, without much belief in your own right, and still less in that of your adversary. If such is the form of ultimate wisdom, then life is a greater riddle than some of us think it to be. I was within a hair's-breadth of the last opportunity for pronouncement, and I found with humiliation that probably I would have nothing to say. This is the reason why I affirm that Kurtz was a remarkable man. He had something to say. He said it. Since I had peeped over the edge myself, I understand better the

meaning of his stare, that could not see the flame of the candle, but was wide enough to embrace the whole universe, piercing enough to penetrate all the hearts that beat in the darkness. He had summed it up. He had judged. "The horror!" He was a remarkable man. After all, this was the expression of some sort of belief; it had candour, it had conviction, it had a vibrating note of revolt in its whisper, it had the appalling face of a glimpsed truth—the strange commingling of desire and hate. (87–88)

71 **"untimely death"**: This speculation is spelled out in the chapter "Midnight on the Coast Highway" at the end of Thompson, *Hell's Angels,* 270: "An un-identified motorcyclist was killed last night when he failed to negotiate a turn on Highway 1."

72 **"willful act"**: In my opinion, what Thompson was looking for here, by rid-ing so close to a crash, was akin to something the writer Michael Ondaatje, in his memoir *Running in the Family,* calls the "great death." Ondaatje's explora-tion of this concept culminates in his chapter "The Passions of Lalla," which is about Ondaatje's maternal grandmother, who stepped off her porch one morning into what had become a predawn expanse of rushing floodwaters and "died in the blue arms of a Jacaranda tree" (113).

72 **"he began to recognize"**: Years later, reflecting on this ride and what he wrote about it that very night—"twenty minutes after coming back from doing it"—he would say:

> One of the few ways I can be almost certain I'll understand some-thing is by sitting down and writing about it. Because by forcing yourself to write about it and putting it down in words, you can't avoid having to come to grips with it. You might be wrong, but you have to think about it very intensely to write about it. So I use writ-ing as a learning tool. (Thompson, *Songs of the Doomed,* 115)

73 **"stayed in Haight-Ashbury much longer"**: From the *Paris Review* inter-view, in Thompson, *Ancient Gonzo Wisdom,* 266: "I still feel needles in my back when I think about all the horrible disasters that would have befallen me if I had permanently moved to San Francisco and rented a big house, joined the company dole, become national affairs editor for some upstart magazine—that was the plan around 1967."

73 **"helping with the edits"**: Years later Bob Geiger would say, in Seymour and Wenner, *Gonzo,* 80: "People think that *Fear and Loathing in Las Vegas* is dedicated to me because they think I was supplying Hunter with drugs, but the main reason is that I would drive down to San Francisco almost every night, and Hunter and I would read through the Hell's Angels manuscript page by page, word by word."

73 **"north of the city"**: In a November 28, 1966, letter to fellow journalist Chuck Alverson, Thompson wrote: "I wanted a book cover photo to counter Random's idea of using some phony design work" (*Proud Highway,* 588).

73    **"struck in the head":** Shortly after the incident, in a letter to Angels' leader
Sonny Barger—who hadn't been on the run to Cloverdale and wasn't there
when Thompson got beat up—Thompson wrote:

> I'm not sure how or why the thing started and I never even saw the
> first thump that got me, but I assume it was a sort of drunken sponta-
> neous outburst that I had the bad luck to get in the middle of. Earlier
> in the day I'd noticed some resentment about my taking pictures, but
> I didn't worry about it because I figured you were straight enough
> to tell me to my face if we had any problems. We've never bullshitted
> each other and I'd grown sort of accustomed to taking you at face
> value. (*Proud Highway,* 585)

73    **"other Angels joined in":** For the dramatic action here I've tried to stay
as close to the description of the event in Thompson, *Hell's Angels,* 272–273,
despite contradictory versions that would later appear in interviews with
Thompson and with others who claimed to be present.

73    **"why it was happening":** Over the subsequent years, Thompson and others would give various explanations as to why he was attacked—because of
a dispute over the money he was making off the book; because he'd gotten
into an argument over the merits of Harleys versus BSAs; or because, after
watching a biker named George Zahn punch his wife and kick his dog, he
intervened, saying, "Any man that will hit a woman is a punk" (which was
pretty much what Bob Geiger had said to *Thompson,* after the fight with
Sandy)—but this sort of reasoning appears to be retroactive; at the moment
the fight erupted and in its immediate wake, he really had no idea why he'd
been attacked . . . apart from the simple reality that they were Hell's Angels
and he was not. William McKeen does an excellent job going through the
many variations of the story; for more, see *Outlaw Journalist,* 110–111.

73    **"lull in the action":** It should be pointed out that this lull occurred after
Tiny had grabbed and prevented another Angel from bringing down a large
rock onto Thompson's head. Thompson, *Hell's Angels,* 273.

74    **"I'm okay":** Carroll, *Hunter,* 106.

74    **"San Francisco":** They'd moved, temporarily, to new apartment on Grattan
Street, only a few blocks away in San Francisco. Thompson, *Proud Highway,*
582.

74    **"growing his face to fit":** cf. George Orwell's "Shooting an Elephant," in
*Collection of Essays,* 152:

> Here was I, the white man with his gun, standing in front of the un-
> armed native crowd—seemingly the leading actor of the piece; but
> in reality I was only an absurd puppet pushed to and fro by the will
> of those yellow faces behind. I perceived in this moment that when
> the white man turns tyrant it is his own freedom that he destroys. He
> becomes a sort of hollow, posing dummy, the conventionalized figure
> of a sahib. For it is the condition of his rule that he shall spend his life
> in trying to impress the "natives," and so in every crisis he has got to

do what the "natives" expect of him. He wears a mask, and his face
grows to fit it. I had got to shoot the elephant.

# Chapter Three

76 **"end of 1966"**: Thompson, *Proud Highway,* 639.

76 **"about 2,500"**: Thompson, *Proud Highway,* 621.

76 **"yet to be paved"**: Salter, *Don't Save Anything,* 273.

76 **"smallest planes"**: These details are drawn from the "History" section of the
Aspen Airport website.

76 **"kept flagging it"**: from Margaret Harrell's outstanding account in *Keep
This Quiet!*, loc. 1495: "Hunter's book had been combed by lawyers, which
was standard procedure. Except the concern went so far as to balk at his use of
the term Pepsi Generation; in context, it might provoke a law suit by Pepsi!"

76 **"kept their heads"**: From my email correspondence (January 5, 2018) with
Margaret Harrell, who sought to clarify her role as Thompson's editor:

> We copy editors, about 5 or 6, were a pool that any editor could re-
> quest—actually stand in line to get! I was typically requested by Jim
> Silberman and Joe Fox. Occasionally by others. They requested me
> to work on novels (i.e., authors with sensitive psyches) and what Jim
> called big complicated books—nonfiction blockbuster types requir-
> ing attention to detail and research.

76 **"As a copy editor"**: At first Thompson resisted Harrell's editorial influence—"am appalled at some of the sentences inserted to 'clarify' my meaning," he wrote her, "which they may or may not do, but I won't have that kind
of writing in my book. I'd rather be obscure"—but he quickly came around.
Harrell, *Keep This Quiet!*, loc. 1279.

76 **"a sort of signature"**: cf. Italo Calvino's "A Sign in Space" (a fabulist narrative about the moment that language was created and used for the first time
in the universe's history):

> So the situation was this: the sign served to mark a place but at the
> same time it meant that in that place there was a sign (something far
> more important because there were plenty of places but there was
> only one sign) and also at the same time that sign was mine, the sign
> of me, because it was the only sign I had ever made and I was the
> only one who had ever made signs. It was like a name, the name of
> that point, and also my name that I had signed on that spot; in short,
> it was the only name available for everything that required a name.
> (*Cosmicomics,* 33)

This passage was written during the same stretch of months that Calvino,
then in his fifties, had been asked to compose a new introduction for the
reissued edition of his novel, *The Path to the Spiders' Nests,* a war narrative that
had been written thirty years earlier and that, in retrospect, he now felt both

terribly embarrassed by and also a tender affection for, it being the very first novel he ever published. The larger point: what must it be like to look back, in all honesty, on that rarest of moments—an instant of creation when you went from having nothing to, unaccountably, finally having *something* by which you might see yourself as distinct?

And in this sense, even though Calvino was ashamed of his first novel and hated to read it again, he understood that each of his subsequent works, no matter how spectacular, would never bridge him across such a terrible chasm of indefinite space as this first novel had: a work that would give shape, for both good and ill, to everything he would ever write afterward.

76 **"perspective on the world"**: Harrell wrote about this process in her memoir, *Keep This Quiet!*, and she expanded on it during a talk in Louisville, at the 2017 GonzoFest, during which she displayed a photocopy of a couple of pages from the original manuscript she and Thompson had worked on—pages that contained her edits alongside his. His appreciation for her editing technique also comes out in the letters she saved from their time together.

76 **"on the phone"**: From Harrell, *Keep This Quiet!*, loc. 1611: "Hunter was still being hounded in November. The lawyers were taking no chances. His book was going through scrutiny not given other books I had worked on. Not at this stage, anyway."

77 **"red and wavy"**: In the Veronica Lake style—cascading and long (January 5, 2018, correspondence with Harrell).

77 **"a bad state for an impressionable hillbilly to come to"**: Harrell, *Keep This Quiet!*, loc. 1567; in the same letter, Thompson had attached two 5 mg pills of Dexedrine (loc. 1568).

77 **"spectacular"**: Thompson, *Proud Highway*, 606.

77 **"meet Harrell for the first time"**: Harrell, *Keep This Quiet!*, loc. 1766:

Hunter stepped in. A giant, six feet four or five, beautifully built, with sandy blond hair and brown eyes. His cheeks dimpled. He didn't speak or reach out to shake my hand. We were beyond that stage, even though it had never been voiced. What he did next would captivate me—by his ability to magically dispel my bountiful self-consciousness. His, too. In one hand was a brown shaving kit . . . And what was inside the bag? Two Ballantine Ales. He took them out and offered them up: one for him, one for me.

78 **"I Hunter Thompson am a writer"**: The entire episode has recently become available on YouTube—"To Tell the Truth—Hunter S. Thompson (February 20, 1967)"—and if you have a chance I highly recommend checking it out.

As you might expect from a similar slice-of-celebrity-life example of mid-1960s television, it vacillates between the banal and the absurd at a fairly predictable clip—except for a handful of moments, by no means inconsequential, during which the show transforms into something that feels deeply misogynistic . . . and in a manner that, in my opinion at least, would've been abundantly clear at the time (as in: I don't think my response can be chalked up to just another by-product of cultural relativism).

Some highlights:

The identity of the contestant who comes on before Hunter Thompson is Wendy Farrington, an Olympic skier who works as a showgirl at a Caribbean resort; the three possible Ms. Farringtons are dressed as such: in the sequins and feathers of an exotic Vegas dancer; in a bikini-top/ striped-pants outfit, as if she were some sort of erotic ringmaster; and as a ski instructor in a tight sweater.

The female contestants who appear *after* Thompson are introduced as thus: "I, Noel Cannon, am a judge in the traffic division of the Los Angeles municipal court. On the bench I have a reputation for toughness; however I have made no compromise between my job and my femininity. At my own expense I decorated my chambers in pink with Louis XIV furniture. I wear bold costume jewelry and dress in the very latest modern style."

And here's a sample of the questions/comments offered by the celebrity judge Tom Poston, an old CBS stableman with the unctuous bearing of a man who's hosted more than his fair share of beauty contests:

"She's a strong healthy girl."
"I voted for #1 because boy did that dress fit her."
"#3, do you like the miniskirt?"
"I voted for #2 because she's so unlikely to be a judge in a formal court looking like that."
"See how different that is—If I woulda said 'I'd like to come up against #1 or #2' it would've been a totally different sound in this audience!"

(At that last comment the studio audience can be heard laughing loudly.)

Poston died in 2007, and his *New York Times* obituary described him thus: "A long-faced, buggy-eyed second banana, Mr. Poston was for a half-century a Paganini of the bewildered, the benighted and the befuddled." To win his last role—that of "a surly, dying clown" on the mid-2000s NBC sitcom *Committed*—he went so far as to pull his pants down during the audition . . . "with electrifying results." (Fox, "Tom Poston, Virtuosic Comic Actor, Is Dead at 85")

78    **"whose philosophy is violence":** When it comes to a general definition of American fascism, that's actually not all that bad a starting point . . .

Though if we're looking for a more specific definition, an excellent starting point is Vice President Henry A. Wallace's description, in the April 9, 1944, edition of the *New York Times:* "[A person] whose lust for money or power is combined with such an intensity of intolerance toward those of other races, parties, classes, religions, cultures, regions, or nations as to make him ruthless in his use of deceit or violence to attain his ends." (Wallace, "Wallace Defines American Fascism")

78    **"At each question"**: At one point Tom Poston asked Thompson: "Did you hear about the musician who was on LSD? He threw himself at the floor and missed. HAWHAWHAW!" Poston then ended his portion of the segment by saying: "I voted for #2, Bud, I thought he was a nice likeable fella, and if I were a Hell's Angel I'd rather beat him up than the other two guys."

78    **"She was dazzled"**: Correspondence with Harrell, January 4, 2018.

78    **"brought physically to life"**: Harrell, *Keep This Quiet!*, loc. 1784–1789.

79    **"unguarded smile"**: Harrell would write of this moment: "With self-revealing amusement, the cutest, most boyish-looking, unassuming guy raised his head; then bent it downward. Sporting short sleeves and a sleeveless jacket, he flashed a modest-looking grin. Watching backstage as he rose out of his seat, not overplaying his hand, dazzled me beyond all description" (Harrell, *Keep This Quiet!*, loc. 1787–1789).

79    **"intoned"**: It was Kitty Carlisle; she stole the show . . . And I'll only add that Ms. Carlisle's cosmopolitan accent was a miracle of inflection and diction and personal style that's not soon to be replicated. Haigh *Azbury,* she pronounced. Ken *Kezey.*

79    **"Surrealistic Pillow"**: Correspondence with Harrell, January 4, 2018. She and Thompson had bought *Surrealistic Pillow,* with Selma Shapiro, that afternoon.

79    **"departing"**: Harrell, *Keep This Quiet!*, loc. 1824.

79    **"Come get into the bed"**: From Harrell's account, in *Keep This Quiet!*, loc. 1815: "I laughed and told him to get into the bed. We completed the passionate attraction that nothing would stop, then and there."

80    **"actually the case"**: Correspondence with Harrell, January 4, 2018.

80    **"passed since"**: Harrell and Thompson would meet up again, in 1991, and resume the affair they'd begun years earlier; for more, see Margaret Harrell's excellent *Keep This Quiet Too!*

80    **"this affair"**: Seymour and Wenner, *Gonzo* 96; Carroll, *Hunter,* 170.

81    **"have another baby"**: Sandy would later say: "I would get pregnant every single time I went off the Pill. I mean I was *instantly pregnant*" (Carroll, *Hunter,* 115).

81    **"She got pregnant again immediately"**: For these details as well as those in the following paragraphs, see McKeen, *Outlaw Journalist,* 115–116; Thompson, *Proud Highway,* 610, 614–619; and Carroll, *Hunter,* 115.

In *Keep This Quiet!* Margaret Harrell writes:

> What he didn't spell out was that in the past six weeks, since the very end of April, his pregnant wife had been bedridden . . . Sandy's terrible situation would continue till around August. She would endure a lingering buildup to a miscarriage. Hunter kept the household going. This came to light for me only in 2008, when Rosalie Sorrels mentioned on the phone what a good father he was, citing how

in this period he looked after his and Sandy's son, three-year-old Juan. Many letters that immediately follow look quite different in this context. (loc. 2217)

81    **"should Sandy's condition change"**: Thompson, *Proud Highway*, 617.

81    **"a national bestseller"**: Already it had sold out its initial print run, more than 25,000 hardcover copies, and by the end of the year, due to additional paperback sales, the total would skyrocket to an astonishing 500,000. Thompson, *Proud Highway*, 613; Thompson, *Fear and Loathing in America*, 14, 18.

81    **"strong initial sales"**: As things were, he only received 10 percent of *all* hardcover sales, which was below the industry standard, from what I can tell ...

81    **"a wretched, predatory document"**: Thompson, *Proud Highway*, 612–613.

81    **"Lynn Nesbit"**: Thompson, *Proud Highway*, 611.

81    **"December 15"**: If Thompson agreed to anything with Random House before this date, then Meredith would be entitled to a percentage of it.

81    **"*next* project"**: Already Thompson had possible topics in mind. The first was a book on the Joint Chiefs of Staff—on the outsized influence these rarely talked about military men had begun to wield on American foreign policy (Thompson, *Proud Highway*, 630–631, 644). But he was also interested in the upcoming presidential contest—terrified by the prospect of Lyndon Johnson's reelection or, worse, his defeat at the hands of a suddenly resurgent Richard Nixon (Thompson, *Proud Highway*, 654–655).

81    **"domestic rhythm"**: The following details are drawn from Thompson's 1966 letters, spanning April to August, in *Proud Highway*, 609–633; from McKeen's *Outlaw Journalist*, 115–116; and from *Gonzo Tapes*, disc 1, track 5, "A Question for the Ages."

81    **"130 acres"**: McKeen, *Outlaw Journalist*, 115.

82    **"*your* next book"**: italics are my own; Thompson, *Proud Highway*, 614–615.

82    **"suspect himself of harboring"**: cf. F. Scott Fitzgerald's *The Great Gatsby* (which Hunter Thompson once copied out by hand, in the winter of 1964, as a means to better understand the rhythm of Fitzgerald's sentences): "Every one suspects himself of at least one of the cardinal virtues and this is mine; I am one of the few honest people that I have ever known" (60).

82    **"likely to lose the baby"**: McKeen, *Outlaw Journalist*, 115.

82    **"six months"**: Carroll, *Hunter*, 115; Seymour and Wenner, *Gonzo*, 66.

82    **"on this planet"**: Carroll, *Hunter*, 152.

82    **"Enter the Brown Buffalo"**: In his book *Autobiography of a Brown Buffalo*, Oscar Zeta Acosta would talk about why he adopted "the Brown Buffalo" both as a personal nickname for himself and also as a more generalized term to describe Chicanos in twentieth-century America: "The buffalo, see? Yes, the animal that everyone slaughtered. Sure, both the cowboys and the Indians are out to get him ... and, because we do have roots in our Mexican past, our Aztec ancestry, that's where we get the brown from" (198).

82 **"The Jerome Hotel":** The bar at which Thompson and Acosta first met has been previously reported as the "Daisy Duck"—Acosta calls it this in *Autobiography of a Brown Buffalo*, and so does Thompson in "Strange Rumblings in Aztlan" and "The Banshee Screams for Buffalo Meat." Such a bar may have existed at one time, though in what capacity remains unclear. HST mentions a "Daisy Duck party at Phil Clark's" in a June 6, 1969 letter (*Fear and Loathing in America*, 122). And Acosta mentioned it to his parents, in a letter dated July 12, 1967, asking that they send him money to "Daisy Duck," though the address didn't necessarily correspond to the bar in question, and there's no mention of meeting Hunter Thompson at it, even though they both claim to have met the first week of July that year (see Hector Calderon's excellent essay "Oscar Zeta Acosta and *The Autobiography of a Brown Buffalo*" in *Narratives of Greater Mexico: Essays on Chicano Literary History*, 106). The Aspen Historical Society has no record of the Daisy Duck ever existing. A similar line of research was conducted by the producers of the PBS documentary *The Rise and Fall of the Brown Buffalo*, and after speaking with them, the best conclusion I can offer is that the name "Daisy Duck" may have been an inside joke / name of an annual party / nickname for a bar—and that, all things considered, the most likely meeting place in July of 1967 between Hunter Thompson and Oscar Acosta would've been the Jerome Bar, which Thompson often frequented and which anyone new to town would've checked out. It was also where Michael Solheim—who knew both Thompson and Acosta independently—would eventually bartend. Of course I could very easily be wrong about all of this—maybe there was an *actual* D.D. bar and the record of its existence has, like so much else, simply been lost; or perhaps it was a nickname for another old Aspen bar like the Red Onion—and in the end I'm not entirely sure. But for what it's worth, I *personally* think that the Jerome Hotel is the right call, which is why I've gone with it here . . .

82 **"oldest landmarks":** The Jerome Hotel and the Red Onion are two of the oldest remaining venues in town.

82 **"everyone was there or had been":** Salter, *Don't Save Anything*, 250. He was describing "the heart of a long democratic period, the 1960s and '70s, when the rich and poor of town, so to speak, rubbed shoulders and were on cordial terms" (ibid., 272).

82 **"center of both":** Salter, *Don't Save Anything*, 260: "There are only two seasons in Aspen—winter and summer. The winter is bigger: more money is spent then."

82 **"Salter added":** Salter, *Don't Save Anything*, 250.

82 **"on horses":** Salter, *Don't Save Anything*, 259.

82 **"holiday weekend":** Acosta, *Autobiography of a Brown Buffalo*, 135.

82 **"with some friends":** The Noonans, Bill and Anne: they were close friends of the Thompsons from Louisville and lived in the guest house on and off at the property in Woody Creek before getting divorced. Carroll, *Hunter*, 115.

83 **"he added wryly":** Thompson, "The Banshee Screams for Buffalo Meat," in Thompson, *Great Shark Hunt*, 511.

83 **"all across the Atlantic and Midwest"**: Out in California, Joan Didion was finishing "Slouching Toward Bethlehem," her feature for the *Saturday Evening Post* on the Haight-Ashbury scene, in which she would write:

> It was not a country in open revolution. It was not a country under enemy siege. It was the United States of America in the late cold spring of 1967 . . . San Francisco was where the social hemorrhaging was showing up. San Francisco was where the missing children were gathering and calling themselves "hippies." (*We Tell Ourselves Stories in Order to Live: Collected Nonfiction*, 67)

Didion had grown up in Sacramento, in an upper-middle-class pioneer-descendant family that during the Depression would've seemed a lot wealthier to others: the sort of family that, like their counterparts in the East—a well-to-do clan of academic New Englanders, for example—had for generations stood apart from the surrounding immigrant population, which in Sacramento at that time would've included my own Italian grandfather, born in 1927 (this is neither here nor there . . . except perhaps within the context of Didion's decision to vote for *Goldwater* in 1964). Regardless, when it came to the Bay Area counterculture scene, Joan Didion had arrived later than most— no worse than if she'd been present from the start.

83 **"Southeast Asia"**: A bit more global context: earlier in the month, at the height of the Six-Day War, the Soviet premier had threatened Lyndon Johnson with nuclear retaliation if the United States refused to restrain Israel. White, *Making of the President: 1968*, 13.

83 **"14,624 dead"**: *Vietnam War*, episode 5.

83 **"white counterparts"**: *Vietnam War*, episode 4.

83 **"friends they had in common"**: Thompson, "Strange Rumblings in Aztlan," 115.

83 **"an idealist"**: From Thompson, "Strange Rumblings in Aztlan," 115:

> He lumbered up to me and started raving about "ripping the system apart like a pile of cheap hay," or something like that . . . and I remember thinking, "Well, here's another one of those fucked-up, guilt-crazed dropout lawyers from San Francisco—some dingbat who ate one too many tacos and decided he was really Emiliano Zapata."

83 **"on the defensive"**: Acosta, *Autobiography of a Brown Buffalo*, 137–139.

83 **"parts unknown"**: Acosta, *Autobiography of a Brown Buffalo*, 71.

83 **"the segregated west side of town"**: On the side of the railroad tracks where the dogs only responded to Spanish commands. Acosta, *Autobiography of a Brown Buffalo*, 78.

83 **"a white girl named Alice"**: This is the name he ascribed to her in Acosta, *Autobiography of a Brown Buffalo*, 118; it may have been a pseudonym.

84 **"converted to the Baptist faith on the spot"**: Acosta, *Autobiography of a Brown Buffalo*, 131.

84    **"lead clarinetist"**: Acosta, *Autobiography of a Brown Buffalo*, 126.

84    **"a self-aware absolute"**: cf. Michael Ondaatje's description of Pat Garrett in *The Collected Works of Billy the Kid:*

> His mind was clear, his body able to drink, his feelings, unlike those who usually work their own way out of hell, not cynical about another's incapacity to get out of problems and difficulties. He did ten years of ranching, cow punching, being a buffalo hunter. He married Apolinaria Guitterrez and had five sons. He had come to Sumner then, mind full of French he never used, everything equipped to be that rare thing—a sane assassin sane assassin sane assassin sane assassin sane assassin sane. (29)

84    **"so-many-million others"**: To quote Acosta's first wife, Bette Davis, in Stavans, *Bandido*, 3: "He was touchingly dear, a charmer, a man of immense talents . . . But he was a victim of a mercilessly racist society, a product of abysmal differences between people. And he lived to personify that victimhood like no one else."

84    **"He ordered more whiskey"**: Acosta, *Autobiography of a Brown Buffalo*, 138.

85    **"the nature of the American system itself"**: Thompson, *Great Shark Hunt*, 115.

85    **"start over again"**: Thompson, *Great Shark Hunt*, 115.

85    **"the electorate"**: I think it's important to take a moment and address, here, what Hunter Thompson's perspective of *fascism* might've been. Perhaps for him, the best definition of the term—of something insidious enough to coagulate around and render inert those ideals on which our two-centuries-old republic had been founded—would perhaps be summarized as an *antonym* to Jeffersonian Democracy, its stark daguerreotype: an occluded system of power that, under the false banner of now-neutralized ideals, encourages the participation of it citizens solely as a means to identify, segregate, and lethally silence any and all forms of dissent.

As a result—and I'm speaking interpretively here—Thompson's conception of *fascism* would've been similar to that of the Italian novelist Umberto Eco, who in 1995 articulated: "Fascism had no quintessence. Fascism was a fuzzy totalitarianism, a collage of different philosophical and political ideas, a beehive of contradictions." These contradictions worked in tandem to bolster, under the premise of our basest tribal and nationalistic instincts, the state's overriding position: *contempt for the weak* (Eco, "Ur-Fascism").

85    **"you'd been forced to accept"**: Thompson, *Great Shark Hunt*, 511.

85    **"he told Thompson that night"**: Thompson, *Great Shark Hunt*, 510–511.

85    **"he called it"**: Thompson, *Great Shark Hunt*, 511.

86    **"white man's turf"**: from a selection of *Autobiography of a Brown Buffalo*, originally published in *Con Safos* and reprinted in Acosta and Stavans, *Uncollected Works*, 167.

86    **"by their obliviousness"**: Thompson, *Fear and Loathing in America*, 97, 107.

86　**"next few months"**: Thompson, *Great Shark Hunt,* 115.

86　**"Thompson gave him a ride"**: The version of their parting depicted here is from the published version of *Autobiography of a Brown Buffalo.* In another version, published in the magazine *Con Safos* (and later included in Acosta's *Uncollected Works,* which was edited by Ilan Stavans), he calls Sandy from the bus stop and gives the idol to her, in order that she pass it on to Thompson (173). Hunter Thompson, in later essays, referred to the scene I've depicted, as do most of the recent biographies about him, including William McKeen's *Outlaw Journalist.* Based on these details, as well as references to the idol "Ebb Tide" in Thompson's collected letters, I've dramatized the version of the meeting that appeared in Acosta's *Autobiography of a Brown Buffalo* (179–182).

86　**"loose, yellowed teeth"**: cf. Michael Ondaatje's *Collected Works of Billy the Kid:*

> And Pat Garrett
> sliced off my head.
> Blood a necklace on me all my life. (2)

Thompson and Acosta's relationship can at times take on the comingled feel of animosity and intimacy that Ondaatje expresses so vibrantly in his fictional rendering of Pat Garrett and Billy the Kid's relationship (though as to which one of them would be the outlaw and which would be sheriff is up to you to decide). In retrospect, this passage from Ondaatje brings to mind a line from Ian Haney López's outstanding book on Acosta's legal career: "Blood is a metaphor not just for race but for human suffering" (López, *Racism on Trial,* 171).

86　**"a plant to the sun"**: cf. Another passage by Michael Ondaatje—when, at the very end of his memoir *Running the Family,* he worried he'd failed to accurately characterize his father, about whom he'd been trying to write truthfully from the start:

> But the book again is incomplete. In the end all your children move among the scattered acts and memories with no more clues. Not that we ever thought we would be able to fully understand you. Love is often enough, towards your stadium of small things. Whatever brought you solace we would have applauded. Whatever controlled the fear we all share we would have embraced. That could only be dealt with one day at a time with that song we cannot translate, or the dusty green of the cactus you touch and turn carefully like a wounded child towards the sun, or the cigarettes you light. (183)

86　**"Where'd you get him?"**: All of the dialogue in this scene is drawn from Acosta, *Autobiography of a Brown Buffalo,* 178–181.

87　**"willingness to look"**: cf. Salter, *Burning the Days,* 73:

> As to what he was made of, what rare element, perhaps in the end I'll know, perhaps he'll tell me in the obscurity, the shade where he has gone. We will stroll aimlessly, as by rivers in France beneath the trees with their huge flat leaves, or along the Rhine, freed from desire and

time, like patients in some hospital, never to leave; he'll tell me what he remembers and I will finally understand.

87    **"over the course of a dinner"**: Thompson, *Fear and Loathing in America*, 22.

87    **"The Death of the American Dream"**: Thompson, *Fear and Loathing in America*, 24–25. Thompson would also reflect on this moment much later in his life, in the 2003 collection *Kingdom of Fear*, loc. 1200–1204:

> The story began in 1968, when Random House gave me $ 5,000 and my editor there said, "Go out and write about 'The Death of the American Dream.'" I had agreed without thinking, because all I really cared about, back then, was the money. And along with the $5K in front money came a $ 7,500 "expenses budget"—against royalties, which meant I'd be paying my own expenses, but I didn't give a fuck about that either. It was a nice gig to get into: Random House had agreed, more or less, to finance my education. I could go just about anywhere I wanted to just as long as I could somehow tie it in with "The Death of the American Dream."

88    **"summer, 1969"**: He described his plan for the book in a January 29, 1968, letter to Jim Silberman, in Thompson, *Fear and Loathing in America*, 25:

> The gig I have in mind is an opening research shot at the Pentagon, featuring attempts to interview the Joint Chiefs . . . by a man who got tired, many months ago, of seeing them referred to as a nameless, yet ominous, cabal that seemed to be in charge of almost everything crucial. I don't really expect these worthies to indulge me, but I think their lack of indulgence will be the beginning of my narrative, to wit: "Who are these people who won't talk to me? Where did they come from and why are they in charge? How far does their power extend? Where does their power originate? Why them, and not me?" And—once we've established some answers in the form of a pattern (or historical framework)—"Where now?"

88    **"just as the summer conventions were kicking off"**: Thompson, *Fear and Loathing in America*, 15–18.

88    **"Richard Milhous"**: A very quick aside: I think it's not unimportant to point out that Richard Nixon's mother, who passed away on September 30, 1967, was also named *Milhous*, as in: HANNAH MILHOUS NIXON.

88    **"cover the primary campaign"**: Thompson left for New York on Friday, February 9, 1968 (Thompson, *Fear and Loathing in America*, 36), where he spent two days hammering out the additional details of his new book contracts (ibid., 42); that weekend he then flew to Boston (Harrell, *Keep This Quiet!*, loc. 2629) and drove to New Hampshire to introduce himself to the Nixon campaign; that Sunday (February 11) Nixon arrived in Manchester for a week of campaigning that would last until Friday, February 15, when, after an event at the Nashua Chamber of Commerce, he drove back to Manchester and boarded a private jet to Florida, where he would unwind and read and, according to Pat Buchanan, work on his tan (Seymour and Wenner, *Gonzo,*

124); after five days of relaxation Nixon would return again to campaign in the New Hampshire primary contest on February 20. For more, see the schedule of Nixon's itinerary during this time, which is available online from the Richard Nixon Presidential Library, "Appointments, Schedules and Appearances Inventory."

88    **"Atlanta or Omaha or Dallas":** This description of the Holiday Inn lobby is drawn from Thompson's recollection of it, four years later, in *On the Campaign Trail '72*, 99: "But then you sort of expected that kind of cheap formica trip from Richard Nixon: all those beefy Midwest detective types in blue sharkskin suits—ex-brokers from Detroit, ex-speculators from Miami, ex gear & sprocket salesmen from Chicago."

88–89  **"long dark sweep of his overcoat":** Buchanan, *Greatest Comeback*, 353.

89    **"in these *damn* headquarters":** Gary Willis characterized Buchanan as such:

> Pat uses his idiosyncratically turned prefix much as the ancient Greeks scattered particles throughout a sentence, to distribute emphases. Before the campaign began, Buchanan described for me his Middle East trip, during which the Israeli war broke out: "The Boss was talking to all these dam-officials in Israel, and he knew as much of the dam-position of the Arabs and Russians as they did. He sat there sketching all the dam-possibilities, and amazed the officials. That's the way he is. Take any political situation in the dam-world, and he has war-gamed it this way and that, considering every which way it might go. (Willis, "What Makes the New Nixon Run?")

89    **"any *damn* credentials":** Thompson, *Fear and Loathing in America*, 95.

89    **"the party's more conservative factions":** Buchanan had been the head of Young Americans for Freedom, a conservative activist group. Willis, "What Makes the New Nixon Run?"

89    **"spent his professional life":** from Hyde's November 30, 2007, obituary in the *New York Times*, Clymer, "Henry J. Hyde, A Power in the House of Representatives, Dies at 83."

89    **"Henry J. Hyde":** Hyde would harass Thompson throughout the New Hampshire trip. Six years later, in 1974, Hyde would win an Illinois congressional seat, and in the House of Representatives he'd work his way up through committees. A fanatical anti-abortion advocate, he helped push through the Hyde Amendment—finally signed by George W. Bush in 2003—that, according to pro-choice activists like Nancy Northrop, amounted to "one of the cruelest injustices perpetrated on American women. For over 30 years, it has allowed antichoice politicians to deprive poor women of medically necessary treatment." (Clymer, "Henry J. Hyde, A Power in the House of Representatives, Dies at 83")

In the 1990s, Hyde led the impeachment charge against Bill Clinton—about which he'd later imply (this would be in 2005) that the proceedings he helped initiate were, for him at least, nothing more than *payback* for what had happened years earlier, during Watergate, to his former boss Richard Milhous

Nixon. "Henry Hyde Says Impeachment Was Revenge for Nixon," *Daily Kos*, April 21, 2005.

In summary: I think it's important to point out that the version of Hyde that Thompson portrayed in the 1968 *Pageant* article—that of a beefy, bigoted, vindictive, former gear-and-sprocket hack from Chicago—has held up well.

88 **"'I'm with *Pageant*'"**: Thompson, *Great Shark Hunt,* 177. Many of the quotes and details here are from Thompson's eventual article on this trip for the July 1968 issue of *Pageant:* "Presenting: The Richard Nixon Doll (Overhauled 1968 Model)," which would be reprinted in *Great Shark Hunt*.

89 **"to do exactly that"**: Thompson, *Fear and Loathing in America*, 94.

89 **"*damn* Levis"**: Thompson, *On the Campaign Trail '72,* 44.

89 **"*damn* ski-jacket"**: "Memoirs of a Wretched Week in Washington," *Boston Globe,* February 23, 1969, reprinted in Thompson, *Great Shark Hunt,* 170.

89 **"Hyde begrudgingly backed off"**: Thompson, *Fear and Loathing in America,* 94.

89 **"Shortly afterward"**: About 30 minutes, Thompson, *Fear and Loathing in America,* 95.

89 **"Nick Ruwe"**: Ruwe's biographical information is drawn from his *New York Times* obituary, Narvaez, "L. Nicholas Ruwe, Ex-Ambassador, 56; Assisted Presidents."

89 **"all rolled into one"**: Thompson wrote in a long June 10, 1968, letter to Ruwe:

> In one of my drafts I took off on this and worked up a long and complicated analogy comparing advance men to horse-trainers and fight managers . . . and I still think it was the most interesting angle I tried to develop, despite the fact that nearly all of it was chopped out for "space reasons." (*Fear and Loathing in America,* 94)

90 **"George really stepped into that one"**: This quote would appear, unattributed, in the subsequent *Pageant* article—Ruwe was referred to as "one of Nixon's advisors"—but in Thompson's June letter to Ruwe the real source was confirmed (*Fear and Loathing in America,* 93).

90 **"Ruwe mentioned a get-together"**: The details of this scene are drawn primarily from Pat Buchanan's account in *Greatest Comeback,* 229–230.

90 **"policy advisor / speech writer / press secretary"**: one of Buchanan's main jobs was to keep a file on everything going on in the news—a compendium of possible questions and answers Nixon could rely upon during an unforeseen crisis, like the recent North Korean attack, that January, on the USS *Pueblo,* which Buchanan drafted the speech for (Willis, "What Makes the New Nixon Run?")

91 **"Madison Avenue veterans"**: Harry Treleaven and Frank Shakespeare.

91 **"the stability it so desperately needed"**: From McGinnis, *Selling of the President,* loc. 461:

America still saw him as the 1960 Nixon. If he were to come at the people again, as candidate, it would have to be as something new; not this scarred, discarded figure from their past. He spoke to men who thought him mellowed. They detected growth, a new stability, a sense of direction that had been lacking. He would return with fresh perspective, a more unselfish urgency.

91 **"enjoying the hell out of this campaign"**: McGinnis, *The Selling of the President,* loc. 3177.

91 **"internal memo"**: McGinnis, *The Selling of the President.* loc. 535. The full quote:

So this was how they went into it: Trying, with one hand, to build the illusion that Richard Nixon, in addition to his attributes of mind and heart, considered, in the words of Patrick K. Buchanan, a speech-writer, "communicating with the people . . . one of the great joys of seeking the Presidency"; while with the other they shielded him, controlled him, and controlled the atmosphere around him.

It was as if they were building not a President but an Astrodome, where the wind would never blow, the temperature never rise or fall, and the ball never bounce erratically on the artificial grass.

91 **"Nick Ruwe admitted"**: Thompson, *Fear and Loathing in America,* 93.

91 **"America's one true *enemy*"**: cf. Don DeLillo's novel *Underworld* (the moment when J. Edgar Hoover, on hand for the infamous 1951 Giants–Dodgers baseball playoff game, reflects on Russia's nuclear capability):

And he thinks of a lonely tower standing on the Kazakh Test Site, the tower armed with the bomb, and he can almost hear the wind blowing across the Central Asian steppes, out where the enemy lives in long coats and fur caps, speaking that old weighted language of theirs, liturgical and grave. What secret history are they writing? (50)

92 **"avoid getting drawn into the next one"**: Buchanan, *Greatest Comeback,* 230.

92 **"more and more American lives"**: This is also drawn from a reflection Thompson wrote at the end of 1967 on the broader meaning of the San Francisco countercultural phenomenon, especially regarding "the painful contradictions in a society conceived as a monument to 'human freedom' and 'individual rights,' a nation in which all men are supposedly 'created free and equal' . . . a nation that any thinking hippy will insist has become a fear-oriented 'warfare state' that can no longer afford to tolerate even the minor aberrations that go along with 'individual freedom'" (Thompson, *Fear and Loathing in America,* 7). A few months later, in a letter to his mother, Thompson would expand upon this point: "Every life lost in Vietnam is a waste and a mockery of human reason. We all know the war's over, in terms of the power struggle, but people will go on being killed right up to the final flag-whistling ceremony" (ibid., 67).

92 **"from beginning to end"**: Fitzgerald, *Great Gatsby,* 154.

92    **"they were still talking heatedly"**: Seymour and Wenner, *Gonzo*, 124;
      Buchanan would remark: "I had a lot more stamina then . . . "

92    **"power & honesty rarely coincide"**: Thompson, *Fear and Loathing in
      America*, 550.

92    **"using their rules against them"**: This quote is from an interview Thomp-
      son did with *Salon* in 2003:

      > I've found you can deal with the system a lot easier if you use their
      > rules—by understanding their rules, by using their rules against them.
      > I talk to a lot of lawyers. You know, I consider Pat Buchanan a friend. I
      > don't agree with him on many things. Personally, I enjoy him. I just like
      > him. And I learn from Pat. (Thompson, *Ancient Gonzo Wisdom*, 317)

93    **"poison toad"**: Thompson, *Great Shark Hunt*, 177.

93    **"fresh, rebranded premise"**: Thompson, *Fear and Loathing in America*, 95.

93    **"typed-up notes"**: Thompson, *Great Shark Hunt*, 177.

93    **"Mr. Nixon runs his own campaigns"**: Thompson, *Great Shark Hunt*,
      182. Hyde, at the end of this exchange, added: "You'd find that out pretty
      quick if you worked for him." To which Thompson replied: "That's a good
      idea. How about it? I could write him a speech that would change his im-
      age in twenty-four hours . . . " But as Thompson would write: "Henry didn't
      think much of the idea. Humor is scarce in the Nixon camp. The staffers tell
      jokes now and then, but they're not very funny."

93    **"peace with honor"**: Thompson, *Great Shark Hunt*, 179:
      > Nixon did confess that he had a way to end the war, but he wouldn't
      > tell how. Patriotically he explained why: "No one with this respon-
      > sibility who is seeking office should give away any of his bargaining
      > positions in advance." (Nixon's wife, Pat, has confidence in his ability
      > to cope with Vietnam. "Dick would never have let Vietnam drag on
      > like this," she says.)

94    **"the candidate himself"**: McGinnis, *Selling of the President*, loc. 2716. Price
      would add:

      > The selection of a President has to be an act of faith. It becomes
      > increasingly so as the business of government becomes ever more
      > incomprehensible to the average voter. This faith isn't achieved by
      > reason; it's achieved by charisma, by a feeling of trust that can't be
      > argued or reasoned, but that comes across in those silences that sur-
      > round the words. The words are important—but less for what they
      > actually say than for the sense they convey, for the impression they
      > give of the man himself, his hopes, his standards, his competence; his
      > intelligence, his essential humanness, and the directions of history he
      > represents. (McGinnis, *Selling of the President*, loc. 2730)

94    **"gathered there to follow him"**: Four years later, looking back on this
      week in *On the Campaign Trail '72*, 99, Thompson would write: "Nixon rarely
      appeared, and when he did nobody in the press corps ever got within ten feet
      of him, except now and then by special appointment for cautious interviews.

Getting assigned to cover Nixon in '68 was like being sentenced to six months in a Holiday Inn."

94 **"his *National Observer* days"**: Thompson, *Fear and Loathing in America*, 41.

94 **"for the first time"**: Bill Cardoso and Thompson would, according to multiple sources, smoke a joint together in the back of the press bus; Cardoso had read *Hell's Angels* and recognized Thompson. Thompson, *Fear and Loathing in America*, 99.

94 **"The Boss"**: Buchanan, *The Greatest Comeback*, 230: "We promised Hunter face time with the candidate, who was skeptical of freelancers."

95 **"February 16"**: Thompson, *Fear and Loathing in America*, 41.

95 **"a short campaign break"**: In *Gonzo* (Seymour and Wenner, 174), Buchanan would explain: "We used to go up to New Hampshire to campaign for two or three days, then take the former vice president down to Florida, where he could relax and get a tan and let our advertising do the talking for us."

95 **"Ray Price approached Thompson"**: Thompson, *Fear and Loathing in America*, 41.

95 **"You've been wanting to talk to the boss?"**: *Playboy* interview, in Thompson, *Ancient Gonzo Wisdom*, 49.

95 **"Come on"**: *New York Times* reporter Bob Semple helped lay the groundwork for the meeting, too; from a letter to Semple on February 20, 1968, in Thompson, *Fear and Loathing in America*, 41:

> Dear Bob . . . Thanks again for the help in Manchester. I kept after Ray Price all day Friday (the day you took off from Boston), and just about the time I gave up I found myself in Nixon's car, with the great man himself bending my ear about pro football. The bastard really knows it; I figured his claiming to be a fan was just another one of his hypes, a pitch for the violence-vote. You're right, I think, in saying he's not a conscious phoney. That complicates my story considerably. I'm not sure what I'll write, but I'll send you a copy if and when it comes out.

95 **"bench of leather"**: I am assuming that the seats of this specific Mercury were leather—an assumption based on my recent and ill-advised bout of time-consuming internet research regarding the 1965–1967 Mercury models . . . All of which is to say: this claim is by no means definitive. In the darkness of this New Hampshire car ride Thompson and Nixon may very well have been bumping along together on *vinyl* seats . . . Or even (*infandum!*) some sort of American pleather . . .

95 **"What did he see?"**: The description here is based on those given by a few writers (such as Norman Mailer in *Miami and the Siege of Chicago* and Gary Willis in his 1968 *Esquire* profile), as well as Thompson's own takes on Nixon's physicality; it also draws on images/televised footage from the time. Additionally, I seem to have conflated (upon further reflection) two images from Denis Johnson's *Train Dreams*, a novella about the life of an itinerant lumberjack in the early-1900s Pacific Northwest:

The World's Fattest Man, who rested on a divan in a trailer that took him from town to town . . . He weighed in at just over a thousand pounds. There he sat, immense and dripping sweat, with a mustache and goatee and one gold earring like a pirate's, wearing shiny gold short pants and nothing else, his flesh rolling out on either side of him from one end of the divan to the other and spilling over and dangling toward the floor like an arrested waterfall, while out of this big pile of himself poked his head and arms and legs. (22)

And:

The strange young hillbilly entertainer Elvis Presley, [whose] private train had stopped for some reason, maybe for repairs, here in this little town that didn't even merit its own station. The famous youth had appeared in a window briefly and raised his hand in greeting [to] the townspeople standing in the late dusk . . . [and] staring into the mystery and grandeur of a boy so high and solitary. (24)

95    **"named it Checkers"**: "Checkers Speech" transcript.

95    **"my school and my church"**: Mailer, "Superman Comes to the Supermart."

96    **"long-extinct species"**: cf. Italo Calvino's "The Dinosaurs" (in which the main character, who'd been living as a dinosaur, manages to survive the extinction of his species):

I prefer not to think back on the period of the great death. I never believed I'd escape it. The long migration that saved me led me through a cemetery of fleshless carcasses, where only a crest or horn or a scale of armor or a fragment of horny skin recalled the ancient splendor of the living creature. And over those remains worked the beaks, the bills, the talons, the suckers of the new masters of the planet. When at last I found no further traces, of the living or of the dead, then I stopped. (97)

96    **"real heavyweight challengers"**: Thompson, *Great Shark Hunt*, 178.

96    **"nothing if not prepared"**: Willis, in his May 1968 *Esquire* profile of Nixon, would write:

I had been told that Nixon's technique, in these midair interviews, is to filibuster on the first question, so I should ask what I really want to know at the outset—"Give him your high hard one right off"—or I might never get him around it. Unfortunately, I had no high hard one. Besides, how does one outtrick Tricky? I knew that for the most intricate Q, he would have a well-prepared A. So I didn't fool with the Vietnam stuff.

96    **"*Green Bay: the overwhelming favorite*"**: From Thompson's *Pageant* article, reprinted in *Great Shark Hunt*, 182: "I'd heard he was a fan, and earlier that night in a speech at a Chamber of Commerce banquet he'd said that he'd bet on Oakland in the Super Bowl, and since Ray Price had arranged for me to ride back to Manchester in Nixon's car, I took the opportunity to ask him about it."

96    **"stronger than the sports-writers claim"**: Thompson, *Great Shark Hunt*, 182.

96    **"knocked off balance"**: Thompson, *On the Campaign Trail '72*, 45.

96    **"very same thing by Bob Geiger"**: The story of this Raiders game and its details were related by Bob Geiger during our interview.

97    **"left of the goalpost"**: Which back then stood at the front of the end-zone—dangerously in play—as opposed to out of bounds at the back, where they're situated now.

97    **"more popular rival"**: All the details in the story about the 1964 Raiders game are from Geiger's account during our interview. But to be clear: Geiger never connected *his* comments about the AFL with Nixon's; I've made this association myself, based on the details Thompson gave regarding the conversation in his 1968 *Pageant* article and in *On the Campaign Trail '72*. In other words: Did Thompson's mind turn to Geiger's story when he heard Nixon talk about the AFL?

       I've tried to stop short of making such a claim (though, if you were to ask me what I personally think, I'd say that it's *probable*, if not assured). Instead, the goal, in placing this flashback here, is to articulate the incongruity of Nixon's expert knowledge—analysis that bore a striking resemblance to the football-based opinions of one of the people Thompson trusted on that subject the most . . .

97    **"design and execution"**: Thompson, *On the Campaign Trail '72*, 45.

97    **"college of origin"**: Afterward, describing this moment in his *Pageant* feature, reprinted in *Great Shark Hunt*, 183, Thompson would write: "It wasn't his factual knowledge that stunned me. It was his genuine interest in the game."

98    **"were true"**: *Playboy* interview, in Thompson, *Ancient Gonzo Wisdom*, 49.

98    **"the entire time"**: This description is based on the one that Thompson gave at the time, in his *Pageant* article (from *Great Shark Hunt*), and during short references from his letters.

       Four years later, recounting the incident, he'd retell it in a more dramatic fashion, and whether or not it actually happened *this* way I'm not sure; for me, paring the drama down to the original feels like the most honest move.

98    **"You almost blew up the plane"**: Thompson, *On the Campaign Trail '72*, 44.

98    **"what a nightmare"**: Thompson, *On the Campaign Trail '72*, 44.

98    **"I didn't realize I was smoking"**: Thompson, *Great Shark Hunt*, 183.

99    **"first twenty pages"**: This equation is based on triple-spaced pages; for a better present-day comparison, imagine that it was probably more like cutting 10 of the first 13 pages in a 30-page document; which means that—if the final heavily edited article was 4,000 words (a rough calculation)—the editors at *Pageant* cast aside about 16 of the 30 pages from his 1968 Nixon article (now we're using a standard word/page calculation: 300 words/page; 30,000 words/100 pages): more than half . . . To Nick Ruwe he wrote: "I submitted around 45 triple-spaced pages, most of them dealing with backstage,

mechanical, seemingly trivial stuff—and 15 of the first 20 of these pages were deleted by the editors; this is sort of like trying to race an 8-cylinder car on 4 sparkplugs" (Thompson, *Fear and Loathing in America*, 93).

99 **"he liked football"**: Is Nixon's declaration of his love for football really all that different from what a child might express? As in: what if the very most enjoyable thing in the world for certain *terrible* men is to eat well-done steak or ride in an enormous plane or sit at the wheel of a big red fire truck and pretend to steer?

99 **"nice guy"**: This is John A. Farrell's phrasing—the author of *Richard Nixon: The Life*. On page 325 he briefly describes how "countercultural journalist Hunter Thompson" received "Nixon's 'nice guy' treatment in a car ride in which they shared their passion for pro football."

100 **"February 14"**: This date is derived from Bob Semple's weekly *New York Times* article on the Nixon campaign, published Sunday, February 18, 1968: "Nixon's Campaign Is Stately, Dignified, Proud—and Slow."

100 *"new makeup he'd been wearing"*: The emphasis here is my own.

100 **"Manchester Holiday Inn"**: White, *Making of the President: 1968*, 6.

100 *"New York Times"*: Under the headline: "Street Clashes Go On in Vietnam, Foe Still Holds Parts of Cities; Johnson Pledges Never to Yield."

101 **"like drunken sailors every day"**: *Vietnam War*, episode 5.

101 **"did the best they could"**: For a recording of Cronkite's broadcast, see the YouTube video "Report from Vietnam (1968)."

101 **"destroy the town to save it"**: *Vietnam War*, episode 5, 42:53.

101 **"two hundred thousand troops"**: White, *Making of the President: 1968*, 125.

101 **"42 percent of the vote"**: White, *Making of the President: 1968*, 153: On the Republican side, Richard Nixon enjoyed "a clear, smashing victory"—winning by a margin of "seven to one" over his closest opponent.

101 **"Robert Kennedy announced his candidacy"**: "Kennedy to Make 3 Primary Races; Attacks Johnson," *New York Times*, March 17, 1968:

> I am today announcing my candidacy for the presidency of the United States. I do not run for the presidency merely to oppose any man, but to propose new policies. I run because I am convinced that this country is on a perilous course and because I have such strong feelings about what must be done, and I feel that I'm obliged to do all I can.

101 **"shocking announcement"**: For a transcript of LBJ's speech, see the entry "The President's Address to the Nation Announcing . . . " from the American Presidency Project, which is archived at the University of California Santa Barbara and can be accessed online.

101 **"home in Woody Creek at the time"**: Thompson, *Fear and Loathing in America*, 49–51.

101   **"destroyed on his feet"**: Thompson, *Fear and Loathing in America*, 50.

101   **"lost a $10,000 advance"**: More than $70,000 by today's standards (currency converter website).

101   **"he'd later write"**: Thompson, *On the Campaign Trail '72*, 123.

102   **"shot through the head and killed"**: Thompson, *Fear and Loathing in America*, 128. Thompson saw it on TV.

102   **"three thousand people were arrested"**: See the entry "Findings on MLK Assassination," which can be found online in the National Archives.

102   **"murder rioters in the streets"**: Farber, *Chicago '68*, 42.

102   **"and the burning"**: Thompson, *Fear and Loathing in America*, 52–53.

102   **"night of the pivotal"**: See the May 25, 2011, article by Joseph A. Palmero in *The Huffington Post*, "Here's What RFK Did in California in 1968."

102   **"Robert Kennedy"**: Earlier in the day, Kennedy was walking along the beach with Theodore White (author of the *Making of the President* series): together they were taking an afternoon break before the vote came in—when suddenly Kennedy saw one of his sons struggling in the surf. The presidential candidate immediately jumped in the water:

> A huge roller came in from the sea, and the bobbing head of one of two children went under. Bobby dived. For a moment one could not see them in the surf until he came up with David, whom he had pulled from the undertow. A large red bruise now marked his forehead where he had bumped either sand or the boy; he chided the boy gently for going beyond his depth, but the boy was safe. (White, *Making of the President: 1968*, 210)

103   **"Kennedy's support for Israel"**: The writer Pete Hamill, a friend of Kennedy's, helped disarm Sirhan. About the assassin he wrote: "He was 24. His rage was fueled by the Six-Day War the previous year and by Kennedy's support for the sale of jet fighters to Israel." (Hamill, "June 5, 1968")

103   **"near the armpit"**: This scene is based on Jules Witcover's account in his book *85 Days: The Last Campaign of Robert Kennedy*, 225–230; others were hit in the legs and lower body by the stray shots, but Kennedy, who'd turned his head to greet Romero, was hit with the first shot at the base of the skull.

103   **"fluid tail of bone"**: cf. Tobias Wolffe's short story, "Bullet in the Brain," reprinted recently in his collection *Our Story Begins*: "The bullet is already in the brain. It won't be outrun forever, or charmed to a halt. In the end it will do its work and leave the troubled skull behind, dragging its comet's tail of memory and hope and talent and love into the marble hall of commerce" (268).

103   **"two former professional athletes"**: The NFL tackle Rosey Grier and Olympic decathlete Rafer Johnson, who helped disarm Sirhan Sirhan.

103   **"Vanderbilt University"**: "Kennedy Charges Johnson Is Divisive."

103   **"He quoted Sophocles"**: In retrospect, Bobby Kennedy really did love his Athenian playwrights. After Martin Luther King Jr.'s assassination that

April—when he announced the news himself to a crowd in Indianapolis—he said: "My favorite poet was Aeschylus. He wrote: 'In our sleep, pain which cannot forget falls drop by drop upon the heart until, in our own despair, against our will, comes wisdom through the awful grace of God.'"

He ended with the statement: "Let us dedicate ourselves to what the Greeks wrote so many years ago: to tame the savageness of man and make gentle the life of this world. Let us dedicate ourselves to that, and say a prayer for our country and for our people."

His speech that day was seen as a major force in helping to make sure Indianapolis avoided the violence that was sweeping the rest of the country. For more, see Higgins, "April 4, 1968."

103    **"American spirit"**: Thompson, *On the Campaign Trail '72*, 372.

104    **"what I should offer"**: Thompson, *Fear and Loathing in America*, 48.

104    **"headed back to Clifford's"**: Clifford, *To Aspen and Back*, 122–123.

104    **"Thompson told Clifford"**: Clifford, *To Aspen and Back*, 123.

105    **"Stop the war!"**: For video of this moment, see the YouTube clip "1968 Democratic Convention, Part 3."

105    **"speaking for the minority"**: Farber, *Chicago '68*, 194.

105    **"won out"**: 1567.75 to 1041.5, Mailer, *Miami and the Siege of Chicago*, 172.

106    **"Chicago police officers"**: Thompson, *Fear and Loathing in America*, 113, 125. Details of the billy-clubbing are taken from both passages.

106    **"lowest knuckles of his spine"**: From Thompson, *Fear and Loathing in America*, 113:

> I had that prized magnetic badge around my neck—the same one that, earlier that day, had earned me a billy-club shot in the stomach when I tried to cross a police line: I'd showed the badge and kept on walking, but one of the cops grabbed my arm. "That's not a press pass," he said. I held it under his face. "What the hell do you think it is?" I asked . . . and I was still looking at the snarl on his face when I felt my stomach punched back against my spine; he used his club like a spear, holding it with both hands and hitting me right above the belt.

106    **"fifteen-thousand-person rally"**: The following stats, quotes, physical details, and stage directions are drawn from David Farber's outstanding *Chicago '68* chapter "The Streets Belong to the People," which has gathered multiple individual sources to articulate a vivid, step-by-step description of the day.

106    **"MOBE"**: MOBE was led by Rennie Davis, Tom Hayden, and David Dellinger. To *Esquire* journalist Terry Southern, Dellinger had said at the beginning of the week, "Our demonstrations shall be entirely peaceful" (Southern, "Grooving in the Chi"). Not that it would necessarily play out that way; for more, see the first two background chapters in Farber, *Chicago '68*.

106    **"Yippies"**: Led by Abbie Hoffman and Jerry Rubin, and also Paul Krassner, who'd become a friend of Thompson's after they met for the first time at the

1966 Berkeley VDC rally—the one in which the Hell's Angels attacked the protestors.

107 **"mainstream contingent":** At one point Allen Ginsberg—beaten and gassed earlier in the week during gatherings at Lincoln Park—attempted to lead everyone in the same "Om" chant he'd introduced, two years earlier, to the Hell's Angels in La Honda.

107 **"clubbing everyone in their way":** For more, see Farber, *Chicago '68*, 196. In retrospect, what happened at the band shell in Grant Park was horrific. The police, after charging the crowd, found the teenager who'd climbed the flagpole and hauled him off. But when one of the MOBE leaders, Rennie Davis, suggested that people link hands, the phalanx of cops surged at him; with their billy clubs they cracked his skull and his face and opened long gashes in his head; he was beaten unconscious. Afterward, as Davis was rushed to the hospital, another MOBE leader, Tom Hayden—undone by the violence he'd just witnessed—grabbed the rally's microphone. Furiously he told everyone to flee the park and head to the Loop: "If blood is going to flow let it flow all over the city!"

107 **"Army-issued launchers":** Farber, *Chicago '68*, 191.

107 **"toward the Stockyards":** The rush of people from Grant Park to the Loop was an extremely chaotic event, as you can imagine. At one point, many of the thousands of fleeing protestors found themselves, by chance, joining up with a small legally permitted march already on its way down Michigan Avenue toward the Amphitheatre—the Poor People's Campaign, an event that the Southern Christian Leadership Council had organized before Martin Luther King Jr.'s assassination (and that included, symbolically, three mule-drawn wagons). Daley had given the permit for the SCLC's march ahead of time, one of the few he'd granted, because he was worried about being perceived as racist—and losing African American votes—if he didn't . . . For more, see Farber, *Chicago '68*, 199.

107 **"four miles to the south":** Farber, *Chicago '68*, 199.

107 **"seven thousand protestors":** Farber, *Chicago '68*, 199.

108 **"toward the lake":** cf. a passage from Vladimir Nabokov's haunting short story "Signs and Symbols": "Straining the corners of his mouth apart by means of his thumbs, with a horrible masklike grimace, he removed his new hopelessly uncomfortable dental plate and severed the long tusks of saliva connecting him to it" (Nabokov, *Stories of Vladimir Nabokov*, 601).

108 **"large blue kit bag at his shoulder":** As Thompson later called this aspect of his apparel: "my friendly blue L.L. Bean kit bag" (*Kingdom of Fear*, loc. 1224).

108 **"what was going on":** From Clifford, *To Aspen and Back*, 125: "Thompson was in Chicago and was clubbed by a cop, gassed and shoved through a store window. He sent me his press badge on which he had scrawled, 'This entitles the bearer to a beating.'" And from Douglas Brinkley's editor's note to Thompson, *Fear and Loathing in America*, xviii: "He witnessed a mob of demonstrators

marching toward a flank of policemen at the corner of Michigan and Balboa. Seconds later, the police charged the protestors with billy clubs waving. Ignoring the press credentials that hung around his neck, the police shoved Thompson against a plate glass window as chaos and violence erupted all around him."

108 **"received word"**: From Farber, *Chicago '68*, 199: Rochford, "after a hurried conference with an SCLC representative, ordered officers to free the mule train [along with the original members of the small poverty march] and allow it, and only it, to continue down Michigan avenue."

108 **"*Clear the intersection*"**: Later, explaining his reasoning, Rochford would say: "I had no intention of allowing a mob to take over the streets" (Farber, *Chicago '68*, 200).

108 **"Chicago police approached"**: The following accounts of violence are individually cited; Farber, who in *Chicago '68* provides some of the most harrowing moments, drew much of his material from three sources: raw CBS news footage; the boxes of testimony compiled by the National Commission on the Causes and Prevention of Violence and stored in the archives of the Lyndon Baines Johnson Library; and from sworn court testimony provided by protestors and police.

108 **"heads of their targets"**: Nearly all of the serious injuries that resulted would be head injuries. Kusch, *Battleground Chicago*, 101.

109 **"up from the lake"**: Arlen, *Living-Room War*, 237.

109 **"cops arrived"**: Arlen, *Living-Room War*, 238–239.

109 **"Kill! Kill! Kill!"**: Farber, *Chicago '68*, 200.

109 **"tried to flee"**: Arlen, *Living-Room War*, 238.

109 **"a young man with a moustache said"**: Arlen, *Living-Room War*, 238.

109 **"television cameraman"**: Arlen, *Living-Room War*, 238.

109 **"attacked him, too"**: Arlen, *Living-Room War*, 238.

109 **"tried to crawl away"**: Mailer, *Miami and the Siege of Chicago*, 179; Farber, *Chicago '68*, 201.

109 **"plainclothes cops"**: Mailer, *Miami and the Siege of Chicago*, 235.

109 **"radio instructions"**: Mailer, *Miami and the Siege of Chicago*, 175.

109 **"chevrons at the shoulders"**: For video of the riot, see the YouTube clip "Chicago Convention the Whole World Is Watching 1968."

109 **"*WAHOO!*"**: Farber, *Chicago '68*, 200.

109 **"closely at his heels"**: Mailer, *Miami and the Siege of Chicago* [via a quoted article by Jack Newfield in the Village], 179–180.

109 **"Fred Dutton"**: This biographical information is drawn from the entry "Frederick Gary Dutton" at www.arlingtoncemetery.net/fgdutton.htm, and from his *Los Angeles Times* obituary (Oliver, "Fred Dutton, 82").

110  **"his pulse fading"**: Witcover, *85 Days,* 232.

110  **"Goodwin said"**: Goodwin, like Dutton, had the misfortune of working for *both* Kennedy brothers on the occasions of their assassinations.

110  **"critic of the war"**: For more on McGovern's position on Vietnam, see Knock, "George McGovern, Vietnam, and the Democratic Crackup."

110  **"our national experience"**: For more on this speech, see the April 26, 1967, *New York Times* article "Excerpts from Senate Exchange on Vietnam War."

110  **"those kids down there"**: Farber, *Chicago '68,* 201.

110  **"filling with blood"**: Knock, *Life and Times of George McGovern,* 408.

111  **"Pat Buchanan"**: Buchannan, *Greatest Comeback,* 325. His hotel room is referenced as "Mr. Nixon's unannounced observation post" in White's *The Making of the President: 1968,* though his name isn't mentioned (345).

111  **"take over society"**: This quote is a combination of passages from pages 181 and 185 in Mailer, *Miami and the Siege of Chicago.*

111  **"played it perfectly"**: See "Address Accepting The Presidential Nomination . . . "

112  **"where the *politics*"**: My emphasis.

112  **"the day pointed us"**: Buchanan, *Greatest Comeback,* 355.

112  **"let alone the country"**: Forty years later, looking back on this moment, Buchanan would reflect: "Hunter Thompson was not entirely wrong when he wrote, 'Richard Nixon is living in the White House because of what happened that night in Chicago'" (Buchanan, *Greatest Comeback,* 364).

112  **"Hubert Horatio Humphrey"**: The description of Humphrey's suite and his behavior within is taken from White, *Making of the President: 1968,* 345–352.

112  **"watching it all up close"**: Afterward Thompson would write:

> For two days and nights I'd been running around the streets of Chicago, writing longhand notebook wisdom about all the people who were being forced, by the drama of this convention, to take sides in a very basic way . . . ("once again," I had written on Monday night, "we're back to that root-question: Which Side Are You On?"). (*Fear and Loathing in America,* 2, 114)

112  **"running skirmishes"**: For more, see Terry Southern's account of the police violence in Lincoln park in his November 1968 *Esquire* article "Grooving in the Chi," which is harrowing.

112  **"antiwar delegate"**: The video of this skirmish can be viewed on YouTube under the entry "Dan Rather Convention Floor Fight 1968."

> "I'm sorry to be out of breath," Rather said during the live broadcast, "but somebody belted me in the stomach."

> Walter Cronkite was not amused: "I think we've got a bunch of thugs here, Dan."

112  **"overwhelming force"**: This undercover police tactic was also used—to much more lethal success—by the FBI and local police departments against Chicano and African American civil rights movements. As such, the violence at the DNC was part of a larger trend; the last four summers in cities across the country there'd been riots and killing and pitched battles between law enforcement and protestors. These riots had occurred for the most part within the poorest and most disadvantaged neighborhoods.

In Chicago, Terry Southern witnessed this tactic firsthand. In "Grooving in the Chi," he wrote:

> Incidentally, one of the most insidious aspects of the entire police operation was the use of "confrontation provocateurs." These were cops dressed like hippies whose job it was to incite the crowd to acts of violence which would justify police intervention or, failing that, to commit such acts themselves. It is curiously significant that their artfully dressed undercover men were so flagrantly conspicuous as to be impossible to miss—not due to their appearance, which was indiscernible from the rest of the crowd, or even the fact that they were encouraging violence, but due completely to the loud, lewd, tasteless stupidity that characterized their every remark and gesture.

113  **"classic pincer formation"**: Eugene McCarthy, watching from his suite, recognized the ancient military tactic immediately; it had been used two thousand years earlier, during the Battle of Cannae, when the superior Roman forces were outflanked by the Carthaginians: "It was to be a holocaust, like at Cannae. The demonstrators, [McCarthy] said, were about to be trapped in Hannibal's double-envelopment movement" (White, *Making of the President: 1968,* 351).

113  **"motorcycle helmet"**: McKeen, *Outlaw Journalist,* 124. It was a Bell motorcycle helmet; Thompson, *Songs of the Doomed,* 123, 288.

113  **"do *anything*"**: From Perry, *Fear and Loathing,* 131:

> Suddenly the police attacked with billy clubs. He found himself surrounded by frantic demonstrators, desperate to flee from a police force run amok. Although his press credentials were prominently displayed on his chest, they seemed not to protect him but to mark him for a special beating. He was hit in the stomach by one of the long riot clubs and could have suffered a serious head injury had he not been wearing a motorcycle helmet that he had decided to take with him at the last minute.

113  **"plate-glass window"**: Kusch, *Battleground Chicago,* 101.

114  **"a few feet away"**: Brinkley's introduction in Thompson, *Fear and Loathing in America,* xvi–xvii.

114  **"cops shoved past"**: Brinkley's introduction in Thompson, *Fear and Loathing in America,* xviii.

114  **"hail of bullets"**: Thompson, *Kingdom of Fear,* loc. 1221.

114 **"shot exploding"**: cf. George Orwell's description of what it felt like to be shot through the throat by a sniper—an incident he'd miraculously survive and then write about in *Homage to Catalonia,* 143:

> Roughly speaking it was the sensation of being *at the center* of an explosion. There seemed to be a loud bang and a blinding flash of light all around me, and I felt a tremendous shock—no pain, only a violent shock, such as you get from an electrical terminal; with it a sense of utter weakness, a feeling of being stricken and shriveled up to nothing. The sand-bags in front of me receded into immense distance. I fancy you would feel much the same if you were struck by lightning. I knew immediately that I was hit, but because of the seeming bang and flash I thought it was a rifle nearby that had gone off accidentally and shot me. All this happened in a space of time much less than a second.

114 **"even heard its report"**: Thompson, *Kingdom of Fear,* loc. 1215: "knowing that at any instant my lungs would be shredded by some bullet that would hit me before I could even hear the shot fired."

114 **"with no escape"**: Thompson, *On the Campaign Trail '72,* 31: "Although I was right in the middle of it the whole time, I have never been able to write about it myself. For two weeks afterwards, back in Colorado, I couldn't even talk about it without starting to cry—for reasons I think I finally understand now, but I still can't explain."

114 **"sort of fear"**: cf. James Salter's essay about flying in combat, "Cool Heads," from his collection of nonfiction *Don't Save Anything,* 70: "Fear is more likely, more distinct, when you see the enemy turning towards you from far off, many of them. They see you and are coming to kill you. Anyone can feel fear."

114 **"Bobby Kennedy"**: cf. Norman Mailer's beautiful passage, in third person, about his experience at the convention.

> From time to time, the reporter thought again of matters which did not balance him. He thought of the fear Bobby Kennedy must have known. This was a thought he had been trying to avoid all night— it gave eyes to the darkness of his own fear—that fear that came from knowing that some of *them* were implacable, *Them!* All the bad cops . . . (*Miami and the Siege of Chicago,* 227)

114 **"slumped against the wall"**: Kusch, *Battleground Chicago,* 101. The victim was a young man from Bethesda, Maryland.

114 **"legs paralyzed"**: This scene—of the paralyzed protestor being beaten— was described in Terry Southern's article "Grooving in the Chi."

115 **"I'm paying fifty dollars a day!"**: Thompson, *Kingdom of Fear,* loc. 1235.

115 **"tear gas"**: In 1972, at the Republican Convention in Miami, Thompson was tear gassed again, and he subsequently offered instructions on how to get it out (as well as a reflection on Chicago):

> Finally, when the gas got so bad that I no longer knew what direction I was moving in, I staggered across somebody's lawn and began

feeling my way along the outside of the house until I came to a
water faucet. I sat down on the grass and soaked my handkerchief
under the tap, then pressed it on my face, without rubbing, until I
was able to see again. When I finally got up, I realized that at least a
dozen cops had been standing within twenty feet of me the whole
time, watching passively and not offering any help—but not beating
me into a bloody, screaming coma, either . . . That was the difference
between Chicago and Miami. Or at least one of the most significant
differences. If the cops in Chicago had found me crawling around in
somebody's front yard, wearing a "press" tag and blind from too much
gas, they'd have broken half my ribs and then hauled me away in
handcuffs for "resisting arrest." I saw it happen so often that I still feel
the bile rising when I think about it. (*On the Campaign Trail '72*, 337)

115   **"his legs crossed"**: The descriptions here of Thompson in the hotel room
are drawn from Thompson, *Kingdom of Fear*, loc. 1239.

116   **"Chicago International Amphitheatre"**: Images here are drawn from
video footage of the convention, including the YouTube entry "Hubert Humphrey Addressed Delegates at the 1968 DNC," and also from this description
by Norman Mailer:

> The Amphitheatre was the best place in the world for a convention.
> Relatively small, it had the packed intimacy of a neighborhood fight
> club. The entrances to the gallery were narrow as hallway tunnels,
> and the balcony seemed to hang over the speaker. The colors were
> black and gray and red and white and blue, bright powerful colors
> in support of a ruddy beef-eating sea of faces. The standards in these
> cramped quarters were numerous enough to look like lances. The
> aisles were jammed. The carpets were red. The crowd had a blood in
> their vote which had traveled in unbroken line from the throng who
> cheered the blood of brave Christians and ferocious lions. (*Miami and
> the Siege of Chicago*, 186)

116   **"other than the amphitheater"**: Michael Arlen, who was on hand as a
reporter for the *New Yorker*, would write about this lack of live footage in his
book *Living-Room War*:

> It's common knowledge by now, to be sure, how Daley and the Dem-
> ocrats combined to cut down the television coverage of the events
> in Chicago by managing the electrical-workers' strike so that there
> wasn't any time left to provide the networks with mobile hookups—
> that, plus preventing the networks' mobile trucks from parking at
> key places on the streets, and making things generally as difficult and
> restrictive as possible. (240)

116   **"press balcony"**: From Thompson, *Fear and Loathing in America*, 126:

> My own preference is MARTIN BORMANN, whom I tried to
> nominate from the press balcony, on several occasions, after Alabama
> and Bull Connor voted for [George] Wallace and Bear Bryant. The
> Jesuit priest sitting next to me kept me from hurling my binoculars

down on [Oklahoma Democratic congressman] Carl Albert . . . and
Daley's thugs, sitting all around me, luckily didn't know who Martin
Bormann is/ was . . . ?? In any case, a vote for Bormann is a vote for
nada—unless everybody who agrees with me votes for Martin, too.

116  **"escaped to Argentina"**: Martin Bormann had died on April 30, 1945—
along with many other Nazis—by suicide, but his demise wouldn't be confirmed until 1972. For more, see Whiting, *Hunt for Martin Bormann.*

117  **"law and order in Chicago"**: Dean Blobaum, "Chicago '68:A Chronology."

117  **"too much for the country to handle"**: This story about Johnson and
Daley is from the *Vietnam War,* episode 7.

118  **"prepared to give"**: For the partial video of Ribicoff's speech, see the You-
Tube entry "Ribicoff vs. Daley at Democratic National Convention 1968."
For the transcript, see "Speech Nominating George McGovern for the U.S.
Presidency."

118  **"Go home!"**: Thompson, *Fear and Loathing in America,* 127.

119  **"I have not time for that"**: Farber, *Chicago '68,* 206.

119  **"just after 11:00 p.m."**: Halfway through the nominating process, a member of the Wisconsin delegation, instead of reporting his state's votes, said,
"Mr. Chairman, most delegates to this convention do not know that thousands of young people are being beaten in the streets of Chicago. And for
that reason, I request the suspension of the rules to relocate the convention
to another city." Chairman Carl Albert interrupted him—banging his gavel
and screaming, "Wisconsin is not recognized for that purpose!" ("1968 Democratic Convention," YouTube.

119  **"Where there is hatred let me sow love"**: Farber, *Chicago '68,* 204.

119  **"without explanation"**: From Thompson, *Kingdom of Fear,* loc. 1280:

> On Thursday night in the Amphitheatre it was not enough for me
> to have a press pass from the Democratic National Committee; I was
> kicked out of my press seat by hired rent-a-cops, and when I pro-
> tested to the Secret Service men at the door, I was smacked against
> the wall and searched for weapons. And I realized at that point that,
> even though I was absolutely right, if I persisted with my righteous
> complaint, I would probably wind up in jail.

119  **"rest of the night"**: From Farber, *Chicago '68,* 204: "At the Amphitheater,
Thursday, the Mayor packed both the press and spectator galleries with his
supporters. Waving banners announcing 'We Love Mayor Daley,' the patron-
age workers and loyalists chanted 'We want Daley, We want Daley,' over and
over."

119  **"broke down crying"**: Thompson, *Fear and Loathing in America,* 119.

119  **"sunrise on Friday morning"**: For more, see Thompson, *Fear and Loathing
in America,* 130:

> Actually, *Ramparts* had a bunch of rooms in the Ambassador, with a
> lot of booze and flesh on the tab—so I ended up there. I got back to

the Hilton around dawn, just in time for the wild aftermath of the cop raid on McCarthy's hq. People running and screaming in the lobby—bleeding, falling, [veteran CBS correspondent] Blair Clark darting wild-eyed from one scene to another.

And from Thompson, *On the Campaign Trail '72,* 32:

At dawn on Friday morning, [McCarthy's] campaign manager, a seasoned old pro named Blair Clark, was still pacing up and down Michigan Avenue in front of the Hilton in a state so close to hysteria that his friends were afraid to talk to him because every time he tried to say something his eyes would fill with tears and he would have to start pacing again.

120    **"McCarthy campaign"**: The details here are mostly taken from White, *Making of the President: 1968,* 359–362.

120    **"Nobody's in charge"**: White, *Making of the President: 1968,* 362.

121    **"letter to a friend"**: Thompson, *Fear and Loathing in America,* 130.

121    **"kick the shit out of them"**: cf. Norman Mailer's last moments at this awful convention (in his book-length account, *Miami and the Siege of Chicago,* which he wrote about himself in the third person): a scene that took place only a few feet away from—and at the same general moment as—Hunter Thompson's sunrise arrival at the Hilton:

The police had charged the McCarthy Headquarters, arrested every kid in sight, beat up on a few, and generally created such consternation that the Senator himself remained in town until Friday afternoon for fear that his children would not be wasted . . .
   On this sunny Friday morning he [Mailer] went into the Hilton. On the steps he met Senator McCarthy's daughter, a lovely and formidable young dark-haired lady, now in a quiet horror over the fury of the bust, and she asked him what he would do about it.
   "I'm going to catch a plane and see my family," he told her, smiling into the proud disapproval of her eyes. "Dear Miss," he could have told her, "we will be fighting for forty years." (237)

## Chapter Four

124    **"wet concrete"**: From Baker, "Gloomy Day Casts a Pall Over Inauguration Mood":

Physically, it was a day out of Edgar Allen Poe, dun and drear, with a chilling northeast wind that cut to the marrow, and a gray ugly overcast that turned the city the color of wet cement. No graves yawned and no lions roared in the streets in the Shakespearean manner, but the gloom of the elements seemed to have infected most of the proceedings.

124   **"the title of peacemaker"**: For the full text of Nixon's speech, see "Inaugural Address, January 20, 1969," available online at UCSB's Presidency Project.

124   **"New Hampshire primary"**: As Douglas Brinkley explained in *Fear and Loathing in America,* 99:

> Boston Globe political reporter Bill Cardoso had introduced himself to Thompson on the Nixon press bus in New Hampshire by saying, "Hey, you're the cat who wrote the Hell's Angels book."They shared a joint, and a bond was struck.

124   **"the newspaper's political bureau"**: In a letter to his new agent, Lynn Nesbit, Thompson wrote:

> Anyway, I told Cardoso that I'd like to write him a weird, free-wheeling piece on Nixon's inauguration, but that I couldn't tell him anything definite until I checked with you, to see if anything else was happening on the fat-money front. If we can't find anything fat, I'd just as soon go ahead and do a short piece for the Globe for $300 and press credentials out of their Washington Bureau. And maybe some minor expenses. (Thompson, *Fear and Loathing in America,* 147)

124   **"Ray Price"**: From "Memoirs of a Wretched Week in Washington," reprinted in Thompson, *Great Shark Hunt,* 172: "Anybody who thinks Nixon wrote that soothing inaugural speech should remember the name, Ray Price. He is Nixon's Bill Moyers, and—like Moyers—a good man to watch for signs of a sinking ship. Price is Nixon's house liberal."

125   **"finally in charge"**: from "Freak Power in the Rockies," reprinted in Thompson, *Great Shark Hunt,* 157.

125   **"Eugene McCarthy had advocated"**: Farrell, *Richard Nixon,* 341.

125   **"in 1961"**: Farrell, *Richard Nixon,* 342.

125   **"might cost him the election"**: The informer in question was a certain forty-five-year-old German emigre on the faculty of Harvard's Department of Government named . . . Henry Kissinger. Farrell, *Richard Nixon,* 638.

125   **"backchannel message"**: The account that follows is based on the 2017 PBS documentary *The Vietnam War,* episode 7, "The Veneer of Civilization," as well as John A. Farrell's insightful investigation in *Richard Nixon: The Life.*

126   **"future peace talks"**: The message was to be delivered by the South Vietnamese Ambassador Bui Diem and also Anna Chennault, a socialite widow of a former US general with extensive East Asian political connections who was known in Washington circles as "The Dragon Lady" (Farrell, *Richard Nixon,* 638).

Farrell, in his endnotes to his Nixon biography, offers an enormous amount of evidence in support of Nixon's treachery; the two most salient examples are a note from H. R. Haldeman's private diary that wasn't discovered until recently—"Keep Anna Chenault working on SVN," Nixon ordered at the time—and, within the same context, the quote: "Any other way to monkey wrench it?" For more, see 637–640 in the Notes section to Farrell, *Richard Nixon*.

126  **"negotiations between governments"**: Farrell, *Richard Nixon*, 342.

126  **"in the middle of a war"**: Recordings of these phone calls were included in *Vietnam War*, episode 7.

126  **"give LBJ a call"**: Nixon also rallied together congressional Republicans, in case this phone call didn't do the trick:

> "Kick them hard," he told Haldeman, to make sure everyone stuck to the same line, should the truth come to light: *This is just a political gimmick by the Democrats that could risk American lives.* (Farrell, *Richard Nixon*, 342)

128  **"White House"**: Details here are drawn from Thompson's *Boston Globe* article and from *On the Campaign Trail '72*, 70–71.

128  **"Vicious dissidence is the style"**: Thompson, *Great Shark Hunt*, 178.

128  **"the first small group was waiting"**: The details for this section are drawn from the *New York Times* articles in the January 21, 1969 issue: Franklin, "Young Demonstrators in Parade"; Belair, "Security Is Evident as Nixon Goes By"; Baker, "Gloomy Day Casts a Pall."

129  **"FOUR MORE YEARS OF DEATH!"**: Baker, "Gloomy Day Casts a Pall."

129  **"HO, HO, HO CHI MINH. N.L.F. IS GONNA WIN!"**: Farrell, *Richard Nixon*, 350.

129  **"TWO. FOUR. SIX. EIGHT. ORGANIZE TO SMASH THE STATE!"**: Thompson, *Great Shark Hunt*, 178.

129  **"ONE. TWO. THREE. FOUR. WE DON'T WANT YOUR FUCKING WAR!"**: Farrell, *Richard Nixon*, 350.

129  **"shattered against the pavement"**: Franklin, "Young Demonstrators in Parade."

129  **"rolling underneath"**: See the firsthand account "The 1969 Inauguration: Horse Manure, Rocks & a Pig" by Greg Simpson on the Wordpress site *Washington Area Spark*.

129  **"nearly stripped naked"**: from Thompson's *Boston Globe* article, reprinted in *Great Shark Hunt*, 179:

> A cop lost his temper and rushed into the crowd to seize an agitator . . . and that was the last we saw of him for about three minutes. When he emerged, after a dozen others had rushed in to save him, he looked like some ragged hippie . . . the mob had stripped him of everything except his pants, one boot, and part of his coat. His hat was gone, his gun and gunbelt, all his badges and police decorations . . . he was a beaten man and his name was Lennox. I know this because I was standing beside the big plainclothes police boss who was shouting, "Get Lennox in the van!"

129 **"threw stones"**: The details of the hail of debris here are drawn from the three *New York Times* articles in the January 21 issue; Thompson's feature in the *Boston Globe;* from Thompson's account in *On the Campaign Trail '72;* and from Craig Simpson's recollection "The 1969 Nixon Inauguration."

129 **"2:45 P.M."**: Franklin, "Young Demonstrators in Parade."

129 **"Vietcong banners"**: Franklin, "Young Demonstrators in Parade."

129 **"The Black Flag of Anarchy"**: Franklin, "Young Demonstrators in Parade."

130 **"half-gallon jug of wine"**: Thompson, *On the Campaign Trail '72,* 70.

130 **"Here comes the president"**: Thompson, *On the Campaign Trail '72,* 70.

130 **"cannonball on wheels"**: Thompson, *On the Campaign Trail '72,* 70.

130 **"what they heard"**: This is a paraphrasing of Thompson's later evaluation in *Kingdom of Fear,* 80:

> It seems to me that the underlying assumption of any public pro-
> test—any public disagreement with the government, "the system,"
> or "the establishment," by any name—is that the men in charge of
> whatever you're protesting against are actually listening, whether
> they later admit it or not, and that if you run your protest Right, it
> will likely make a difference.
>
> Norman Mailer made this point a long time ago when he said
> that the election of JFK gave him a sense, for the first time in his life,
> that he could actually communicate with the White House. Even
> with people like Johnson and Mac Bundy—or even Pat Brown or
> Bull Connor—the unspoken rationale behind all those heavy public
> protests was that our noise was getting through and that somebody
> in power was listening and hearing and at least weighing our protest
> against their own political realities . . . even if these people refused to
> talk to us. So in the end the very act of public protest, even violent
> protest, was essentially optimistic.

130 **"heavy issues"**: The rest of the quote, which is also part of the reflection in *Kingdom of Fear,* 82:

> John Kennedy on Cuba and the Bay of Pigs, Martin Luther King
> Jr. on Vietnam, Gene McCarthy on "working behind the scenes
> and within the Senate Club," Robert F. Kennedy on grass and long
> hair and what eventually came to be Freak Power, Ted Kennedy on
> Francis X. Morrissey, and Senator Sam Ervin on wiretaps and pre-
> ventive detention. Anyway, the general political drift of the 1960s
> was one of the Good Guys winning, slowly but surely (and even
> clumsily sometimes), over the Bad Guys . . . and the highest exam-
> ple of this was Johnson's incredible abdication on April Fool's Day
> of 1968.

131 **"fighting among themselves"**: Thompson, *Great Shark Hunt,* 168.

131 **"shallow, stagnant water"**: Which is to say: this is how Washington, DC, smells to *me,* now, after eight winters of living here.

131 **"toward the Mall"**: From the *Boston Globe* feature, in Thompson, *Great Shark Hunt,* 172:

> It was cold, and getting colder. I zipped up my ski jacket and walked fast across the Mall. To my left, at the base of the monument, a group of hippies was passing a joint around . . . and off to the right a mile or so away, I could see the bright dome of the Capitol . . . Mr. Nixon's Capitol.

131 **"*Mr. Nixon's City*"**: Thompson, *Great Shark Hunt,* 176.

131 **"Edmund Burke"**: Thompson, *Songs of the Doomed,* 10.

131 **"means to flourish"**: From a 2001 interview Thompson did with *Yahoo!,* in Thompson, *Ancient Gonzo Wisdom,* 287: "Are you familiar with Edmund Burke's dictum that the only thing necessary for the triumph of evil is for good men to do nothing? The first time I heard that, I think, was from Bobby Kennedy in 1968, and it just stuck with me."

131 **"at a loss"**: From the ending to his *Globe* article, in Thompson, *Great Shark Hunt,* 172–173: "Suddenly I felt cold, and vaguely defeated. More than eight years ago, in San Francisco, I had stayed up all night to watch the election returns . . . and when Nixon went down I felt like a winner."

131 **"about to break"**: cf. Joseph Conrad's ending to *Heart of Darkness,* 96— when the narrator Charles Marlow, upon returning to Europe, meets with Mr. Kurtz's grieving fiancée: "I heard her weeping; she had hidden her face in her hands. It seemed to me that the house would collapse before I could escape, that the heavens would fall upon my head, but nothing happened. The heavens do not fall for such a trifle."

131 **"Richard Nixon"**: Thompson, *On the Campaign Trail '72,* 389.

132 **"a lucrative assignment"**: The article would be titled "Those Daring Young Men in Their Flying Machines . . . Ain't What They Used to Be!" It would be published in September. In a February 11, 1969, letter to Jim Silberman he'd write:

> Tomorrow, for instance, I will mark the 10th anniversary of my discharge from the Air Force by going back to an AF base to do an article on test pilots. I told them I'd be back someday. Ten years ago those pigs made me spend a week painting a latrine, over and over again, 12 hours a day for 6 days—the same four vomit-green walls. And now they tell me they're going to put a driver at my disposal. . . . Yes Sir, whatever you need. . . . Ho, ho. . . . Yeah. . . . Which means I'm taking off for Los Angeles and Edwards AFB in a few hours. I'll be there (at the Continental Hotel after a few days at the base) until Feb 23 or so. I'll also be drifting around the East LA barrio with my Brown Power man, Oscar Acosta. There's a good article—and even a book—in that action. (Thompson, *Fear and Loathing in America,* 160)

132 **"Hyatt Continental Hotel"**: His room fees were paid for through the Random House expense account that was part of his "Death of the American

Dream" book—an account that was starting to spiral out of control. Thompson, *Fear and Loathing in America*, 163.

132　**"most well-known attorneys in the state":** From Thompson, "Strange Rumblings in Aztlan," 176.

132　**"East LA":** For more on the Walkouts, a seminal moment in the Chicano movement, see Munoz, *Youth, Identity, Power,* as well as Correa, *Chicano Nationalism.*

132　**"up to forty years in prison":** Ian Haney López's *Racism on Trial: The Chicano Fight for Justice* looks at Acosta's legal brilliance—the lasting precedent he set with this case—in excellent detail.

132　**"Mexican-American community":** López explains this legal defense in detail in *Racism on Trial,* 31.

132　**"police practices":** From Moore, *Love and Riot,* 41: "His great jump in basic thinking—which he would describe to anybody willing to listen—was to forget everything he learned in law school and to start the legal process by assuming that everything was political."

133　**"police custody":** See Acosta's moving account of these unprosecuted murders—as well as his attempt to draw attention to them—in *Revolt of the Cockroach People,* 92–99.

133　**"in the way his *own* clients were":** Vigil, *Crusade for Justice,* 147.

133　**"Mexican-American community":** Acosta would say: "I contend that all grand juries are racist since all grand jurors have to be recommended by Superior Court judges and that the whole thing reeks of subconscious, institutional racism" (López, *Racism on Trial,* 133).

In *Racism on Trial,* López quotes transcripts of the grand jury challenge—which would prove to be an enormous embarrassment for the judges who, testifying under oath, were forced to admit that the only people of Mexican-American descent they knew were the workers and housekeepers they employed. For more, see *Racism on Trial,* 98.

133　**"out to get me":** Thompson, *Fear and Loathing in America,* 86.

134　**"little energy bombs":** Decades later, these notebook installments would be published as "First Visit from Mescalito," in Thompson, *Songs of the Doomed,* 126–137.

134　**"written in his journal":** These revealing journal entries—about Thompson's struggle to balance amphetamine and alcohol—were published as an essay at the beginning of the second edition of his letters, *Fear and Loathing in America,* 5–11.

134　**"The Devil and Daniel Webster":** This is a reference to a 1936 Steven Vincent Benet short story—concerning a classic Faustian bargain—that was later made into a 1941 film.

134　**"I've never had mescaline":** Thompson, *Songs of the Doomed,* 130.

135　**"without sobbing":** Sandy describes what it was like for Thompson to come back from the 1968 DNC in the film *Gonzo* (Gibney, 2008).

135   **"Hunter was a patriot"**: Gibney, *Gonzo.*

135   **"*Politics is the art of controlling your environment*"**: Thompson, *Kingdom of Fear,* loc. 416.

136   **"helped found the CCA"**: James Salter helped found the CCA in tandem with Aspen residents Bob Lewis, Robin Molny, Fritz Benedict, David Michaels, and Dr. Harold Harvey. Herchenroeder, "'Hippie Lawyer' Recalls Battle of Aspen."

136   **"Bernard Shir-Cliff"**: April 17. Thompson, *Fear and Loathing in America,* 171.

136   **"*Hell's Angels* sales"**: More than $100,000 by today's standards.

136   **"George Stranahan"**: Many years later, Stranahan would become the proprietor of the Flying Dog beer brand.

136   **"he and Sandy would own their own place"**: See McKeen, *Outlaw Journalist,* 126; and Thompson, *Fear and Loathing in America,* 183, 208, as well as this May 23 letter to his mother from p. 181:

>   I spent hours on the midnight phone, settling a very complicated deal to buy this place. Since I have no income of record, no property, no credit, no job history, no education and no advancement prospects—it takes a considerable amount of fine haggling to get hold of a $ 77,000 property in the midst of a spiraling land market. I think I've sent pictures of this house, which is part of the deal—along with the smaller, next-door house that Noonan is living in, and about 25 acres with a spectacular view and another fine house-site. You'll have to get out here and see the whole thing, once it's settled. I assume it's set, but I won't be sure until around mid-July—about the same time Sandy is due.

136   **"University of Kentucky"**: See Thompson's April 27, 1969, letter to his mother in Thompson, *Fear and Loathing in America,* 173:

>   I had a hell of a lot of options that Jim doesn't have in this goddamn war-maddened world. I'm not sure what I'd do today if my only choice was between staying at UK or getting drafted or going to jail or leaving the country. In all honesty, I think I'd leave the country . . . although I wouldn't want to and I'd feel I was being driven out. But I'd feel like a ghoulish hypocrite if I told anybody these days to grit his teeth and obey orders. Nobody kids themselves anymore about the military building character or anything else worth building. So, if a check now and then can help buy options, I figure it's nothing lost and a chance of something gained.

136   **"Owl Farm"**: *Owl Farm* appears to be an homage to Jack London's name for the grand estate he built—and then lost to fire—in Sonoma, only a few miles from where the Thompsons had lived. It's also a reference, it seems, to Thompson's schedule: he worked at night and slept during the day. In addition, he seems to have had a thing for owls; as Sandy would say years later:

"Hunter named it Owl Farm because he had a fetish about owls. He had owls everywhere" (Carroll, *Hunter*, 116).

136   **"affinity for guns"**: Thompson, *Fear and Loathing in America*, 167.

136   **"140 pages"**: Thompson, *Fear and Loathing in America*, 179.

137   **"he wrote Shir-Cliff in May"**: Thompson, *Fear and Loathing in America*, 177.

137   **"past six months"**: Thompson, *Fear and Loathing in America*, 169.

137   **"the previous year"**: Another feature he'd been working on, which would eventually be killed by *Playboy* but revived later by the new *Scanlan's Monthly*, was a profile on the famous Olympic skier Jean Claude Killy—the reporting on which actually took him back, ten months after the fact, to the Chicago amphitheater, where Killy was participating in the 1969 Chicago Auto Show. In a letter to Jim Silberman he'd write:

> My first encounter with Killy, for instance, was at the Chicago Auto Show—in the goddamn Stockyards Amphitheatre, all those ghosts, with Killy and O. J. Simpson selling Chevrolets in the same big room where Carl Albert once peddled Hubert Humphrey . . . christ, what a nightmare. (Thompson, *Fear and Loathing in America*, 164)

And from the eventual article Killy itself:

> We left the Merchandise Mart and zapped off on a freeway to the Auto Show—and suddenly it registered: The Stockyards Amphitheatre. I was banging along the freeway in that big car, listening to the others trade bull / fuck jokes, trapped in the back seat between Killy and Roller, heading for that rotten slaughterhouse where Mayor Daley had buried the Democratic party. I had been there before, and I remembered it well. Chicago—this vicious, stinking zoo, this mean-grinning, Mace-smelling boneyard of a city; an elegant rock-pile monument to everything cruel and stupid and corrupt in the human spirit. (Thompson, *Great Shark Hunt*, 72)

137   **"I feel like Johnny Appleseed"**: Thompson, *Fear and Loathing in America*, 185.

137   **"little pistol"**: Carroll, *Hunter*, 119.

137   **"west side of town"**: All of the details and quoted dialogue depicted in the following hospital scene are drawn directly from two sources:
Sandy and Anne Noonan's accounts in Carroll, *Hunter*, 119–120; and Sandy's account in Seymour and Wenner, *Gonzo*, 68–69.

138   **"conflicting Rh factors"**: For a more details on the medical nature of Rh factors, see this explanatory pamphlet "The Rh factor, How It Can Affect Your Pregnancy," from the American College of Obstetricians and Gynecologists.

138   **"as if an enormous gate had been closed on her"**: About this moment Sandy would recount: "It was like an incredible iron gate had been slammed in my face" (Carroll, *Hunter*, 119).

139 **"Roaring Fork River"**: They buried the baby on the land that the Noonans had recently purchased. Carroll, *Hunter,* 120.

139 **"what had happened"**: Carroll, *Hunter,* 120.

139 **"forty miles due west of Aspen"**: "US Department of Energy Management"; "A Nuclear Device Fired in Colorado." See also the historic footage of Walter Cronkite's newscast that day, available on YouTube under the entry "Walter Cronkite's Historic Footage of Project Rulison."

139 **"Hunter Thompson included"**: At the time Thompson had begun writing a feature, which hadn't been commissioned by anyone, on the AEC's project to fracture and release, with fission explosions, the rock containing the gas reserves—a process that, today, we'd call "nuclear fracking." In a September 24, 1968, letter to Acosta (Thompson, *Fear and Loathing in America,* 207) he lamented:

> I am sitting here working on a long article on the AEC and the oil companies and these fucking death bombs they are setting off in Colo, Nev, etc. . . . and I don't have the vaguest fucking idea where to send it. Look around you and see what has happened, in the past few years, to the handful of national magazines that used to print mean shit about the fatbellies. This fucking polarization has made it impossible to sell anything except hired bullshit or savage propaganda.

140 **"surface of the mountain"**: The nuclear blast at Rulison was part of the Plowshare program—experiments that sought to apply America's atomic arsenal toward peaceful uses, such as the building of tunnels and artificial harbors. At the time the Soviets were trying the same thing, even going so far as to divert a river into a recently formed blast crater, creating an artificial lake. The problem, of course, was that nuclear weapons, no matter how well designed, *irradiate the shit* out of whatever substance they contact. A few years later, the Austral oil company would claim that the natural gas they siphoned from the Rulison explosion was less than 1 percent contaminated, meaning it was safe to be used by the public, but they soon realized that nobody in their right mind would be willing to turn on their stove and flood their house with gas that carried in its essence the traces of a nuclear explosion . . . In short, the Plowshare program wasn't a *marketable* strategy. Eventually these experiments in nuclear fracking would give way to the water-based kind with which we're now familiar. (Fact Sheet)

140 **"Thompson wrote afterward"**: Thompson, *Fear and Loathing in America,* 207.

140 **"Humanistic Institute"**: Thompson, in an op-ed for the *Aspen Illustrated News* on September 24, 1969, titled "For Whom the Bell Tolls" (reprinted in Watkins, *Freak Power,* 24–25), wrote, "The meeting was scheduled for 8:00 sharp at the Institute, exactly five hours after the bomb went off in Rulison."

140 **"new hotels and condominiums"**: The clients these developers hoped to attract—a wealthy, seasonal crowd—first needed to be made to feel, during this transitional period, as comfortable as possible, hence the discrimination against unfavorables like hippies.

140   **"Carrol Whitmire"**: Stonington, "Former Sheriff Dies in Arizona."

141   **"Frank Lloyd Wright"**: See Berger, "City Should Save the Hearthstone House."

141   **"hoping to see flames"**: Thompson, *Fear and Loathing in America*, 199.

141   **"Everything that could possibly go wrong here, has"**: Thompson, *Fear and Loathing in America*, 200.

142   **"forgetting the whole thing"**: Thompson, *Fear and Loathing in America*, 203.

142   **"paralysis and desperation"**: Thompson, *Fear and Loathing in America*, 205.

142   **"they were my children, too"**: Carroll, *Hunter*, 127.

142   **"against overdevelopment"**: Clifford, *To Aspen and Back*, 135–137.

143   **"after midnight"**: Clifford, *To Aspen and Back*, 136.

143   **"straighten out this town"**: Seymour and Wenner, *Gonzo*, 100.

143   **"political power to change the town"**: In Peggy Clifford's depiction (*To Aspen and Back*, 136), Edwards agreed to run while on the phone that night, but in Thompson's depiction—his 1970 *Rolling Stone* article "Freak Power in the Rockies" (reprinted in Thompson, *Great Shark Hunt*, 116), he and Salter and Solheim met again with Edwards the next day to finally sell him on the idea.

143   **"Why not?"**: Thompson, *Great Shark Hunt*, 154.

143   **"even vaguely resembling their own terms"**: Thompson, *Great Shark Hunt*, 144.

144   **"1,600 possible votes at stake"**: Thompson, *Great Shark Hunt*, 146.

144   **"den mother"**: Watkins, *Freak Power*, 30; Peggy Clifford describes Eve Homeyer in detail:

> Eve Homeyer, with her pale red hair, the wardrobe of a country club matron and a sharp tongue, was our true adversary. She stressed the need for moderation and fiscal conservativism . . . She was quite willing to support anything that might win votes for her, and frequently noted that she was a traditionalist who understood and appreciated the free enterprise system. Her principle asset, however, was that she was not anything like Edwards. Edwards scared a great many people, who called him "socialist" or worse. (Clifford, *To Aspen and Back*, 139)

144   **"she wrote"**: Watkins, *Freak Power*, 32–33.

144   **"radio spots"**: The region still lacked a local television station.

144   **"JOE EDWARDS FOR MAYOR"**: Watkins, *Freak Power*, 29, 31.

144   **"overall capacity for growth"**: Clifford, *To Aspen and Back*, 137; Watkins, *Freak Power*, 32–33.

145   **"was nervous"**: Thompson, *Great Shark Hunt*, 149.

145   **"has made millionaires"**: Thompson, *Great Shark Hunt*, 150.

145 **"Dr. Robert "Bugsy" Barnard":** As Thompson recounted in his *Rolling Stone* article "Freak Power in the Rockies," in Thompson, *Great Shark Hunt,* 141:"The retiring mayor, Dr. Robert 'Buggsy' Barnard, had been broadcasting vicious radio warnings for the previous 48 hours, raving about long prison terms for vote-fraud and threatening violent harassment by 'phalanxes of poll-watchers' for any strange or freaky-looking scum who might dare to show up at the polls."

145 **"newly registered voters":** Guido's abiding hatred for hippies was mentioned in his 2002 obituary in the *Aspen Times:* Harvey, "Meyer, All-Around Local Character, Dies at Age 85."

145 **"one of them yelled":** The dialogue and details here are drawn from Thompson's "Freak Power in the Rockies," reprinted in Thompson, *Great Shark Hunt,* 153–155.

145 **"rest of the day":** Clifford, *To Aspen and Back,* 140.

146 **"Bemused":** Thompson, *Great Shark Hunt,* 148: "I'd been awake and moving around like a cannonball for the last fifty hours, and now—with nothing left to confront—I felt the adrenalin sinking."

146 **"he'd write":** from a November 19, 1969, letter to Silberman, in Thompson, *Fear and Loathing in America,* 216.

146 **"wake of Chicago":** Later, in his *Rolling Stone* article "Freak Power in the Rockies," Thompson would interrogate his own reasons for working so hard on the Edwards campaign:

> I'm still not sure what launched me. Probably it was Chicago—that brain-raping week in August of '68. I went to the Democratic Convention as a journalist, and returned a raving beast. For me, that week in Chicago was far worse than the worst bad acid trip I'd even heard rumors about. It permanently altered my brain chemistry, and my first new idea—when I finally calmed down—was an absolute conviction there was no possibility for any personal truce, for me, in a nation that could hatch and be proud of a malignant monster like Chicago. Suddenly, it seemed imperative to get a grip on those who had somehow slipped into power and caused the thing to happen. But who were they? Was Mayor Daley a cause, or a symptom? . . .
> So in truth it was probably a sense of impending doom, of horror at politics in general, that goaded me into my role in the Edwards campaign. (*Great Shark Hunt,* 155–157)

146 **"caused the thing to happen":** Thompson, *Great Shark Hunt,* 156.

146 **"protect the town's image":** This quote is from an "advertisement" for the Aspen Wallposter Thompson wrote that's reprinted in Hinckle, *Who Killed Hunter Thompson?,* 62–63.

146 **"instead of merely destroying it":** Thompson, *Kingdom of Fear,* 83.

147 **"a ten year delayed honeymoon":** Thompson, *Fear and Loathing in America,* 214.

147 **"decades younger":** Thompson, *Fear and Loathing in America,* 214, 226.

147 **"long since aggressively dissipated":** Thompson, *Fear and Loathing in Las Vegas*, 178.

148 **"late-season snow":** This detail is from a letter written by James Salter on April 30, 1970, reprinted in Salter, *Memorable Days*, 18.

148 **"his wife, Ann":** Salter and his first wife, Ann Altemus, would divorce in 1975. The next year he'd begin living in Aspen with the writer Kay Eldredge; they'd eventually marry in 1998. For more, see *Conversations with James Salter*, loc. 240.

148 **"near the Meadows":** James Salter would write about his house in Aspen in *Don't Save Anything*, 267: "In the winter the snow came down, heavy and white, unending, like silent applause . . . It's hard to think of a feeling of greater well-being: storm without, fire within."

148 **"uncrowded":** From a discussion I had with James Salter on October 17, 2014, during which I had the chance to ask him about what he'd been doing during the bombing of Pearl Harbor; about his favorite moment from his lifetime of skiing; about what he'd loved most about living in Honolulu after World War II; about his friendship with Peter Matthiessen; and even about his opinions on tennis. He also discussed, briefly, his relationship with Hunter Thompson. For more of Salter's work, see Paumgarten, "Postscript: James Salter, 1925–2015."

148 **"They talked about writing":** The dialogue and details that follow are taken from my discussion with Salter. To clarify: here are my notes from his comments on Thompson (composed two days after our conversation):

> Talk about HST. Says that Aspen was a small town. HST into big things, like running for sheriff. Needed to be center of scene. Loud drunk. Spilling things at table. Best times with HST were at friend's house, female writer they both knew, could talk to him there. Never went to HST's house. Too many admirers/flock of worshippers. Had HST over to his own house often. Story about Derby: HST upset about career, not sure what to do next, Hell's Angels' book had just come out, Salter suggests that HST return to Louisville and write about hometown—Kentucky Derby. Became Kentucky Derby Is Decadent and Depraved. Said that HST was a beautiful writer when he was at his best. Really beautiful writer.

148 **"He was forty-four":** James Salter's biographical information is based on the time line provided at the beginning of his collection of interviews, *Conversations with James Salter*, and also on his memoir *Burning the Days*.

149 **"shooting down another":** Salter described this moment decades later in his memoir *Burning the Days*, 158: "A few hits in the right wing, then tremendous joy, at closer range a solid burst in the fuselage . . . The MIG, now funeral craft that bore nothing, was falling from thirty thousand feet, spinning leisurely in its descent until its shadow unexpectedly appeared on the hills and slowly moved to join it in a burst of flame."

149    **"literary career"**: In 1970 Salter was working on short stories and screen-plays. The year before he'd directed the film *Three*, starring Charlotte Rampling and Sam Waterston. *Conversations with James Salter*, loc. 232.

149    **"understood the despair"**: cf. Salter, *A Sport and a Pastime*, 15:

> Autun, still as a churchyard. Tile roofs, dark with moss. The amphi-theatre. The great central square: the Champs de Mars. Now, in the blue of autumn, it reappears, this old town, provincial autumn that touches the bone. The summer has ended. The garden withers. The mornings become chill. I am thirty, I am thirty-four—the years turn dry as leaves.

149    **"Kentucky Derby"**: This story—the origin of Thompson's Kentucky Derby piece—is also relayed by Douglas Brinkley in the introduction to *Fear and Loathing in America*, xvi (Brinkley refers to Salter as a "dear friend" of Thompson's) and by Thompson in *Songs of the Doomed*, 147.

149    **"plus $500 for expenses"**: Thompson, *Fear and Loathing in America*, 293.

149    **"Woody Creek"**: Hinckle, *Who Killed Hunter Thompson*, 88.

149    **"agreed to send out an illustrator"**: Thompson's suggestion for an artist, the *Denver Post* cartoonist Pat Oliphant, was unavailable.

149    **"the Derby itself"**: Thompson, *Fear and Loathing in America*, 293.

149    **"into Cambodia"**: Beecher, "Rising Peril Seen."

149    **"both abroad and at home"**: For the transcript of this speech, see "Address to the Nation on the Situation in Southeast Asia," from The Presidency Project.

150    **"terminal identity crisis"**: Thompson, *Great Shark Hunt*, 17.

150    **"exceptionally wise idea"**: Thompson, *Fear and Loathing in America*, 296.

151    **"Thompson said to him"**: "Kentucky Derby Is Decadent and Depraved," reprinted in its original form in Hinckle, *Who Killed Hunter Thompson?*, 211.

151    **"maybe talk things over"**: Steadman, *Joke's Over*, 12.

151    **"Steadman was a talented"**: "He's good," Thompson wrote to Hinckle about Steadman after the trip, "probably better than anybody working in this country—but they didn't like him in Louisville" (*Fear and Loathing in America*, 296).

151    **"acclimate himself"**: Steadman, *Joke's Over*, 13.

151    **"Thompson would write"**: "Kentucky Derby Is Decadent and Depraved," reprinted in its original form in Hinckle, *Who Killed Hunter Thompson?*, 214.

151    **"the members' wives"**: Steadman, *Joke's Over*, 14.

151    **"a can of Mace"**: In the collected letters there's no direct mention of the Mace attack—Thompson brings up Mace in an aside to Silberman while talking about the Derby in May 1970, but that's about it . . . in the end, your guess is as good as mine. See Steadman, *Joke's Over*; Hinckle, *Who Killed Hunter Thompson?*; Carroll, *Hunter*; and the ESPN 30/30 short *Gonzo @ The Derby* for more.

152 **"five hundred antiwar protestors"**: Kifner, "4 Kent State Students Killed by Troops."

152 **"invites tragedy"**: Semple, "Nixon Says Violence Invites Tragedy."

152 **"referred"**: Agnew actually called them "tomentose exhibitionists," using an absurdly obscure botanical term for *covered in hair.* Semple, "Nixon Says Violence Invites Tragedy."

152 **"predictable and avoidable"**: Semple, "Nixon Says Violence Invites Tragedy."

152 **"Youth in its protest must be heard"**: "Text of Hickel Letter."

152 **"Kent State victims"**: Bigart, "War Foes Here Attacked by Construction Workers."

152 **"killing two more students"**: *Vietnam War,* episode 9.

153 **"growing up there"**: Thompson, *Fear and Loathing in America,* 296.

153 **"series of organizational headers"**: See original article, which was reprinted recently in Hinckle, *Who Killed Hunter Thompson?,* 202–227.

153 **"just hours before the deadline"**: Hinckle, *Who Killed Hunter Thompson?,* 88.

153 **"finer, meatier edge"**: Thompson, *Fear and Loathing in America,* 295.

153 **"Horrible way to write anything"**: Thompson, *Fear and Loathing in America,* 295.

153 **"ever read"**: Thompson, *Fear and Loathing in America,* 337.

153 **"part exaggeration/fiction"**: Seymour and Wenner, *Gonzo,* 127.

153 **"It's totally gonzo"**: Carroll, *Hunter,* 124; Seymour and Wenner, *Gonzo,* 126.

153 **"start of the piece"**: "The Kentucky Derby Is Decadent and Depraved" employed two main stylistic conceits: 1) the reporter's dramatization of personal experience as a means to articulate the true nature of the event itself; and 2) an impressionistic, real-time process of composition, free of the reconstructive scaffolding and editorial compromises of subsequent drafts.

154 **"line of attack"**: Thompson's brilliant stylistic shift was, at its heart, a *rhetorical* one—the sort that George Orwell had lit upon, a generation earlier, in his attempt to illuminate the horror of British imperialism: instead of investigating and reporting on the atrocities inflicted on indigenous populations (a tactic his audience in London had numbed to), Orwell started showing how the colonial system destroyed the young British men whose task it was to carry out its unjust policies—how *he,* as an administrator in Burma forced to hang prisoners and shoot elephants, had been morally compromised.

As a corollary, this is similar to the sort of satire that the comedian Stephen Colbert employed in *The Colbert Report:* by turning himself into a gross exaggeration of already exaggerated right-wing media figures—and then, on occasion, interviewing said figures on his show, parroting their own extremes back at them in a way that even they couldn't help but see—Colbert laid bare the hypocrisy of this right-wing point of view.

154 **"We can do without your kind in Kentucky"**: "Kentucky Derby Is Decadent and Depraved," reprinted in its original form in Hinckle, *Who Killed Hunter Thompson?*, 226–227.

154 **"doomed atavistic culture"**: Hinckle, *Who Killed Hunter Thompson?*, 215.

154 **"a candidate for sheriff of that community"**: Hinckle, *Who Killed Hunter Thompson?*, 227.

155 **"dark Levi's jeans"**: Watkins, *Freak Power*, 124–126.

155 **"meant as a talisman"**: Thompson, *Stories I tell Myself*, 207; Aspen Wallposter no. 7: "Aztec 'eternal life' pendant, a gift from Emiliano Zapata's grand-daughter . . . " (reprinted in Watkins, *Freak Power*, 184–185)

155 **"tennis hat"**: This description of Thompson's white cap is from Ripley, "'Freak Power' Candidate."

155 **"my long-haired opponent"**: Watkins, *Freak Power*, 124–127; Reprints of *Aspen Times* articles from October 15 and October 29, 1970.

155 **"a packed house"**: The third candidate, Glenn Ricks, former undersheriff, refused to attend the first debate, calling it "a three-ring circus." Watkins, *Freak Power*, 124.

155 **"the interests of the few"**: Watkins, *Freak Power*, 70.

156 **"The Last, Best Hope of Man"**: Watkins, *Freak Power*, 70.

156 **"whatever's right"**: Watkins, *Freak Power*, 73.

156 **"the political processes still work"**: From Ripley, "'Freak Power' Candidate": "He wants to prove to the disenchanted—the 'freaks'—that the political processes still work."

156 **"I want the job real bad"**: This film, *Show Down at Aspen*, was shown on December 11, 1970, as part of the program "This Week," a public affairs series produced by Thames TV.

157 **"won't get any votes"**: Watkins, *Freak Power*, 149.

157 **"any talent for remaining aloof"**: Clifford, *To Aspen and Back*, 153.

157 **"Colorado Revised Statutes"**: Watkins, *Freak Power*, 126; "Shrieval Candidates Speak at SatA," *Aspen Times*, October 15, 1070, 7B.

157 **"when I need a gun I want it there"**: Watkins, *Freak Power*, 126; "Shrieval Candidates Speak at SatA."

158 **"widened the generation gap to a chasm"**: More from his answer:

> The young people now look upon law enforcement as their bitter enemy. They consider cops to be narrow minded fascists who send out informants to spy and set them up for arrests, which can result in fantastic jail sentences . . . Approximately 50% of felony cases filed in Pitkin County in the last three years have been possession of marijuana. (Watkins, *Freak Power*, 130; "Sheriff Candidates Discuss Issues")

158 **"we're going to get a revolution"**: *Show Down at Aspen* (film).

158  **"sociologist-type ombudsman":** "Sheriff Candidates Discuss Issues," *Aspen Times,* October 29, 1970, 7B.

159  **"not only wise but necessary":** *Show Down at Aspen* (film).

159  **"actually destroy Aspen":** *Show Down at Aspen* (film).

159  **"Lorraine Herwick":** From Wallposter no. 4:

> As a sheriff's deputy four years ago Whitmire was plotting to unseat his boss, then Sheriff Lorraine Herwick, a gentle and straightforward man who had never been stung by the power-bee of corporate ambition-politics—and who lost his job because of it. Herwick saw his role as one of maintaining the civic peace, rather than terrifying the citizenry, and when Whitmire challenged his leadership by hinting at all the criminal horrors that he (Herwick) had never even known about, the elderly ex-sheriff was shocked. (Watkins, *Freak Power,* 54)

159  **"not for the money":** *Show Down at Aspen* (film).

159  **"Pitkin county":** *Show Down at Aspen* (film).

159  **"lifetime achievement":** As sheriff, Whitmire's slow-burn personality was probably seen as a strength; at last he'd attained a job rich in the Western tradition of individuality and action that aligned perfectly to his deeply laconic nature.

160  **"besieged":** By 1970, all of Whitmire's deputies were required to wear cowboy hats and boots and black bolo ties. The gun he personally carried in his holster had an engraved, ivory-colored handle. "To me, marijuana is still a narcotic," he said after the debates. In conversations with his constituents he professed that the prospect of *someone else* becoming sheriff represented an existential threat to the community as a whole—and specifically to "the older people and the young children who are coming up." (*Show Down at Aspen* [film])

160  **"a list of targets on which he himself had been included":** Wallposter no. 4, reprinted in Watkins, *Freak Power,* 54.

160  **"Black Panthers and Weathermen":** Wallposter no. 4, reprinted in Watkins, *Freak Power,* 54.

161  **"The thing about satire":** Such tactics—both Whitmire's and Thompson's—were not new. To quote "Il Duce's Portraits," Italo Calvino's essay about what it was like to grow up under Benito Mussolini:

> In one of the affectionate games that people used to play at the time with children of one or two years, the adult would say, "Do Mussolini's face," and the child would furrow his brow and stick out angry lips . . . The image of Mussolini came to me filtered through the sarcastic discourse of adults (certain adults), which jarred with the chorus of praise.

161  **"a monomaniacal Swiss hotelier":** To the British film crew, Guido Meyer had said (regarding Hunter Thompson and the hippies): "To get rid of this

problem, I would get a business man that mean business, that stand up and have backbone . . . He say; 'okay now, we are going to do a job'—within the law, no shooting if possible . . . and these freaks will be thrown in jail" (*Show Down at Aspen* [film]).

161    **"return to America"**: From Guido Meyer's 2002 obituary in the *Aspen Times*:

> When Guido Jr. spoke immediately after Stephanie and Alie, he recalled being sent away to boarding school in Switzerland around the same time the hippie movement was taking off in Aspen and the rest of the United States. It was only after Richard Nixon won the presidency in 1968 that Guido allowed his children to return to school in the United States. Apparently, Guido Jr. noted, Nixon's election restored his father's confidence in the nation's future. (Harvey, "Meyer, All-Around Local Character, Dies At Age 85")

161    **"Lyndon Johnson"**: Wallposter no. 1, in Watkins, *Freak Power,* 42.

162    **"way of life"**: Wallposter no. 1, in Watkins, *Freak Power,* 42.

162    **"Victorian painting and wallpapering"**: Wallposter no. 4 advertisement, reprinted in Watkins, *Freak Power* 53. Thompson and Solheim had first met in Idaho, in 1964, when he was still writing for the *National Observer.* Solheim moved to Aspen at the end of the 1960s to take over the Jerome Bar, but the transition got delayed; in 1972 he would finally take over and run the bar (Salter, *Don't Save Anything,* 259).

162    **"Ed Bastian"**: Seymour and Wenner, *Gonzo,* 105.

162    **"try something else"**: Peggy Clifford, "May the Best Man Win," *Aspen Times,* October 29, 1970, 12-B, reprinted in Watkins, *Freak Power,* 164.

162    **"He wants too pure a world"**: *Show Down at Aspen* (film).

162    **"bearded, and muscular"**: Clifford, *To Aspen and Back,* 151.

163    **"slowly stirred his drink"**: Clifford, *To Aspen and Back,* 151.

163    **"Anyone know where I can find him?"**: From the *Aspen Times* account, reprinted in Watkins, *Freak Power,* 158: "Bromley . . . ordered a double bourbon and pulled out a switch-blade to stir it with, then announced he was a friend of Hunter Thompson and wanted to know where he could find him."

163    **"if you win the election"**: Perry, *Fear and Loathing,* 145.

163    **"sped off"**: Clifford, *To Aspen and Back,* 150; Thompson, *Kingdom of Fear,* 74.

163    **"up to our ankles"**: Watkins, *Freak Power,* 158.

163    **"guns and explosives"**: Thompson, *Kingdom of Fear,* 74.

164    **"former English major at Columbia"**: Thompson, *Kingdom of Fear,* 74.

164    **"I'm here on federal business"**: Seymour and Wenner, *Gonzo,* 107.

164    **"clearly just violated"**: From Thompson's letter to Jann Wenner, reprinted in Thompson, *Fear and Loathing at Rolling Stone,* 108.

165    **"SDS"**: *Aspen Times,* "Editorial: A Sheriff's Agent."

165 **"brutally illogical extreme"**: Thompson, *Kingdom of Fear,* 73.

166 **"greedy fascist dreams"**: Thompson, *Kingdom of Fear,* 86.

166 **"his political opponent's headquarters demonstrates"**: *Aspen Times,* "Editorial: A Sheriff's Agent."

166 **"a self-portrait"**: The *Aspen Times* had wanted a photograph of Bromley to run with their October 29 article, and that Wednesday, a friend of Thompson's, Paul Davidson, had driven to Boulder and approached the ATF agent at his home address. From *Kingdom of Fear,* 76:

> Davidson got the picture we needed by knocking on the agent's door and saying that he was so impressed with the wonderful chopper outside that he just had to get a shot of it—along with the proud owner. So Bromley—ever alert—posed for the photo, which ran a day later in the Aspen *Times.* . . . We sent Bromley a copy of the published photo/story . . . and he responded almost instantly by mailing me a threatening letter and another, very personal, photo of himself that he said was a hell of a lot better.

166 **"SEE YOU SOON"**: *Aspen Times,* "Baxter, Whitmire, and Williams Win."

167 **"Backlash Potential"**: Thompson, *Great Shark Hunt,* 153.

167 **"more than a dozen calls"**: Wallposter no. 7, in Watkins, *Freak Power,* 184–185.

167 **"a margin of 197 votes"**: *Aspen Times,* "Election Results," November 5, 1970, 1A, reprinted in Watkins, *Freak Power,* 173.

167 **"kick around anymore"**: *Aspen Times,* "Baxter, Whitmire, and Williams Win."

167 **"he was relieved"**: Clifford, *To Aspen and Back,* xv.

168 **"resign in disgrace"**: Whitmire's obituary alluded to this incident—he left office on August 9, 1976, midway through his third four-year term, under political pressure from a three-week investigation by then district attorney Frank Tucker. However, the real story was finally explained by another longtime Aspen sheriff, Bob Braudis, at a 2014 symposium:

> Braudis then shifted the conversation toward former Aspen Sheriff Dick Kienast, who was elected sheriff in 1976 after, according to Braudis, former Sheriff Carrol Whitmire was caught stealing public money. "[Whitmire] was told he could either leave town or be prosecuted," Braudis said. (McLaughlin, "Trio Shares Stories of the '70s")

168 **"the way it should be, I think"**: Thompson, *Fear and Loathing in America,* 344.

## Chapter Five

170 **"Ford Pinto"**: Thompson, *Fear and Loathing in America,* 383. The Pinto went on sale in September 1970, so this model—most likely the sedan but possibly

the hatchback, which became available in February—would be in relatively pristine condition. And even though the Pinto would be recalled for safety issues later in the decade—for good cause—in March 1971 it was probably seen by someone like Hunter Thompson as an intriguing rental option, akin today to a sleek Mazda sedan.

170 **"about four miles away"**: This information about Acosta's residence was generously provided by Ricardo Lopez, a producer of *The Rise and Fall of the Brown Buffalo*, the 2018 PBS documentary by Phillip Rodriguez. During an interview in Los Angeles on January 12, 2017, Lopez and I then drove together along the route that's described here.

170 **"staying at a boardinghouse"**: Specifically: The Hotel Ashmun, 4534 Whittier Boulevard; in 1971 Thompson's room was $5.80 a night, the most expensive in the house. Thompson, "Strange Rumblings in Aztlan," 109.

170 **"a few thin bars of shade remained"**: The description of shadow and light is based on personal observation; it's taken from the notes I made during a trip to Los Angeles on April 1, 2016, during which I retraced Thompson and Acosta's journey from East LA to Beverly Hills, and then across the desert to Las Vegas and back.

170 **"smog brightening the sky"**: Descriptions of the smog throughout this chapter are drawn from Acosta, *Revolt of the Cockroach People*, 50, 204; and from Burton Moore's *Love and Riot*, 46. Moore's book is an autobiographical recounting of his relationship with Acosta during the late 1960s and early 1970s.

170 **"surrounding neighborhood"**: These riots took place on August 29, 1970, and January 31, 1971.

170 **"a rock or two"**: Thompson's subsequent article on these events ("Strange Rumblings in Aztlan") is shot through with apprehension over the prospect of another riot; also, in his detailed recounting of the two previous riots, he uses many of the images I've drawn on for this scene; additional imagery is based on Acosta's account of what it was like to watch the film of the August 29 riot in *Revolt of the Cockroach People*, as well as clips from the footage itself in Phillip Rodriguez's outstanding 2014 documentary *Ruben Salazar*.

171 **"millions of dollars in damages"**: August 29 riot: 4 dead, over a million dollars in damages; and January 31 riot: 1 dead, half a million dollars in damages. For more, see López, *Racism on Trial*, 193–195.

171 **"low-sixties"**: Descriptions of temperature and weather are based on research done through Wunderground's historical weather data website.

171 **"seen as an outsider"**: Oscar Acosta dramatizes this conceit in *The Revolt of the Cockroach People*, 176–181, especially in relation to the Denver civil rights leader Corky Gonzales; also see Acosta's letter to Thompson in Thompson, *Fear and Loathing in America*, 176–178.

171 **"*gabacho*"**: From Douglas Brinkley's footnote in Thompson, *Fear and Loathing in America*, 759: "Gabacho is Spanish for 'Frenchman' or 'Frenchified Spaniard.'"

171 **"put every one of us away for five years"**: Thompson, "Strange Rumblings in Aztlan," 132.

171 **"Thompson's first thought"**: Thompson, "Strange Rumblings in Aztlan," 132.

171 **"stay away altogether"**: These threats are articulated in "Strange Rumblings in Aztlan," in the "Jacket Copy" essay, and in Thompson's elegy for Acosta, "The Banshee Screams for Buffalo Meat," all reprinted in Thompson, *Great Shark Hunt,* 94–95, 132.

171 **"but nothing like this"**: On his first day in town, after drinking with Acosta and other activists in his room at the boardinghouse until sunrise, Thompson went to use his bathtub . . . only to discover that someone had linked a naked copper wire between the faucet and the wall-socket: a live, deadly circuit:

> But my room had no shower. And somebody, that night, had managed to string a naked copper wire across the bathtub and plug it into a socket underneath the basin outside the bathroom door. For what reason? Demon Rum, I had no idea. Here I was in the best room in the house, looking for the shower and finding only an electrified bathtub. (Thompson, "Strange Rumblings in Aztlan," 113)

171 **"since 1968"**: Thompson, *Fear and Loathing in America,* 220.

171 **"covering the rally"**: The rally was held in what was then called Laguna Park—later it was renamed Ruben Salazar Park; for more, see *Ruben Salazar* (film, 2014).

172 **"Crusade for Justice"**: The details in this paragraph are drawn from *Ruben Salazar* (film, 2014) and from Thompson's reportage in "Strange Rumblings in Aztlan," 111–114.

172 **"Ruben Salazar and a colleague"**: This colleague was Guillermo Restrepo, a twenty-eight-year-old cameraman and reporter who would witness, firsthand, everything that was to follow. For more, see Restrepo's testimony in *Ruben Salazar* (film, 2014).

172 **"killing him instantly"**: *Ruben Salazar* (film, 2014). An excellent account of the riot can be found in the opening to Escobar, "Dialectics of Repression," 1485:

> The Los Angeles County Sheriff's Department, responding to a minor disturbance, declared the demonstration an unlawful assembly and ordered the park vacated. Before the mass of people had a chance to leave the park and, indeed, well before most people knew that police had ordered them to disperse, sheriff's deputies charged the crowd, shooting tear gas and beating fleeing demonstrators with nightsticks. Many people panicked as they were crushed against the line of deputies and fought pitched battles with them.

172 **"not just for journalists"**: Thompson, "Strange Rumblings in Aztlan," 116.

172 **"get to the bottom of it"**: Thompson first started writing the article in September, just after Salazar's death, but *Scanlan's* went bankrupt in the middle

of his reporting; he resurrected it for *Rolling Stone,* and the goal for the new version was to combine the 1971 unrest with his investigation into Salazar's murder that took place six months earlier.

172  **"the movement's leaders"**: Thompson, "Strange Rumblings in Aztlan," 110.

173  **"sheriff's deputies and spokesmen"**: Most prominently, Lieutenant Norman Hamilton, who Thompson refers to as "the Sheriff's nervous mouthpiece" (Thompson, "Strange Rumblings in Aztlan," 122).

173  **"2,025-page"**: Thompson, "Strange Rumblings in Aztlan," 149.

173  **"switched immediately to Spanish"**: Thompson, "Strange Rumblings in Aztlan," 117.

173  **"rampant police brutality"**: Thompson talks about this struggle in his "Jacket Copy" essay, in *Great Shark Hunt,* 94–96.

173  **"five thousand dollars' worth"**: Thompson, *Fear and Loathing in America,* 332.

173  **"American Express and Diners Club accounts had been frozen"**: Thompson, *Fear and Loathing in America,* 357.

173  **"worried his Carte Blanche card would be next"**: He signed up for a new Carte Blanche card, using his Diners Club (which was about to be revoked) as leverage; the Diners Club card was canceled by March 9, 1970, when Scanlan's was still in business (Thompson, *Fear and Loathing in America,* 357).

173  **"back taxes"**: Thompson, *Fear and Loathing in America,* 332.

173  **"possible staff writer gig"**: Thompson, *Fear and Loathing in America,* 369.

173  **"beginning to double back on him"**: He describes this in his previously unpublished 1968 essay that opens Thompson, *Fear and Loathing in America,* 5–11.

174  **"tiny eyewindow"**: Thompson, "Strange Rumblings in Aztlan," 136.

174  **"midsized living room"**: This scene is based on Thompson's descriptions of the house in "Strange Rumblings in Aztlan," as well as from descriptions in Moore, *Love and Riot,* 93–95, and Acosta, *Revolt of the Cockroach People,* 209.

174  **"shot and killed by law enforcement"**: Munoz, *Youth, Identity, Power,* 206.

174  **"accused (falsely)"**: An undercover officer in the LAPD, Fernando Zumaya, had infiltrated the Brown Berets and then set these fires himself; Acosta was able to prove this during his cross-examination of Zumaya, who, as a police officer, was the only person among the activists with access to the upper floors of the hotel where the fires occurred. As a result, the charges against the activists were eventually dropped. López, *Racism on Trial,* 36.

174  **"Governor Ronald Reagan"**: López, *Racism on Trial,* 36–38.

174  **"guns and knives"**: Thompson, "Strange Rumblings in Aztlan," 135–136.

174  **"gasoline, soap, and oil"**: Acosta, *Revolt of the Cockroach People,* 120.

174 **"enormous amount of marijuana"**: in a 1998 interview with *Arena* magazine, reprinted in Thompson, *Ancient Gonzo Wisdom,* 251, Thompson refers to it as a "pound of weed"; he also calls it "a big bag of marijuana."

174 **".357 Magnum Colt Python handgun"**: 1996 *Rolling Stone* interview with Peter O'Rourke, in Thompson, *Ancient Gonzo Wisdom,* 201.

174 **"begging for justice"**: Thompson, "Strange Rumblings in Aztlan," 136.

174 **"This legal bullshit ain't makin' it"**: Thompson, "Strange Rumblings in Aztlan," 136.

174 **"The day of blood will come"**: Moore, *Love and Riot,* 95.

174 **"The FBI had opened multiple files on him"**: Stavans, *Bandido,* 7; see the PBS documentary *The Brown Buffalo* for more. In our January 12, 2017, interview, producer and researcher Ricardo Lopez, who's been conducting FoIA requests on Acosta for decades, suggested that there were *multiple* FBI files on Acosta.

175 **"grand juries"**: These interrogations did not go over well with the judges, and you can probably imagine why:

> OSCAR ZETA ACOSTA: Do you know any Mexican-Americans, Judge?
> JUDGE JOSEPH LEE CALL (B. 1904): Well, that gentleman that is a gardener at my house is Mexican American. I just signed his citizenship papers. I guess now he is a double-fledged citizen, if that's what you mean.
> OZA: Do you know any persons of Mexican descent who were born here in this country?
> JLC: Mexican descent? If I do, I can't recall them . . .
> (*Racism on Trial,* 98.)

175 **"the most powerful figures in Los Angeles"**: "The Banshee Screams for Buffalo Meat," in Thompson, *Great Shark Hunt,* 501.

175 **"on the porch"**: Thompson, *Great Shark Hunt,* 94–96.

175 **"teenage militants"**: Thompson, "Strange Rumblings in Aztlan," 135–136.

175 **"their uneasiness"**: Thompson, *Fear and Loathing in America,* 447. Acosta wrote to Thompson: "Would anyone in his right mind believe that Rudy, Benny, and Frank would have talked to you without me?" Acosta's bodyguards seem to have agreed, in retrospect, to allow their names to be mentioned in the subsequent article: Benny Luna and Rudy Sanchez gave full names; Frank, perhaps using an alias, only gave his first name.

176 **"dusty and dry"**: This description is drawn from my personal experience visiting the site—research that was conducted April 1, 2016, and January 12, 2017.

176 **"he finally said"**: O'Rourke *Rolling Stone* interview, in Thompson, *Ancient Gonzo Wisdom,* 202.

176 **"*El Pueblo's* crowded living room"**: Thompson, *Fear and Loathing in America,* 366.

176 **"The cops never lose"**: Thompson, "Strange Rumblings in Aztlan," 134.

176   **"about to come down"**: Thompson, "Strange Rumblings in Aztlan," 148.

176   **"pair of slacks"**: Perhaps this incident refers to Marlene Dietrich instead; the source, unfortunately, is the entry "Hotel of Stars" in the gossip website *Seeing Stars*.

176   **"her first movie contract here"**: Ibid.

177   **"lived just up the road"**: Joan Didion's address in the early 1970s was 7406 Franklin Avenue, Los Angeles, CA 90046. The house was enormous, extravagant, and secluded (you should disregard her description of it in *The White Album*, throughout which she attempted to paint herself as less conservative/affluent than she and her husband, Gregory Dunne, actually were). Years later, this house would be turned into headquarters for the Shumei America spiritual organization.

On a side note, Hunter Thompson and Joan Didion would finally meet, for the first and possibly only time, in November 1973, during a dinner party at the Bel Air house of Max Palevsky, a billionaire who supported both *Rolling Stone* and George McGovern's 1972 presidential bid. Said meeting went pretty much how you'd expect. From a December 25, 1973, letter to Greg Jackson at ABC News, in Thompson, *Fear and Loathing in America*, 566: "I met [Gregory Dunne] & his wife about a month ago, incidentally, at a dinner party at Palevsky's; they seemed like inordinately quiet people. Or maybe it was just because of my own standard-brand behavior—drunk, speedy & raving."

177   **"come to expect elsewhere"**: The details of the Polo Lounge are drawn from an afternoon I spent there, on April 1, 2016, a spring Friday almost exactly forty-five years to the day after Thompson and Acosta decamped to its patio section.

177   **"near the palm trees"**: Thompson, *Fear and Loathing in Las Vegas*, 6.

177   **"extra ice"**: For more on Thompson's peculiar culinary tastes, see Carroll, *Hunter*, 144.

177   **"Salazar's death"**: Steadman, *Joke's Over*, 68–69.

177   **"all this pressure"**: The details and quotes in the subsequent three paragraphs are drawn from the essay "Jacket Copy," in Thompson, *Great Shark Hunt*, 94–95.

177   **"closing in"**: Thompson, *Fear and Loathing in Las Vegas*, 12.

178   **"I agree . . . "**: Jacket Copy," in Thompson, *Great Shark Hunt*, 94.

179   **"By all accounts"**: see López, *Racism on Trial*, 233–236. For an in-depth look at the bombing campaign, as well as a letter from Acosta to Thompson that references it directly, see Acosta, *Uncollected Works*, 136; and Moore, *Love and Riot*, 60–61.

179   **"buildings, schools, and banks"**: For an extensive list of sites that were bombed, see Moore, *Love and Riot*, 60–61.

179   **"had been killed"**: López, *Racism on Trial*, 233.

179   **"since he'd last seen"**: Acosta and Thompson saw each other during Thompson's sheriff campaign, in November 1970; they also talked by phone in February 1971; see Thompson, *Kingdom of Fear,* 91–92.

179   **"possibility of surveillance "**: the fear of wiretaps, especially on phone calls, was a constant issue.

179   **"knew Acosta better"**: Moore makes this point in *Love and Riot,* 58.

179   **"out of town for the weekend?"**: Perry, *Fear and Loathing,* 157.

179   **"Acosta was intrigued"**: "Jacket Copy," in Thompson, *Great Shark Hunt,* 94.

180   **"from Tom Vanderschmidt"**: Thompson, *Fear and Loathing in America,* 376.

180   **"overcommitting himself"**: Draper, *Rolling Stone Magazine,* 175.

180   **"pay $300 up front"**: Thompson, *Fear and Loathing in America,* 382.

180   **"to accept the gig"**: Draper, *Rolling Stone Magazine,* 175.

180   **"who knew when"**: "Jacket Copy," in Thompson, *Great Shark Hunt,* 94.

181   **"the call you've been waiting for"**: Thompson, *Fear and Loathing in Las Vegas,* 8.

181   **"the hell out of town"**: Yvette C. Doss, "The Lost Legend of the Real Dr. Gonzo," *Los Angeles Times,* June 5, 1998.

181   **"in preparation"**: Thompson, *Fear and Loathing in Las Vegas,* 8.

181   **"real privacy"**: "Jacket Copy," in Thompson, *Great Shark Hunt,* 95: "In a big red convertible with the top down, there is not much danger of being bugged or overheard."

181   **"his credit card"**: Thompson, *Fear and Loathing in America,* 383.

181   **"In their possession"**: For this trip, they wouldn't have psychedelic substances like mescaline or LSD. Two months after this trip, Jim Silberman, Thompson's editor at Random House, wrote in a letter: "You know it was absolutely clear to me reading Las Vegas 1 [what was to become the first half of *Fear and Loathing in Las Vegas*] that you were not on drugs," to which Thompson wrote back: "This is true," and went on to explain that the account of the first part of the trip "was a very conscious attempt to *simulate* a drug freakout—which is always difficult, but reading it over I still find it depressingly close to the truth I was trying to recreate." By "drugs" they both seem to be talking about psychedelics, as opposed to the Dexedrine capsules Thompson consumed regularly, and later in this same letter Thompson explains that *after* the trips to Vegas, he and a friend "ate a bunch of mescaline and went to a violent, super-jangled car race," where they "experienced the same kind of bemused confusion with the reality that Raoul Duke & his attorney had to cope with in Vegas." He ends by asking Silberman to keep his opinions of Thompson's "drug diet" that weekend to himself: "As I noted, the nature (& specifics) of the piece has already fooled the editors of *Rolling Stone.* They're absolutely convinced, on the basis of what they've read, that I spent my expense money on drugs and went out to Las Vegas for a ranking freakout."

In interviews over the subsequent decades, Thompson would contradict himself—he later claimed that everything he wrote in *Fear and Loathing in Las Vegas* was true—but this letter to Silberman, coupled with comments from the audio tapes he made during his April return to Vegas for the district attorneys' convention on narcotics and dangerous drugs suggests that they really did only bring Dexedrine and marijuana. The context makes sense, too, considering the impromptu nature of their trip and/or the general difficulty of obtaining these substances at the last minute.

For more, see Thompson, *Fear and Loathing in America*, 375–444, as well as *Gonzo Tapes*, discs 2 and 3.

181   **"the marijuana":** 1998 Interview with *Arena Mag*, in Thompson, *Ancient Gonzo Wisdom*, 252.

181   **"spotted a hitchhiker":** This scene is drawn from the responses Thompson gave in the 1996 interview in *Rolling Stone* with Peter O'Rourke, reprinted in Thompson, *Ancient Gonzo Wisdom*, 209:

> We happened to pick up this kid on another road, not on the road from L.A. to Las Vegas. I was driving; it was the first time around— the red car. I saw a kid hitchhiking. A tall, gangly kid. I said, "What the hell?" and I pulled over: "Hop in." "Hot damn," he said, "I never rode in a convertible before." And I said, "You're in the right place." I was really pleased. That was a true thing. I identified with him. I almost said, "You want to drive?"

182   **"hit the road":** Weingarten, *Gang That Wouldn't Write Straight*, 250.

182   **"Acosta: You remind me . . . ":** 1/11/70, Thompson, *Fear and Loathing in America*, 255.

182   **"Thompson: I want to have a place . . . ":** 1/20/70, ibid., 273.

182   **"Acosta: Mankind is doomed . . . ":** 1/11/70, ibid., 255.

182   **"Thompson: True—and all the more reason . . . ":** 1/20/70, ibid., 273.

183   **"Acosta: The struggle is just as much . . . ":** 1/11/70, ibid., 252.

183   **"Thompson: You've got yourself so wired up . . . ":** 1/20/70, ibid., 273.

183   **"Acosta: In fact, I am superior to Christ . . . ":** 2/10/70, ibid., 281.

183   **"Thompson: One of these days . . . ":** 3/9/70, ibid., 285.

183   **"Acosta: You dumb motherfucker . . . ":** 1/11/70, ibid., 254.

183   **"the movement":** The early protests were organized by the Young Chicanos for Community Activism (YCCA) which would later become the Brown Berets.

183   **"everyone involved":** Other groups were present, too, such as MeCHA.

183   **"caught by surprise":** The young activists gathered at a local coffee shop, La Piranya, but the harassment was so extreme—they were jailed for curfew violations, even though they were indoors—they moved to the basement of the Episcopal Church of the Epiphany.

183   **"the emerging concept of 'Aztlan'"**: This concept was articulated in detail during a conference in Denver in March 1969, organized by activist Corky Gonzales's Crusade for Justice. López, *Racism on Trial,* 214.

In *Youth, Identity, Power,* Carlos Munoz Jr., who attended the conference and had been one of the students charged with conspiracy during the '68 walkouts, offers this definition:

> Aztlan was the name used by the Aztecs to refer to their place of origin. Since the Aztecs had migrated to central Mexico from "somewhere in the north," Chicano activists claimed that Aztlan was all the southwestern United States taken from Mexico in the 1846–1848 US-Mexican War. This included California, Texas, New Mexico, most of Arizona, large parts of Colorado, Nevada, and Utah, and a piece of Wyoming. (94)

183   **"Aztlan had become"**: From López, *Racism on Trial,* 215: "'Aztlan!' emerged as one of the great rallying cries of the Chicano movement, and today it continues to evoke notions of peoplehood and ancestral belonging."

183   **"rallying point"**: From López, *Racism on Trial,* 218: "Every celebration of Aztlan and every declaration of Chicano irredentism functioned first as a statement about Mexican descent and racial non-whiteness. In the language of the Chicano movement, nation meant race."

183   **"marginalized American citizens"**: From the handbill of the Denver Crusade for Justice Conference, in Munoz, *Youth, Identity, Power,* 94: "Brotherhood unites us, and love for our brothers makes us a people whose time has come and who struggle against the foreigner 'Gabacho' who exploits our riches and destroys our culture . . . We are Bronze People with a Bronze Culture . . . We are Aztlan."

183   **"Special Operations for Conspiracy"**: Correa, *Chicano Nationalism,* 79.

184   **"They even went so far"**: From Correa, *Chicano Nationalism,* 79.

> These agent provocateurs would intentionally incite and cause violence amongst group members or toward authorities. In doing so, they would please their superiors and move up in rank. In turn, their superiors would then persuade the public that the Brown Berets were a group of subversives who were espousing Communism and inciting violence.

184   **"use deadly force"**: Vigil, *Crusade for Justice,* 152.

184   **"continuous and aggressive investigative attention"**: Correa, *Chicano Nationalism,* 90.

184   **"a threat to the national security"**: Hoover made this statement in an internal memo on 3/27/68; Correa, *Chicano Nationalism,* 82.

184   **"could sense it everywhere"**: Stavans, *Bandido,* 122.

184   **"Ruben Salazar"**: This biographical sketch is based on Phillip Rodriguez's outstanding documentary *Ruben Salazar* (film 2014).

185 **"tone down his coverage"**: The LAPD and sheriff's department were especially image conscious—a result of their ties to Hollywood—and they were worried about looking bad even if they didn't think any changes were necessary; for more on LA law enforcement in the 1960s—the overarching logic of its approach—see the chapter "Law Enforcement and Legal Violence" in López, *Racism on Trial*, 134–154.

185 **"the city's power structure"**: i.e., Mayor Sam Yorty, Sheriff Peter Pitchess, and Police Chief Edward Davis.

185 **"5:30 p.m."**: López, *Racism on Trial*, 194.

185 **"Tom Wilson"**: See *Ruben Salazar* (film, 2014) in which Wilson speaks about his role in the event. (For what it's worth: Tom Wilson is, in my opinion, a monster. He blew off Salazar's head and from his testimony afterward: he thinks he was in the *right*.)

185 **"started to fall apart"**: Thompson would dramatize the difficulty of this case—the process through which he came to understand the events surrounding Salazar's murder—in Thompson, "Strange Rumblings in Aztlan," 120–132.

185 **"a deadly ten-inch projectile"**: Thompson, "Strange Rumblings in Aztlan," 128.

185 **"not that Thompson thought for a moment"**: Thompson, "Strange Rumblings in Aztlan," 123.

185 **"the evidence alone didn't suggest"**: Thompson, "Strange Rumblings in Aztlan," 131:

> Nobody who heard that testimony could believe that the Los Angeles County sheriff's department is capable of pulling off a delicate job like killing a newsman on purpose. Their handling of the Salazar case—from the day of his death all the way to the end of the inquest—raised serious doubts about the wisdom of allowing cops to walk around loose on the street.

185 **"something more complex"**: Much of the context and information provided here on law enforcement's approach to the Brown Berets has been gained through email interviews with Ernesto B. Vigil, which I conducted between September 6, 2016, and October 6, 2016. Thompson—in "Strange Rumblings in Aztlan," in letters to his editors Jim Silberman and Jann Wenner, and also in his "Jacket Copy" essay—discussed his attempt to piece all of these threads together: how he eventually arrived at the conclusion that Salazar was the victim of a larger conspiracy, one that Vigil and also Ricardo Lopez, who participated in Phillip Rodriguez's PBS documentaries *Ruben Salazar* and *The Brown Buffalo,* spent decades researching.

In a June 2, 1971, letter to Silberman, in *Fear and Loathing in America,* 397, Thompson wrote:

> The way I saw it, Ruben Salazar was a journalist, not a Chicano— and I personally believe they shot him intentionally, but I couldn't prove that (all my research and interviews were done *before* the [coroner's] inquest—before the cops would talk to the press—and the

only reason I resurrected the story was that the result of the inquest incredibly confirmed the story I'd put together in the first days after the murder.

185   **"frightening escalations":** From the "Jacket Copy" essay in Thompson, *Great Shark Hunt*, 95: "It had worked out nicely, in terms of the Salazar piece—plenty of hard straight talk about who was lying and who wasn't, and Oscar had finally relaxed enough to talk to me straight."

186   **"deadly escalation":** For more on this, see Ernesto Vigil's testimony in *Ruben Salazar* (film 2014), as well as his expertly researched *Crusade for Justice*.

187   **"a few loose ends":** Weingarten, *Gang That Wouldn't Write Straight*, 243–247.

187   **"near the border of Floyd Lamb State Park":** F. Andrew Taylor, "The City: In Search of Thompson's Vegas," *Las Vegas Sun*, 1997, reprinted at http:// totallygonzo.proboards.com/thread/124/search-thompsons-vegas.

187   **"cool desert wind":** Thompson, *Fear and Loathing in Las Vegas*, 29.

187   **"cruised the Strip":** Taylor, "The City"; Thompson, *Fear and Loathing in Las Vegas*, 41.

188   **"Desert Inn":** See the napkin note in Thompson and Corbett, *Gonzo*, 168.

188   **"he talked about":** Thompson, *Fear and Loathing in America*, 411.

188   **"ride to the airport":** 1998 interview with *Arena Mag*, in Thompson, *Ancient Gonzo Wisdom*, 252.

189   **"Acosta had left behind":** The details of his hotel room and the lobby at dawn are drawn from Thompson's "Jacket Copy" essay; O'Rourke's *Rolling Stone* interview with Thompson; the *Paris Review* interview with Douglas Brinkley and Terry McDonell and George Plimpton; the 1998 *Arena Mag* interview; and from moments that are corroborated by these nonfiction sources in the subsequent fictionalized recounting of it all in Thompson, *Fear and Loathing in Las Vegas*, 69–87.

189   **"prison":** Marijuana laws in Nevada in 1971 were exceptionally harsh; possession of even a small amount could result in a felony.

190   **"called room service":** Thompson, *Fear and Loathing in Las Vegas*, 72.

190   **"put on the only album":** From Thompson's *Paris Review* interview, "The Art of Journalism No. 1," reprinted in Thompson, *Ancient Gonzo Wisdom*, 274: "Through all the *Las Vegas* stuff I played only one album. I wore out four tapes. The Rolling Stones' live album, called *Get Yer Ya-Ya's Out* with the in-concert version of 'Sympathy for the Devil.'" Lyrics from this album appear throughout *Fear and Loathing in Las Vegas*.

190   **"Sympathy for the Devil":** On the album, during the run up to this song—as the crowd hums and Keith Richards tunes his guitar, you could hear, with startling clarity, specific shouts from the audience. Suddenly a woman near the stage began to yell at Mick Jagger. "Paint It Black," she demanded. Her voice was slurred and hostile. "Paint It Black! Paint It Black, Paint It Black You Devil! Paint It Black!" Over which can then be heard the first chords of "Sympathy for the Devil," a song that, by all accounts, was based on one of

the very best books to come out of the twentieth century, Mikhail Bulgakov's *The Master and Margarita,* in which the Devil, "wearing an expensive grey suit and imported shoes of a matching color," appears in 1930s Moscow with the immediate if secondary goal of humiliating, through a series of hilarious tricks and ruses, the spineless leaders of the Soviet literary intelligentsia—the very same group that under Stalin had said nothing as writers like Osip Mandelstam were condemned and sent to their deaths (6).

The song itself still has a haunting feel, all these decades later. "*I shouted out, who killed the Kennedys," Jagger sings, "when after all, it was you and me.*"

190 **"he filled his notebook with"**: McKeen, *Outlaw Journalist,* 164.

191 **"*You are not guilty*"**: Thompson, *Fear and Loathing in Las Vegas,* 87.

191 **"Around him"**: This scene is mostly drawn from two passages:

From a November 28, 1996, *Rolling Stone* interview with P. J. O'Rourke, in Thompson, *Ancient Gonzo Wisdom,* 201:

> Oscar had left me there with a pound of weed and a loaded .357 and some bullets in his briefcase . . . I couldn't pay the bill. And I was afraid. And I was waiting for the right hour to leave the hotel through the casino . . . And earlier I'd slowly, you know, moved stuff down to the car, small amounts, in and out. But there was one really big, metal Halliburton that there was no way to get out. I was trying to pick the right time to leave. I remember at 4:30 in the morning, a poker game was going on, nothing but poker games. I just walked through the casino nonchalantly carrying the Halliburton. I was afraid, I was afraid of taking off, you know, in a red car, on the only road to L.A.

And Thompson, *Fear and Loathing in Las Vegas,* 69–74, which provides a detailed description—including this depiction, from page 57, of the same early-morning scene:

> Now off the escalator and into the casino, big crowds still tight around the craps tables. Who *are* these people? These faces! Where do they come from? They look like caricatures of used-car dealers from Dallas. But they're *real.* And, sweet Jesus, there are a hell of a *lot* of them—still screaming around these desert-city crap tables at four-thirty on a Sunday morning. Still humping the American Dream, that vision of the Big Winner somehow emerging from the last-minute pre-dawn chaos of a stale Vegas casino.

191 **"an older clientele"**: This could be said for almost every hotel in Las Vegas in the early 1970s; for more, see Thompson's references to the nature of the town throughout *Fear and Loathing in Las Vegas,* especially on pages 44 and 193; as well as Joan Didion's essay "Marrying Absurd" in *We Tell Ourselves Stories in Order to Live.*

192 **"Thompson was positive"**: This scene is based on Thompson's explanation of the trip back in *Songs of the Doomed,* 153; in his 1996 interview with O'Rourke; and in his "Jacket Copy" essay.

192 **"the bargaining phase"**: Thompson, *Songs of the Doomed,* 153–154.

193   **"Thompson kept pulling over":** O'Rourke *Rolling Stone* interview, in Thompson, *Ancient Gonzo Wisdom*, 201.

193   **"captured his subjective experience":** In retrospect, this Monday morning drive would come to represent one of the clearest examples of Gonzo Journalism: a form of instant reportage that, published without revision or editing, articulates the undiminished immediacy of the subject matter.

193   **"Gonzo Journalism":** from "Jacket Copy" in Thompson, *Great Shark Hunt*, 95, in which he attempted to define his concept of Gonzo Journalism: "The writing would be selective & necessarily interpretive—but once the image was written, the words would be final; in the same way that a Cartier-Bresson photograph is always (he says) the full-frame negative. No alterations in the darkroom, no cutting or cropping, no spotting . . . no editing."

Not that such a thing is ever completely possible: Even in the moment itself, the act of telling the story becomes a form of artifice—something so inherently dense as to occlude the natural window that is meant to open out on what's *really happening.* As Thompson would clarify:

> In the end I found myself imposing an essentially fictional framework on what began as a piece of straight / crazy journalism. True Gonzo reporting needs the talents of a master journalist, the eye of an artist / photographer and the heavy balls of an actor. Because the writer must be a participant in the scene, while he's writing it—or at least taping it, or even sketching it. Or all three. Probably the closest analogy to the ideal would be a film director / producer who writes his own scripts, does his own camera work and somehow manages to film himself in action, as the protagonist or at least a main character. (*Great Shark Hunt*, 95)

193   **"He'd reached the anonymity":** From Thompson, *Fear and Loathing in Las Vegas*, 83: "safety, obscurity, just another Freak in the Freak Kingdom."

193   **"he drove to Pasadena":** The details of his week at the racetrack motel are drawn from his "Jacket Copy" essay and his 1996 *Rolling Stone* interview with O'Rourke.

193   **"for the next five days":** David Felton, his new editor at *Rolling Stone,* lived in Pasadena. Now that the reporting on the Salazar story was done, it made sense to post up somewhere close, so they could get things ready for publication as quickly as possible.

194   **"1971 spring racing":** The season was about to culminate with the Santa Anita Derby, which would be won by "Jim French," a remarkably durable thoroughbred in the midst of a historic Triple Crown run. *Chicago Tribune,* "Thoroughbred, Auto Industries Join Hands Today," June 19, 1971.

194   **"he worked without distractions":** O'Rourke *Rolling Stone* interview, in Thompson, *Ancient Gonzo Wisdom*, 208.

194   **"in Rolling Stone no. 81":** Thompson, *Fear and Loathing in America*, 395. At 19,200 words it was the longest article the magazine had yet to publish.

194   **"the use of *indiscriminate* force"**: From Thompson, "Strange Rumblings in Aztlan," 119: "Being a sheriff's deputy in East L.A. was not much different from being a point man for the American Division in Vietnam. 'Even the kids and old women are VC.'"

194   **"the malignant reality"**: Thompson, *Great Shark Hunt,* 131.

194   **"the standard Mitchell-Agnew theme"**: For three years the current administration had been harping on "Law and Order" and domestic security as central themes. Spiro Agnew had repeatedly attacked the press, threatening legal action against broadcast networks and referring to members of the media as "unelected elites" inherently biased toward the current president. (See his November 13, 1969 speech in Des Moines, which was quite a doozy . . . ) Over the past decade J. Edgar Hoover had relied on the unconstitutional Counter Intelligence Program to subvert, with intimidation and blackmail and lethal violence, civil rights and antiwar movements. And then there was Richard Nixon, whose treasonous tactics had helped him secure the Oval Office in the first place—and who, over the course of the next two years, would increasingly reject the basic tenants of the American system to secure and expand his sphere of personal power. The video of the Des Moines speech can be found under the entry "Spiro Theodore Agnew" at the website *American Rhetoric.*

195   **"convince his old friend"**: In this sense, Ruben Salazar's killing was really just an extension of a top-down antagonism toward transparency and accountability and equal rights: the unfortunate but logical outcome for a culture that continued to equate power with moral superiority—and, in turn, societal disadvantage with degeneracy.

Hunter Thompson, based on his experience, still believed that it was possible to expose and fight back against these trends through traditional means— via existing media outlets like *Rolling Stone.* Oscar Acosta, after everything that had happened, now saw things differently.

195   **"met for the first time"**: For more on this meeting—and on Thompson and Wenner's relationship in general—see chapter 8, 174–205, of Joe Hagan's biography *Sticky Fingers,* which vividly dramatizes the moment that their paths initially crossed; Hagan also explores the initial rush of friendship between the two of them, as well as the mutual collaboration, admiration, resentment, disappointment, and distrust that, along with decades of financial haggling, would mark their interactions.

195   **"they'd both been living"**: William McKeen's *Outlaw Journalist* also sketches out Wenner's background in a deft manner, and his take on the relationship between the two men is insightful on a cultural level: Wenner is described as "the prototype of the hip young capitalist." McKeen also writes: "The rap against Wenner was that he was the ultimate groupie, that he started *Rolling Stone* as a way to meet the Beatles." For more, see McKeen's chapter "Epiphany," 139–143.

195   **"many of the same people"**: As well as Warren Hinckle, who'd been Wenner's higher up at the *Ramparts* operation in the mid-1960s.

195    **"intrigued and off-balance"**: Thompson would later describe his own behavior at their first meeting as "a flagrantly cranked-up act." During a break in their discussion Wenner shook his head and said to a colleague, "I know I'm supposed to be the youth representative in the culture, but what the fuck is *that?*" (Hagan, *Sticky Fingers,* 175).

195    **"your story in RS"**: Hagan, *Sticky Fingers,* 175.

196    **"Keep it up"**: Perry, *Fear and Loathing,* 161.

197    **"April 26 to Thursday April 29"**: Thompson, *Fear and Loathing in America,* 349.

197    **"still pumping out"**: cf. Joan Didion's essay "At the Dam," in Didion, *We Tell Ourselves Stories in Order to Live,* 326:

> The star map was, he had said, for when we were all gone and the dam was left. I had not thought much of it when he said it, but I thought of it then, with the wind whining and the sun dropping behind a mesa with the finality of a sunset in space. Of course that was the image I had seen always, seen it without quite realizing what I saw, a dynamo finally free of man, splendid at last in its absolute isolation, transmitting power and releasing water to a world where no one is.

197    **"more than a hundred minutes of dialogue"**: These tapes were released as *The Gonzo Tapes* in 2008, to accompany Alex Gibney's documentary *Gonzo,* by Shout Factory. Unless noted, everything you're reading in this section is drawn from my own transcripts of them.

198    **"for a picture"**: Thompson, *Fear and Loathing in America,* 407.

198    **"walked over to Caesars Palace"**: This scene is taken from Thompson and Corbett, *Gonzo,* which features Thompson's photography and notes. On page 168 there's a snapshot of a single handwritten sheet—"Horrible Scene at C-Palace"—which provides the first part of the dialogue that's relayed here. But behind this sheet (in the photo) the next page of the notebook bleeds through. And, long story short, after scanning the image into my computer I was able to erase the writing from the first page and reveal most of what was written on the second . . . the details of which are provided here. I am not a technically savvy individual, and I'll simply add this process took a great many hours of work that probably should've been spent, in retrospect, on *writing . . .*

203    **"At dawn the next morning"**: This trip to the airport is also drawn from the same notepad images in Thompson and Corbett, *Gonzo;* as with the scene at Caesar's I used the imaging technique to unearth the writing from the page beneath the one that was showing (169).

205    **"Later that night"**: The details in this scene are drawn from a phone interview I conducted with Bruce Innes on March 23, 2017; from Thompson's May 9, 1971, letter to Jim Silberman in Thompson, *Fear and Loathing in America,* 382; and from general descriptions of the Circus Circus and its owner in Thompson, *Fear and Loathing in Las Vegas.*

205    **"its owner"**: For more, see the "Jay Sarno" entry in *Online Nevada Encyclopedia.*

205   **"that begins"**: At least this is how the song "Chicago" starts up when it's played live on Crosby, Stills, Nash & Young's *4 Way Street;* did Bruce Innes state this lyric about Daley before he began the song? In our interview I didn't ask, but *4 Way Street* had been released a few weeks earlier, on April 7, 1971, so it's not a huge stretch to depict "Chicago" beginning this way—a song that Innes *did* play that night and that is clearly about Mayor Daley and the 1968 DNC and the trial that followed . . .

206   **"The Circus-Circus . . . "**: Thompson, *Fear and Loathing in Las Vegas,* 46.

206   **"After five days in Vegas . . . "**: Thompson, *Fear and Loathing in Las Vegas,* 193.

206   **"134-judge bench"**: López, *Racism on Trial,* 36.

206   **"in a consistent and lawyerlike manner"**: López, *Racism on Trial,* 36.

206   **"Over the course of the proceedings"**: López, *Racism on Trial,* 37–38.

206   **"working as a provocateur"**: López, *Racism on Trial,* 38–39.

206   **"In May"**: The details and dialogue in this scene are based on Oscar Acosta's description of it in his October 1971 letter to Thompson, as well as Thompson's June 1971 letter to Jim Silberman (*Fear and Loathing in America,* 397, 445).

207   **"On August 28"**: This scene is based on The *Los Angeles Times* article recounting the event, "Biltmore Trial Lawyer Arrested," August 29, 1971, as well as a *Los Angeles Herald Examiner* article, which is described in Stavans, *Bandido,* 84.

207   **"didn't have a prescription"**: From Acosta, *Autobiography of a Brown Buffalo,* 171: "Fifteen mgs. of amphetamine moves you just about right when you've got a hangover and the sheriff's looking for you. If you're used to them, of course. I'd been taking them ever since I started Law School. I worked as a copy boy for the S.F. Examiner . . . One of the other copy boys had a whole room full of various drugs."

207   **"evicted"**: Moore, *Love and Riot,* 98.

207   **"divorced"**: Stavans, *Bandido,* 69.

207   **"move back in"**: Thompson, *Fear and Loathing in America,* 446.

207   **"acquitted on all counts"**: López, *Racism on Trial,* 232.

208   **"he wrote nonstop in the basement"**: Carroll, *Hunter,* 143.

208   **"It was fun to write . . . "**: Thompson, *Great Shark Hunt,* 97.

208   **"San Francisco in"**: Thompson, *Fear and Loathing in Las Vegas,* 67–68.

208   **"the grim meat-hook realities"**: Thompson, *Fear and Loathing in Las Vegas,* 178.

209   **"in this doomstruck era"**: Thompson, *Fear and Loathing in Las Vegas,* 178.

210   **"It wouldn't be a *journalistic* assignment"**: The details of their plans for the 1972 election are drawn from Hagan, *Sticky Fingers,* 218–219.

210 **"Max Palevsky"**: Palevsky's biographical details are drawn from Hagan, *Sticky Fingers*, 219.

210 **"The plan was"**: Hagan sums it up nicely in *Sticky Fingers*, 202–203:

> Putting aside the Vietnam assignment, Wenner plotted instead to get Thompson press credentials for the White House . . . In Max Palevsky, *Rolling Stone* now had entrée to Washington power . . . The idea was to harness the newly empowered youth vote to take on Richard Nixon on an antiwar platform. Palevsky offered to be his lead financial backer, staking him $300,000. For Wenner and Thompson, the path forward seemed clear: *Rolling Stone* could serve as the journalistic wing of the McGovern campaign, with Thompson stirring the shit with his patented Fear and Loathing.

210 **"free to savage"**: From *Boys on the Bus,* a book on the campaign by *Rolling Stone*'s Timothy Crouse—Thompson's colleague and partner and helper extraordinaire—who at the time was in his midtwenties: "Thompson was free to write the unmentionable" (314).

210 **"the most decent man"**: Thompson, *On the Campaign Trail '72,* 111.

211 **"relocating them"**: In the oral history *Gonzo* (Seymour and Wenner, 146), Wenner would say:

> We would have full-time coverage of a professional election in our rock & roll magazine. What we thought of right at the beginning—we were trying to make some kind of splash—was that he'd move to Washington. Well, that may or may not have been the smartest idea. But it got him there. We put him on payroll with a salary of $17,000 a year, which was big for us then.

211 **"You dumb cocksucker . . . "**: Thompson, *Fear and Loathing in America,* 448.

211 **"I have no regrets . . . "**: Thompson, *Fear and Loathing in America,* 447.

211 **"Did you even so much as . . . "**: Thompson, *Fear and Loathing in America,* 448.

212 **"some fucking native"**: Thompson, *Fear and Loathing in America,* 447.

212 **"My God!"**: McKeen, *Outlaw Journalist,* 176.

212 **"You stupid fuck"**: Thompson, *Fear and Loathing in America,* 476.

212 **"What kind of journalist"**: "The Banshee Screams for Buffalo Meat," in Thompson, *Great Shark Hunt,* 511.

213 **"He had a lawyer's"**: "The Banshee Screams for Buffalo Meat," in Thompson, *Great Shark Hunt,* 515; I've cut out part of this quote, a reference to Acosta's predilection for LSD (which was very real) because 1) Thompson harps on this in the earlier passages taken from his letters, and 2) I think it's important to keep the focus on Acosta's belief in the power of truth: a belief that his relationship with psychedelics no doubt affected, but that also, in the end, existed as a sort of rich gossamer thread throughout the course of his deeply complex life—a consistency of belief that feels, in retrospect, deeply abiding.

## Chapter Six

216 **"namely me"**: Thompson, *On the Campaign Trail '72*, 99.

216 **"beating Richard Nixon in the fall"**: Thompson, *On the Campaign Trail '72*, 142.

216 **"nearest opponent"**: *New York Times*, "Muskie Maintains Gallup Poll Lead."

217 **"disgracefully bad"**: This was *Newsweek*'s national correspondent Dick Stout.

218 **"I've ever been subjected to"**: Thompson, *On the Campaign Trail '72*, 89.

218 **"Monty Chitty"**: Forty years later, William McKeen tracked Monty Chitty down and did an excellent interview with him about the incident; for more, see *Outlaw Journalist*, 187–200.

218 **"Peter Sheridan"**: The biographical information on Peter Sheridan is drawn from three sources:
Scully, *Living with the Dead*, 279–280.
Benson and Menconi, *Comin' Right at Ya*, 47–48.
Patoski, *Willie Nelson*, 330–331.

218 **"claiming LSD as a sacrament"**: The BooHoo Bible claimed, among other things, that the ultimate goal of mankind was to someday bombard and annihilate the planet of Saturn. For more, see http://okneoac.org/millbrook/ch35.

218 **"the campaign's advance man"**: Thompson, *On the Campaign Trail '72*, 94. The person Sheridan knew was Richie Evans, a Muskie advance man; Evans, when he heard Sheridan had arrived, completely disappeared from sight.

218 **"cause a scene"**: Sheridan wanted to leave his hat at the coat check:
> But when he tried to check his hat, the manager coiled up like a bull-snake—recognizing something in "Sheridan's" tone of voice or maybe just the vibrations that gave him a bad social fear, and I could see in his eyes that he was thinking: "O my God—here it comes. Should we mace him now or later?" (Thompson, *On the Campaign Trail '72*, 94)

219 **"Sunshine Special"**: The full quote from Thompson, *On the Campaign Trail '72*, 94:
> "To hell with that," I said. "Take the train with us. It's the presidential express—a straight shot into Miami and all the free booze you can drink. Why not? Any friend of Richie's is a friend of Ed's, I guess— but since you can't find Evans at this hour of the night, and since the train is leaving in two hours, well, maybe you should borrow this little orange press ticket, just until you get aboard."

219 **"kept the BooHoo under control"**: Thompson, *On the Campaign Trail '72*, 98.

219 **"wind gusting from the west"**: Historical weather data from Wunderground.

219   **"an ugly little wop"**: Thompson, *On the Campaign Trail '72*, 98.

219   **"car no. 300"**: Naughton, "Muskie Thrives on an Old Campaign Method."

220   **"expensively orchestrated trip"**: $50,000 total, most likely: Thompson, *On the Campaign Trail '72*, 115.

221   **"cut short his remarks"**: Thompson, *On the Campaign Trail '72*, 89.

221   **"Afterward Peter Sheridan"**: Eventually Peter Sheridan would end up in Austin, where he'd become Willie Nelson's close friend and bodyguard. In 1980, in California, while riding a Harley-Davidson that Nelson had purchased for him, he'd be sideswiped and killed.

221   **"Freak Kingdom"**: Thompson, *On the Campaign Trail '72*, 93.

221   **"fellow correspondents"**: Crouse, *Boys on the Bus*, 313.

221   **"candidate like Muskie"**: The "Sunshine Special" story would become a favorite of the Grateful Dead's Jerry Garcia. From Scully, *Living with the Dead*, 279–280: "Jerry loves this hippie Paul Bunyan fable, a tale of a freewheeling freak creating havoc in the camp of the sanctimonious and hypocritical."

221   **"possible general election face-off"**: Thompson, *On the Campaign Trail '72*, 107.

222   **"what was really going on"**: Timothy Crouse explores this issue, which he coined as "Pack Journalism," in depth in his book *Boys on the Bus*, 7–8.

222   **"one-off thing"**: from Thompson, *On the Campaign Trail '72*, 4: "When I went to Washington I was determined to avoid this kind of trap. Unlike most other correspondents, I could afford to burn all my bridges behind me—because I was only there for a year, and the last thing I cared about was establishing long-term connections on Capitol Hill."

222   **"next year's crop"**: Thompson, *On the Campaign Trail '72*, 127.

222   **"dangerously unstable"**: Thompson, *On the Campaign Trail '72*, 238.

222   **"by sundown on Labor Day"**: Thompson, *On the Campaign Trail '72*, 142. The rest of the quote: "If I were running a campaign against Muskie I would arrange for some anonymous creep to buy time on national TV and announce that twenty-two years ago he and Ed spent a summer working as male whores at a Peg House somewhere in the North Woods. Nothing else would be necessary."

222   **"had been housed"**: Farrell, *Richard Nixon*, 425.

222   **"chief of staff"**: Farrell, *Richard Nixon*, 425.

223   **"enemies' list"**: Farrell, *Richard Nixon*, 484. The enemies list initially included twenty names, from Dick Gregory to Allard Lowenstein.

223   **"Hunter Thompson called it"**: Thompson, *On the Campaign Trail '72*, 53.

223   **"break down weeping"**: Broder, "Muskie Denounces Publisher."

223   **"destruction of an opponent"**: Broder would reevaluate his coverage of this moment years later in a February 1987 essay; see Broder, "The Story That Still Nags at Me."

224 **"West African ceremonies"**: Thompson, *On the Campaign Trail '72*, 147.

224 **"find himself accused"**: The full quote, from Thompson, *On the Campaign Trail '72*, 97:

> The Boohoo incident haunted me throughout the campaign. First it got me barred from the Muskie camp, then—when investigations of the Watergate Scandal revealed that Nixon staffers had hired people to systematically sabotage the primary campaigns of almost all the serious Democratic contenders—the ex-Muskie lieutenants cited the Boohoo incident as a prime example of CREEP's dirty work. Ranking Muskie lieutenants told congressional investigators that Sheridan and I had conspired with Donald Segretti and other unnamed saboteurs to humiliate Muskie in the Florida primary. The accusation came as a welcome flash of humor at a time when I was severely depressed at the prospect of another four years with Nixon. This also reinforced my contempt for the waterheads who ran Big Ed's campaign like a gang of junkies trying to send a rocket to the moon to check out rumors that the craters were full of smack.

224 **"full of smack"**: Thompson, *On the Campaign Trail '72*, 97.

224 **"That winter"**: The details here about their time in Washington, DC, are drawn from Carroll, *Hunter*, 151–160.

224 **"twenty-five percent"**: Carroll, *Hunter*, 152.

225 **"a lot of speed"**: Carroll, *Hunter*, 156.

225 **"in his own world"**: Carroll, *Hunter*, 153.

225 **"I remember myself smoking"**: Carroll, *Hunter*, 152.

225 **"I was drunk"**: Carroll, *Hunter*, 153.

225 **"with Thompson"**: Hagan, *Sticky Fingers*, 218–219.

226 **"in 1968"**: With General Curtis LeMay as his running mate; still, Wallace won forty-six electoral votes in 1968, an astonishing amount.

226 **"fire & brimstone *performance*"**: Thompson, *On the Campaign Trail '72*, 139.

226 **"rock star"**:, Thompson, *On the Campaign Trail '72*, 166.

226 **"anger and dissatisfaction"**: In an August 8, 1972, radio interview Thompson did with WBZ Boston (reprinted in Thompson, *Ancient Gonzo Wisdom*, 10), he compared the grievances of Wallace voters to those he'd heard from the Hell's Angels half-a-decade earlier:

> It's the kind of people who I saw in a place like Serb Hall in Milwaukee, this really rabid, relatively same kind of crowd. It was a crowd that had come out there for no other reason than to see Wallace. They told me that they were there because he was the one person in American politics who really made sense when you cut through the bullshit and get things done. They wanted to get the truth back. As much as I was appalled by it, the whole mood, I was struck by

the intensity they were feeling. There are people in this country who really feel that they are not only left out, but that the world is deaf to them.

227   **"fucking them over for so long"**: Thompson, *On the Campaign Trail '72*, 253.

227   **"honest solutions"**: Thompson, *On the Campaign Trail '72*, 253.

227   **"see his name in the paper"**: Bremer's motivation wasn't ideological; he simply wanted to see his name in the papers, to be famous. For more, see David Montgomery's December 1, 2015, *Washington Post* article "Arthur Bremmer's Shot Gov. Wallace to Be Famous," www.washingtonpost.com /lifestyle/magazine/he-shot-george-wallace-to-be-famous-now-he-lives -in-silence/2015/12/01/700b1d26-78d7-11e5-bc80-9091021aeb69_story .html?utm_term=.5fc84ef81505.

227   **"for history"**: Crouse, *Boys on the Bus*, 314.

228   **"US position on Israel"**: Thompson, *On the Campaign Trail '72*, 227–228. Making your political opponent deny outlandishly false claims was, as Thompson would write, nothing new:

> This is one of the oldest and most effective tricks in politics. Every hack in the business has used it in times of trouble, and it has even been elevated to the level of political mythology in a story about one of Lyndon Johnson's early campaigns in Texas. The race was close and Johnson was getting worried. Finally he told his campaign manager to start a massive rumor campaign about his opponent's life-long habit of enjoying carnal knowledge of his own barnyard sows.
> "Christ, we can't get away calling him a pig-fucker," the campaign manager protested. "Nobody's going to believe a thing like that."
> "I know," Johnson replied. "But let's make the sonofabitch deny it." McGovern has not learned to cope with this tactic yet. Humphrey used it again in California, with different issues, and once again George found himself working overtime to deny wild, baseless charges that he was: (1) Planning to scuttle both the Navy and the Air Force, along with the whole Aerospace industry, and (2) He was a sworn foe of all Jews, and if he ever got to the White House he would immediately cut off all military aid to Israel and sit on his hands while Russian-equipped Arab legions drove the Jews into the sea.

228   **"Japanese Current"**: Thompson, *On the Campaign Trail '72*, 118.

229   **"dishonest old hack"**: Thompson, *On the Campaign Trail '72*, 190.

229   **"rabid skunk"**: Thompson, *On the Campaign Trail '72*, 258.

229   **"brain-damaged old vulture"**: Thompson, *On the Campaign Trail '72*, 170.

229   **"American politics today"**: Here's the full quote of Thompson's comparison of Humphrey to Nixon, in Thompson, *On the Campaign Trail '72*, 186:

> With the possible exception of Nixon, Hubert Humphrey is the purest and most disgusting example of a Political Animal in American politics today. He has been going at it hammer and tong twenty-five

hours a day since the end of World War II—just like Richard Nixon, who launched his own career as a Red-baiting California congressman about the same time Hubert began making headlines as the Red-baiting Mayor of Minneapolis. They are both career anti-Communists: Nixon's gig was financed from the start by Big Business, and Humphrey's by Big Labor . . . and what both of them stand for today is the de facto triumph of a One Party System in American politics.

229    **"straight-shooting believer"**: From Thompson, *Ancient Gonzo Wisdom,* 14–15: "I like him, personally. I think he's a good, very straight politician. For a politician, he's one of the most honest people I've ever seen . . . He's a very reasonable kind of guy."

229    **"Thompson would write"**: Thompson, *On the Campaign Trail '72,* 111. The full quote: "He is probably the most honest big-time politician in America; Robert Kennedy, several years before he was murdered, called George McGovern 'the most decent man in the Senate.'"

229    **"elect almost anybody"**: Thompson, *On the Campaign Trail '72,* 256.

230    **"Don't take a taxi"**: Carroll, *Hunter,* 160.

231    **"the correct side of history"**: The biographical information on McGovern here is from the 2006 documentary film *One Bright Shining Moment,* directed by Stephen Vittoria.

232    **"calling your name"**: Thompson, *On the Campaign Trail '72,* 170.

232    **"within the structure's basement"**: Thompson references this moment in two of his *Rolling Stone* articles: "Fear and Loathing at the Watergate: Mr. Nixon Has Cashed His Check," and "Fear and Loathing in Limbo: The Scum Also Rises," both of which were later anthologized in *The Great Shark Hunt.*

On the night of June 17th I spent most of the evening in the Watergate Hotel: From about eight o'clock until ten I was swimming laps in the indoor pool, and from 10:30 until a bit after 1:00 AM I was drinking tequila in the Watergate bar with Tom Quinn, a sports columnist for the now-defunct Washington Daily News.

Meanwhile, upstairs in room 214, Hunt and Liddy were already monitoring the break-in, by walkie-talkie, with ex-FBI agent Alfred Baldwin in his well-equipped spy-nest across Virginia Avenue in room 419 of the Howard Johnson Motor Lodge. Jim McCord had already taped the locks on two doors just underneath the bar in the Watergate garage, and it was probably just about the time that Quinn and I called for our last round of tequila that McCord and his team of Cubans moved into action— and got busted less than an hour later.

All this was happening less than 100 yards from where we were sitting in the bar, sucking limes and salt with our Sauza Gold and muttering darkly about the fate of Duane Thomas and the pigs who run the National Football League. (Thompson, 246–247)

233 **"blue subaqueous timbre to the light"**: cf. Denis Johnson's poem "The Circle": "The scene had a subaqueous timbre . . . that shines in the dreams I have when I sleep" (from *The Throne of the Third Heaven of the Nations Millennium General Assembly: Poems Collected and New*, 117).

234 **"with his handgun"**: Farrell, *Richard Nixon*, 468.

234 **"install listening devices for the first time"**: Farrell, *Richard Nixon*, 471–472.

234 **"came upon"**: For more, see this recent 2012 article from the *Washingtonian*, which is fascinating: Craig, "The Bartender's Tale."

235 **"the administration that had ordered it"**: For more see Emery, *Watergate*, 143–144.

235 **"Thompson wrote bitterly"**: Thompson, *On the Campaign Trail '72*, 369.

236 **"died violently"**: Farrell, *Richard Nixon*, 496; *Vietnam War*, episode 9.

236 **"medical background"**: Thompson, *On the Campaign Trail '72*, 304–315.

237 **"Democratic counterpart"**: Thompson, *On the Campaign Trail '72*, 324.

237 **"martini-sipping GOP delegates on the other"**: Thompson, *On the Campaign Trail '72*, 358.

238 **"floor demonstrations"**: Crouse, *Boys on the Bus*, 165.

238 **"rented Impala convertible"**: Thompson, *On the Campaign Trail '72*, 316.

238 **"Collins Avenue"**: Details from this scene have been taken from three sources: Thompson, *On the Campaign Trail '72*, 357–369; the film *Operation Last Patrol*; and the Top Value Television feature *Four More Years*.

238 **"Sergeant Ron Kovic"**: He would later be portrayed by Tom Cruise in the 1989 Oliver Stone film *Born on the Fourth of July*.

239 **"Pete McCloskey"**: McCloskey had challenged Nixon in that year's New Hampshire primary on an antiwar platform (similar to McCarthy's 1968 run), garnering 11 percent of the vote—a decision that drove the paranoid president wild with anger—and as the Watergate scandal developed, McCloskey would become the first Republican to call for Nixon's impeachment.

239 **"You can't get in through here!"**: The dialogue is from the Top Value TV feature *Four More Years*.

240 **"Miami Beach"**: Thompson, *On the Campaign Trail '72*, 364.

240 **"disturbing the peace"**: Thompson, *On the Campaign Trail '72*, 368.

240 **"bad pornographic film"**: Thompson, *On the Campaign Trail '72*, 328.

241 **"He's shown us how"**: *Four More Years* (film).

242 **"in a certain sense, true"**: Thompson had run as an independent, and the weekend before the 1969 sheriff election, the Republican and Democratic parties of Aspen had joined forces against the Freak Power Ticket, so as to avoid splitting the vote—a betrayal by the Democrats that Thompson hadn't expected.

242 **"square of paper"**: This was a beautifully ironic reference to Mayor Daley's shameless sewer-worker demonstrations four years earlier in Chicago when, just before Hubert Humphrey's acceptance speech, Daley had flooded the floor with union members of the city's public works, many of whom carried freshly printed signs that read "We Love Mayor Daley!"

243 **"against chairs other delegates were still standing on"**: Thompson, *On the Campaign Trail '72*, 336.

244 **"White House press pass"**: Crouse, *Boys on the Bus*, 260.

244 **"he said to another reporter"**: Bob Greene of the *Chicago Sun Times* (*On the Campaign Trail '72*, 377).

245 **"American flag"**: McDonell, *An Accidental Life*, 115.

245 **"Thompson called him"**: Thompson, *On the Campaign Trail '72*, 376.

245 **"Thompson tried to ask him"**: Crouse, *Boys on the Bus*, 260–261.

245 **"walked up to him"**: McDonell, *An Accidental Life*, 116.

247 **"the Werewolf"**: This passage, from *On the Campaign Trail '72*, 392, is followed by one of my very favorite that Hunter Thompson would ever write—an imagined scene in which Nixon transforms into the beast Thompson has always known him to be:

> At the stroke of midnight in Washington, a drooling red-eyed beast with the legs of a man and a head of a giant hyena crawls out of its bedroom window in the South Wing of the White House and leaps fifty feet down to the lawn . . . pauses briefly to strangle the Chow watchdog, then races off into the darkness . . . towards the Watergate, snarling with lust, loping through the alleys behind Pennsylvania Avenue, and trying desperately to remember which one of those four hundred identical balconies is the one outside Martha Mitchell's apartment. . . .
>
> Ah . . . nightmares, nightmares. But I was only kidding. The President of the United States would never act that weird. At least not during football season.

247 **"in us"**: Thompson, *On the Campaign Trail '72*, 392, 389, 391–392.

247 **"$2,000 worth of revenue space"**: Hagan, *Sticky Fingers*, 222.

247 **"Zoo Plane"**: The details of the Zoo Plane come from Crouse's description of it in *Boys on the Bus*, 347–351, and Thompson's mention of it during the extended self-interview portion of his "November" chapter in *On the Campaign Trail*, 394–433.

248 **"physical and spiritual collapse"**: In a December 17, 1972, letter to McGovern aide Sandy Berger, Thompson wrote, in *Fear and Loathing in America*, 499: "I am coming more & more to grips with the notion that getting on the Zoo Plane permanently fucked up my life."

248 **"he wrote"**: Thompson, *On the Campaign Trail '72*, 228.

248 **"this madness"**: Thompson, *On the Campaign Trail '72*, 387–388.

248  **"23 percentage points"**: White, *Making of the President: 1972,* 373–374.

248  **"broke down in tears"**: Seymour and Wenner, *Gonzo,* 172. The full quote from George McGovern:

> He had a couple more questions he wanted to put to me, so I had one final interview with him in my office. He teared up more than once. He took it very hard. There was no question in my mind that he grieved over it, and that he was serious. He alternated between a sort of sweet fury and genuine grief. He couldn't even stand to look at me. (172–173)

248  **"some hope for the future"**: from a 2005 interview with McGovern in *One Bright Shining Moment* (film).

249  **"He couldn't do it"**: The details of this section are drawn from the Author's Note to Thompson, *On the Campaign Trail '72;* and from Hagan, *Sticky Fingers,* 281. Hagan describes the final push to finish the book as catastrophic: "The effort almost broke Thompson."

249  **"to hell with the consequences"**: Thompson, *On the Campaign Trail '72,* 4.

249  **"testament to its ruin"**: cf. the ending to *The Wasteland,* by TS Eliot, of whom Thompson was a fan:

> These are fragments I have shored against my ruins

250  **"American politics"**: Thompson, *On the Campaign Trail '72,* 469.

250  **"my friends"**: Rugaber, "McCord Tells Senate of New Watergate Names."

250  **"astonishing reach"**: Farrell, *Richard Nixon,* 508.

250  **"destroyed evidence"**: Farrell, *Richard Nixon,* 479–480, 502.

251  **"all resigned"**: The banner headline in the May 1, 1973, *New York Times:* "NIXON ACCEPTS ONUS FOR WATERGATE."

251  **"as he liked to call himself"**: For more on Senator Sam Ervin, see Hunter, "Sam Ervin, Country Lawyer."

251  **"daily five-hour broadcast"**: Thompson, *Great Shark Hunt,* 258.

251  **"to his body"**: In his interview with McGovern at the end of *On the Campaign Trail '72,* 447, Thompson described a recent visit to an Aspen doctor: "He said in all of his years in medicine, about fifteen or twenty years ... he'd never seen anybody with as bad a case of anxiety as I had. He said I was right on the verge of a complete mental, physical, and emotional collapse. At that point I began to wonder how the hell you or anyone else survived."

251  **"literary writer"**: Thompson added that he wanted to go back to constructing his work in a careful, revised manner again: "I think it's about time I get back in the habit of writing at least a second draft of my gibberish, instead of lashing all this last-minute lunacy into print for no reason except to fill space or justify some ill-conceived headline in RS" (Thompson, *Fear and Loathing in America,* 514).

251  **"people he cared about"**: He was trying to resist requests from his editors to do more articles; he wanted to travel less: "The central horror of my (and

Sandy's) life at the moment is that I seem to have somehow set myself up for a travel / writing schedule in 1973 that looks very much like a replay of 1972— which would no doubt be as intolerable for the people in the RS production dept. as it would be for me" (Thompson, *Fear and Loathing in America,* 513).

251 **"time Now for time Later":** Thompson, *Fear and Loathing in America,* 514.

251 **"the plan":** He told Wenner that he wanted to tone things down:

> At that point, presuming the story works, we can get back on something approaching a normal schedule . . . but my gut feeling at the moment is that we should probably keep the contract in a state of limbo until I have time to sit back here on the porch and re-assess my commitments, which seem to be getting more & more out of hand. (Thompson, *Fear and Loathing in America,* 513)

252 **"reporting assignments":** Thompson, *Fear and Loathing in America,* 521–522.

252 **"plan a conference":** see the December 25, 2007, article in the *Las Vegas Sun,* "Hunter S. Thompson, How All Went Wrong in Elko."

252 **"newspapers and magazines":** Thompson, *Fear and Loathing in America,* 515–516.

252 **"New York Post":** See the entry for this book on Simon & Schuster's website for a more complete list of reviews.

253 **"stolen files and perjury":** Rugaber, "Hearing Is Told That Magruder Had File Moved."

253 **"June 25":** See Lowy, "Fred Thompson Aided Nixon on Watergate."

253 **"just north of the Capitol":** See the entry "The Kennedy Caucus Room" on the United States Senate website.

253 **"Nixon's staff":** Baker, *Family of Secrets,* 224.

253 **"very polite FBI agent":** Thompson, *On the Campaign Trail '72,* 259.

254 **"regardless of the law":** See the YouTube entry "Watergate Hearings: John Dean's Opening Statement (1973)."

254 **"published in the *New York Times*":** For Dean's testimony see the June 28, 1973 transcript of it in the *New York Times.*

254 **"John Dean":** Thompson and Dean would actually meet, in 1978—during the filming for a BBC production on Thompson's life—and the two of them would recount the Watergate hearings. Thompson would explain how he'd watched Dean on the television from Woody Creek (out on his porch) and been amazed at the power of Dean's testimony: "I honestly didn't believe you could pull it off. I admired it tremendously" (BBC, *Omnibus: Hunter Thompson*).

254 **"knew it all along":** This passage is a (near) direct quote from John Farrell's outstanding biography on Nixon—from the chapter "A Third-Rate Burglary," which details Dean's involvement in the scandal: "Later on, when the cover-up collapsed, Senator Howard Baker, who had a gift for pithy

encapsulation, would reduce the issue to: 'What did the president know, and when did he know it?' The answer is that Nixon knew it all, and he knew it all along" (*Richard Nixon*, 480).

254 **"get to Washington as soon as possible"**: Thompson, *Great Shark Hunt*, 262.

254 **"arrived in mid-July"**: The details of this trip are taken from "Fear and Loathing at the Watergate, Mr. Nixon Has Cashed His Check," Thompson's September 27, 1973, article in *Rolling Stone*, reprinted in Thompson, *Great Shark Hunt*.

255 **"aware of listening devices, yes sir"**: "Transcripts," *New York Times*, July 17, 1973.

255 **"yellow pencil"**: Thompson, *Great Shark Hunt*, 268.

255 **"on hand for the magazine"**: For more on Leibovitz's relationship with *Rolling Stone*—with Jann Wenner and his wife, Jane, with whom she lived for an extended period—see the chapter "Whatever Gets You Thru the Night" in Hagan, *Sticky Fingers*, 265–267.

255 **"on his way to the bathroom"**: Steadman, *Joke's Over*, 104–105.

255 **"witness it live"**: Thompson, *Great Shark Hunt*, 275–276.

256 **"$1500 a month"**: Thompson, *Great Shark Hunt*, 252.

256 **"signed copy"**: Thompson, *Fear and Loathing in America*, 544.

256 **"his wife, Eleanor"**: Thompson, *Fear and Loathing in America*, 558. Eleanor was a fascinating figure; she had met George at a high school debate in South Dakota—in which she and her partner defeated him—a story I find especially touching . . . (Ambrose, *The Wild Blue*, 45)

Also, see this passage from the end of McKeen's *Outlaw Journalist*, 364—an excellent description of George McGovern's speech at Thompson's 2005 funeral, which the senator gave despite the fact that Eleanor was in the hospital at the time, recovering from a heart attack:

> Senator McGovern, the featured speaker, focused on Hunter's *Campaign Trail* book. "At the end of the book, on the last page, Hunter has a list and he says it's 'Ten things I wish I had done during the campaign.' And what he said for number ten was 'I wish I had spent a week on a deserted Caribbean island with Eleanor McGovern.'" The crowd laughed. "I didn't think so kindly of that, but we've stayed in touch over the years and everything. And when I went to the hospital yesterday to talk to Eleanor—Eleanor insisted that I come—and she said, 'George, since you'll be the last one to talk to Hunter before they shoot his ashes up, tell him I wished I had spent that week with him, too.'"

256 **"Seventeenth and R Streets"**: Thompson, *Fear and Loathing in America*, 529.

256   **"Steadman and a few others"**: Steadman, *Joke's Over,* 98–99; Seymour and Wenner, *Gonzo,* 159.

256   **"Sing 'Masters of War' for the Senator"**: Steadman, *Joke's Over,* 98.

257   **"rarified air to be fixed in"**: Thompson, *Fear and Loathing in America,* 530.

257   **"took that as a compliment"**: Seymour and Wenner, *Gonzo,* 159.

257   **"in ecstatic cahoots on that fact all the time"**: Fitzgerald, *Great Gatsby,* 154.

257   **"normally dormant potential"**: Thompson, *Great Shark Hunt,* 250.

258   **"What will Nixon do?"**: Thompson, *Great Shark Hunt,* 276.

258   **"strike back"**: Thompson, *Great Shark Hunt,* 275.

258   **"he pushed too far"**: Thompson, *Great Shark Hunt,* 262.

258   **"January 1, 1974"**: Thompson, "Fear and Loathing in the Bunker."

259   **"fail to learn something from it"**: Thompson, *Great Shark Hunt,* 242.

259   **"Oscar Acosta wrote to Hunter Thompson"**: Thompson, *Fear and Loathing in America,* 542.

259   **"a weekend together in Mexico"**: *Gonzo Tapes,* Disc 4, Tracks 5–11.

259   **"20 percent cut of the film rights"**: 20 percent of $7,500, which was what Acosta thought Thompson had received.

259   **"and wish me well, as I do you"**: Thompson, *Fear and Loathing in America,* 561–562.

260   **"past two years"**: Thompson, *Fear and Loathing in America,* 562.

260   **"*The Rise and Fall of General Z*"**: Stavans, *Bandido,* 120.

260   **"last will and testament"**: Composed January 13, 1974. Acosta, *Uncollected Works,* 305.

260   **"June 1974"**: Acosta, *Revolt of the Cockroach People,* 259.

260   **"gone badly"**: The details and speculation here are drawn in part from the afterword written by Acosta's son, Marco, to Acosta, *Revolt of the Cockroach People,* 259–262.

260   **"a storm off the Pacific coast"**: Acosta, *Revolt of the Cockroach People,* 259–262.

260   **"Acosta was gone"**: At the end of his first book, *The Autobiography of the Brown Buffalo,* Acosta had written,

> Ladies and gentlemen . . . my name is Oscar Acosta. My father is an Indian from the mountains of Durango. Although I cannot speak his language . . . you see, Spanish is the language of our conquerors. English is the language of our conquerors. . . . No one ever asked me or my brother if we wanted to be American citizens. We are all citizens by default . . . I am neither a Mexican nor an American. I am neither a Catholic nor a Protestant. I am a Chicano by ancestry and a Brown Buffalo by choice. Is that so hard for you to understand? (199)

261 **"about these transcripts":** He said this quote directly to John Dean, when the two of them met in 1978, during the taping of the BBC film *Omnibus: Hunter Thompson.*

261 *"The Cocaine Papers"*: Thompson, *Fear and Loathing in America,* 592.

261 **"David Felton":** Hagan, *Sticky Fingers,* 282.

261 **"a participatory take on the text":** Thompson, *Fear and Loathing in America,* 592. That July, in a letter to Wenner, Thompson wrote: "Enclosed, meanwhile, is the tape I mentioned & also the typed translation of a 15-page outburst I lashed together on a night when I was probably as deep in the throes of cocomania as I'll ever get. My idea was to get as crazed as possible on the stuff, then try to write something . . . and these 6 (enc.) pages are the result" (ibid.).

261 **"dilettantes and celebrities and rich people":** Carroll, *Hunter,* 158.

261 **"audio recordings":** *Gonzo Tapes,* disc 4, tracks 12–17.

261 **"he noted":** "Freud Cocaine Papers," *Gonzo Tapes,* disc 4, tracks 13 and 14.

262 **"more than a week":** 6/18/74–6/28/74, from *Gonzo Tapes.*

262 **"David Felton would later reflect":** Hagan, *Sticky Fingers,* 282.

262 **"fascinating short pieces":** i.e., "The Banshee Screams for Buffalo Meat," among others.

262 **"his more sustained work once had":** Douglas Brinkley, the presidential historian and executor of Thompson's literary estate, would say of the work that Thompson produced in the 1960s and early 1970s:

> He really worked hard . . . It's unbelievable, the amount of work he did, the thinking and trying to make each sentence count. He wasn't eating acid then. He was eating speed—that was his drug of choice, to keep him writing all night. He was not as much fun as he painted himself to be. He was a work beast, and it shows in the quality of anything he wrote in that period. (McKeen, *Outlaw Journalist,* 324)

263 **"he could never climb back":** McKeen, *Outlaw Journalist,* 349. The full quote:

> "He was a tortured, tragic figure," Sandy would say many years afterward. "I do not think he was a great writer. I think he clearly had great potential, both as a writer and a leader. However, he fell—dramatically and a very, very long time ago. Hunter wanted to be a great writer and he had the genius, the talent, and, early on, the will and the means. He was horrified by whom he had become and ashamed—or I really should say tortured. He knew he had failed. He knew that his writing was absolutely not great. This was part of the torture. And yet, he could never climb back. The image, the power, the drugs, the alcohol, the money . . . all of it . . . he never became the great American writer he had wanted to be. Nowhere close. And he knew it."

263 **"listen to this tape":** Carroll, *Hunter,* 170–171.

263   **"extramarital relationship"**: Seymour and Wenner, *Gonzo*, 95–96. In the early 1970s Thompson also had an affair with Sally Quinn, a print and television journalist who would marry Ben Bradlee, the executive editor of the *Washington Post* (ibid., 197).

263   **"she said to him"**: Carroll, *Hunter*, 175.

263   **"the two of them would separate"**: Seymour and Wenner, *Gonzo*, 219.

263   **"In 1978"**: Thompson, *Stories I Tell Myself,* 75.

264   **"from Grant to Harding to Nixon"**: Drew, *Washington Journal,* 265.

264   **"unseasonably cool"**: Drew, *Washington Journal,* 332.

264   **"CBS News"**: Drew, *Washington Journal,* 388.

264   **"Stay the hell out of this!"**: Drew, *Washington Journal,* 391.

264   **"from Richard Nixon to Gerald Ford"**: Drew, *Washington Journal,* 390.

264   **"he's quitting!"**: Thompson, *Great Shark Hunt,* 306.

265   **"battery-powered TV set"**: The full quote from Leibovitz, *Annie Leibovitz at Work,* 29:

> I was waiting there. Hunter was back at the hotel. Every reporter on the planet was at the White House, and Hunter was in the swimming pool at the Hilton with a battery-powered TV set. When Nixon walked down the red carpet toward the helicopter that would take him away, there were dozens of press photographers, most of them shooting with long lenses to get in tight, since the news magazines didn't have room for large pictures. Everyone pretty much moved away after Nixon was inside the helicopter and the door was closed. The guards began rolling up the carpet. It wasn't the kind of picture that most magazines would want to run or had room to run then, but a lot can be told in those moments in between the main moments. When it became apparent to the editors at *Rolling Stone* that Hunter was not going to file a story in time, they decided to run my pictures as the story, along with some old pieces we had published on Nixon. I had the cover and eight pages of pictures inside. Hunter's story ran two issues later and was pegged to Ford's pardon of Nixon. It was very long and included a scene Hunter concocted in which he gets out of the swimming pool and takes a cab to the White House and arrives at the Rose Garden.

265   **"East Room"**: Wooten, "Tears at Parting."

266   **"could only have been the hyena"**: Thompson, *Great Shark Hunt,* 315.

266   **"rapidly approaching deadline"**: Seymour and Wenner, *Gonzo*, 183.

# BIBLIOGRAPHY

## Books and Articles

Acosta, Oscar Zeta. *The Autobiography of a Brown Buffalo*. New York: Vintage, 1989.
———. *Revolt of the Cockroach People*. New York: Vintage Books, 1989.
Acosta, Oscar Zeta, and Ilan Stavans. *Oscar "Zeta" Acosta: The Uncollected Works*. Evanston: Arte PuìBlico Press, 1996.
Ambrose, Stephen E. *The Wild Blue*. New York: Simon and Schuster, 2012.
Apple, R. W. "Nixon Accepts Onus for Watergate." *New York Times*. May 1, 1973.
Arlen, Michael J. *Living-Room War*. Syracuse, NY: Syracuse University Press, 1997.
Baker, Russ. *Family of Secrets: The Bush Dynasty, America's Invisible Government, and the Hidden History of the Last Fifty Years*. New York: Bloomsbury, 2010.
Baker, Russell. "Gloomy Day Casts a Pall over Inauguration Mood." *New York Times*. January 21, 1969.
Beecher, William. "Rising Peril Seen." *New York Times*. April 30, 1970.
Belair, Felix, Jr. "Security Is Evident as Nixon Goes By." *New York Times*. January 21, 1969.
Benson, Ray, and David Menconi. *Comin' Right at Ya: How a Jewish Yankee Hippie Went Country, or, the Often Outrageous History of Asleep at the Wheel*. Austin: University of Texas Press, 2015.
Berger, Bruce. "City Should Save the Hearthstone House." *Aspen Times*. February 21, 2007.
Bigart, Homer. "War Foes Here Attacked by Construction Workers; City Hall Is Stormed." *New York Times*. May 9, 1970.
Broder, David. "Muskie Denounces Publisher," *Washington Post*. February 27, 1972.
———. "The Story That Still Nags at Me." *Washington Monthly*. February 1987.
Buchanan, Patrick J. *Greatest Comeback: How Richard Nixon Rose from Defeat to Create the New Majority*. New York: Crown, 2015.
Bulgakov, Mikhail. *The Master and Margarita*. New York: Penguin, 2016.
Calderon, Hector. *Narratives of Greater Mexico*. Austin: University of Texas Press, 2004.

Calvino, Italo. *Cosmicomics.* New York: Harcourt Brace, 1968.

———. "Il Duce's Portraits." *New Yorker.* June 19, 2007.

———. *Invisible Cities.* New York: Harcourt Brace, 1974.

Carroll, E. Jean. *Hunter.* New York: Dutton, 1993.

Drew, Elizabeth. *Washington Journal.* New York: Overlook Press, 2014.

Clifford, Peggy. *To Aspen and Back: an American Journey.* New York: St. Martin's Press, 1980.

Clymer, Adam. "Henry J. Hyde, a Power in the House of Representatives, Dies at 83." *New York Times.* November 11, 2007.

Conrad, Joseph. *Heart of Darkness & Selections from Congo Diary.* New York: Modern Library, 1999.

———. *The Nigger of the "Narcissus" and Other Stories.* New York: Penguin, 2007.

Correa, Jennifer G. *Chicano Nationalism.* Stillwater: Oklahoma State University, 2006.

Crouse, Timothy. *The Boys on the Bus.* New York: Random House Trade Paperbacks, 2003.

DeLillo, Don. *Underworld.* New York: Scribner, 2015.

Dickerson, John. "Never Goldwater." *Slate.* May 12, 2016. http://www.slate.com/articles /news_and_politics/politics/2016/05/never_goldwater_the_failed_attempt_to _wrest_the_1964_gop_nomination_from.html.

Didion, Joan. *We Tell Ourselves Stories in Order to Live: Collected Nonfiction.* New York: Knopf, 2006.

Dodgson, Rick. *It's All a Kind of Magic: The Young Ken Kesey.* Madison: University of Wisconsin Press, 2013.

Doss, Yvette L. "The Lost Legend of the Real Dr. Gonzo." *Los Angeles Times.* June 5, 1998.

Eco, Umberto. "Ur-Fascism." *New York Review of Books.* June 22, 1995. www.nybooks .com/articles/1995/06/22/ur-fascism/.

Eliot, T. S. "The Waste Land." www.poetryfoundation.org/poems/47311/the-waste-land.

Emery, Fred. *Watergate.* New York: Touchstone, 1995.

Eppridge, Bill. "June 5, 1968: The Last Hours of RFK." *New York Magazine.* http:// nymag.com/news/politics/47041/index5.html.

Escobar, Edward J. "The Dialectics of Repression, the Los Angeles Police Department and the Chicano movement, 1968–1971." *Journal of American History.* March 1993.

Farber, David. *Chicago '68.* Chicago: University of Chicago Press, 1994.

Farrell, John A. *Richard Nixon, the Life.* New York: Doubleday, 2017.

Fitzgerald, F. Scott. *The Great Gatsby.* New York: Scribner, 1995.

Fox, Margalit. "Tom Poston, Virtuosic Comic Actor, Is Dead at 85." *New York Times.* May 2, 2007.

Franklin, Ben A. "Young Demonstrators in Parade Throw Smoke Bombs and Stones at Nixon's Car." *New York Times.* January 21, 1969.

Gladwell, Malcolm. "Running from Ritalin." *New Yorker.* February 2, 1999.

Hagan, Joe. *Sticky Fingers.* New York: Knopf, 2017.

Hamill, Pete. "June 5, 1968: The Last Hours of RFK." *New York Magazine.* May 26, 2008. http://nymag.com/news/politics/47041/index5.html.

Hamilton, David. "In an Innertube, on the Amazon." *Michigan Quarterly Review* 29, no. 3. 1990. https://quod.lib.umich.edu/m/mqrarchive/act2080.0029.003/1:10 ?view=toc.

Harrell, Margaret. *Keep This Quiet!* Raleigh: Saeculum University Press, 2011.

Harvey, Allyn. "Meyer, All-Around Local Character, Dies at Age 85." *Aspen Times.* July 23, 2002.

Herbers, John. "Kennedy Charges Johnson Is Divisive." *New York Times.* March 22, 1968.

Herchenroeder, Karl. "'Hippie Lawyer' Recalls Battle of Aspen," *Aspen Times.* December 15, 2013.

Higgins, Will. "April 4, 1968: How RFK Saved Indianapolis." *Indianapolis Star.* April 2, 2015.

Hinckle, Warren. *Who Killed Hunter Thompson?* San Francisco: Last Gasp, 2017.

Hunter, Marjorie. "Sam Ervin, Country Lawyer, Feels 'Pretty Good.'" *New York Times.* September 9, 1983.

Johnson, Denis. *Jesus' Son.* New York: Harper Collins, 1992.

———. *Train Dreams.* New York: Farrar, Straus and Giroux, 2011.

———. *The Throne of the Third Heaven of the Nation's Millennium General Assembly: Poems Collected and New.* New York: Harper Perennial, 1996.

Kenney, Brian. *The Footloose American.* Portland: Broadway Books, 2014.

Kifner, John. "4 Kent State Students Killed by Troops," *New York Times.* May 5, 1970, 1.

Knock, Thomas J. "George McGovern, Vietnam and the Democratic Crackup." *New York Times.* December 5, 2017.

———. *The Rise of a Prairie Statesman: The Life and Times of George McGovern.* Princeton, NJ: Princeton University Press, 2016.

Kusch, Frank. *Battleground Chicago: The Police and the 1968 Democratic National Convention.* Chicago: University of Chicago Press, 2008.

Leary, Timothy. "A Review: The Neo-American Church Catechism and Handbook." In *The Boo Hoo Bible* by Art Kleps. San Cristobal: Toad Books, 1971.

Leibovitz, Annie, and Sharon DeLano. *Annie Leibovitz at Work.* New York: Jonathan Cape, 2011.

Levasseur, Jennifer, and Kevin Rabalais, eds. *Conversations with James Salter.* Oxford: University Press of Mississippi, 2015.

Loiederman, Roberto. "The Darker Side of a Night with Hunter Thompson." *Los Angeles Times.* February 27, 2005.

López, Ian Haney. *Racism on Trial: The Chicano Fight for Justice.* Cambridge, MA: Harvard University Press, 2009.

Lowy, Joan. "Fred Thompson Aided Nixon on Watergate." *Washington Post.* July 7, 2007.

Mailer, Norman. *In the Red Light: A History of the Republican Convention of 1964.* Seattle: Amazon Digital Services, 2016.

———. *Miami and the Siege of Chicago.* New York: Random House, 2016.

———. "Superman Comes to the Supermarket." *Esquire.* November, 1960.

Martin, Douglas. "Angus Cameron, 93, Editor Forced Out in McCarthy Era." *New York Times.* November 23, 2002.

Maxwell, William. *So Long, See You Tomorrow.* New York: Knopf, 2011.

McDonell, Terry. *An Accidental Life.* New York: Knopf, 2016.

McGinnis, Joe. *The Selling of the President.* New York: Byliner, 2012.

McKeen, William. *Outlaw Journalist.* New York: Norton, 2009.

McLaughlin, Michael. "Trio Shares Stories of the '70s." *Aspen Times.* July 14, 2014.

McWilliams, Carey. *The Education of Carey McWilliams.* New York: Simon and Schuster, 1979.

McWilliams, Susan. "This Political Theorist Predicted the Rise of Trumpism." *The Nation.* December 15, 2016.

Menand, Louis. "Out of Bethlehem." *New Yorker.* August 24, 2015.

Mishak, Michael J. "Hunter S. Thompson, How All Went Wrong In Elko." *Las Vegas Sun.* December 25, 2007.

Montgomery, David. "Arthur Bremer Shot Gov. George Wallace to Be Famous. A Search for Who He Is Today." *Washington Post*. December 1, 2017.

Moore, Burton. *Love and Riot*. Mountain View, CA: Floricanto Press, 2003.

Munoz, Carlos, Jr. *Youth, Identity, Power*. New York: Verso, 2007.

Nabokov, Vladimir. "Signs and Symbols." *The Stories of Vladimir Nabokov*. New York: Knopf, 2011.

———. *Speck, Memory*. New York: Vintage, 1989.

Narvaez, Alfonso. "L. Nicholas Ruwe, Ex-Ambassador, 56; Assisted Presidents." *New York Times*. May 4, 1990.

Nash, Tom. "Hunter S. Thompson's Appropriately NSFW FBI File." Muckrock. October 9, 2012, www.muckrock.com/news/archives/2012/oct/09/inside-hunter -s-thompsons-fbi-file/.

Naughton, James. "Muskie Thrives on an Old Campaign Method, Whistle-Stopping." *New York Times*. February 20, 1973.

Nelson, Maggie. *The Argonauts*. Minneapolis: Graywolf Press, 2016.

Oliver, Myrna. "Fred Dutton, 82; Key Aide to Kennedys and Gov. Pat Brown." *Los Angeles Times*. June 27, 2005.

Ondaatje, Michael. *The Collected Works of Billy The Kid*. New York: Knopf, 2011.

———. *Running in the Family*. New York: Knopf, 2011.

Orwell, George. *A Collection of Essays*. New York: Mariner Books, 1970.

———. *Homage to Catalonia*. New York: Mariner Books, 2015.

Palermo, Joseph A. "Here's What RFK Did in California in 1968." *Huffington Post*. May 25, 2011.

Passmore, Kevin. *Fascism: A Very Short Introduction*. Oxford: Oxford University Press, 2014.

Patoski, Joe Nick. *Willie Nelson: An Epic Life*. New York: Little, Brown, 2008.

Paumgarten, Nick. "Postscript: James Salter, 1925–2015." *New Yorker*. June 21, 2015.

Perry, Paul. *Fear and Loathing: The Strange and Terrible Saga of Hunter S. Thompson*. New York: Thunder's Mouth Press, 1992.

Ripley, Anthony. "'Freak Power' Candidate May Be the Next Sheriff in Placid Aspen, Colo." *New York Times*. October 19, 1970.

———. "A Nuclear Device Fired in Colorado." *New York Times*. September 11, 1969.

Rugaber, Walter. "Hearing Is Told That Magruder Had File Moved." *New York Times*. May 18, 1973.

———. "McCord Tells Senate of New Watergate Names." *New York Times*. March 26, 1973.

Salter, James. *Burning the Days*. New York: Random House, 1997.

———. *Don't Save Anything*. Berkeley, CA: Counterpoint Press, 2017.

———. *Memorable Days: The Selected Letters of James Salter and Robert Phelps*. Berkeley, CA: Counterpoint Press, 2007.

———. *A Sport and a Pastime*. New York: Macmillan, 2007.

Scully, Rock. *Living with the Dead: Twenty Years on the Bus with Garcia and the Grateful Dead*. New York: Cooper Square Press, 2001.

Semple, Robert, Jr. "Nixon Says Violence Invites Tragedy." *New York Times*. May 5, 1970.

———. "Nixon's Campaign Is Stately, Dignified, Proud—and Slow." *New York Times*. February 2, 1968.

———. "Nixon Says Violence Invites Tragedy." *New York Times*. May 5, 1970.

Seymour, Corey, and Jann Wenner. *Gonzo: The Life of Hunter Thompson*. New York: Little, Brown, 2007.

Shirley, Craig. "The Bartender's Tale: How the Watergate Burglars Got Caught." *Washingtonian*. June 6, 2012.

Simpson, Craig. "The 1969 Nixon Inauguration: Horse Manure, Rocks & a Pig." *Washington Area Spark*. January 9, 2013. https://washingtonspark.wordpress.com/2013/01/09/the-1969-nixon-inauguration-horse-manure-rocks-a-pig/.

Southern, Terry. "Grooving in the Chi." *Esquire*. November 1968.

Stavans, Ilan. *Bandido*. Evanston, IL: Northwestern University Press, 2003.

Steadman, Ralph. *The Joke's Over*. New York: Houghton Mifflin Harcourt, 2006.

Stonington, Joe. "Former Sheriff Dies in Arizona." *Aspen Times*. March 28, 2006.

Thompson, Anita. *Ancient Gonzo Wisdom*. Cambridge, MA: Da Capo Press, 2009.

Thompson, Hunter. *Fear and Loathing at Rolling Stone*. New York: Simon and Schuster, 2012.

———. *Fear and Loathing in America*. New York: Simon and Schuster, 2000.

———. *Fear and Loathing in Las Vegas*. New York: Vintage, 1998.

———. "Fear and Loathing in the Bunker." *New York Times*. January 1, 1974.

———. *Fear and Loathing: On the Campaign Trail '72*. New York: Simon and Schuster, 2012.

———. *The Great Shark Hunt*. New York: Simon and Schuster, 2003.

———. *Hell's Angels*. New York: Random House, 2012.

———. *Kingdom of Fear*. New York: Simon and Schuster, 2003.

———. "The Motorcycle Gangs: Losers and Outsiders," *The Nation*, May 17, 1965.

———. *The Proud Highway*. New York: Random House, 2012.

———. *Songs of the Doomed*. New York: Simon and Schuster, 2003.

Thompson, Hunter, and Ben Corbett. *Gonzo*. Los Angeles: AMMO Books, 2009.

Thompson, Juan. *Stories I Tell Myself*. New York: Knopf, 2016.

Vigil, Ernesto B. *The Crusade for Justice*. Madison: University of Wisconsin Press, 1999.

Wallace, Henry A. "Wallace Defines 'American Fascism.'" *New York Times*. April 9, 1944.

Watkins, Daniel Joseph. *Freak Power: Hunter S. Thompson's Campaign for Sheriff*. Aspen, CO: Meat Possum Press, 2015.

Witcover, Jules. *85 Days: The Last Campaign of Robert Kennedy*. New York: HarperCollins, 2016.

White, Theodore. *The Making of the President: 1964*. New York: HarperCollins, 2010.

———. *The Making of the President: 1968*. New York: HarperCollins, 2010.

———. *The Making of the President: 1972*. New York: HarperCollins, 2010.

Whiting, Charles. *The Hunt for Martin Bormann*. Yorkshire: Penn & Sword, 2010.

Whitmer, Peter. *When the Going Gets Weird*. New York: Hyperion, 1993.

Wolfe, Tom. *The Electric Kool-Aid Acid Test*. New York: Macmillan, 2008.

———. "The Last American Hero Is Junior Johnson. Yes!" *Esquire*. March 1965.

Wolff, Tobias. *Our Story Begins*. New York: Vintage, 2009.

Wooten, James T. "Tears at Parting." *New York Times*. August 10, 1974.

## Additional Articles

*Aspen Times*. "Baxter, Whitmire, and Williams Win." November 5, 1970.

———. "Editorial: A Sheriff's Agent." October 29, 1970.

———. "Shrieval Candidates Speak at SatA." October 15, 1970.

*Daily Kos.* "Henry Hyde Says Impeachment Was Revenge for Nixon." April 21, 2005. www
.dailykos.com/stories/2005/04/22/108614/-Henry-Hyde-says-Impeachment
-was-revenge-for-Nixon.

*Kirkus Reviews.* "Ask Me for Tomorrow: Review." April 15, 1964.

*New York Times.* "Muskie Maintains Gallup Poll Lead." February 20, 1972.

———. "Excerpts from Senate Exchange on Vietnam War." April 26, 1967.

———. "Excerpts from Testimony before the Senate Committee Investigating Watergate." July 17, 1973.

———. "Text of Hickel Letter," May 7, 1970.

## Video

*The Rise and Fall of the Brown Buffalo.* Dir. Phillip Rodriguez. 2018.

*BBC Omnibus: Hunter S. Thompson.* 1978.

*Four More Years.* Top Value Television. 1972.

*Gonzo: The Life and Work of Dr. Hunter S. Thompson.* Dir. Alex Gibney. 2008.

*One Bright Shining Moment: The Forgotten Summer of George McGovern.* Dir. Stephen Vittoria. 2005.

*Operation Last Patrol.* Dir. Frank Cavestani and Catherine Leroy. 1972.

*Ruben Salazar: Man in the Middle.* Dir. Phillip Rodriguez. 2014.

*Show Down at Aspen.* Thames TV. 1970.

"Spiro Theodore Agnew." *American Rhetoric.* www.americanrhetoric.com/speeches/spiro
agnewtvnewscoverage.htm.

*The Vietnam War.* Dir. Ken Burns and Lynn Novick. Episode Four: "Resolve." 2017.

*The Vietnam War.* Dir. Ken Burns and Lynn Novick. Episode Five: "This Is What We Do."
2017.

*The Vietnam War.* Dir. Ken Burns and Lynn Novick. Episode Seven: "The Veneer of
Civilization." 2017.

*The Vietnam War.* Dir. Ken Burns and Lynn Novick. Episode Nine: "A Disrespectful
Loyalty." 2017.

"Nelson Rockefeller Addresses 1964 Convention." C-SPAN Video Archives. www.c-span
.org/video/?c3807346/governor-nelson-rockefeller-addresses-64-convention.

"Ralph 'Sonny' Barger Confronts VDC." San Francisco Bay Area Television Archive.
https://diva.sfsu.edu/collections/sfbatv/bundles/225552.

"We Shall March Again." University of California, Berkeley, Art Museum and Pacific
Rim Archive. https://archive.org/details/cbpf_000034.

## YouTube Videos

"1968 Democratic Convention," YouTube. www.youtube.com/watch?v=1Iye1NQy1NY.

"1968 Democratic Convention, Part 3." YouTube. www.youtube.com/watch?v=LB8
gkkbf_Zk.

"Chicago Convention the Whole World Is Watching 1968." YouTube. www.youtube
.com/watch?v=7_9OJnRnZjU.

"'Daisy Girl' Rare 1964 Lyndon Johnson Political Ad." YouTube. www.youtube.com
/watch?v=9Id_r6pNsus.

"Dan Rather Convention Floor Fight 1968." YouTube. www.youtube.com/watch?v
=wItUjFU1i4M.
"Goldwater 1964 Acceptance Speech." YouTube. www.youtube.com/watch?v=RF
Siyueal7Q.
"Hubert Humphrey Addressed Delegates at the 1968 DNC." YouTube. www.youtube
.com/watch?v=zhLcNXLzlNA.
"Ribicoff vs. Daley at Democratic National Convention 1968." YouTube. www.youtube
.com/watch?v=Gj9TkjL87Rk.
"To Tell the Truth—Hunter S. Thompson (February 20, 1967)." YouTube. www.youtube
.com/watch?v=f9_V5FrM4CI&feature=youtu.be.
"Walter Cronkite's Historic Footage of Project Rulison." YouTube. www.youtube.com
/watch?v=HwAAqXsrZ58.
"Walter Cronkite: Report from Vietnam (1968)." YouTube. www.youtube.com/watch
?v=Nn4w-ud-TyE.
"Watergate Hearings: John Dean's Opening Statement (1973)." YouTube. www.youtube
.com/watch?v=-cVdsMJ-nEg.

## Audio

Thompson, Hunter S. *The Gonzo Tapes: The Life and Work of Dr. Hunter S. Thompson.* Los
Angeles: Shout Factory, 2008.

## Interviews

Geiger, Robert. Interview, April 27, 2017.
Harrell, Margaret. Interview, January 5, 2018; correspondence, January 4, 2018.
Innes, Bruce. Interview, March 23, 2017.
Lopez, Ricardo. Interview, January 12, 2017.
Salter, James. Conversation, October 17, 2014.
Vigil, Ernesto. Correspondence, September 6, 2016, and October 6, 2016.

## Transcripts

Dean, John. "Transcript of White House Memo on Dean's Senate Testimony." *New York
Times.* June 28, 1973.
Goldwater, Barry. "Goldwater's 1964 Acceptance Speech." *Washington Post.* July 16, 1964.
Johnson, Lyndon. "The President's Address to the Nation Announcing Steps to Limit the
War in Vietnam . . ." March 31, 1968. www.presidency.ucsb.edu/ws/?pid=28772.
Nixon, Richard. "Address Accepting the Presidential Inauguration . . ." August 8, 1968.
www.presidency.ucsb.edu/ws/?pid=25968.
Nixon, Richard. "Address to the Nation on the Situation in Southeast Asia." April 30,
1970. www.presidency.ucsb.edu/ws/?pid=2490.
Nixon, Richard. "The Checkers Speech." September 23, 1952. www.presidency.ucsb
.edu/ws/?pid=24485.
Nixon, Richard. "Inaugural Address." January 20, 1969. www.presidency.ucsb.edu/ws
/?pid=1941.

Ribicoff, Abraham. "Speech Nominating George McGovern for the U.S. Presidency." August 28, 1968. www.americanrhetoric.com/speeches/abrahamribicoff1968dnc .htm.

Rockefeller, Nelson. "Remarks on Extremism at the 1964 Republican National Convention." July 14, 1964. http://rockarch.org/inownwords/nar1964text.php.


## Misc.

Unpublished letter from Angus Cameron to Hunter Thompson, June 7, 1965. The Alfred A. Knopf Collection at the Ransom Center (archive), University of Texas at Austin. Knopf 477.8, boxes 250–251.

Unpublished letter from Hunter Thompson to Gordon Lish, September 3, 1965. The Genesis West Collection at the Ransom Center, University of Texas at Austin. MS-1572, container 3-1.

"US Department of Energy Management: Rulison, Colorado, Site Fact Sheet." Department of Energy. www.lm.doe.gov/rulison/Sites.aspx.

"Findings on MLK Assassination." In JFK Assassination Records. National Archives. www.archives.gov/research/jfk/select-committee-report/part-2-king-findings .html#page-header.

Currency Converter. https://data.bls.gov/cgi-bin/cpicalc.pl.

Historical Weather Data. Weather Underground. www.wunderground.com/history/.

"Hotel of Stars." Seeing-Stars: The Ultimate Guide to Celebrities and Hollywood. www .seeing-stars.com/Hotels/BeverlyHillsHotel.shtml.

"A Chronology." Chicago '68. http://chicago68.com/c68chron.html.

"Oral History Interview with Frederick S. Farr." California State Archives State Government Oral History Program. http://archives.cdn.sos.ca.gov/oral-history/pdf /farr.pdf.

"The Rh factor, How It Can Affect Your Pregnancy." The American College of Obstetricians and Gynecologists. www.acog.org/-/media/For-Patients/faq027.pdf?dmc =1&ts=20180104T0822284366.

"Frederick Gary Dutton." Arlington National Cemetery Website. www.arlington cemetery.net/fgdutton.htm.

"Appointments, Schedules and Appearances Inventory." The Richard Nixon Presidential Library. www.nixonlibrary.gov/forresearchers/find/textual/inventories/inventory _appointments.pdf.

"History." Aspen Airport. http://aspenairport.com/about-aspen-airport/history.

"The Kennedy Caucus Room." United States Senate. www.senate.gov/artandhistory /history/common/briefing/Caucus_Room.htm.

"Jay Sarno." *Online Nevada Encyclopedia*. www.onlinenevada.org/articles/jay-sarno.

# INDEX

**Timothy Denevi** is an assistant professor in the MFA program at George Mason University. His first book, *Hyper: A Personal History of ADHD,* was published in 2014. He received his MFA in nonfiction from the University of Iowa. His essays can be found online in *The Atlantic, New York, Salon, Time, The Paris Review,* and *Literary Hub,* where he serves as the nonfiction editor. He lives near Washington, DC, with his wife and children.

PublicAffairs is a publishing house founded in 1997. It is a tribute to the standards, values, and flair of three persons who have served as mentors to countless reporters, writers, editors, and book people of all kinds, including me.

I. F. STONE, proprietor of *I. F. Stone's Weekly*, combined a commitment to the First Amendment with entrepreneurial zeal and reporting skill and became one of the great independent journalists in American history. At the age of eighty, Izzy published *The Trial of Socrates*, which was a national bestseller. He wrote the book after he taught himself ancient Greek.

BENJAMIN C. BRADLEE was for nearly thirty years the charismatic editorial leader of *The Washington Post*. It was Ben who gave the *Post* the range and courage to pursue such historic issues as Watergate. He supported his reporters with a tenacity that made them fearless and it is no accident that so many became authors of influential, best-selling books.

ROBERT L. BERNSTEIN, the chief executive of Random House for more than a quarter century, guided one of the nation's premier publishing houses. Bob was personally responsible for many books of political dissent and argument that challenged tyranny around the globe. He is also the founder and longtime chair of Human Rights Watch, one of the most respected human rights organizations in the world.

. . .

For fifty years, the banner of Public Affairs Press was carried by its owner Morris B. Schnapper, who published Gandhi, Nasser, Toynbee, Truman, and about 1,500 other authors. In 1983, Schnapper was described by *The Washington Post* as "a redoubtable gadfly." His legacy will endure in the books to come.

Peter Osnos, *Founder*